ALSO BY AMBER GUINNESS

A House Party in Tuscany
Italian Coastal

WINTER IN TUSCANY

*To Dada, Matthew and Milo, three adored men,
who taught me to delight in a cold winter's night.*

❖❖❖

COSY RECIPES AND THE *QUANTO BASTA* WAY

WINTER IN TUSCANY

✦✦✦

AMBER GUINNESS

Photography by Valentina Solfrini

T&H

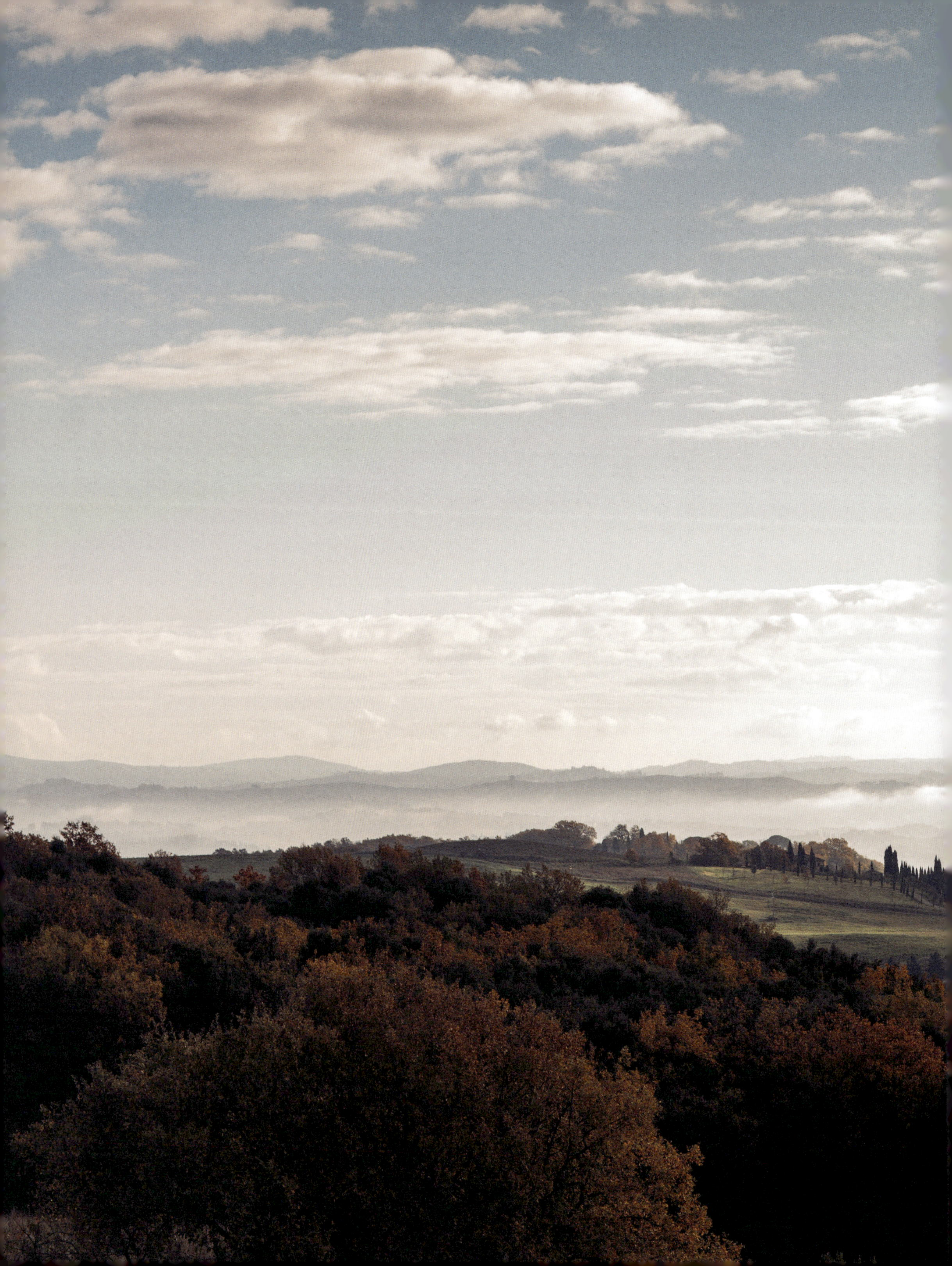

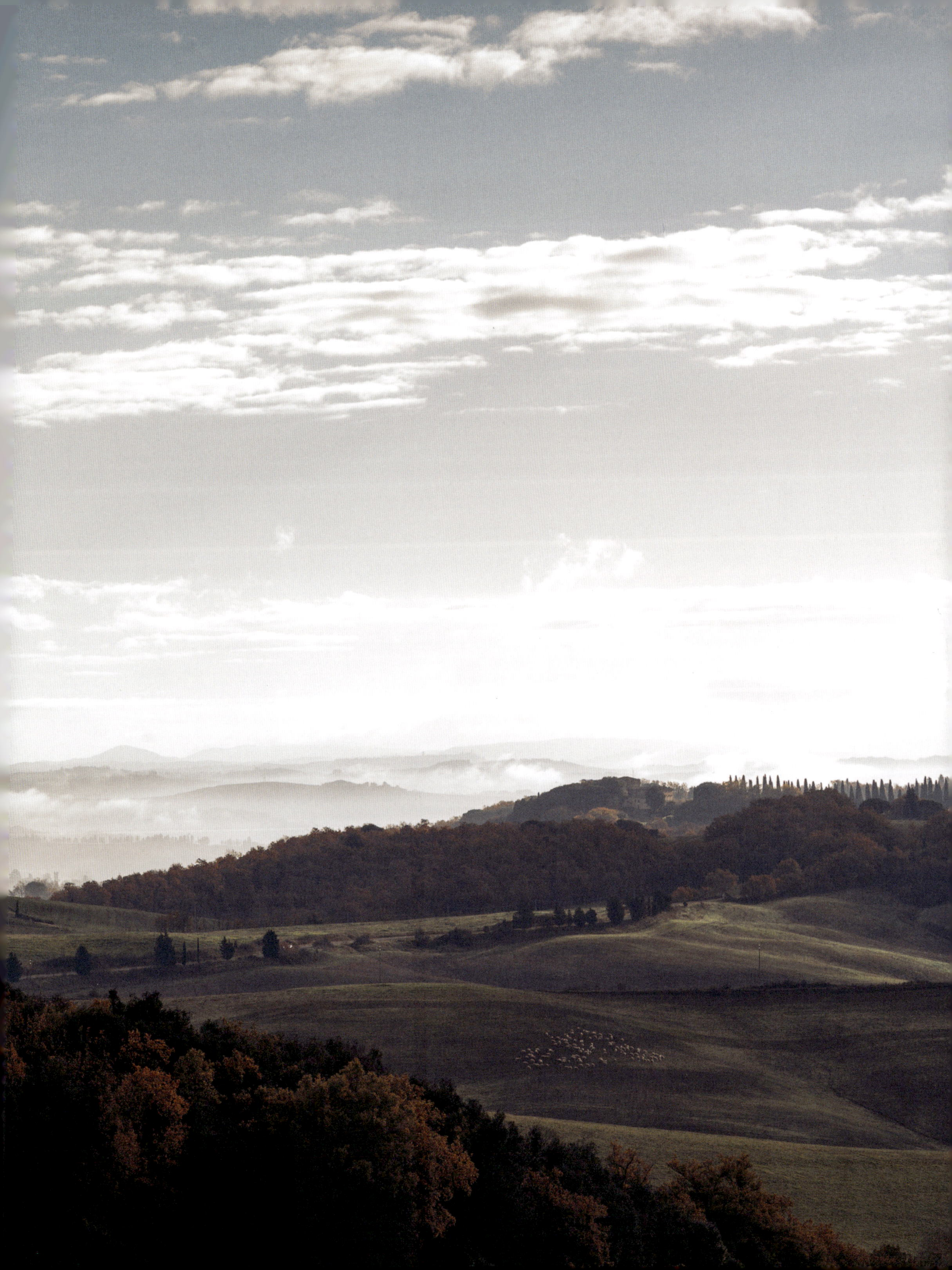

RISTORANTE
DA
MARIO
CUCINA
CASALINGA
TOSCANA
TAGLIERI SALUMI
FORMAGGI
FOCACCE CON
RUCOLA-POMODORINI
FORMAGGIO-SALCICCIA
TARTAR-DI-FASSONA

CONTENTS

INTRODUCTION ... 10
A BRIEF HISTORY OF TUSCAN FLAVOURS ... 16
THE TUSCAN PANTRY ... 20
WINES OF TUSCANY ... 26
TUSCAN COOKING: THE 'QUANTO BASTA' WAY ... 32
MENUS ... 36

✦✦✦✦✦

RECIPES

ANTIPASTI ✦ BEFORE THE MEAL ... 42

MINESTRE ✦ COMFORTING SOUPS ... 68

PRIMI ✦ PASTA & GRAINS ... 98

PIATTI DI MEZZO ✦ VEGETARIAN MAINS ... 128

SECONDI DI CARNE ✦ MEATY MAINS ... 162

CONTORNI ✦ SIDES ... 186

DOLCI ✦ SWEETS ... 216

✦✦✦✦✦

AROUND US AT ARNIANO ... 86
FLORENCE ... 148
SIENA ... 204

✦

ACKNOWLEDGEMENTS ... 250   INDEX ... 252

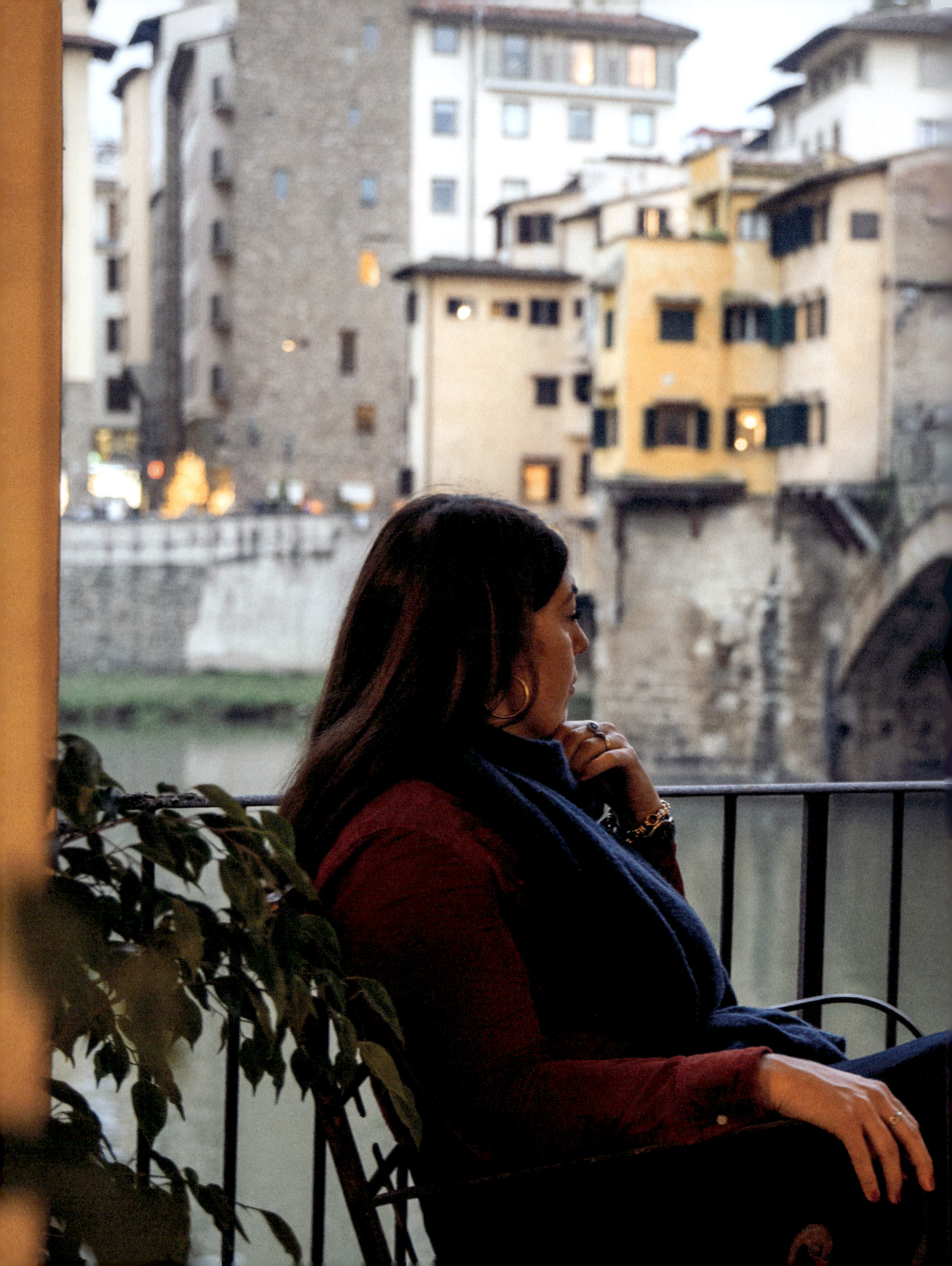

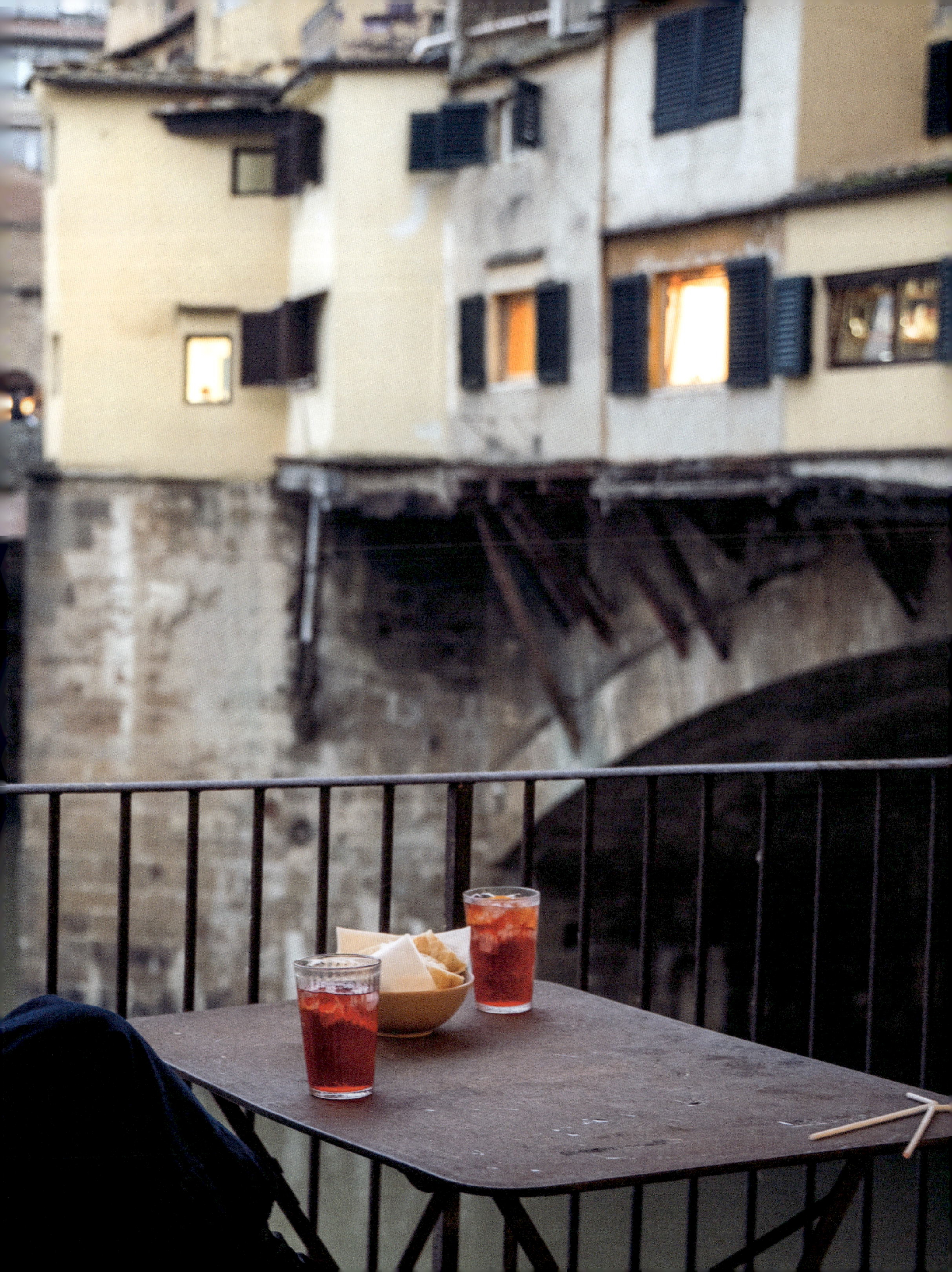

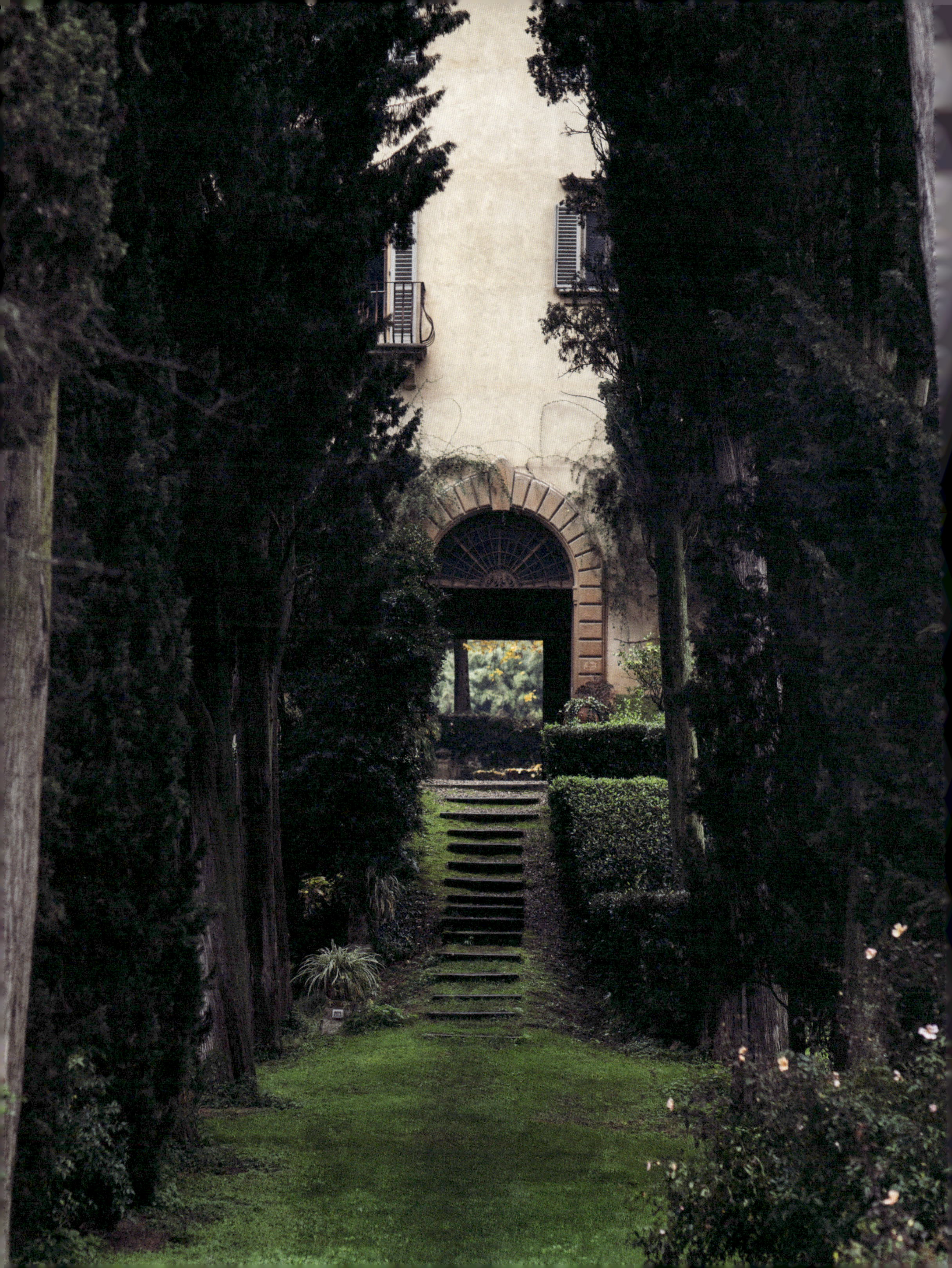

INTRODUCTION

ALTHOUGH PEOPLE ASSOCIATE Tuscany with balmy summer days and the incessant cacophony of cicadas, it is the colder months that are my favourite here. As the temperatures begin to drop in October, there is a sense of respite after the long languid months of searing heat, and a general feeling of reclamation in one of Italy's most visited regions as everyone who works in restaurants, wineries and hotels has a moment to catch their breath after a busy season. Autumn is also a time of hard work for the region, as the bounty of these fertile lands is harvested and turned into celebrated produce famous the world over – full-bodied, ruby-red wines; the new season's thick acid-green olive oil; plump, tasty porcini mushrooms, and musky seductive white truffles. The festive season soon comes and goes and we pass into the quiet cold months of the new year. There is a calm which makes this the most wonderful time to explore Tuscany's cities and little towns, all so full of treasures. It's the time I most love to visit Siena's glorious black and white cathedral, or to see Fra Angelico's frescoes in the monastery of San Marco in Florence, or brave the marathon of beauty that is the Uffizi.

OPPOSITE:– A secret garden in Florence, belonging to the family of my friends Violet and Savannah

As a child growing up in the Val d'Ombrone, between Siena and the famous wine-making town of Montalcino, the school terms dictated our family's movements. We were firmly planted at home from September to June, immediately leaving to spend the summer holidays with family in England. As a result, summer is not the time I most associate with home, but rather, cosy winter nights by the roaring waist-height fire in our kitchen, on which my dad would often roast meat or chestnuts. Being a large, stone farmhouse designed to lose heat in the summer, our house, Arniano, was (and is) very difficult to heat. I remember sitting like sardines on the sofa with my sister, Claudia, and our parents, Jasper and Camilla, to keep each other warm as we watched TV – and there was always a heavy reliance on electric blankets to avoid the nasty shock of jumping into a freezing cold bed.

Luckily, the cold is often accompanied by crisp sunny days and blue skies here, and as we look out towards Montalcino the view is still dominated by the muted green of the cypress, beech, ilex and pines that line the valley. Beyond sits Monte Amiata, the highest point in sight – and one which, when flecked with white, is an exciting one as we can hop in the car and be skiing on its three runs within an hour or so. Once, in 1996, the snow came down from the mountain and covered the whole valley in a deep thick white blanket. It was Boxing Day and my parents had friends with kids staying. They had left us eight children at the house with a sitter while they went to dinner with some friends near Montalcino. Halfway through the meal they realised how heavily the snow was falling and they jumped up from the table, leaving their food uneaten as they leapt into their cars for fear of being snowed out from us. They were too late and had to be rescued by the fire brigade from the side of the road, where they'd got themselves stuck on a snowbank. They were brought home in a fire truck, much to our excitement. Snow like that is rare, though, with 2010 the only other year I remember being like it. Winter days are short and evenings close in early, but mercifully the cold blue skies make it bearable, much more so than when the temperatures rise a little and we are accosted by dark clouds and heavy downpours.

I have always loved winter. These are the months when Tuscany's best-known dishes come into their own: *ribollita*; deep black beef *peposo*; *pici al ragu* – all perfect antidotes to the icy winds outdoors. They lift the spirits on dark nights when it's most needed. This is when I most enjoy being holed up in the kitchen or in the hustle and bustle of a cosy trattoria, hiding from the biting chill in the air or rain. It is also my favourite time for eating, the colder months calling for steaming bowls of warming soups, meaty pastas, buttery polenta and deeply flavoured slow-cooked meats.

Here in Tuscany, the concept of making something tasty from very little is a culinary art that was born from necessity in this historically very poor area – though nowadays, this making do with what is to hand has come to define Tuscany's cuisine in and of itself, overtaking the more fussy, complicated dishes that were served on the tables of noble families. The enduring success of the region's 'cucina povera' dishes springs from the use of quality ingredients – often with very little done to them except the application of heat and patience. In the case of one of the region's most frugal recipes, *zuppa di pane* (bread soup), this is taken to the extreme, as it literally consists of water, bread and olive oil.

Tuscany's frank, rugged and decisive flavours are unapologetically celebrated now more than ever, though they have been appreciated throughout history. The Renaissance architect Filippo Brunelleschi apparently discovered *peposo* (a stew made from cheap cuts of beef, red wine and pepper) while visiting the potters at Impruneta on an expedition to find materials to build Tuscany's largest cathedral. When he tried this dish, cooked for hours in the kilns in which their bricks and pots

FOLLOWING LEFT:–
Santa Maria del Fiore seen from Via dello Studio

FOLLOWING RIGHT:–
Chiara preparing for service in the kitchen of Trattoria Cammillo

were fired, he thought it so good that he arranged for stalls to be set up around the Santa Maria del Fiore building site to feed workers helping to construct the now world-famous cathedral of Florence. Bettino Ricasoli, a 19th century nobleman said to have formulated the precise blend of grape varieties that has come to define and characterise chianti wine, exclaimed while eating a plate of *panzanella* (a Tuscan summer salad made of bread, onion, vinegar and tomatoes) in Siena that the food was *Una cucina povera che può stare sul tavolo di un re* – A cuisine for the poor, fit for the table of a king. It seems he really believed this: legend has it that when King Emmanuel visited Castello di Brolio, just north of Siena, in the 1860s, Ricasoli had the gumption to serve the King this poorest of dishes.

The ability to make do with what is to hand – *l'arte di arrangiarsi* – means that for every traditional 'Tuscan' dish, there is no one definitive version or recipe, despite what some may claim. Within the same area you can often go from house to house and find slightly different cooking methods, textures, herbs or seasonings used to make ostensibly the same thing. It's an attitude that can be summed up in the saying *A occhio e quanto basta*, meaning that you make something by eye, and with as much as you need.

Leaf through any cookbook originally written in Italian and you will note that in the list of ingredients for each recipe, there is a distinct lack of hand-holding for the reader. Salt will be included in the list of needed items, as will the ubiquitous *olio EVO (extra vergine oliva)*, but instead of listing the number of teaspoons or tablespoons you need, they'll be followed by the initials 'q.b.' – meaning *quanto basta*, or 'as much as is needed'. These two letters represent so much of what Italian cooking is about. They illustrate in black and white how preparing a meal doesn't need to be the exacting affair that many people find it to be. There's no need, when preparing a savoury meal, to painstakingly measure out tablespoons of olive oil when a generous glug will do the trick. The concept of *quanto basta* invites us to cook in the way that I believe leads to the most straightforward, tasty and rewarding food – which is that if you add ingredients little by little and taste as you go along, the quantities (within reason) don't matter quite so much as we might think and 'mistakes' are usually rectifiable. If that glug of olive oil was a bit too generous, add more of the other ingredients and the result won't be oily. Aside from baking, where exactness is required to set off the necessary chemical reactions, the 'q.b.' approach to cooking is essentially the basis for all good, simple food that Italy is so famous for, as, through necessity, Italians came up with ways of applying cooking processes to frugal ingredients in order to make them tasty, delicious and nutritious.

This approach is what this book is about and what defines the recipes. They are a collection of dishes that give you the rugged, decisive flavours of Tuscan cuisine, with shortcuts where available, allowing you to use whatever glass you happen to have to hand as a measuring cup, and to pour a few glugs of oil into a pan without getting out the measuring spoons, and to substitute with what you have and not worry too much about following 'the rules' – as no Tuscan ever did.

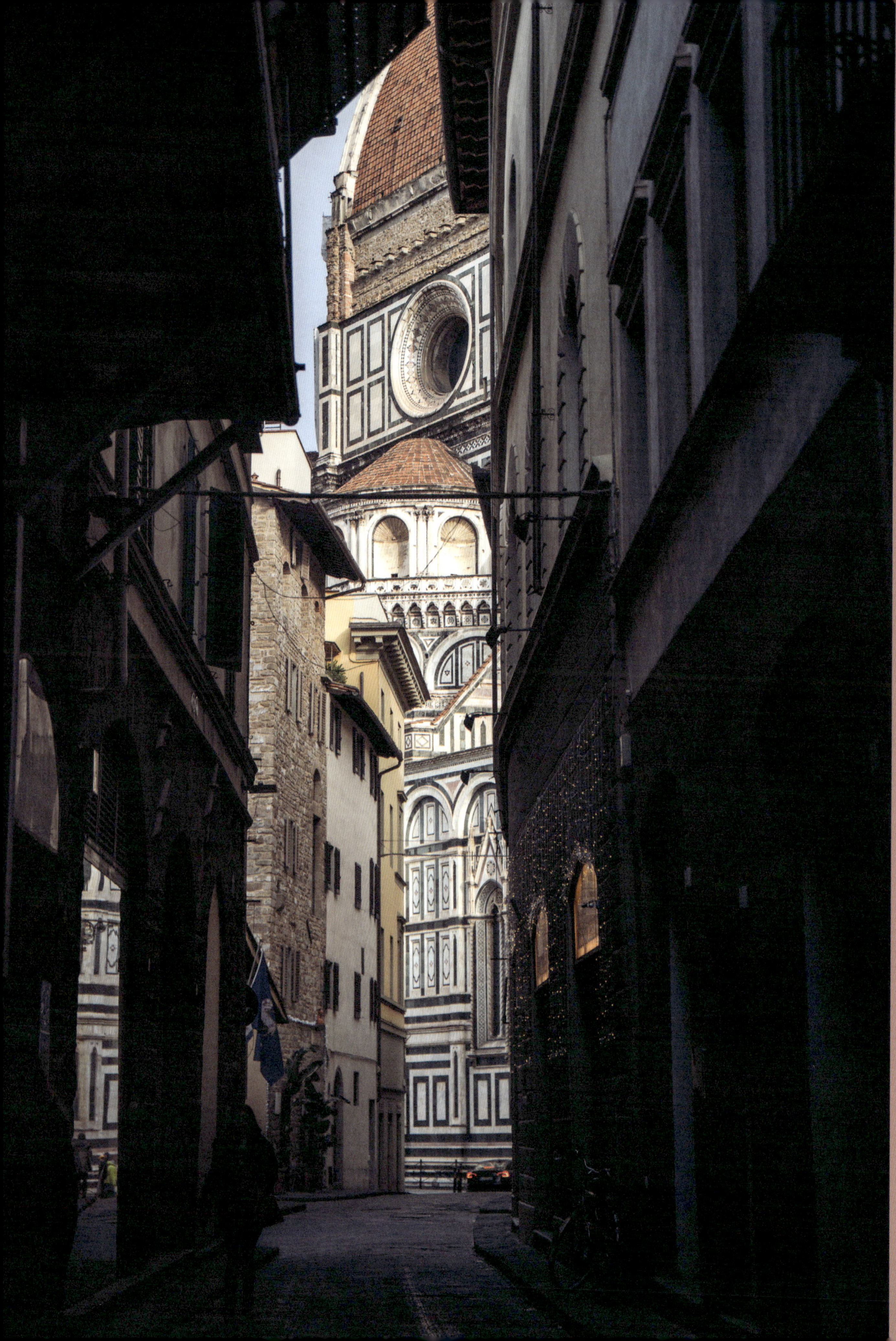

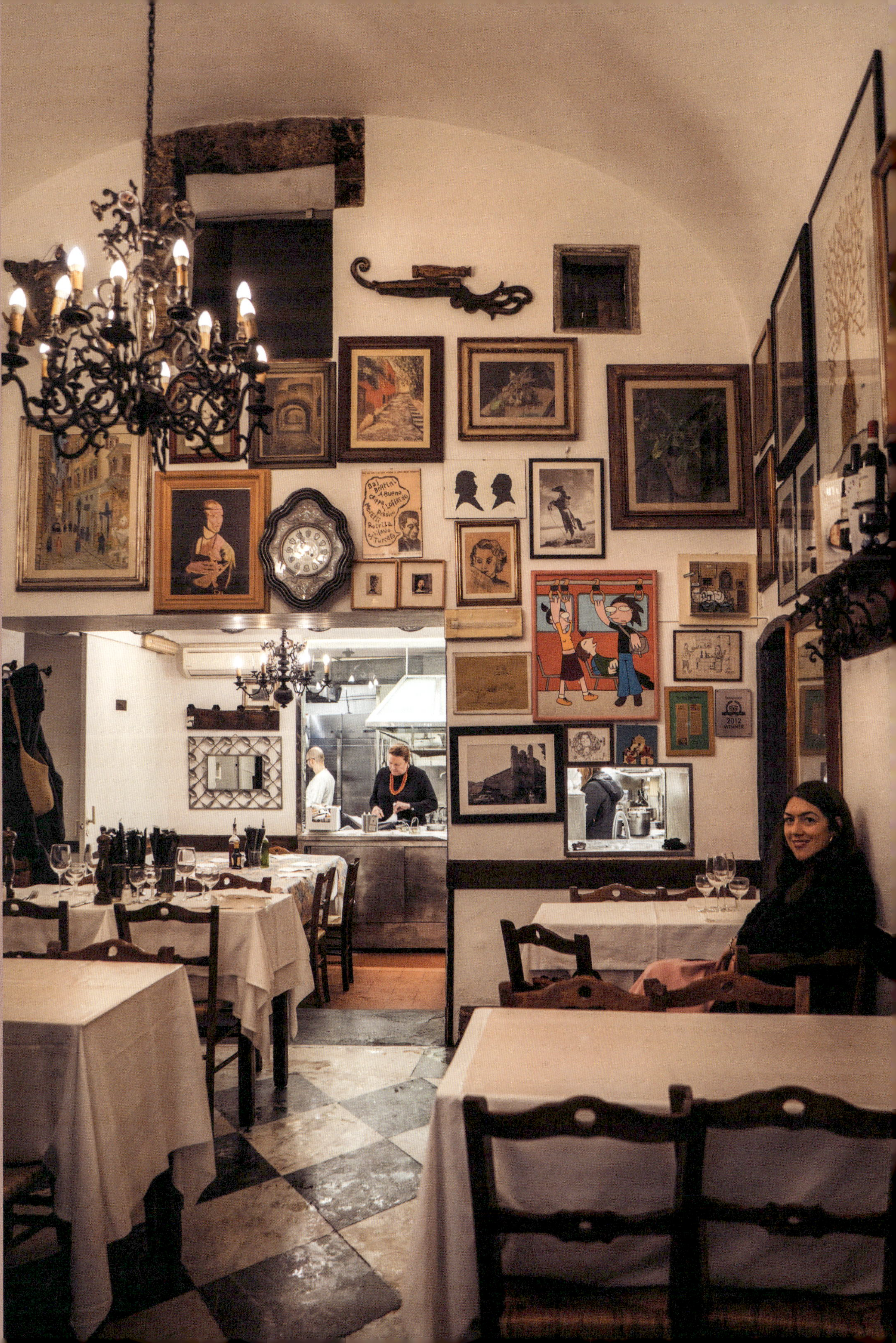
2012
WINNER

Trattoria Buzzin

OGGI S'È FATTO:

Crostone Cavolo Nero, Burratina e Acciughe — 14.-
Insalatina di Puntarelle, Rucola e Grana — 14.-
Ribollita — 10.-
Lasagne fatte in casa — 15.-
Pici Cavolo Nero, Salsiccia e Crema di Parmigiano — 15.-
Polpo alla Griglia con Purè di Ceci — 20.-
Filetto di Manzo al Pepe Verde e Spinaci — 26.-

SPECIALE:
Risottino al Cavolo Nero e Scamorza Affumicata — 14.-

A BRIEF HISTORY OF TUSCAN FLAVOURS

✦✦✦✦✦

DESPITE A COMMON assumption that Tuscan food is mostly meat-based, it does in fact include lots of vegetables, beans and pulses. To this day Tuscans are known throughout the rest of Italy as *i mangiafagioli* – 'the bean eaters' – referring to the ubiquitous accompaniment of *fagioli al fiasco* to most dishes: cannellini beans simmered very gently overnight in a glass jar with sage and rosemary, and dressed in very good olive oil.

Beans came to Italy in the early 1500s after Columbus and Vespucci brought them back from their voyage to the Americas. However, the Tuscan tradition of eating spelt, lentils and other pulses stretches back much further to when the region was known as Etruria, or 'Etruscan land', two thousand or so years ago. Cave drawings, artefacts and accounts from visiting Greeks described the twice-daily banquets held by noble Etruscans with sumptuous tables decorated with flowers and fine cutlery, giving the sense that food was as huge a part of everyday life for the Etruscans as it is for modern-day Tuscans. One archaeological dig of an Etruscan settlement uncovered over 500 varieties of seeds, grains and plants, including olives, grapes, figs, spelt and hazelnuts. Our local olive press is called 'Frantoio Etrusco', in reference to the ancient tradition of olive pressing in the area, and to an excavation near our home, Arniano, which found one of the most significant Etruscan settlements, including many artefacts that have ended up in our local museum, the most interesting of which to me are the fairly advanced kitchen utensils they used. It was a cuisine inherited by the Romans and little changed by them, remaining fairly frugal and based predominantly on pulses such as lentils and spelt, particularly in soups.

OPPOSITE:– Ferruccio Bartarelli preparing sage for service. His father co-founded Trattoria Casalinga in Florence in 1963.

Writings from the 1500s point to a cuisine much more similar to the one we know today, referring to dishes we still eat, such as *crostini neri* (crostini with chicken liver pate) and *peposo* (beef stew). Meat, eaten in a nose-to-tail fashion, is still a huge part of culinary life. I know no self-respecting Tuscan who won't rhapsodise on the delectability of *lampredotto* (stewed Florentine tripe eaten in a bread roll), *fegatelli* (pork liver and sage dumplings in lace fat), and – possibly the most challenging for those unused to this sort of cooking – *cibrèo*, a stew of chicken hearts, liver, cockscomb, wattle and testicles, said to have been a favourite dish of Catherine de Medici, and one that prides itself on wasting absolutely no part of the animal. Offal aside, some of Tuscany's most emblematic dishes are meat-based, the most famous being *bistecca alla fiorentina* – Florentine T-bone steak, cut three or four fingers high and cooked over coals until charred outside but rare inside. Any non-touristy restaurant will almost certainly refuse to cook this for you any other way than rare; I have seen many who like their meat well cooked told to order something else. *Arista di maiale*, herby slow-cooked pork loin, is another typical, popular and tasty *secondo* in Tuscany.

Vegetables are always strictly seasonal, and everyone you speak to will be excited at any given point in the year about what is – or is about to be – in season. In autumn, it is the mushrooms, with families spending their Sunday afternoons in the woods with torches on their heads to spot the best bounty. Most families I know have at least one competent *fungaiolo* among them who has passion enough for foraging to have learnt or been taught by a parent or grandparent to distinguish between the delicious edible varieties and the fatal. Chestnuts begin to fall from the trees on the mountain and are roasted over an open fire in special frying pans with holes in to let in some of the flames and slightly char the nuts, lending a smoky flavour to the meaty flesh. A recipe purported to date back to the Etruscans involves cooking the chestnuts with onions and chickpeas and half blending this into a thick, hearty soup that is slightly sweet from the chestnuts. A few Tuscan desserts, such as *castagnaccio*, use chestnut flour, as it was cheaper than wheat flour and naturally sweet, and so required less sugar, which was expensive. As we move into winter, the artichokes return and are celebrated in a huge variety of ways: deep-fried, chopped up into raw salads, stewed with olive oil to top thin slices of veal escalopes, or simply sautéed and covered in egg for a fabulous frittata (page 133). Bitter-leafed radicchio is cooked, roasted or served as a salad. There is also great excitement at the first frost, as the biting cold is wonderful for cavolo nero, the ultimate Tuscan green. Its thick, dark green water-repellent leaves, which are similar to kale and almost look like crocodile skin, are tenderised by the cold, and are enjoyed stewed in soups, blanched and blended into pesto, and sautéed in chilli and garlic as a side dish.

This is a fabulous aspect of Tuscan cuisine – that throughout history the cooking style has been based on what was available, with a focus on bringing out the best of whatever is being cooked. The results are tasty and straightforward, and the region so confident in their deliciousness that its dishes have endured beyond the days of want and deprivation. So much so that they have been exported to foreign lands. When Catherine de Medici married King Henry II and moved to the French court, it is said she brought with her many of her favourite Florentine dishes, which then evolved into many of the famous ones we associate with French food: *carabaccia* (Florentine onion soup), *papero con melarancio* (duck cooked with bitter orange), *salsa di fegato* (chicken liver pate), and *salsa colla*, a predecessor of bechamel sauce.

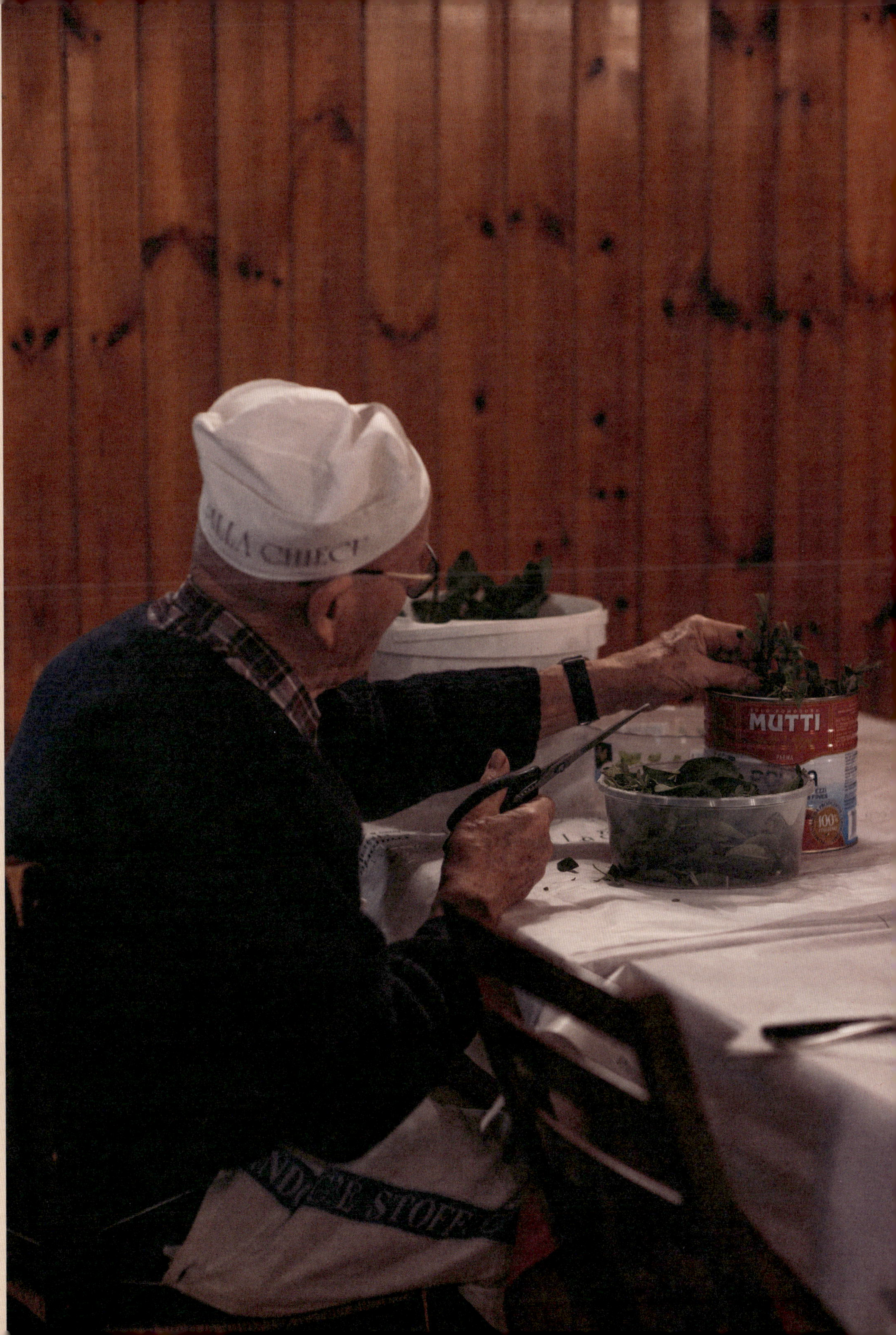
MUTTI

OOH COSO...
CI VOI ANDÀ
DOVE SI METTE
LA SALVIA AI
TORDI?
MOLINARI
BARBIERI

THE TUSCAN PANTRY

AFTER THE FALL of the Roman empire and the invasions of the barbarians, regional Italian cooking started to emerge as people weren't part of one Empire as they had been under the Romans. Venetian cooking, for instance, became strikingly different from Tuscan as they traded with the Orient, which influenced their ingredients and flavours, whereas Tuscan cuisine always stayed very much tied to its own local produce. Here are some of the ingredients you'll typically find in a Tuscan kitchen, and throughout the recipes in this book.

OPPOSITE:– Locanda il Paradiso in Chiusure

AGLIONE

This is a type of elephant garlic grown in the Val di Chiana, between Arezzo, Cortona and Chiusure. It's huge, but has a much milder flavour than regular garlic, meaning that it is very easy to digest and doesn't lead to the dreaded 'garlic breath' – which is why it is also known as *l'aglio del bacio* ('kissing garlic'). When crushed and very gently cooked in oil, it almost froths and melts into its own sauce, which when paired with tinned or fresh tomatoes makes one of the most wonderful accompaniments for pici (thick Tuscan noodles made from flour and water), known as *pici all'aglione* (page 126). You can substitute normal garlic for aglione by using half the amount called for in the recipe, but you'll need to remove the central green shoot – known as the germ – to make it a little milder.

ARTICHOKES

Fresh artichokes can look rather alarming. The inedible tough exterior and menacing-looking talons at the end of each leaf don't seem as though they could possibly be protecting anything you'd want to eat, let alone such a deliciously nutty, tender heart. Tuscans are particularly adept at using artichokes in many dishes. Globe artichokes aren't so common here, but a whole host of varieties are grown across the region, including the Sardinian variety, which is fabulous steamed and dressed in good olive oil and served with a hunk of pecorino. Near us, the hamlet of Chiusure is famous for harvesting spring *carciofini* (baby artichokes) and preserving them in olive oil with peppercorns, bay leaves and other herbs, to be served alongside silky slices of prosciutto or *finocchiona* (Tuscan fennel seed-infused salami). I love artichokes in all shapes and sizes, particularly when fried, served in a salad or frittata (page 133) or as an accompaniment to meat. I find the process of preparing them very meditative, and if I am only cooking for four, it really takes no time at all to pull off the tough outer leaves, trim the stems, slice the hearts in half and remove the hairy choke. Where possible, I have indicated in the recipes when you can substitute jarred artichokes for fresh ones – but in some instances there really is no point.

CANNELLINI BEANS

These magical beans are a key ingredient for many of Tuscany's most classic dishes, such as *ribollita*, and make the perfect accompaniment to Tuscany's simply grilled meats in the form of *fagioli al fiasco* (cannellini beans cooked very gently overnight in a glass beaker with garlic and herbs – see my version on page 198), and *fagioli all'uccelletto* (beans in tomato sauce). When whizzed up, they give soups a velvety creaminess which means you don't have to resort to butter or indeed cream to make a steaming bowl of soup on a cold winter's night feel cosy and warming – surely better for our health, and great for anyone who follows a vegan diet. I always have a few tins or jars of pre-cooked cannellini beans in my cupboard to stir through a simple vegetable stew (page 80), to make a creamy soup base for a spelt soup (page 84) or *pasta e fagioli* (see variation on page 84). As I love *fagioli al fiasco* but am often in a hurry, I have come up with a recipe for Garlicky rosemary cannellini beans (page 198) using tinned beans to give the same satisfying effect. Dried cannellini are always the tastiest and most economical option, when you have the time and foresight to soak them ahead; the soaking water can then be used to cook the beans, in a satisfying no-waste solution which also adds nutrition and flavour. To cook dried beans, treat them in the same way as dried chickpeas (see facing page).

CAVOLO NERO

Probably the most emblematic of Tuscan vegetables, cavolo nero – or 'black cabbage' – is a brassica with no head, instead growing long, elegant dark green leaves, similar to kale. The leaves feel a little rubbery, look a bit like dinosaur skin and are water repellent. Growing from autumn and into the new year, they are at their best after the first frost, which tenderises the leaves. They need cooking to become edible, and to prepare them, you simply pull along the tough white stem to strip away the more tender leaves, discarding the stalk. Cavolo nero is one of my favourite vegetables, and I love it stirred through soups, blanched and stir-fried with garlic and chilli, or whizzed into a pesto to dress pasta.

CHESTNUTS

Chestnuts signal the arrival of the colder months in Tuscany, when they are sold in their dark brown pods in netted bags, ready to be scored with a knife (so they don't explode) and roasted in their skins over an open fire. To do this, my dad always used a special wooden-handled frying pan with holes in the bottom, which he'd place directly on the embers of the fire to slowly roast the chestnuts, and we would then all peel them and eat them together in front of the telly. Chestnuts are naturally sweet, nutty and brittle in texture, and have long been an invaluable source of nutrition throughout the region. On Monte Amiata, the mountain that dominates our view from Arniano, locals were historically cut off from the plains where wheat was grown for flour, so they opted to use chestnuts instead, which were abundantly available, milling the nutty meat into a flour for making *pane dei poveri* (poor man's bread), pasta and cakes, including the celebrated Tuscan dessert, *castagnaccio* – a dense, sweet chestnut cake with pine nuts that was developed by the women on the mountains who were always trying to think of new ways to use chestnut flour and make it more palatable.

CHICKPEAS

Nutritious, filling and full of protein, *ceci* (chickpeas) have been a stalwart of the Tuscan pantry for millennia, used in soups since the Etruscans ruled these lands – one of which, *zuppa etrusca* (page 83), is still enjoyed today. Chickpeas are still blended into soups and stews, or served simply with very good olive oil, rosemary, sea salt and pasta to make *pasta e ceci*, one of the most rewarding and warming bowls of food you can imagine on a winter's night. One of my favourite options for my *contorno* (side dish) is often just chickpeas dressed in olive oil. Rehydrating dried chickpeas is incredibly easy, but you'll need to plan ahead. Simply leave them to soak for at least 12 hours in plenty of water with a teaspoon of bicarbonate of soda (baking soda), some herbs (rosemary, sage and bay leaves) and a few garlic cloves, after which time they will have magically plumped up. They will then need gentle simmering for about an hour and a half. Despite rehydrated beans being better in flavour and more economical, for ease I usually keep some glass jars of *ceci giganti* (giant chickpeas) in my pantry, which are more expensive but have a great flavour and don't require much cooking time. I love using these to make a quick, tasty and nutritious supper, such as the Sausage, lentil & chickpea stew on page 173.

EGGS

I love eggs. They are the reason I don't think I could ever be a vegan, though I would probably be quite happy as a vegetarian. They are also happily, very good for you, being rich in protein and a host of vitamins and minerals. Happy chickens make happy eggs, so I always opt for the best I can find and afford. When buying eggs in the UK or Europe, check the serial number printed on the shell, which lets you cut straight past any misleading language on the packaging. The first digit of the serial number will range from 0 up to 3, which will immediately tell you whether the eggs are Organic (0), Free Range (1), Barn Laid (2) or the dreaded Battery Cage (3). It also helps you save money, as an intensely yellow yolk is not always an indicator of a high-quality egg but just more clever branding. Some farms feed their chickens paprika and marigold leaves to achieve that colour, which isn't bad in itself, but generally means the eggs will be more expensive – when, really, the important point is that the eggs are actually free range, or even better, organic.

Large eggs are apparently painful for the hens to lay, so I usually avoid anything bigger than medium, and have used only organic medium-sized room-temperature eggs in all the recipes in this book.

FLOURS

Italians have a whole variety of flours that are milled to different degrees of fineness. The finest is '00', which is typically used to make cakes, pastries and fresh pasta as it yields a very soft texture. The next one up is '0', which is still fairly fine. Both of these have a low protein content and can be substituted with plain or all-purpose flour for the recipes in this book.

LENTILS AND SPELT

Spelt is high in fibre, and rich in iron, magnesium and potassium, and in Italy has always been felt to hold particular health benefits such as lowering cholesterol and being good for the digestive system. It keeps well once cooked, ready to be stirred through a thick, hearty soup, or in the warmer months turned into *insalata di farro*, a cold salad in which the spelt is seasoned and mixed with lots of grilled vegetables. It can also be used as a more nutrition-packed substitute for rice in 'speltotto' (page 114).

Lentils have always been popular in this historically poor area, being so affordable and very high in protein. Tradition dictates that they must be eaten on New Year's Eve to bring wealth and prosperity, with pork sausages, pig's trotter or pork loin the usual accompaniment.

OLIVE OIL

Cold-pressed extra virgin olive oil is one of the great joys of living in Tuscany. Its unctuous green colour and peppery taste are one of the highlights of November when the olives are harvested and the *olio nuovo* (new oil) is pressed. Using very good cold-extracted olive oil is perhaps the easiest way to elevate the simplest salad to the sublime, but as it is expensive, don't use it for cooking. Good olive oil is expensive; there isn't really a way around that. Keep it for that *filo d'olio crudo* (drizzle of raw oil) at the end of assembling a dish or to douse your toast in. For cooking, I'm not too fussy and I'm happy with a more economical ordinary olive oil from the supermarket, so long as it's labelled as being 'single origin'. It's important to keep a beady eye on labels to make sure you aren't buying stuff that is laced with seed oils. Avoid those on which the small print says it is a blend of olive oils from different countries, as that is when they usually add lower-grade oils to bulk it out and make it cheaper.

PANCETTA

Salt-cured pork belly, pancetta is tasty and goes delightfully crispy when fried. It adds a fabulous salty, meaty element to many pasta dishes, particularly when paired with green vegetables. I always use unsmoked pancetta, as I find the flavour of smoked pancetta too overpowering, but this is down to personal taste. You can buy pancetta as ready-cut *cubetti*, or lardons, or in flat round slices, which you can chop into little pieces. If you have a good deli, you can buy pancetta in thick slices to dice your own lardons – or even better, ask for *guanciale*, salt-cured pig cheek (the essential ingredient of any true carbonara) to add even more salty fat to your dish.

PARMESAN

I always have a hunk of parmesan in my fridge, as I know I will always be able to feed myself if I haven't been to the shops. As long as I have olive oil, parmesan and some pasta or rice, I will be okay. Parmesan brings a salty flavour to any dish and that umami edge that we all love. It's also a lovely and easy thing to bring out before dinner, as you can leave a hunk on the table next to a knife and people can slice off pieces of parmesan to snack on. Grating your own parmesan really does make all the difference when serving it over pasta. I never buy ready-grated packets from the supermarket, as I suspect they add some nasty stuff to stop it clumping together and drying out. Most importantly, it doesn't taste as good. I try to see grating cheese as a moment of meditation or the chance to listen to some music or a podcast.

PECORINO

Southern Tuscany is famous for its pecorino, as there is plenty of grazing for the sheep whose milk will be turned into this delicious cheese. Our local flock often get lost and bumble through our garden at Arniano, and we are alerted to their presence by the jingle-jangle of the bells around their necks. Pecorino di Pienza, from Tuscany's cheese-making capital of Pienza in the Val d'Orcia, is famed for its tangy, nutty flavour and generally comes in three forms of maturity. *Fresco*, hardly matured at all, is a white super-mild cheese that is fabulous with tender young broad beans in spring, or bruleed under sugar (page 50); it can be substituted with emmental or a mild cheddar. *Semi-stagionato* is the orange-rinded, more flavoursome pecorino that I serve as part of an *aperitivo* and it is great with a glass of wine or Prosecco. *Stagionato* is a very nutty, brittle, mature cheese which works beautifully with something sweet, such as a slice of pear or a drizzle of truffle-infused honey. A *semi-stagionato* or *stagionato* works wonderfully as a substitute for parmesan for grating over your pasta or 'speltotto' (page 114). At Casalinga, a family-run trattoria in Florence, they use these instead of parmesan in their pestos.

POLENTA

Polenta, or cornmeal, is a coarse flour milled from corn. When cooked with water, it thickens into a thick, nutritious paste that makes a hearty accompaniment to Tuscan stews and vegetables. It is often served in a more liquid loose form, sometimes with wilted greens stirred through. Any leftovers are often rolled out into an even layer and allowed to solidify to fry or grill over the fire in true waste-not-want-not fashion. Soon after being brought to Italy from the Americas in the 1500s, corn became a dominant crop, having a much higher yield than native grains, and so polenta became a dietary staple for peasant farmers – and in dire harvest years such as 1763 and 1767, it was attributed with having saved the country from famine. In leaner times, polenta might have been dressed only with a little oil, but a truly delicious plate of polenta involves fat, and lots of it – lashings of butter and grated cheese, or, in the case of polenta 'lasagna' (page 119), bechamel sauce.

ROSEMARY

Rosemary is possibly the most used herb in Tuscan cooking. It accompanies most roasts, is scattered over potatoes ready for the oven, is added to focaccia dough and is generally considered one of the quickest ways to inject flavour into most dishes. It's a hardy herb that grows in abundance all over Tuscany under even the most exacting circumstances, and we have bushes and bushes of it at home at Arniano where the soil is predominantly clay, which is famous for being impossible to grow anything in. When I lived in London I used to keep buying little packets of rosemary sprigs and realised what a ridiculous waste of money this was. A little rosemary plant is not much more expensive than a few sprigs in plastic, and yields so much more. This plant now happily lives on my windowsill, ready for its smaller sprigs to be snipped off for cooking, and has the added benefit of giving off a lovely scent.

I never use dried rosemary. Whenever a recipe in this book calls for rosemary, it is always fresh.

SAUSAGES

In Italy, sausages are very plump, fatty and meaty. The meat is minced to have a large grain, and they don't add any breadcrumbs or filler. I know this from experience, having helped turn the handle on the mincing machine at our neighbour's farm as a child. The sausages are almost always grilled over an open fire or barbecue and are delicious. They're served with cannellini beans (*salsicce e fagioli*) or little green lentils (*salsicce e lenticchie*), particularly around New Year as the combination is said to bring prosperity. When buying sausages for any of the recipes in this book, try to get large organic sausages, with the highest possible meat content.

STRACCHINO

Stracchino is a creamy soft white cheese made of cow's milk. It's sold in little plastic tubs, as its consistency is essentially similar to panna cotta, and it has a pleasant tangy acidity that pairs well with most flavours. It's absolutely wonderful spread on toast and topped with the new season's extra virgin olive oil in November, or with the best of the summer's tomatoes in August. Sadly, it can be difficult to find outside of Italy, which is why, whenever I put it on the breakfast or lunch table for guests, people exclaim at its deliciousness and ask why on earth they have never heard of it. Stracchino is often used as part of an *aperitivo* or antipasto here in Tuscany, and is also mixed with sausage meat to make the ultimate wine bar (*enoteca*) menu staple: grilled sausage and stracchino crostone (page 58). If you can't find stracchino, a ripe young brie is a good substitute, as is cream cheese, or even taleggio, though this has a much more dominant flavour, and none has the lovely acidic backnote of stracchino, so will be more rich.

TOMATO CONCENTRATE

Often sold in satisfying tubes rather like toothpaste, tomato concentrate is one of the handiest things to have in one's fridge. It is a thick, dense paste with an intensely strong tomato flavour that needs cooking or bulking out with other ingredients. When I am cooking for myself, this is a much more handy and economical option than an entire tin of peeled plum tomatoes, as I can just add a tablespoon of tomato concentrate to get the same effect without having half a tin of tomatoes hanging around. Real *estratto di pomodoro* (tomato concentrate) dates back centuries to parts of Italy and the Mediterranean where the sun is intense and heats any surface it reaches. In Sicily they would traditionally cook down tomatoes to reduce their water content, strain them to eliminate any seeds or skins, then spread this over wooden boards and leave it to dry in the sun. Once all the moisture had been extracted, the paste would be scraped off and put in jars. This is an experience people can still take part in at the Anna Tasca Lanza cookery school near Palermo. It was in the 1950s that Ugo Mutti managed to industrialise the process and seal tomato concentrate in toothpaste tubes.

I always try to buy the slightly more expensive varieties (still quite cheap) as the lower-quality ones are laced with lots of sugar. When I use tinned tomato, I exclusively use whole peeled plum tomatoes, as they stew and break down much better than chopped ones. I just use the end of a wooden spoon to break up the tomatoes, and always add water to the empty tin and swish it around to get any last bits of tomato to add to the pan. Given the insidious underbelly of the tinned tomato market that has come to light in recent years, where many immigrants are brought in to harvest the tomatoes in hideous conditions and treated little better than slaves, I encourage you to buy the best quality you can afford, as the bigger brands producing 'higher' quality goods are less likely to be involved in these practices.

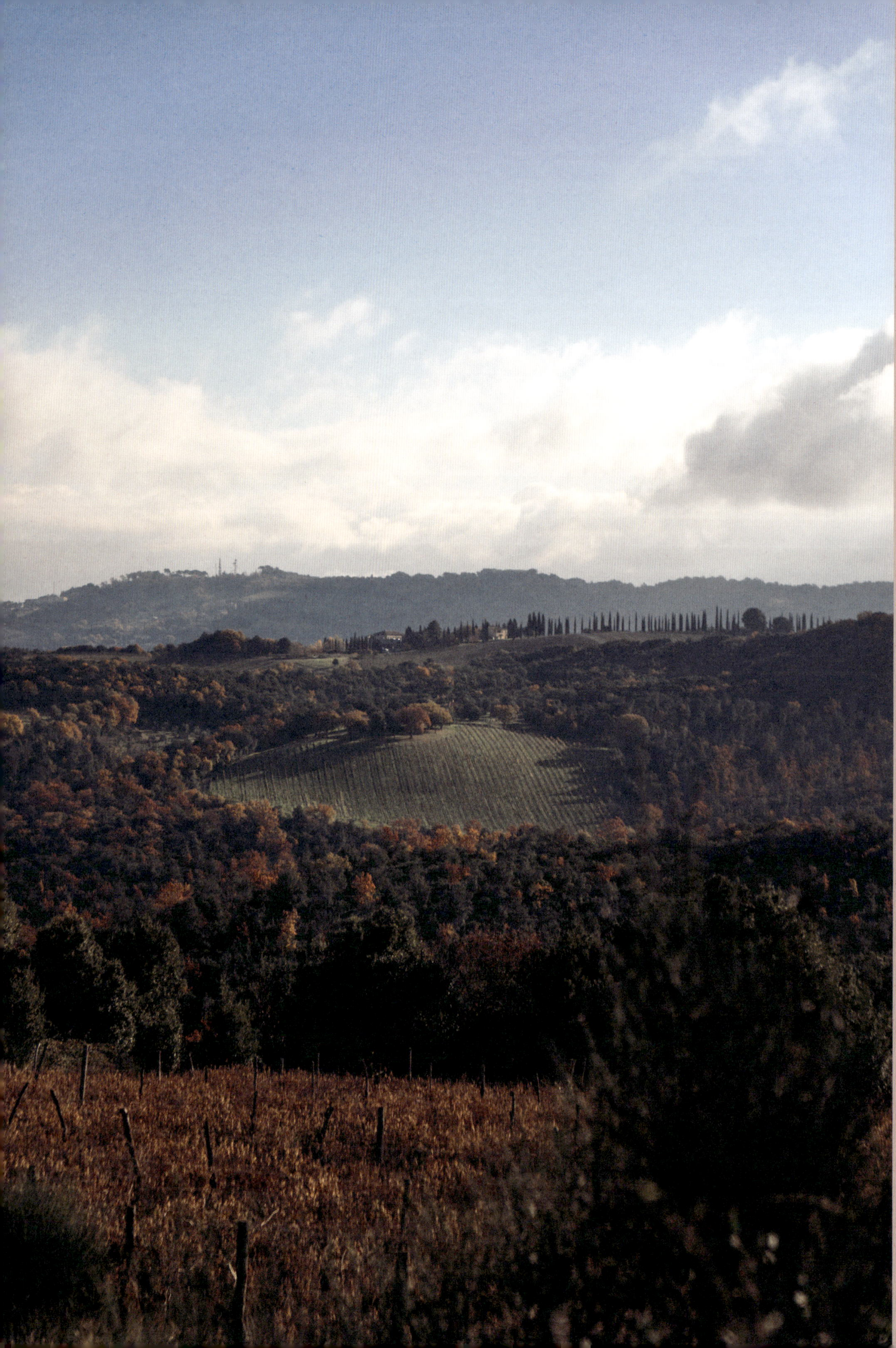

WINES OF TUSCANY

◆◆◆●◆◆◆

TUSCANY HAS A great variety of wines: Nobile di Montepulciano, Vernaccia di San Gimignano and the coastal Super Tuscans, which include famous brands such as Tignanello and Ornellaia. Because Tuscany is so hyper local, the wines I know best are inevitably the ones produced near where I grew up – those from Chianti, which sits to the north of us, and from Montalcino to the south. Following are some thoughts and notes on wines from these territories. And though I am no wine expert, I am friends with a great many, including my friend Carolina, who I met on my first day at primary school in Buonconvento and who is now a well-respected sommelier at Castiglion del Bosco, an incredible winery founded by the Ferragamo family and famed for producing some of the finest brunelli. Running their wine members' club takes Carolina across the globe to extol the fabulousness of their reds, and it is to Carolina that I am indebted for educating me on all matters viticultural.

OPPOSITE:– Looking over vineyards towards Montalcino

MONTALCINO

From Arniano, we can see the hilltop town of Montalcino on the other side of the valley. The town's name is synonymous with its biggest export – wine. Brunello di Montalcino is now world famous, but until 1980, when it was awarded its DOCG (Denominazione di Origine Controllata e Garantita) designation, it was just local table wine made from sangiovese, the dominant grape in Tuscan winemaking. A very refined, full-bodied wine, brunello is made from the grape clone Sangiovese Grosso (large), which has a thicker skin than its cousin Sangiovese Piccolo (small), which is used to make chianti.

Brunello is expensive because only the finest grapes from the highest points of any given vineyard are used, and the wine then has to be aged for a minimum of five years. This means storing and moving the wine from oak barrel to cement barrel and back again over the course of half a decade before it's able to be released. Bold and well structured, brunello pairs very well with Tuscany's heartier meaty fare.

The other wine from this area is Rosso di Montalcino. More affordable than brunello, it has a higher level of acidity, a lovely ruby-red colour, and feels lively and vibrant to drink. As it's a little less smooth it goes well with cheese, particularly pecorino as an *aperitivo*, or any cheesy main dish such as Baked fennel & pasta with bechamel (page 144), as its acidity works well with fat.

The altitude at which the vines grow around Montalcino gives the grapes their punchy flavour as they are exposed to the sun in summer, but then also to low temperatures in winter. However, a late frost in March when the plants are budding can lead to disaster. When this happens, the vineyards will light little fires a few metres between each of the vines to stop the buds falling off and potentially jeopardising September's grape harvest.

There are many good winemakers in Montalcino. Some of my favourites for both rosso and brunello are Castiglion del Bosco, Sesti, Castello Romitorio and Tenuta Buon Tempo. All are located in beautiful places, make excellent wine and use sustainable organic farming practices.

CHIANTI CLASSICO

Chianti Classico wines come from the hills south of Florence and north of Siena, a clearly defined territory whose boundaries were originally outlined by Cosimo III de' Medici in 1716 as being the only place allowed to label its bottles as being a 'Chianti Classico' – a designation that still stands. Nowadays this pocket of Tuscany is one of eight subregions that make up the vast area known more loosely as Chianti, which stretches from the foothills of the Apennine Mountains to south of Siena (and includes Montalcino) – but a Chianti Classico will always be from these very specific hills.

This small portion of the wider Chianti region is still a much larger area than Montalcino (about 78,000 hectares compared with Montalcino's 28,000), and is made up of four municipalities: Castellina in Chianti; Gaiole in Chianti; Radda in Chianti; and Greve in Chianti (where my parents lived before we moved to Arniano). The hills around these parts are much more densely wooded than around us south of Siena, and the vineyards are shoehorned into small patches of land between the forests. Some of the wineries here are centuries old. Our friend Giovanni Mazzei's family have been making delicious reds in the small hamlet of Fonterutoli, just outside Castellina in Chianti, since 1435 – and the Ricasoli family for even longer, since 1101.

In 1924 the wineries from the four municipalities came together and decided to protect their classic viticultural methods and founded the Chianti Classico Consortium, choosing as their symbol the black rooster, which was used by the league of medieval winemakers centuries before (and can be seen in Giorgio Vasari's mid-1500s painting *Allegory of Chianti* in Palazzo Vecchio in Florence). The outline of the black cockerel printed on the neck of the bottle now instantly tells you that the wine you are picking up is a Chianti Classico. This wine is very different from those from Montalcino, being medium bodied and more acidic. Like Rosso di Montalcino, chiantis are lighter than brunelli and perfect with rich food as their acidity balances it out.

Chianti Classico comes in three grades, determined by its age and specific grape content. *Annata* is a table wine which has to be aged for at least twelve months, whereas the slightly superior *riserva* has to be aged for twenty-four months. Both the *annata* and *riserva* must be made using at least 80 per cent sangiovese grapes and 20 per cent red grape varieties approved by the consortium (including merlot, syrah, canaiolo rosso and cabernet sauvignon, among others). The third and highest grade is the *Gran Selezione*, which must be made using 90 per cent sangiovese and up to 10 per cent grapes indigenous to the area.

There are hundreds of excellent wineries in the hills between Siena and Florence. Our firm favourites are Castello di Fonterutoli from the Mazzei family, Rocca di Montegrossi, Querceto di Castellina and Castello di Ama, which also houses a remarkable contemporary art collection, allowing one to take in some culture along with a wine tasting.

OPPOSITE:– The *vinsantaia* at Castello Sonnino

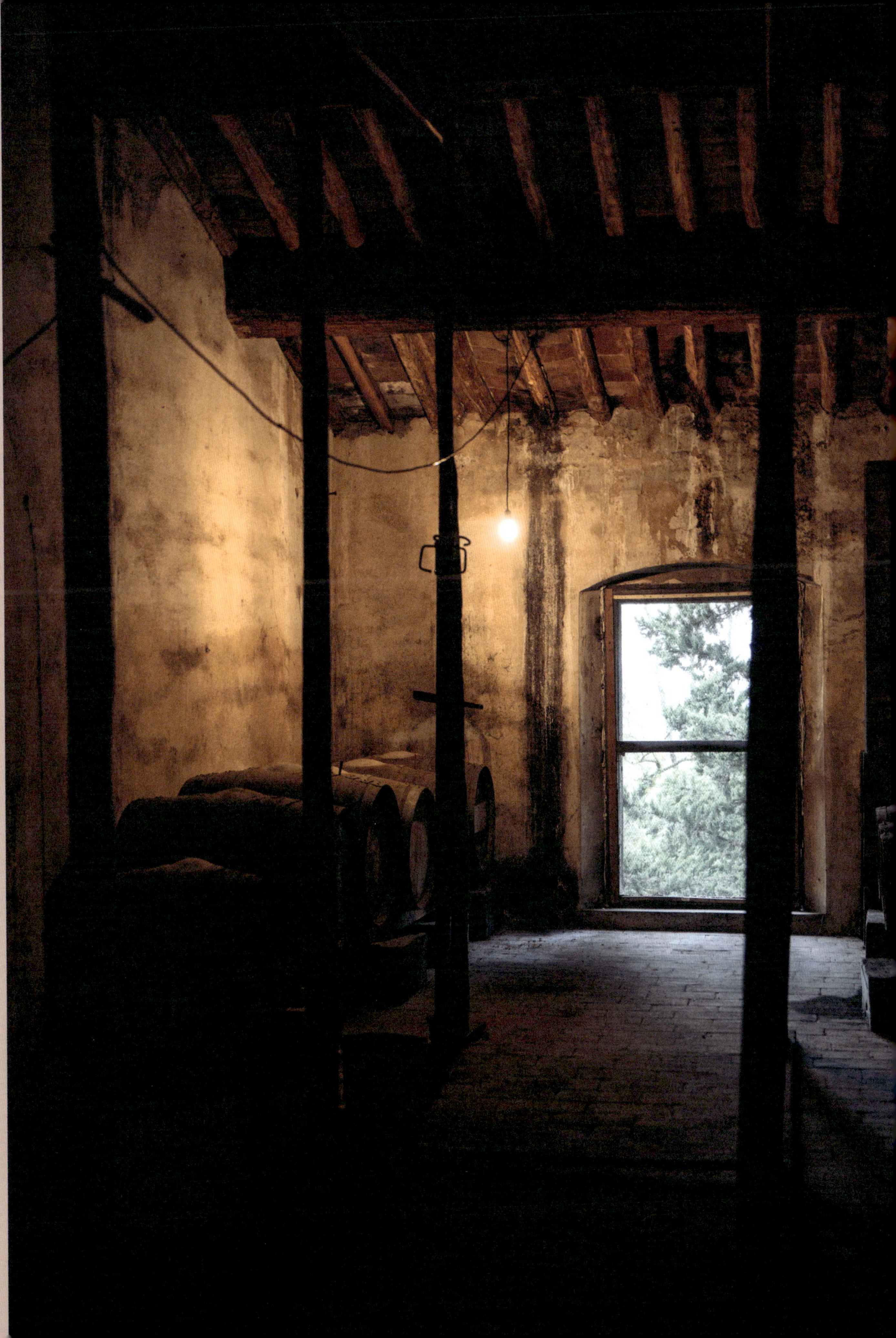

30

CLOCKWISE FROM TOP LEFT:—
Barrels at Castello Sonnino; Having a lesson
in wine from Don Andrea at Monte Oliveto
Maggiore; A doorway at Sant'Antimo;
Vintage bottles of Brunello di Montalcino

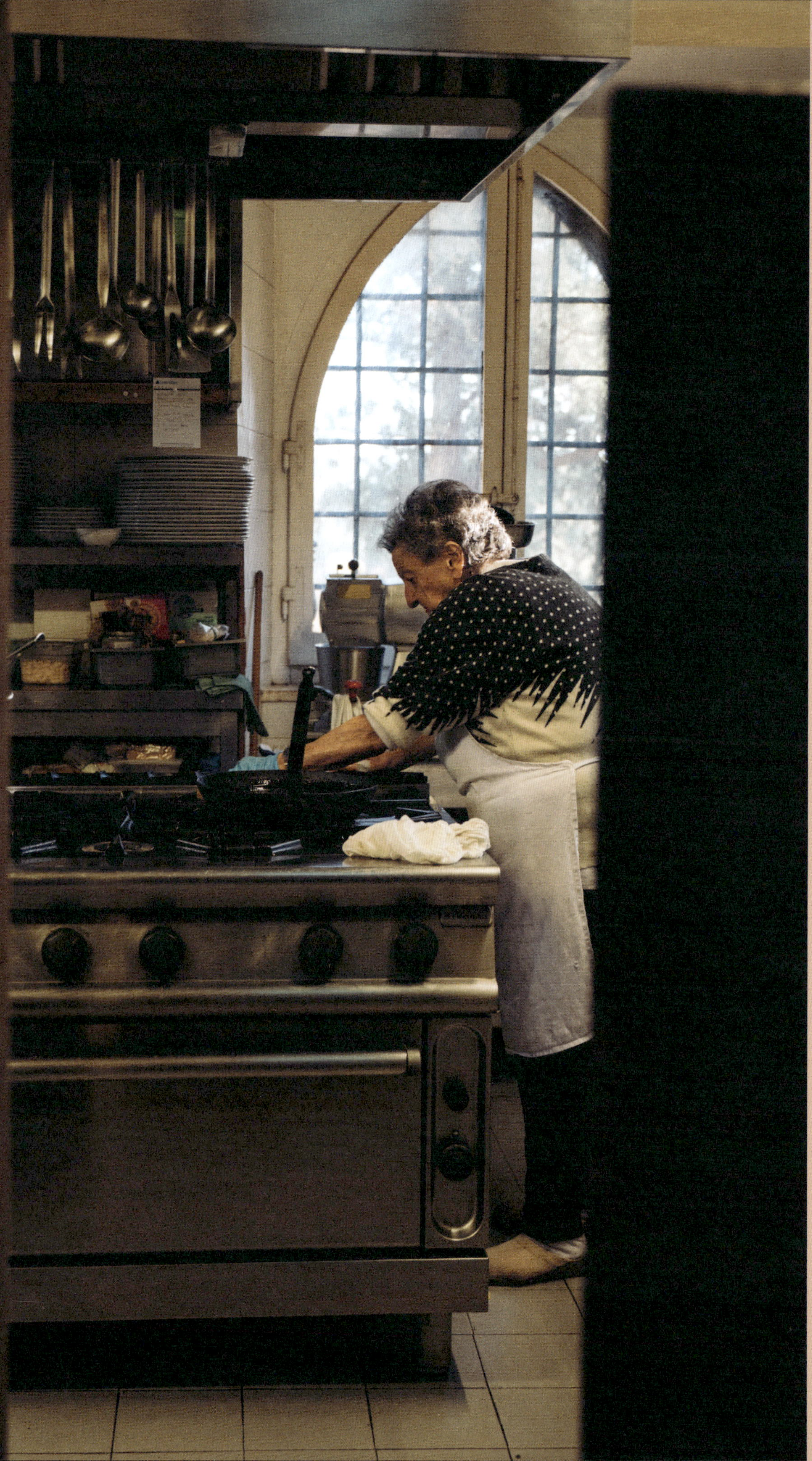

TUSCAN COOKING:
THE '*QUANTO BASTA*' WAY

THE MOST COMMON conversation I have with my Tuscan friends and neighbours over a meal is usually about what we've eaten in the days preceding, and what we might eat at the next meal. What one is cooking for dinner will be discussed over a morning coffee standing at the bar, while buying a newspaper, or in the queue at the pharmacy. The other day, I got caught up in a heated but friendly conversation between a barista and a customer over the best way to cook *lampredotto* (Florentine tripe stew). These discussions are most often with a total stranger who, having seen what produce you have in your basket, will strike up a conversation about what you plan on doing with your tomatoes, artichokes or porcini. After you've answered, you'll be in for some unsolicited advice on the best way to prepare them – though this never includes exact quantities, weights or timings. It's assumed you'll figure it out. This is what the idea of *quanto basta* is all about: you add as much olive oil, flour, butter or salt as is needed, and you cook, bake or fry the dish until it's ready. For instance, when a legendary local cook, Grazia, very kindly showed me her method for making pici, she tipped half a bag of flour into a bowl and started adding water. When I asked how much flour she thought she was using, just to note it down, she said, *Beh, ci vuole la farina che prende* – 'Well, we need as much flour as it takes.' While being quite so loose with measures makes me a bit anxious, I do love the sentiment behind it – that of not stressing too much, or not taking cooking too seriously, but instead using your taste, touch, instinct and a bit of common sense to make something pretty tasty.

OPPOSITE:– The family-run kitchen at Ristorante La Torre at Monte Oliveto Maggiore

OPPOSITE:– Tossing my emergency rosemary spaghetti

Another part of the *'quanto basta'* attitude to cooking – and something I have learnt over my years of cooking in lots of different kitchens – is that one's own way is usually the best method. There is no point veering off your own techniques if these are what work for you. If you're using a dessert spoon instead of a tablespoon to measure your ingredients, or slightly dodgy scales, or if your oven has a quirk and only cooks on the left-hand side, none of it really matters too much. As long as you are familiar with these variances and work with them consistently, you will find your way around them to get the desired result. If you are familiar with your oven's idiosyncrasies, for instance, then you will know how to bake a cake in it. And as long as you are measuring all the ingredients with the same thing, whether it be a dessert spoon rather than a tablespoon, the proportions will still be correct for baking – there might just be a bit less or a bit more cake. A lot can also be said for tasting as you go along – it's quite difficult to burn, oversalt, under-season or overcook a dish if you are regularly checking and tasting it. To me, tasting and adding a little bit of this or that as needed is the cornerstone of delicious food, as it allows you to cook the *'quanto basta'* way.

With this in mind, this book is a collection of cosy, hearty recipes that I love to make and eat in winter, and that are either classically Tuscan or Tuscan influenced, and not too prescriptive. I say 'influenced', as I am often keen to impart delicious Tuscan flavours without having to dedicate the time and patience that these often require – so I will always flout tradition to take a shortcut where I can, as I believe in working with the time that our busy modern lives allow.

Thinking of time and menu planning, I have created a list of recipes that you can make *al volo* (on the fly, or in a rush), taking less than 30 minutes to throw together, and ones you can make *con calma* (calmly in a quiet moment) – dishes that are suited to weekend cooking, or can be broken down into stages and brought together at the end. There are also some recipes that are simply easier to make in big batches, such as a classic *ragu* which, due to the number of hours it takes to cook, is worth making a large amount and freezing for a last-minute supper another time. You'll find a list of which dishes you can batch-cook or make ahead on page 39.

Aside from a chicken liver pate, I haven't included the classic offal-based Tuscan recipes as I don't eat them often, and find the ingredients difficult to buy outside Italy (sometimes even outside Tuscany). It's also rare to meet someone who wasn't born and raised in Tuscany who shares the local enthusiasm for them – though of course, conscious-minded omnivores everywhere should really be eating as much of these sorts of dishes as possible. I just wish I were adventurous enough to be one of them.

All the recipes in this book have been tested in a fan-forced oven, and temperatures are given in both Celsius and Fahrenheit. If using a conventional oven, increase the temperature by about 20°C (70°F).

Unless otherwise specified, the recipes in this book are for four people, as this is how I like to host and entertain on winter nights – to curate a cosy, intimate evening with a couple of good friends surrounded by lots of candlelight, glasses of chianti, and a delicious warming something to eat.

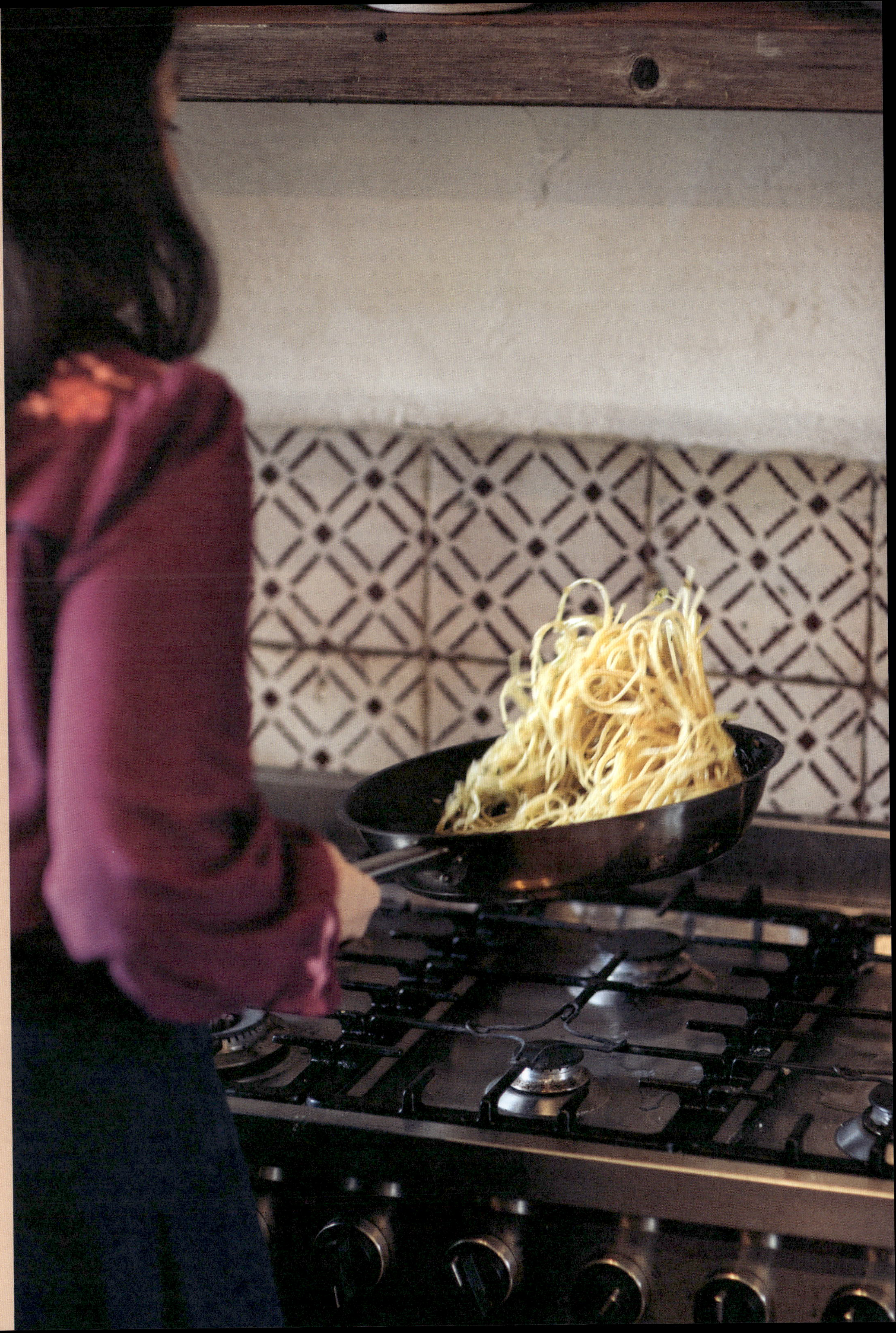

✦✦✦✦✦ MENUS ✦✦✦✦✦

A FEW KITCHEN SUPPERS TO IMPRESS

Serve any of the bread-based starters from a board on the kitchen table along with drinks while you chat or your guests keep you company as you finish cooking.

Menu No.01

Crostini with chicken liver pate . . . . p. 62

Herby roast pork loin with potatoes . . . p. 170
Cabbage tossed 'in the pan' . . . . . p. 197

Cantucci & vin santo semifreddo . . . . . p. 229

◆

Menu No.02

Juliette's mustardy artichoke crostini . . . . p. 66

Lemony meatballs . . . p. 179
Garlicky rosemary cannellini beans . . . . p. 198
Roasted baby onions . . . p. 194
Cavolo nero tossed 'in the pan' . . . p. 197

William's chocolate & rosemary olive oil mousse . . . . . . p. 230

◆

Menu No.03

Sausage & stracchino crostone . . . p. 58

Chestnut gnocchi with butter & sage . . . p. 120
OR Chestnut gnocchi (p. 120) with ragu (p. 116)

Chocolate & Amarena cherry cake . . . . p. 233

◆

Menu No.04

Fennel in lemony anchovy sauce . . . p. 54

Grazia's radicchio, sausage & rice timballo . . . . p. 174
Cabbage, apple & walnut salad . . . p. 202

Quince tarte tatin . . . p. 227

A FEW COSY KITCHEN SUPPERS

Menu No.01
Crostini with cavolo nero & cannellini beans . . . P. 65
Pici with garlicky tomato sauce . . . P. 126
OR Pici with cheese & pepper sauce . . . P. 127
Orange, polenta & thyme cake . . . . P. 234

Menu No.02
Juliette's mustardy artichoke crostini . . . P. 66
Mama's malfatti in broth . . . P. 76
Chocolate & Amarena cherry cake . . . . P. 233

Menu No.03
Baked porcini with cheese, honey & thyme . . . P. 57
Black pepper stew . . . . P. 176
Garlicky rosemary cannellini beans . . . P. 198
Red wine panna cotta with Jessica's grilled pears . . . P. 224

Menu No.04
Sausage, lentil & chickpea stew . . . . P. 173
Cantucci & vin santo semifreddo . . . . P. 229

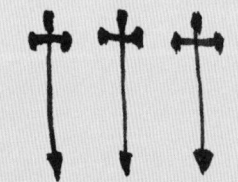

Menu No.05
Crostini with cavolo nero & cannellini beans . . . P. 65
'Good time' radicchio, gorgonzola & walnut lasagne . . . P. 143
Cabbage, apple & walnut salad . . . . P. 202
Ricciarelli with coffee . . . . P. 238

DISHES TO MAKE 'AL VOLO'

These recipes can be ready in 30 minutes or less.

ANTIPASTI

Chiara's bruleed pecorino ... P. 50

Baked porcini with cheese, honey & thyme ... P. 57

Fennel in lemony anchovy sauce ... P. 54

Juliette's mustardy artichoke crostini ... P. 66

Crostini with cavolo nero & cannellini beans ... P. 65

Crostini with chicken liver pate ... P. 62

Sausage & stracchino crostone ... P. 58

COMFORTING SOUPS

If you have your stock ready, or are using shop bought, these can be pulled together very quickly.

Mama's malfatti in broth ... P. 76

Egg & parmesan 'shreds' in broth . P. 79

Nara's spelt & cannellini bean soup . P. 84

Etruscan chestnut & chickpea soup . P. 83

PRIMI

Drunkard's spaghetti ... P. 105

Orecchiette with brussels sprouts & pancetta ... P. 110

Fusilloni with cavolo nero, walnut & pecorino pesto ... P. 106

Tonnarelli with artichokes & prosciutto ... P. 109

Saffron 'speltotto' from the monks of Monte Oliveto ... P. 114

PIATTI DI MEZZO

Artichoke frittata ... P. 133

Dada's baked leeks in bechamel ... P. 134

Baked fennel & pasta with bechamel ... P. 144

'Good time' radicchio, gorgonzola & walnut lasagne ... P. 143

SECONDI CARNE

Lemony escalopes ... P. 183

Florentine steak ... P. 166

DOLCI

William's chocolate & rosemary olive oil mousse ... P. 230

Matthew's orange & cinnamon salad ... P. 237

A few *cantucci* biscuits and a glass of vin santo

DISHES TO MAKE 'CON CALMA'

These recipes are not quick, but can be prepared in stages when you have time.

ANTIPASTI

Fried salty 'cuddles' with prosciutto & stracchino ... P. 49

The dough for these needs a few hours to prove, but the actual hands-on time needed to bring the dough together and to shape and fry the 'coccoli' is fairly minimal.

COMFORTING SOUPS

Vegetable stock ... P. 72

Chicken and beef bone broth ... P. 73

These soup bases take a few hours to simmer, but can be made ahead and stored in the fridge or frozen in convenient portions to throw together a meal at the last minute.

PRIMI

'Fake' meat sauce ... P. 102

Long slow cooking gives the vegetables the impression of being a thick and meaty ragu, so the process can't be rushed. But you can make the sauce ahead and keep it in the fridge to dress your pasta when you're ready to eat.

Ragu ... P. 116

There is no getting around the fact that a good ragu takes 3 hours to cook, but if you make a big batch all at once, you can freeze what you don't need in convenient portions to dress a last-minute plate of pasta or cheesy polenta or use in a lasagne.

Sienese pici ... P. 122

Shaping pici for four can be meditative, but rather longish if you aren't doing it in the moment with friends. You can make the pasta dough up to 3 days ahead and leave it in the fridge. The pici can be shaped and rolled a few hours ahead and refrigerated on a large plate or tray; just make sure you coat them well in semolina so they don't stick together.

SECONDI

Black pepper stew ... P. 176

Marinating and long slow cooking is what makes a relatively cheap cut of meat very tender in this stew, but it is even more delicious the next day, so it's a great dish to make ahead or in stages. Besides the long simmering time, it's actually very hands-off and quick to throw together.

Sausage, lentil & chickpea stew ... P. 173

Another wonderful dish that is even more delicious the next day, if you have the time to prepare it ahead.

Lemony meatballs ... P. 179

You can prepare the meatball mixture and shape the meatballs (which takes time) up to a day ahead and leave in the fridge until ready to cook.

DOLCI

Cantucci & vin santo semifreddo ... P. 229

This is a dessert to make when you have space and time, as it takes a few bowls and lots of washing up. It also needs time to set in the freezer, which means you can make it up to 5 days ahead and freeze until ready to serve.

Chocolate & Amarena cherry cake with ricotta ... P. 233

Florentine apple 'pancake' cake ... P. 223

Red wine panna cotta with Jessica's grilled pears ... P. 224

This is very quick to throw together, but the panna cotta requires time to set. Happily, you can make the panna cotta 5 days ahead and leave it in the fridge until serving.

Quince tarte tatin ... P. 227

You can poach the quince quarters the day before and refrigerate them in their poaching liquid in an airtight container until needed.

THIS SPREAD:— A wintery dinner at Arniano

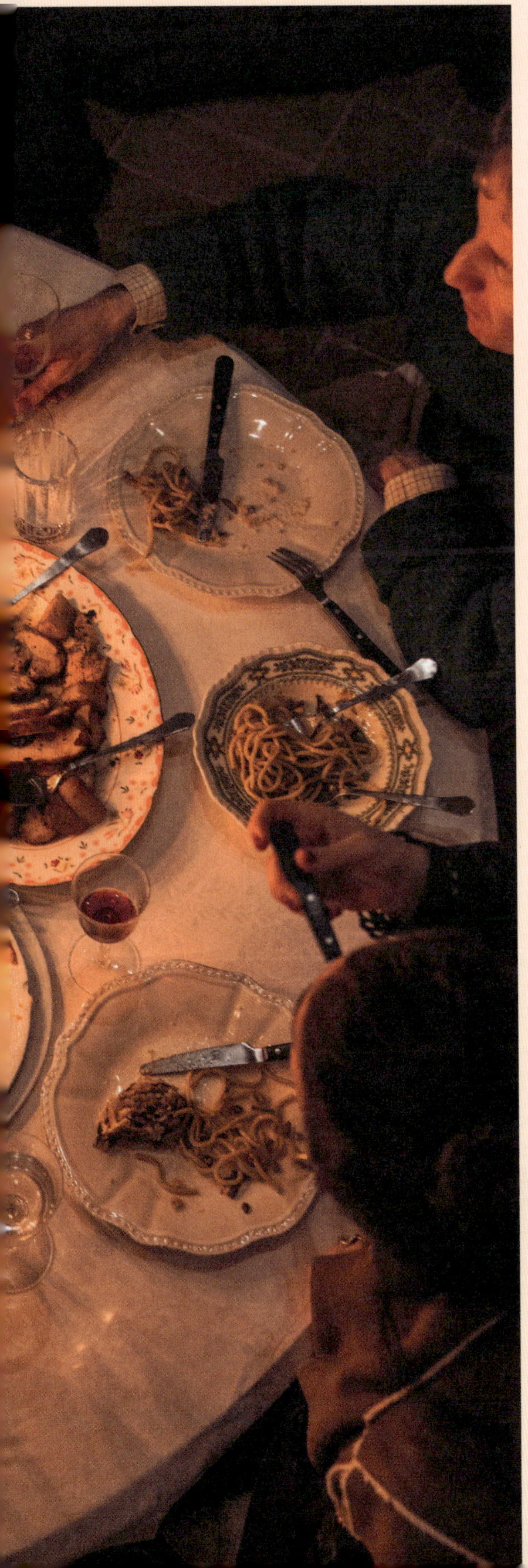
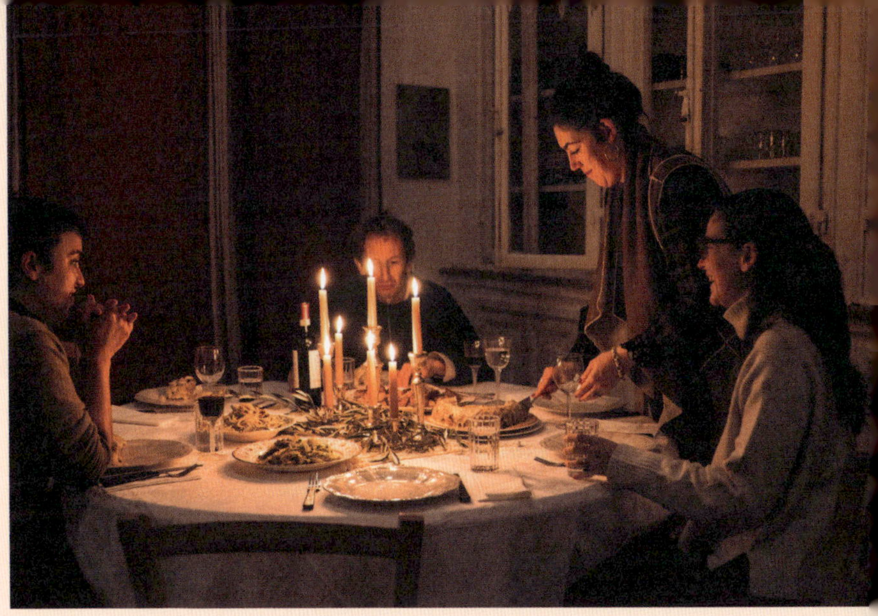
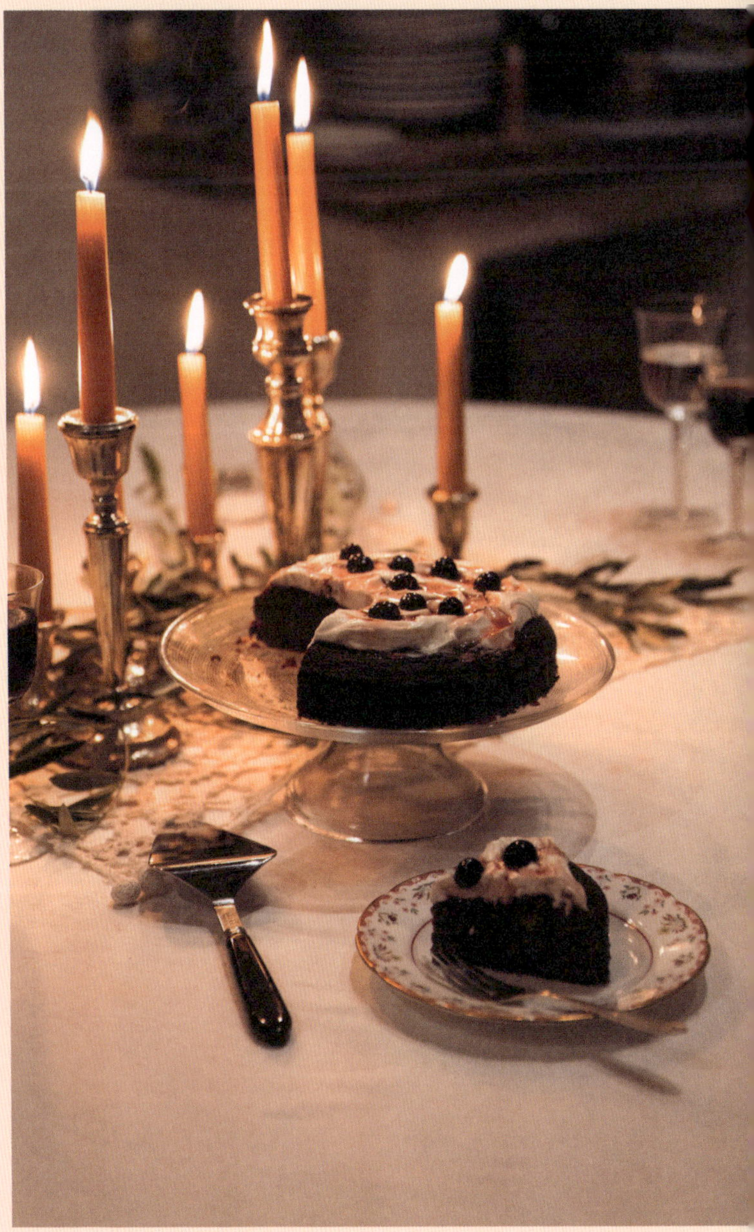

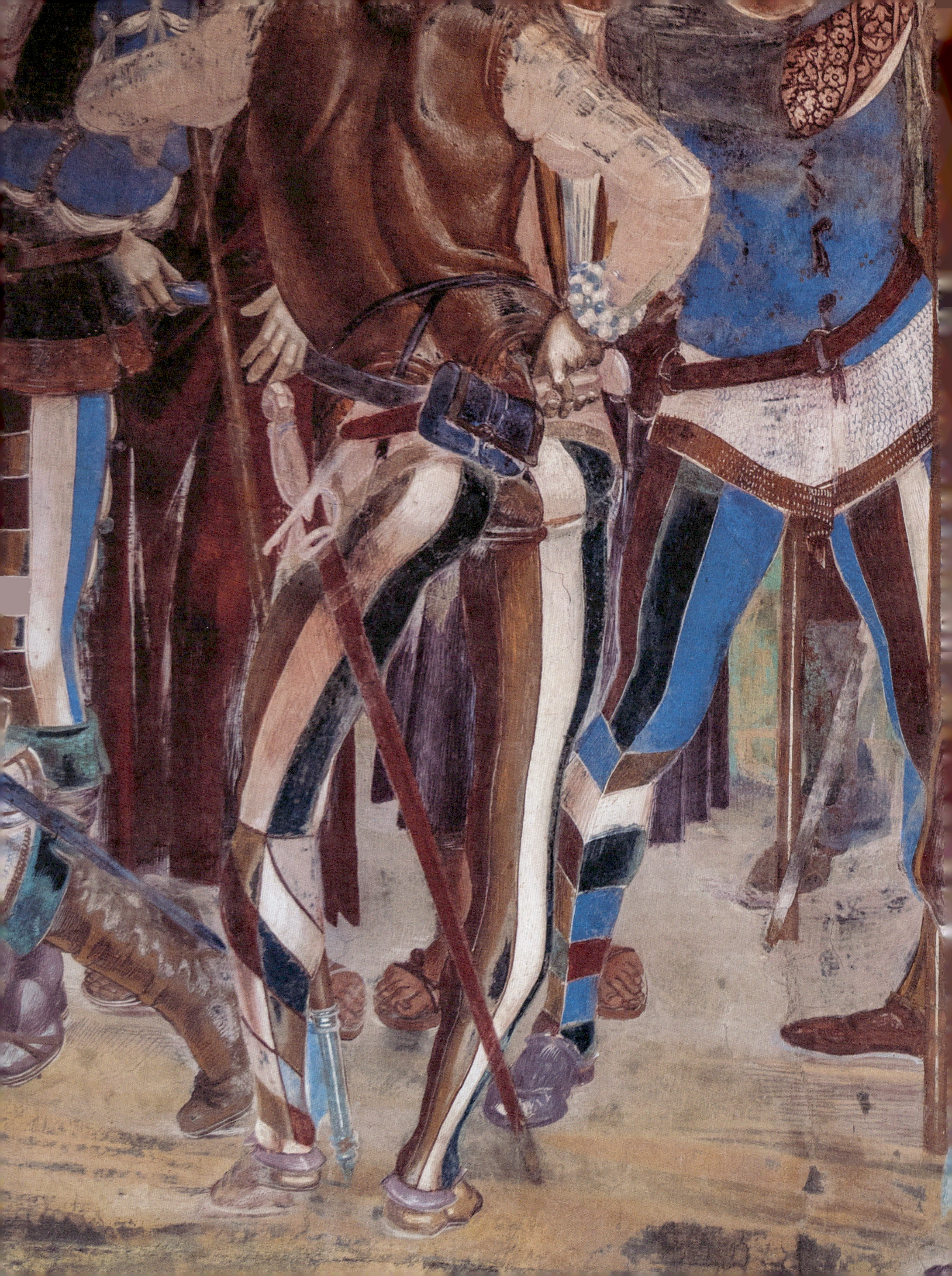

ANTIPASTI

BEFORE THE MEAL

Antipasti make up an important section of the menu of any self-respecting trattoria in Tuscany. They constitute the part of the meal that is designed to abate your hunger, to stave off your desperation for food and open up your appetite for the serious business of enjoying the main dishes to follow. I have a friend who takes this philosophy so seriously that when having a meal with colleagues or clients, he will stop for a *crostino* en route to the restaurant so as to really keep the wolf (and more importantly his 'hanger') from the door when in company.

Antipasto is an amalgam of the Latin words for 'before' (ante) and 'meal' (pasto), so it literally means 'before the meal'. A moment for catching your breath after a long morning or day, to catch up with your dining companions and munch on something delicious and satisfying while deciding what to order.

In Tuscany, the antipasti menu is often where you'll find the produce of whatever season you happen to be in most celebrated; in the colder months, the offerings might include an artichoke salad, or *puntarelle* (chicory or bitter greens) dressed with an anchovy sauce, or *pinzimonio* – seasonal raw vegetables sliced beautifully and served with a little bowl of the new season's olive oil in late autumn and winter.

An antipasto can be hot and is often deep-fried – fried porcini mushrooms, sage leaves or artichokes are a delight in the colder months. Toasted bread is often involved, though sometimes this might be as simple as a *tagliere* – a plate of cold cuts and pecorino cheese, which Tuscans so particularly excel at. Thick slices of *finocchiona* (fennel seed–infused salami), prosciutto Toscano (a saltier, leaner and more rugged version of its counterpart from Parma) and *soppressata* (a delicious, fatty and salty salami made in true top-to-tail fashion, so it's best not to ask what's in there) all lend support to the theory that Tuscan bread is unsalted because the accompaniments for it are so tasty and well seasoned that the bread doesn't need any additional salt. (The more common theory is that salt was historically omitted as it was once heavily taxed, but I prefer the more apocryphal culinary version.)

Unsalted Tuscan bread is also the base for one of the most popular and well-known antipasti, *crostini* (which aptly takes its name from the Latin for 'crust'). These crunchy, toasted pieces of stale bread – also known as bruschetta when topped with fresh tomatoes and basil in summer – are like a little blank canvas for whatever vegetables, cheese or meat you fancy, and are one of the quickest antipasti or snacks for feeding friends and family.

Crostini are also a fabulous base for vegetable toppings. You'll find two of my favourite ones on pages 65 and 66, as well as a recipe for the Tuscan classic, *crostini neri* – crostini with chicken liver pate (page 62).

DELICIOUS ANTIPASTI THAT REQUIRE NO COOKING:-

PECORINO CON PERE, MIELE E NOCI – Arrange a cheeseboard with a hunk of pecorino, walnuts, a small jar of truffled honey and slices of pear. Eat slices of the cheese with the pear and walnuts and drizzle over a little honey as you go.

BURRO E ACCIUGHE – Place a small plate of good-quality anchovy fillets on the table alongside a pat of very cold unsalted butter and toasted unsalted Tuscan bread or white sourdough. Use a butterknife to spread the cold butter on the toast – ideally thickly enough that you can see your teeth marks when you bite into it – and top with an anchovy fillet or two.

PINZIMONIO – Arrange a mixture of sliced seasonal raw vegetables (such as radishes, fennel, celery, baby artichokes and carrots) alongside a bowl of good new-season olive oil and a small bowl of sea salt. Dip the vegetables in the oil and sprinkle with a little salt as you go.

FETTUNTA – An 'oily slice' (*fetta* meaning 'slice', and *unta* meaning 'oily') for when the new-season olive oil is available in November. Toast unsalted Tuscan bread or white sourdough, and simply drizzle liberally with acid-green new olive oil and a little sea salt.

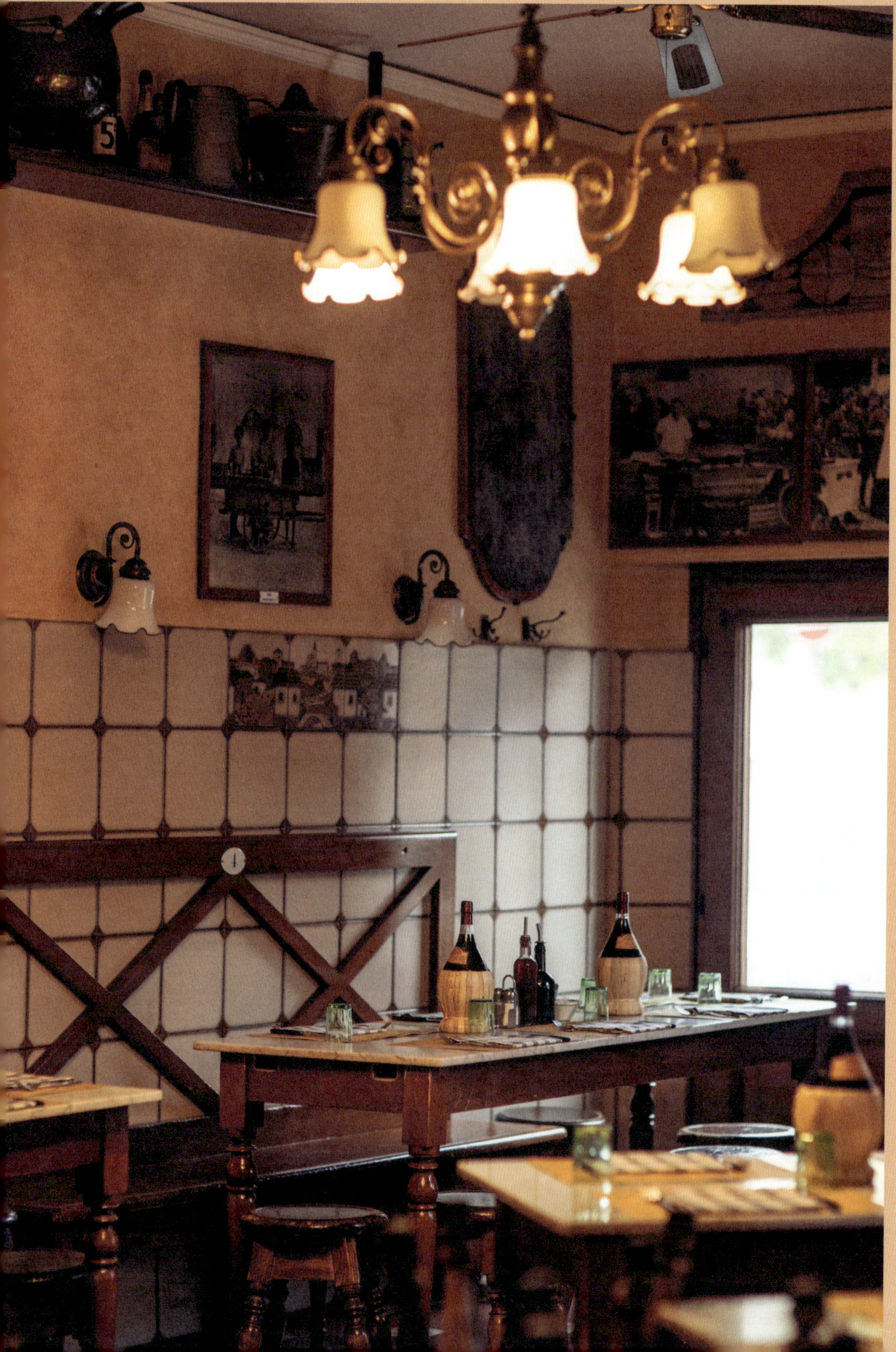

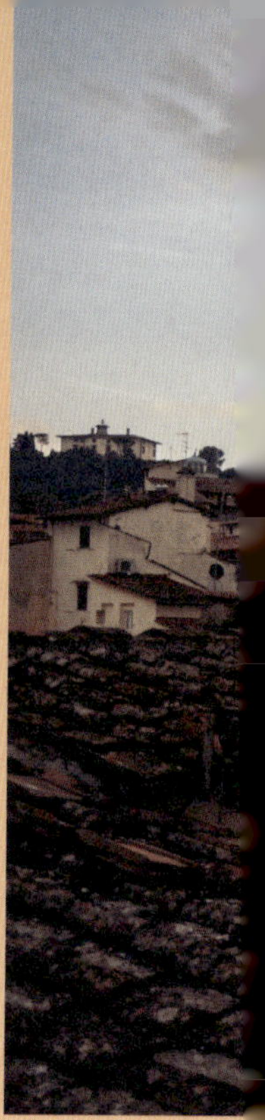

CLOCKWISE FROM BOTTOM LEFT:— Alla Vecchia Bettola in a quiet moment before service; Looking at the rooftops of Oltrarno from our flat; Lunch at Trattoria Cammillo

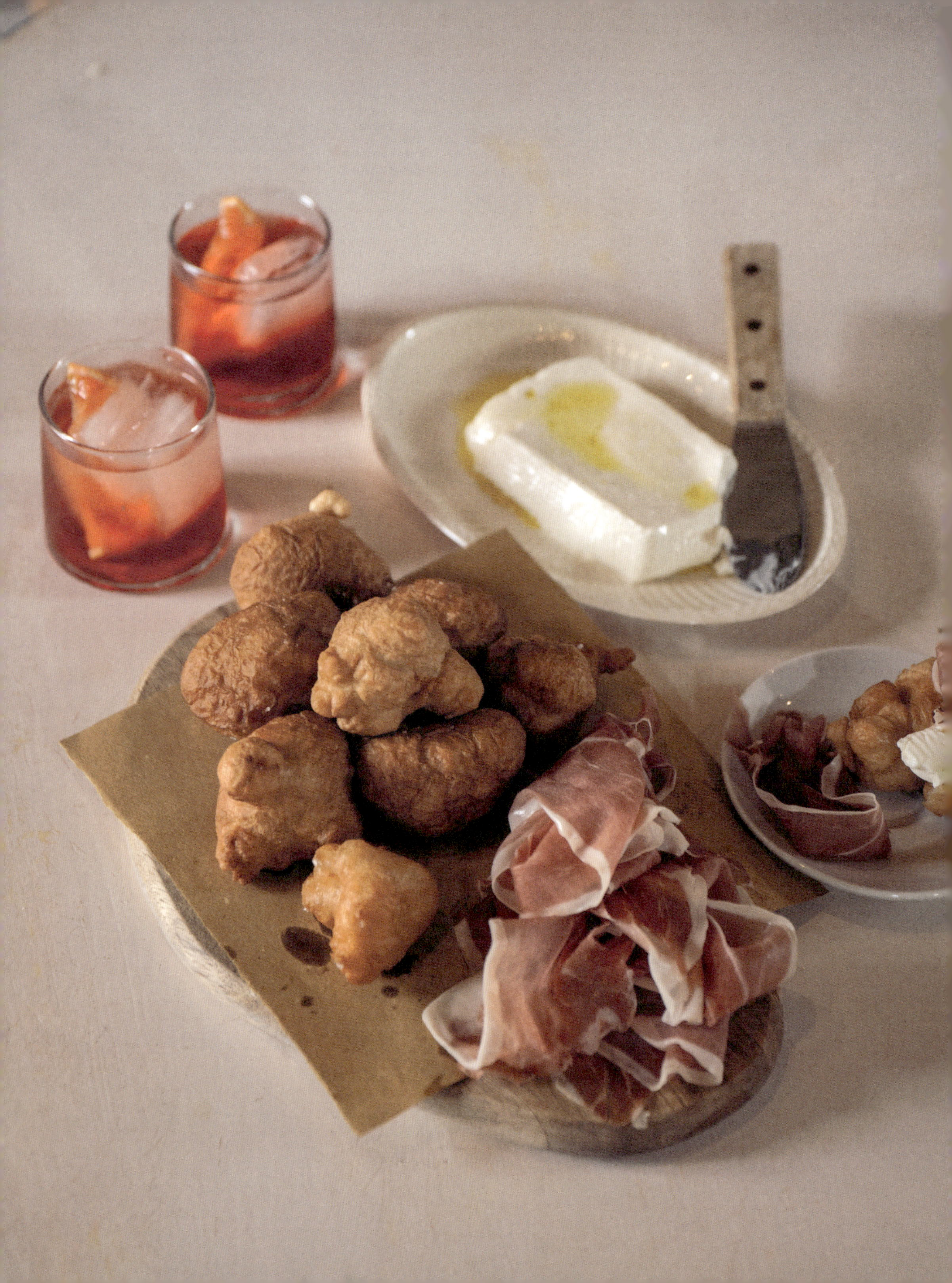

Coccoli con prosciutto e stracchino

Fried salty 'cuddles' with prosciutto & stracchino

SERVES 4

10 g (¼ oz) dried yeast
200 ml (7 fl oz) tepid water
1 teaspoon sugar
200 g (7 oz) '00' flour
1 tablespoon olive oil
½ teaspoon fine sea salt
vegetable oil, for deep-frying

TO SERVE
fine sea salt
stracchino
prosciutto di Parma (prosciutto Toscano)

Coccoli, or cuddles, are a Florentine street food made of deep-fried yeasted dough, served with prosciutto and stracchino (a wonderfully creamy and slightly tangy cheese made from cow's milk). Fried dough in various forms is popular all over Tuscany, and near us in the countryside is a restaurant that brings you a plate of *coccoli* when you sit down – not served with anything, just covered in fine salt. It is the perfect way to get your juices going as you peruse the menu.

This dough is very loose and liquid, looking more like a bubbling monster in the bowl than a usual bread dough, but the *coccoli* come out very light and airy. You will need two spoons to drop the mixture into the hot oil to fry. Traditional recipes also include lard and broth, but I love the simplicity of using just flour, water and yeast.

These are perfect to make on weekends as they are delicious, low effort and impressive. The dough requires no kneading, taking only a few moments to bring together before being left to sit for a few hours, ready to be sizzled briefly in hot oil and served alongside something cold and fizzy.

Instead of stracchino, you can serve the *coccoli* with cream cheese, a young ripe brie or some taleggio.

PREPARATION:– A few minutes
PROVING:– 2 hours
FRYING:– 10 minutes

Mix the yeast with the water and sugar in a bowl, stirring well until the yeast has fully dissolved and looks creamy. Tip the flour into a separate bowl, make a well in the centre, pour in the yeast mixture and stir together thoroughly. The mixture will be quite liquid. Add the olive oil and salt and stir again.

Cover the bowl and leave the dough to double in size over the next 2 hours.

When the dough has risen, two-thirds fill a wide deep frying pan with vegetable oil. Turn the heat to medium–high and leave the oil to heat up for a few minutes. An easy way to check it's ready is to put a little piece of the dough in the oil: when the oil starts sizzling, it's ready. You want the oil to be around 170°C (325°F) to get the perfect golden colour; any hotter and the *coccoli* will burn.

Take a tablespoon of the dough and use another tablespoon to gently nudge it off into the oil. Repeat with a few more tablespoons of the dough, being careful not to overcrowd the pan. Leave to fry for about 5 minutes, turning occasionally so the *coccoli* cook evenly.

Using a slotted spoon, transfer the *coccoli* to a plate lined with paper towel to soak up any excess oil while you finish frying the remaining dough.

Sprinkle the cooked *coccoli* generously with fine sea salt and serve right away with soft stracchino cheese and prosciutto. You can either break the *coccoli* apart and make a little sandwich, or scoop up some stracchino then bite into some ham, it's totally up to you.

Pecorino brulèe

Chiara's bruleed pecorino

SERVES 4

8 slices of pecorino fresco ('fresh' pecorino), each about 1 cm (½ inch) thick

5 tablespoons caster sugar

TO SERVE

prosciutto di Parma (prosciutto Toscano) (optional)

My friend Chiara, who owns our favourite restaurant Trattoria Cammillo down the road from us in Florence, came up with this joyous and simple starter: sugar sprinkled onto pecorino fresco and blow-torched so it caramelises, forming a beautiful glassy top. It's key with this dish to use a kitchen blow torch and a young pecorino which has not been matured for long and still has a dense springy texture, as it pairs so well with the crack of the sugar when slightly melted by the blow torch. At a pinch, a more mature pecorino romano works too, but you could also try a mild cheddar, emmental or even camembert.

PREPARATION:— A few minutes
COOKING:— A few minutes

Lay the cheese slices on a heatproof serving plate and sprinkle evenly with the sugar.

Using a small cook's blow torch set to low, begin flaming the sugar from a distance, so that you don't blow the sugar away before it sets. Keep the flame moving across all the cheese slices so that you don't burn them, and adjust the blow torch distance as needed, until the sugar has melted and browned.

Once you have a glassy caramel top, serve immediately with a fork, either on its own or with some thinly sliced prosciutto.

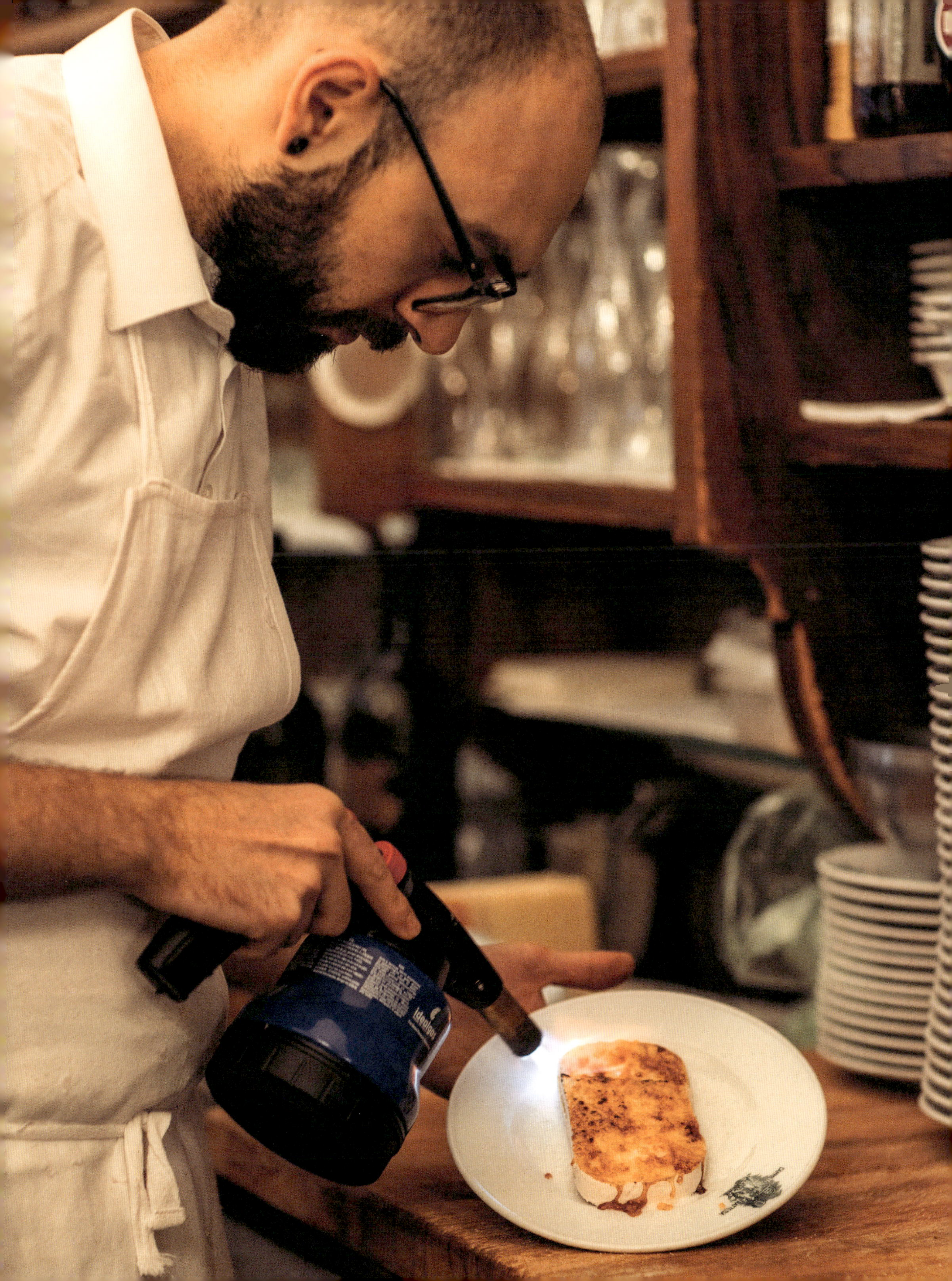

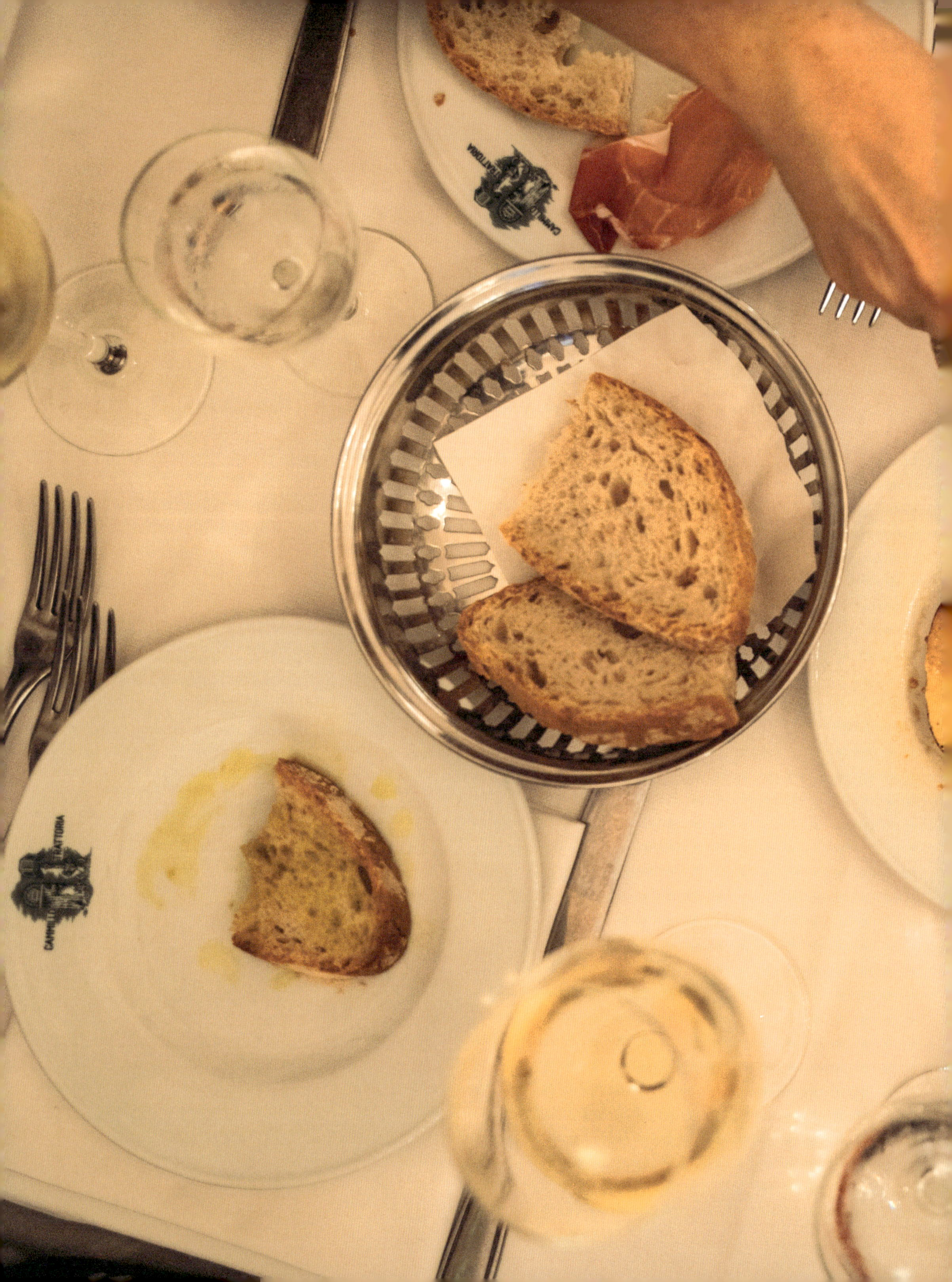

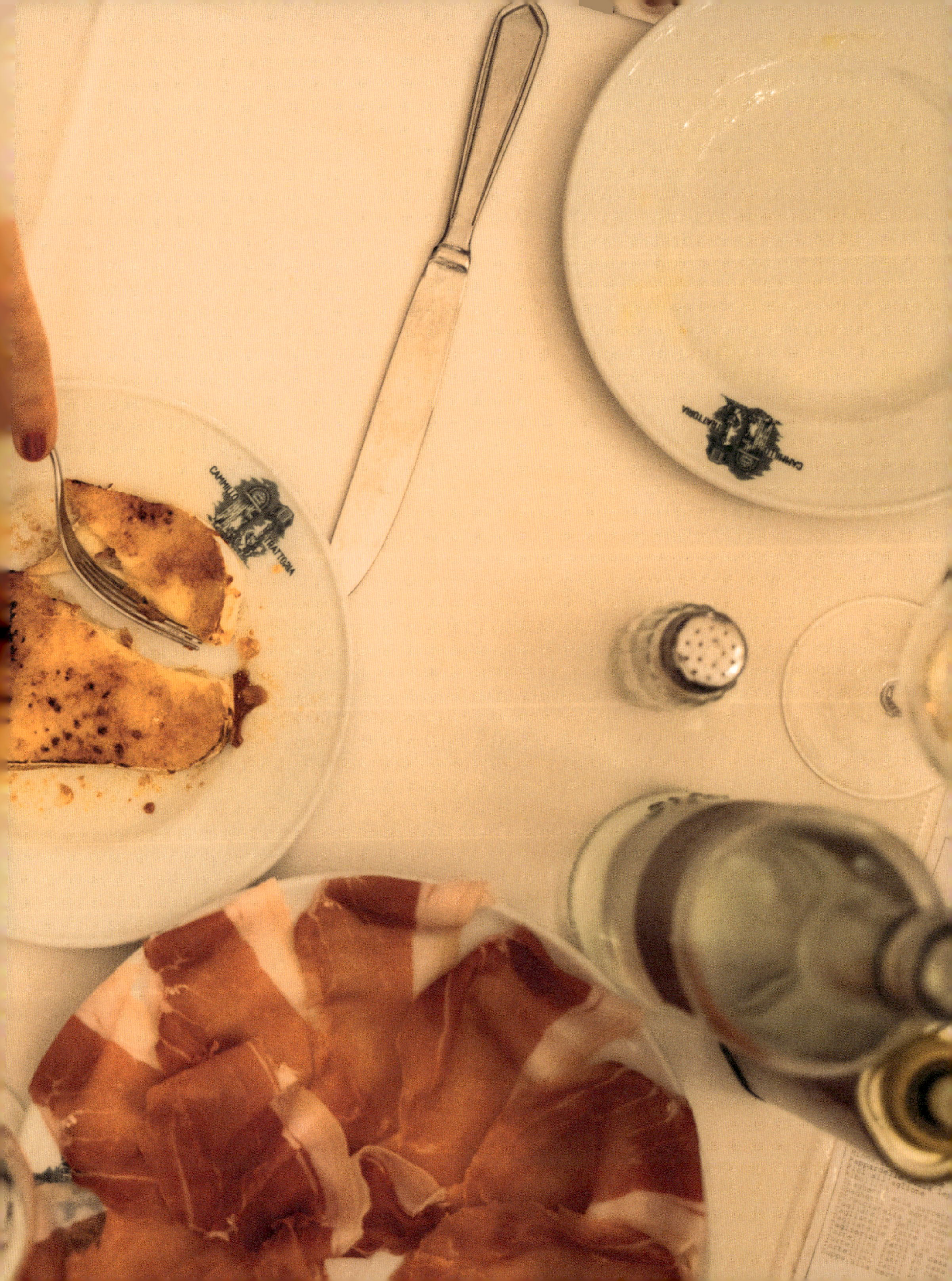

Finocchi alle puntarelle

Fennel in lemony anchovy sauce

SERVES 4

2 large fennel bulbs

1 small tin or jar of good-quality anchovy fillets

1 garlic clove, crushed

juice of ½ lemon

good-quality olive oil

freshly ground black pepper

A joy of the colder months is the return of bitter leaves such as chicory, and more specifically *puntarelle* – a pale-stemmed, green-tipped bitter chicory, a head of which looks like a children's drawing of a monster's claw. In Rome, and in many restaurants in Tuscany, *puntarelle* are passed through a special wire mesh to turn the leaves and stems into thin curled fronds, which are then soaked in iced water before being drained, dried and dressed in a lemon and anchovy sauce. If you can find *puntarelle*, I do recommend using it in this salad (you can finely chop the *puntarelle* with a sharp knife instead of using wire mesh, which is much less fiddly) – but as fennel is much easier to get hold of outside Italy, I have included it here instead.

I am not specifying exact quantities for the dressing in this recipe because the proportions are really based on personal preference. Some like it more lemony (me), and some prefer it to taste very anchovy-y (my husband), so in our home we compromise by giving whoever makes the dressing the power to decide.

PREPARATION:– A few minutes
COOKING:– A few minutes

Slice the woody base off the fennel bulbs. Remove any woody tops, and the outer layer if it is very thick and tough, so you are left with the tender core. If your fennel bulbs are on the smaller side, you may not need to remove a layer.

Slice the bulbs in half lengthways and place on a chopping board, cut side down. Slice lengthways as thinly as you can, transferring all the fennel to a serving bowl.

In a separate bowl, mash about a tablespoon of anchovy fillets (I normally use about four fillets, my husband eight) with a fork. (Alternatively, you can make the anchovy sauce using a pestle and mortar.) Once mashed, add the garlic, and slowly add the lemon juice and 2–3 tablespoons olive oil, whisking constantly and tasting as you go. Adjust the quantities to taste. If you would like it more acidic, add a drop more lemon juice; if you want the sauce to taste more of anchovy, mash in more anchovy. You want a loose dressing that will coat the fennel, so don't be afraid to add more lemon juice or oil, just taste as you go.

When ready to serve, add a few cracks of black pepper, pour the sauce over the fennel and toss thoroughly. Eat immediately.

OPPOSITE:– *Puntarelle* in anchovy sauce at Trattoria del Carmine in Florence

> **VARIATION:–** If you can't find fennel or it's obscenely expensive, use thinly sliced crisp white cabbage instead.

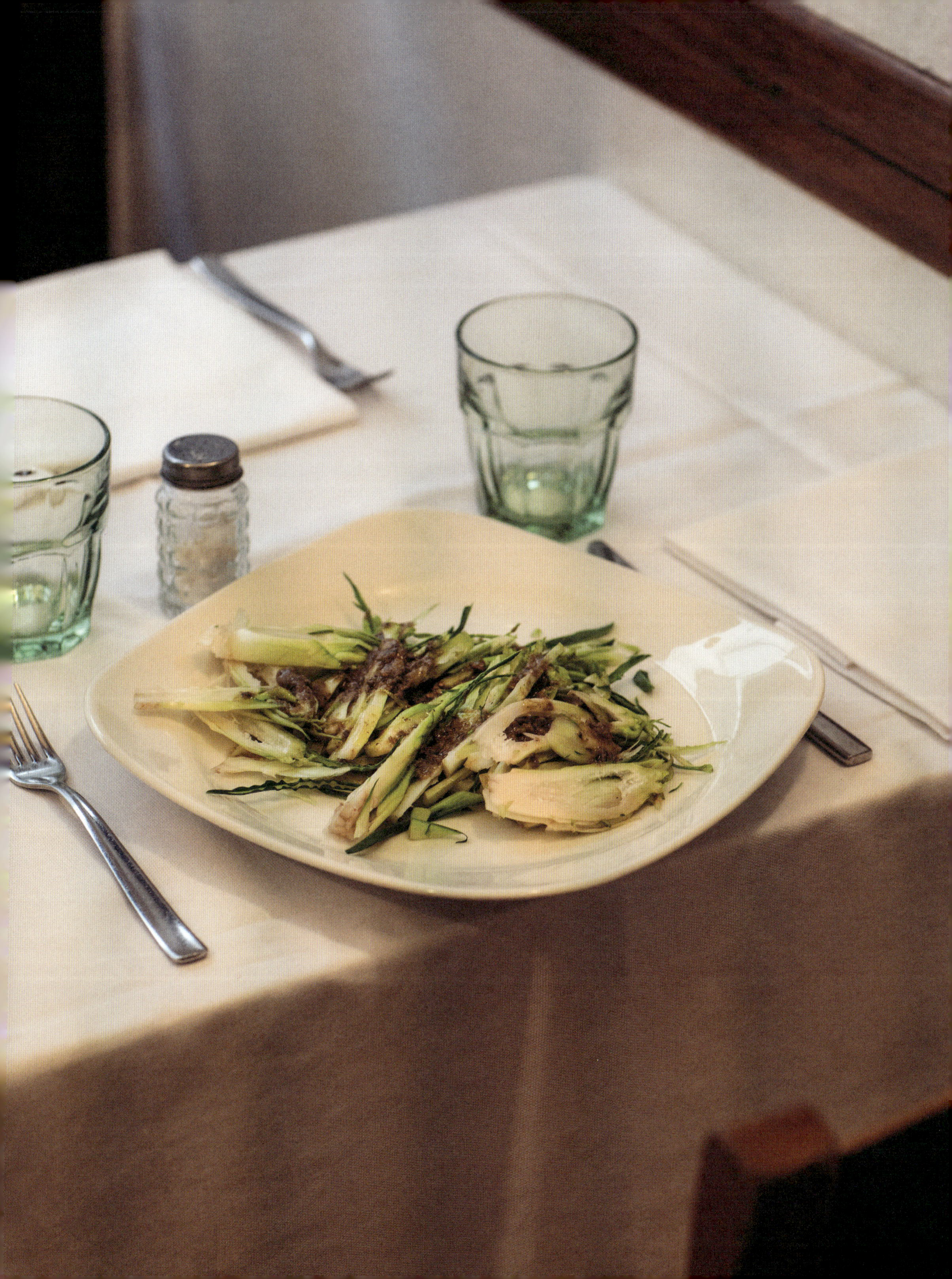

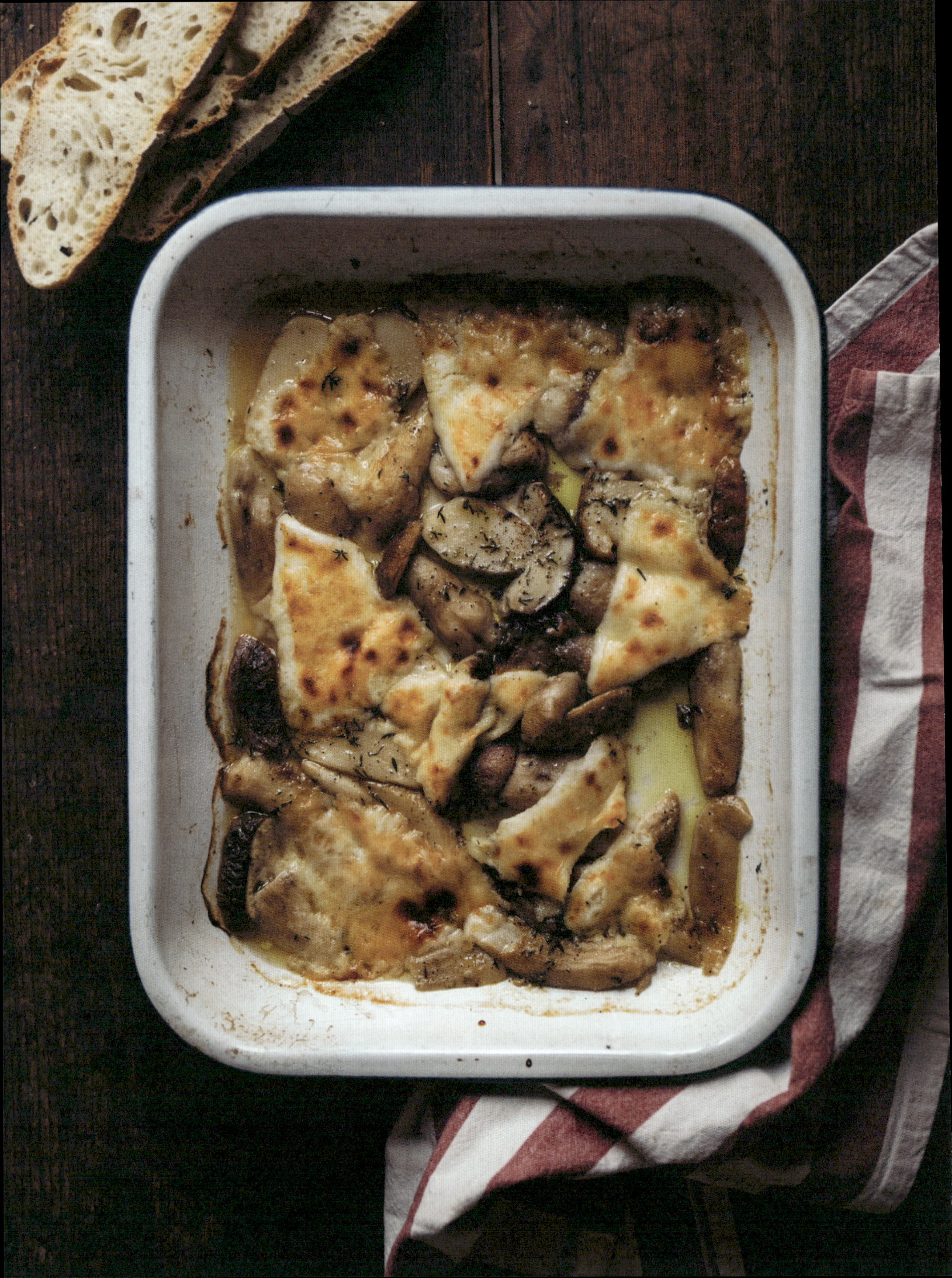

Porcini al forno con pecorino, miele e timo

Baked porcini with cheese, honey & thyme

SERVES 4

4 large porcini mushrooms, or 400 g (14 oz) mushrooms of your choice

1 tablespoon olive oil

sea salt and freshly ground black pepper

a few thyme sprigs, leaves picked

8 slices of fresh pecorino, emmental or mild cheddar

4 tablespoons runny honey

TO SERVE

good crusty bread

I love this as a very speedy and delicious starter. The meaty mushrooms with the melted cheese, honey and thyme are a lovely combination when eaten with very good crusty bread. If you can't get fresh porcini, this recipe also works well with portobello, shiitake, oyster and chanterelle mushrooms – just roast them without the cheese for a few minutes first. I've even used pre-sliced white mushrooms from the supermarket. These threw out a lot more moisture, but this was no bad thing, as it called for more bread to soak up the sweet honey mushroomy juices alongside the melted cheese.

PREPARATION:– 5–10 minutes
BAKING:– 10–15 minutes

Preheat the oven to 200°C (400°F) fan-forced.

Clean the mushrooms using a clean brush or tea towel to rub away any dirt. Cut away any roots or particularly earthy bits.

Slice the mushrooms lengthways about 5 mm (¼ inch) thick. Transfer to a roasting tin large enough to lay the mushrooms out in a single layer. (If you've bought pre-sliced mushrooms, put them directly in the roasting tin.) Drizzle with the olive oil, season with salt and black pepper and toss, then arrange so that the mushrooms aren't piled up on top of each other. Scatter the thyme over, then lay the cheese slices on top and drizzle with the honey.

Bake for 10–15 minutes, until the mushrooms are cooked and the cheese is bubbling.

Serve hot, with a loaf of crusty bread.

Crostone di salsicce e stracchino

Sausage & stracchino crostone

SERVES 4

4 large slices of white sourdough bread (preferably a little stale)

2 sausages, about 100 g (3½ oz) each

6 tablespoons stracchino cheese

olive oil

Different from a *crostino* (*-ino* indicating something smaller), a *crostone* (the suffix *-one* meaning bigger) is a much heftier, large affair. Unlike a *crostino*, which is designed to get the appetite going but not to properly sate it, these will most often be served in *enoteche* (wine bars) as a tasty and sturdy stomach-lining accompaniment to a robust glass of chianti.

PREPARATION:— A few minutes
BAKING:— 20 minutes

Preheat the oven to 170°C (325°F)/150°C (300°F) fan-forced.

Take the slices of bread and line on a baking tray. If the toast slices are very long, cut in half. Put in the oven for up to 5 minutes, until lightly golden and a bit dried out. Turn the slices over halfway through, so that they dry evenly. Remove from the oven.

Turn the oven up to 200°C (400°F).

Slice down the side of the sausages with a knife and remove the sausage meat from their casing. Transfer to a bowl and break up the meat with a fork.

Add the stracchino and mix together until you have an amalgamated mixture.

Using a tablespoon, divide the mixture equally onto each piece of bread and smooth out to the edges using the back of the spoon. Drizzle lightly with a little olive oil and put back in the oven.

Bake for 10 minutes until the cheese is bubbling and browning and the sausage meat has cooked. Remove from the oven and leave to rest for 5 minutes, until cool enough to handle. If the pieces of bread are particularly big, you may need a knife and fork.

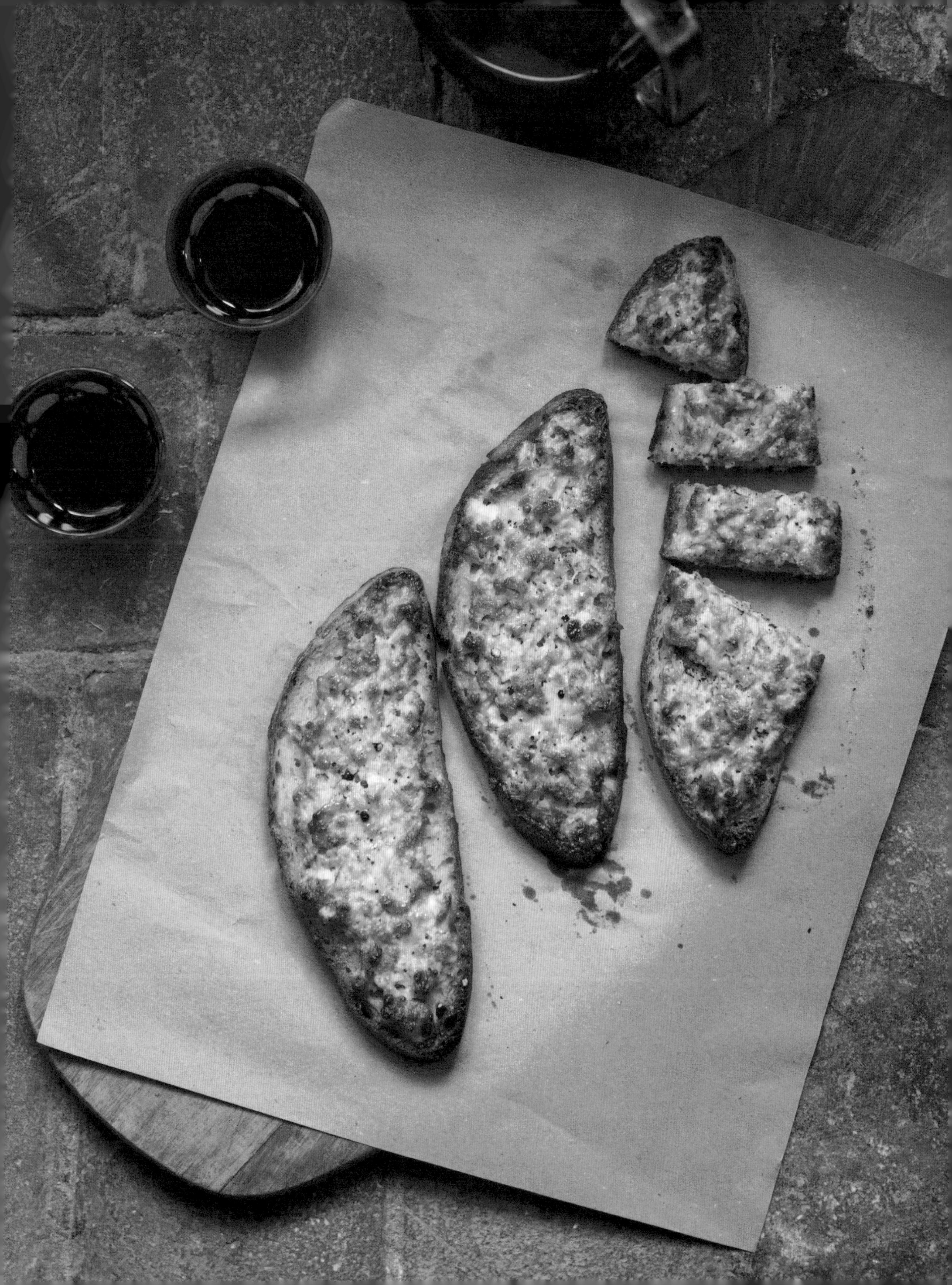

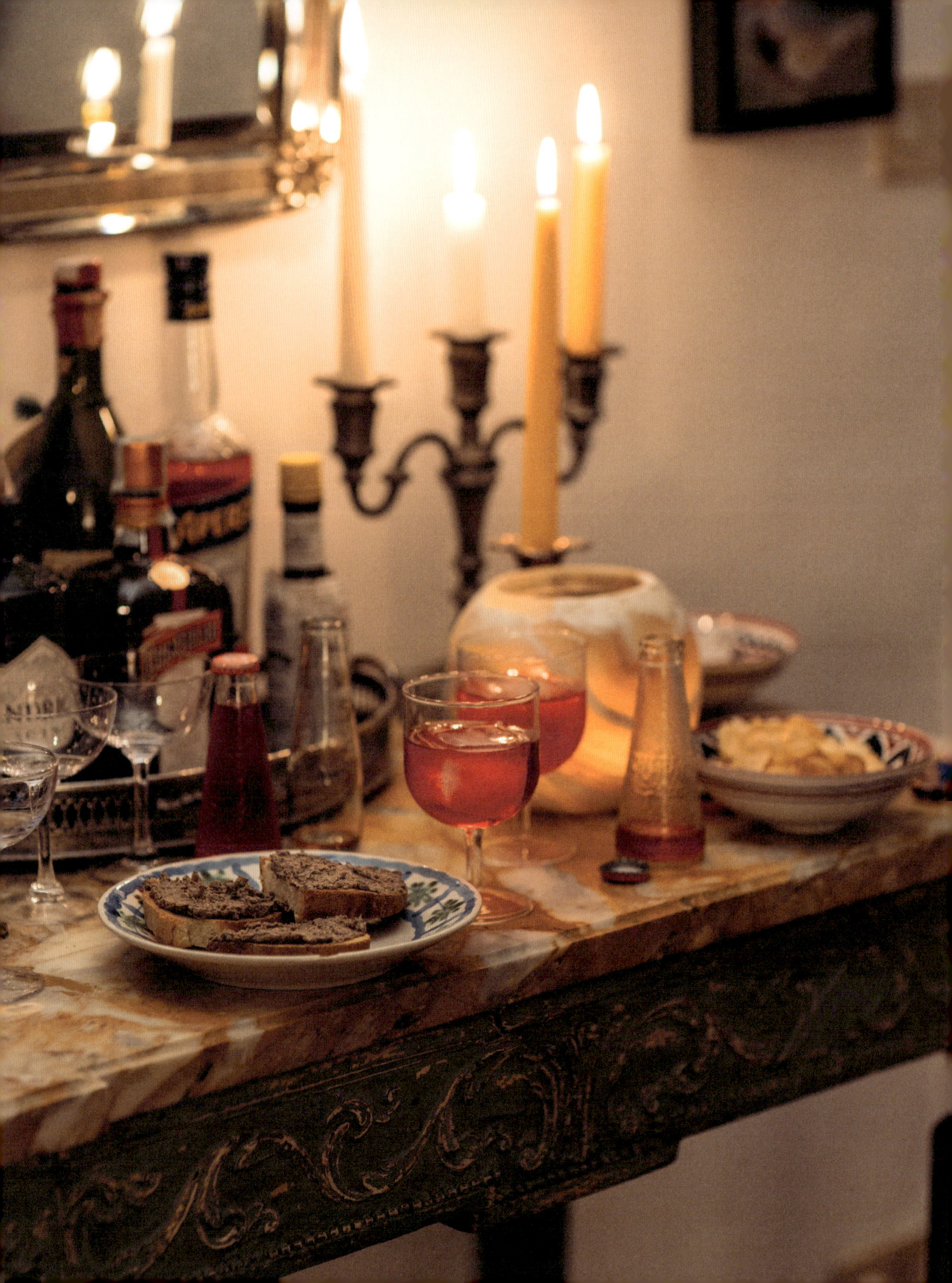

Crostini

SERVES 4

4 large slices of white sourdough bread (preferably a little stale), cut 1 cm (½ inch) thick

Here's a quick recipe for Tuscan *crostini* – which is essentially, toast – ready to be topped with whatever ingredients you fancy. As well as cheese or meat, *crostini* are also a fabulous base for vegetable toppings. I have included two of my favourite ones on the following pages. My friend Juliette's mustardy artichoke crostini (page 66) is her go-to antipasto for a party. It's delicious, moreish and made of relatively inexpensive ingredients, so is wonderful for a crowd – while the Crostini with cavolo nero & cannellini beans (page 65), from Trattoria La Casalinga in Florence, makes a wonderful and filling winter warmer which is just as perfect for a quick lunch as a starter to a dinner party.

PREPARATION:– A few minutes
COOKING:– 7 minutes

Preheat the oven to 150°C (300°F) fan-forced. Cut the bread to your preferred size for your chosen topping. (After it's been in the oven, the toasted bread will be too brittle to slice cleanly without shattering.)

Lay the bread slices on a baking tray and toast in the oven for 5–7 minutes, until golden and completely dry, turning the slices over halfway through so they dry evenly.

Remove the crostini from the oven and set aside until ready to serve. Once cooled completely, you can keep them in an airtight container for up to 2 days before topping.

Crostini neri

Crostini with chicken liver pate

SERVES 4

CHICKEN LIVER PATE

300 g (10½ oz) chicken livers

olive oil

½ red onion, very finely chopped

sea salt

½ wine glass of vin santo, or a sweet dessert wine

50 g (1¾ oz) unsalted butter

2 anchovy fillets, preserved in oil

1 tablespoon brined capers, rinsed and finely chopped

100 ml (3½ fl oz) chicken stock

Crostini (page 61), to serve

Salsa di fegato (chicken liver pate) is one of Tuscany's most emblematic dishes, and has been served with *crostini* since medieval times. Any restaurant in the region will almost certainly have *crostini neri* or *crostini Toscani* on the menu, but no two versions will ever be the same. Some restaurants will serve bread dipped in broth topped with the warm, loose pate; elsewhere it will be a room-temperature dense spread on toasted crunchy bread (my preferred variation). The chicken livers are cooked with onion, capers, a tiny bit of anchovy and a dash of sweet wine to come together into a salty, earthy delight. As a child it was always a huge treat to go to the deli section of the supermarket and order *salsa di fegato* from a large tub behind the glass counter. It really is delicious and doesn't taste intense – just like a mouthful of umami. It's a great thing to make at the start of the week and keep in the fridge, ready to spread on *crostini* as a starter if you have friends or family coming over.

I have upped the vin santo to make the pate a little sweeter, but you can halve the amount if you would like the more traditional version.

PREPARATION:– 5 minutes
COOKING:– 30 minutes

Slice the chicken livers into small pieces, discarding any stringy bits. Pat dry with paper towel or a clean tea towel.

In a large, deep frying pan, heat a few glugs of olive oil, along with the finely chopped onion and a little salt. Cook gently over a medium heat for about 3 minutes, until the onion is translucent. Add the chicken liver and cook for a few minutes, stirring often. Once the chicken liver has browned, pour in the vin santo and cook over a lowish heat for 5–8 minutes, until all the wine has evaporated and the liquid has reduced.

Remove from the heat and leave to cool for a few minutes before transferring to a food processor, keeping the pan handy for the next step. Pulse a few times until you have a rough, granular-looking mixture, a bit like a thick hummus. Set aside.

Add the butter and anchovy fillets to the frying pan over a medium heat. When the butter starts to melt and the anchovies dissolve, add the chopped liver mixture, along with the capers, and stir until amalgamated. Add half the chicken stock, stir, then add the rest. Cook over a low heat for another 10 minutes, until your pate has reduced to a thick sauce-like consistency.

Serve the *crostini* warm or at room temperature, spread with the pate.

The pate will keep in a clean glass jar or container in the fridge for up to 3 days.

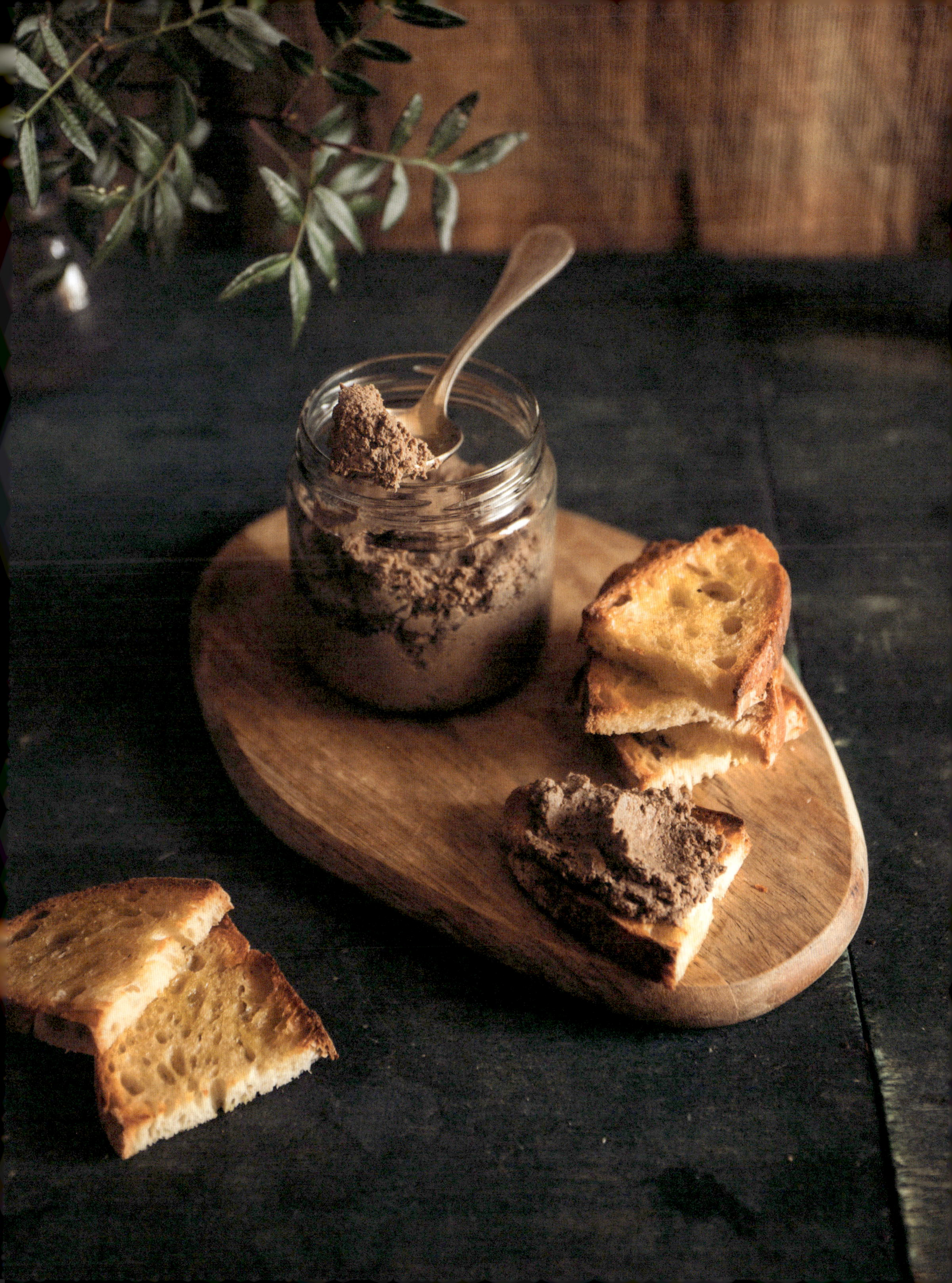

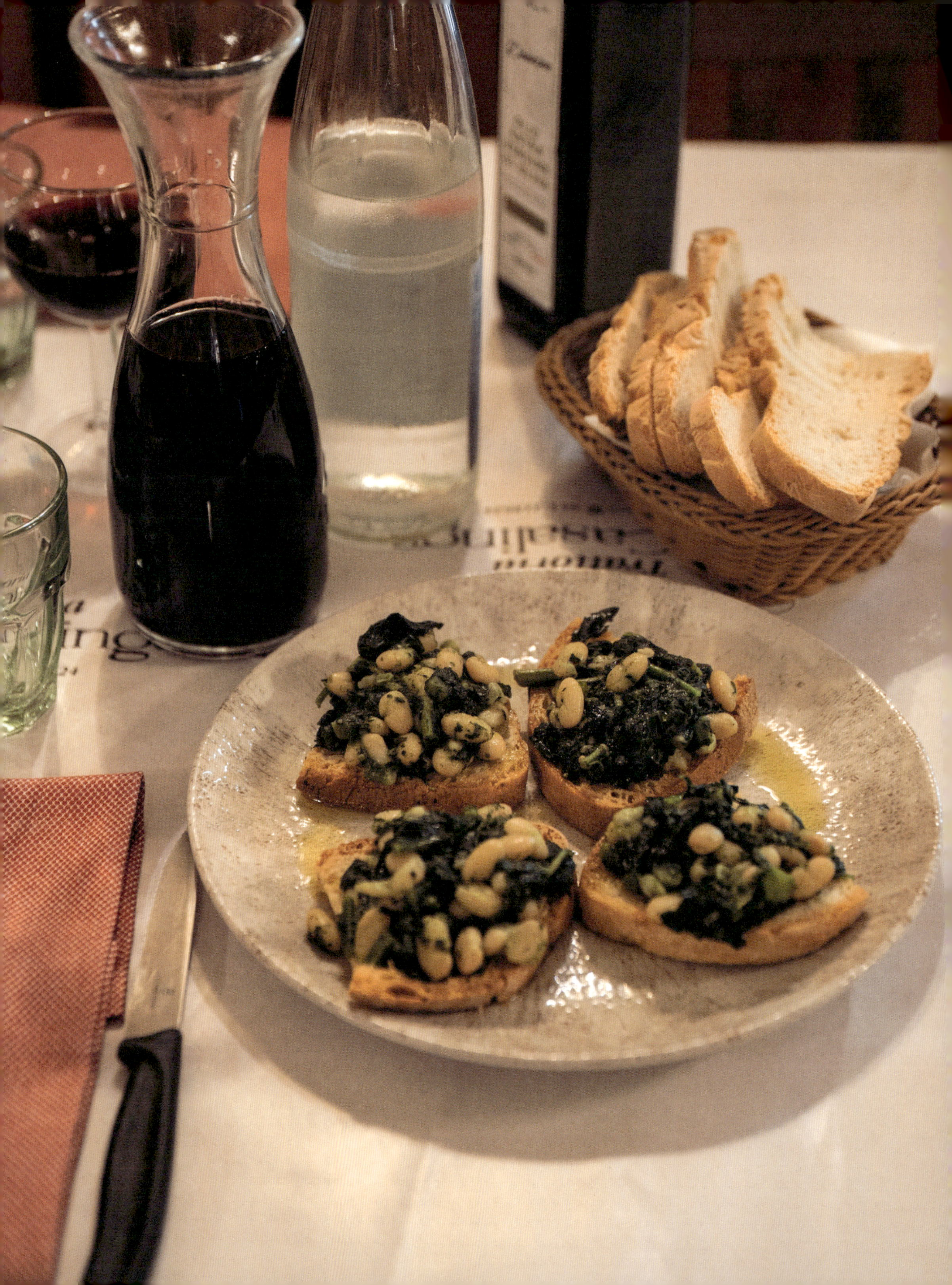

Crostini con cavolo nero e cannellini

Crostini with cavolo nero & cannellini beans

SERVES 4

large handful of chopped cavolo nero leaves, or a large handful of whole cavolo nero, leaves removed from the stalks

olive oil

1 garlic clove, sliced in half

chilli flakes

sea salt

1 small tin or jar of cannellini beans, drained

Crostini (page 61), to serve

COOKING & ASSEMBLING:– **15 minutes**

Bring a small pan of salted water to the boil and cook the cavolo nero until dark green and completely wilted – about 8 minutes. Drain well and finely chop.

In a wide frying pan, heat 2 tablespoons of olive oil with one of the garlic halves and a pinch of chilli flakes. Once sizzling, add the cavolo nero and toss with the garlicky oil, stir-frying for a few minutes. Add a generous pinch of sea salt and discard the garlic. Stir in the cannellini beans and warm through for 2–3 minutes.

Arrange the *crostini* on a serving board and rub each piece lightly with the remaining garlic half. Drizzle with a little olive oil, sprinkle with sea salt, then top each one with a heaped tablespoon of the warm cavolo nero and cannellini bean mixture. Finish off with a drizzle more oil, salt and chilli flakes if you like and serve with napkins alongside.

Crostini con carciofi e senape

Juliette's mustardy artichoke crostini

SERVES 4

5 tablespoons mayonnaise

2 teaspoons dijon mustard

sea salt and freshly ground black pepper

pinch of paprika

½ teaspoon chilli powder, or to taste

5 tablespoons grated parmesan

2 small jars of artichoke hearts

Crostini (page 61), to serve

zest of ½ lemon

PREPARATION:– A few minutes
COOKING:– 20 minutes, plus resting time

Preheat the oven to 160°C (315°F) fan-forced.

In a bowl, mix the mayonnaise with the mustard, a pinch of salt, a few grinds of black pepper, the paprika and chilli. Mix through 2 tablespoons of the parmesan and taste, then adjust the seasoning as necessary.

Drain the artichokes well of all their liquid, then roughly chop them, so there are still a few chunky pieces of artichoke. Mix the artichokes through the mustardy mayonnaise.

Transfer the artichoke mixture to a wide, shallow ovenproof dish, smoothing it out with the back of a spoon. Evenly sprinkle with the remaining parmesan and finish with a few more grinds of black pepper. Bake for 20 minutes, or until the top is bubbling and browned.

Remove from the oven and allow to rest for at least 10 minutes, or up to a few hours.

When you're ready to assemble, spoon some of the artichoke mixture onto the crostini and finish with a little lemon zest and black pepper and serve from a board or serving plate alongside napkins. Alternatively, you could bring the dish to the table and leave everyone to make their own *crostini*, or use it as a dip.

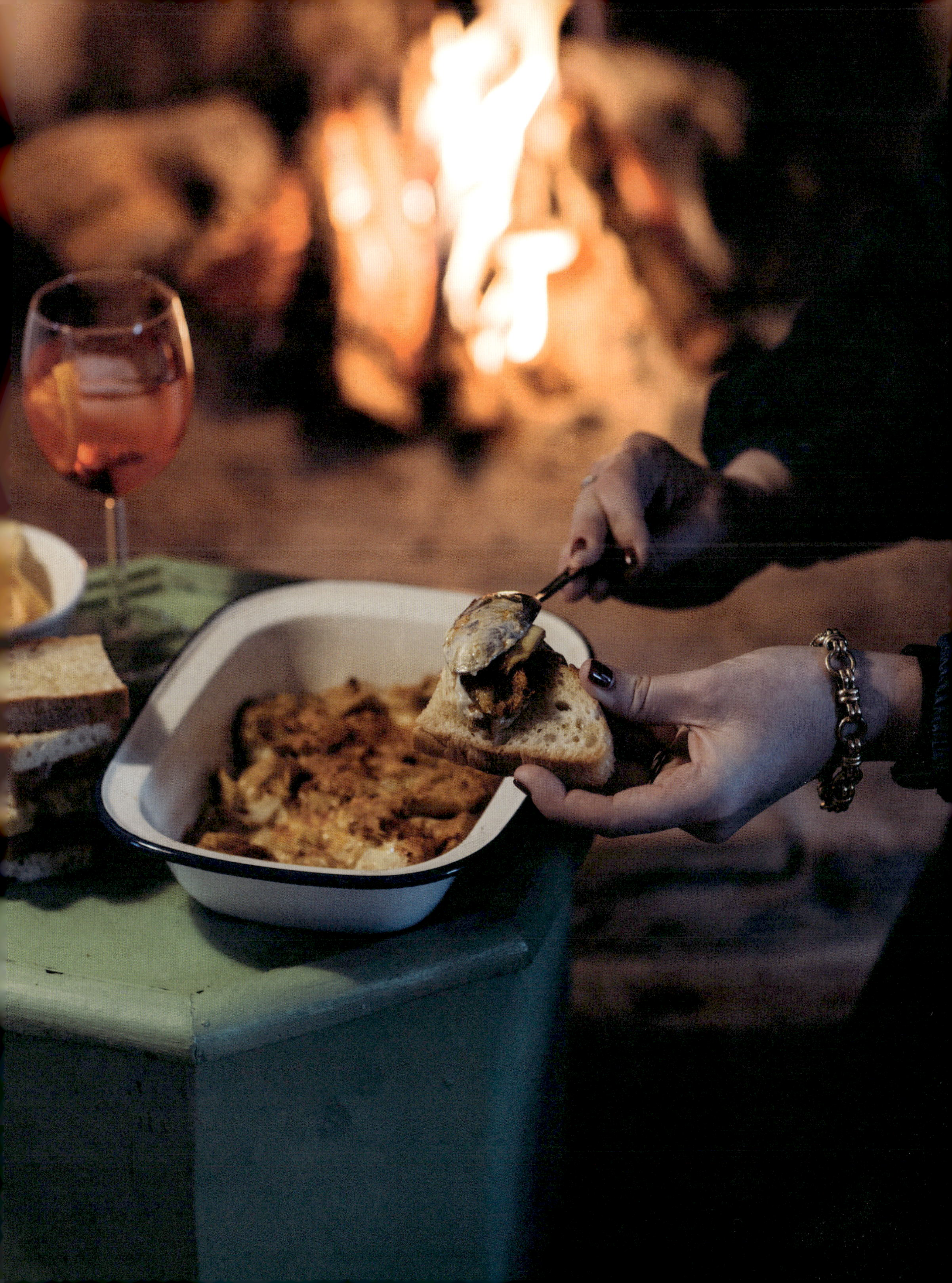

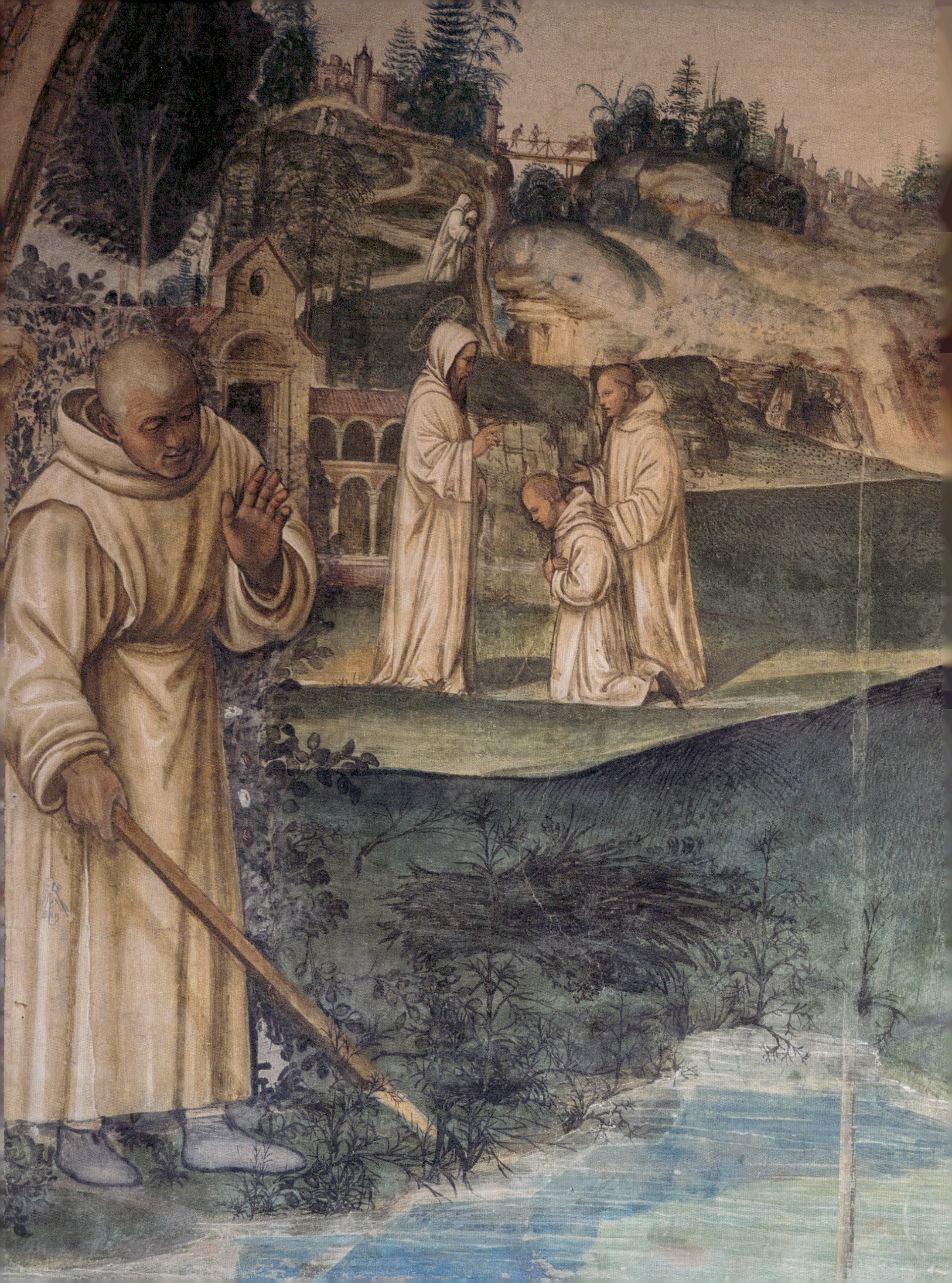

MINESTRE

COMFORTING SOUPS

WHENEVER I AM asked what comfort food is to me, my answer is always a broth-based one. When a steaming bowl of well-made broth – *brodo* – is placed in front of me, either on its own as a humble-looking amber-coloured liquid, or with the added joy of fresh tortellini or round balls of *malfatti* (ricotta and spinach dumplings) bobbing about in it, I always see it as an act of love and care on the part of the person who made it.

A good broth can be transporting, feeling oddly indulgent and at the same time cleansing and virtuous. When made well, you can't believe that this much flavour and luxury can come from a boiled chicken, a bunch of vegetables or leftover bones. One of the most satisfying parts of cooking is to be efficient with meals and to get more than one meal from a single ingredient. Particularly in the case of meat, being a meat eater who tries to see it as a luxury enjoyed a few times a week and not every day, I find great satisfaction in making broth from any leftover bones or meat scraps and extracting every last bit of goodness from the meat I've eaten.

Wonderful recipes from all over the country show the Italian proficiency for elevating a stock by adding another element: *tortellini in brodo* from Bologna, or *stracciatella* (egg and parmesan in soup) from Rome. I love how, when a stock is very good, or a kitchen takes pride in their broth, there is a respect for the depth of flavour that has been achieved. It takes patience to make a good one – which is why it is all the more delicious when someone else makes it for you. In restaurants near us in Florence, both smart and humble, there will often be *tazza di brodo* (cup of broth) on the menu. One of the plainest variations of a clear soup is *pastina in brodo* – mini pasta shapes cooked and served in broth (see page 73).

In Italy, a *brodo* is a clear liquid which has extracted all the flavour and goodness from a chosen ingredient, whether it be vegetables, meat or fish. Deriving from the word *inzuppare* ('to soak up'), a *zuppa* (soup) traditionally means any liquid meal that has bread in it as the vehicle to soak the liquid. A *minestra* is a soup with vegetables and possibly some rice or pasta. All of these terms, however, can also be used as a more generic word for 'soup'. In our busy modern world where convenience and speed has influenced culinary traditions – eating on the go, standing at a bar or on the street – soups are seen as the ultimate home comfort: a bowl of liquid is very messy to eat on the move with a spoon, meaning the best way to consume them is at the table with your family.

When I was growing up and now in my own house, variously adorned broths have always been a staple midweek family supper and dinner party dish, which is why this chapter is dedicated to sharing a few favourites with you, including *zuppa di farro* (Nara's spelt & cannellini bean soup, page 84), and an ancient Etruscan chestnut and chickpea soup (page 83) – two cosy, thick, hearty Tuscan soups the region is famous for.

If you haven't got round to making your own stock, there is a stock cube that I use all the time and that is entirely different from, and superior to, any I have ever had outside of Italy – a brand by Star called 'Il Mio Dado Classico' (the most widely sold in Italy). The packaging features an illustration of a 1950s housewife wearing a pearl necklace and eating a spoonful of *pastina in brodo*. They, of course, are now on the list of evil ultra-processed foods, but they're an indulgence I can't let go of as they remind me of my childhood. If you can, try to get hold of some for your pantry, as they are magical and will work well with all the recipes in this book. Good quality shop-bought chicken or bone broth will also work well.

The following recipes are for four people, perfect for a cosy night in on your own or gossiping with close friends and family by the fire, but if you are fewer, it is still worthwhile making the full quantity of the meat or vegetable broths on pages 72 and 73, so you can freeze any leftover broth for another time. As a general guide, the perfect bowl of broth is about 175 ml (6 fl oz) per person.

Brodo vegetale

Vegetable stock

MAKES 1.5 LITRES (51 FL OZ)

olive oil

2 large tomatoes

2 onions (red, white or golden), sliced in half

3 celery sticks (or more if you have them knocking around in the bottom of the fridge)

3 carrots, roughly chopped

1 potato, peeled and roughly chopped into chunks

1 bay leaf

handful of flat-leaf parsley stalks

1 teaspoon whole peppercorns

2 teaspoons fine sea salt

This stock almost feels like it needs no recipe, as it is more of an 'odds and sods' affair based on what you have wilting in your fridge – but here's a guide to how I make vegetable stock when I feel like being meat-free, or am making a risotto or soup for vegetarian friends.

Other vegetables I sometimes add if I have them left over from making another dish are cavolo nero stalks, fennel tops, sweet potato and turnip.

PREPARATION:– a few minutes
COOKING:– 1½ hours

Put a couple of glugs of olive oil in a large saucepan over a medium heat. Add the tomatoes, cut side down. Without moving them, let them cook for 3–5 minutes, until they are sizzling and have a little colour on them. Add the remaining ingredients except the salt and stir, leaving to cook for another few minutes. Pour in 3 litres (101 fl oz) cold water and bring to the boil.

Turn down the heat and gently simmer, uncovered, for 1½ hours, checking occasionally to make sure the water isn't boiling off too quickly and reducing too much.

Drain the stock, discarding the vegetables and aromatics. Stir the salt through and your broth is now ready to use in soups, risottos or any of the following recipes.

The broth will keep in a tightly sealed container in the fridge for up to a week, or can be frozen for up to 6 months.

Brodo di carne

Chicken & beef bone broth

MAKES 1.5 LITRES (51 FL OZ)

1 chicken carcass left over from a roast chicken, or 2 raw chicken legs or thighs

250 g (9 oz) piece of boiling beef

250 g (9 oz) beef bones

1 onion, peeled and sliced in half

1 potato, peeled

3 large carrots, peeled

3 celery sticks

large bunch of flat-leaf parsley stalks

1 teaspoon peppercorns

sea salt

'Bone' broth is now a buzzword for health, but in Italy it's been made since time immemorial as the base for nutritious, frugal meals. Whereas outside of Italy you might have to go to your butcher to ask for bones, here in the supermarket meat counter they have always sold beef bones for adding to broths or enriching the flavour of a *bollito misto* (boiled mixed meats). I love this recipe as it's so hands off, only requiring you to put the ingredients in a pot and keep an eye on it for a few hours.

If you are making this broth ahead, or you have some left over, freeze it in batches either in labelled zip-lock bags or in ice trays to toss into soups and stews, and use within 6 months of freezing.

PREPARATION:– 5 minutes
COOKING:– 3 hours

Place all the ingredients in a very large pot and cover with about 4 litres (135 fl oz) cold water.

Bring to the boil, then turn the heat right down and leave to cook, uncovered, for about 40 minutes. Partially cover with a lid and simmer for 2 hours, checking occasionally and skimming off any foam that forms on top with a slotted spoon.

After 2 hours, take the lid off and allow the broth to reduce by about one-quarter, which should take 20–30 minutes. Taste the liquid; it may need a few pinches of salt.

Remove from the heat and drain the broth through a colander set over a bowl. Strain again through a sieve or a tea strainer, if you have one. Stir in another 2 teaspoons salt and allow to cool.

Once cooled, refrigerate for about an hour. The stock should have set, and a thin layer of fat hardened on the surface. Scoop the fat away with a spoon and your broth is now ready to reheat and use as you wish in soups, risottos or any of the following recipes.

The broth will keep in a tightly sealed container in the fridge for 3 days, or can be frozen for up to 6 months.

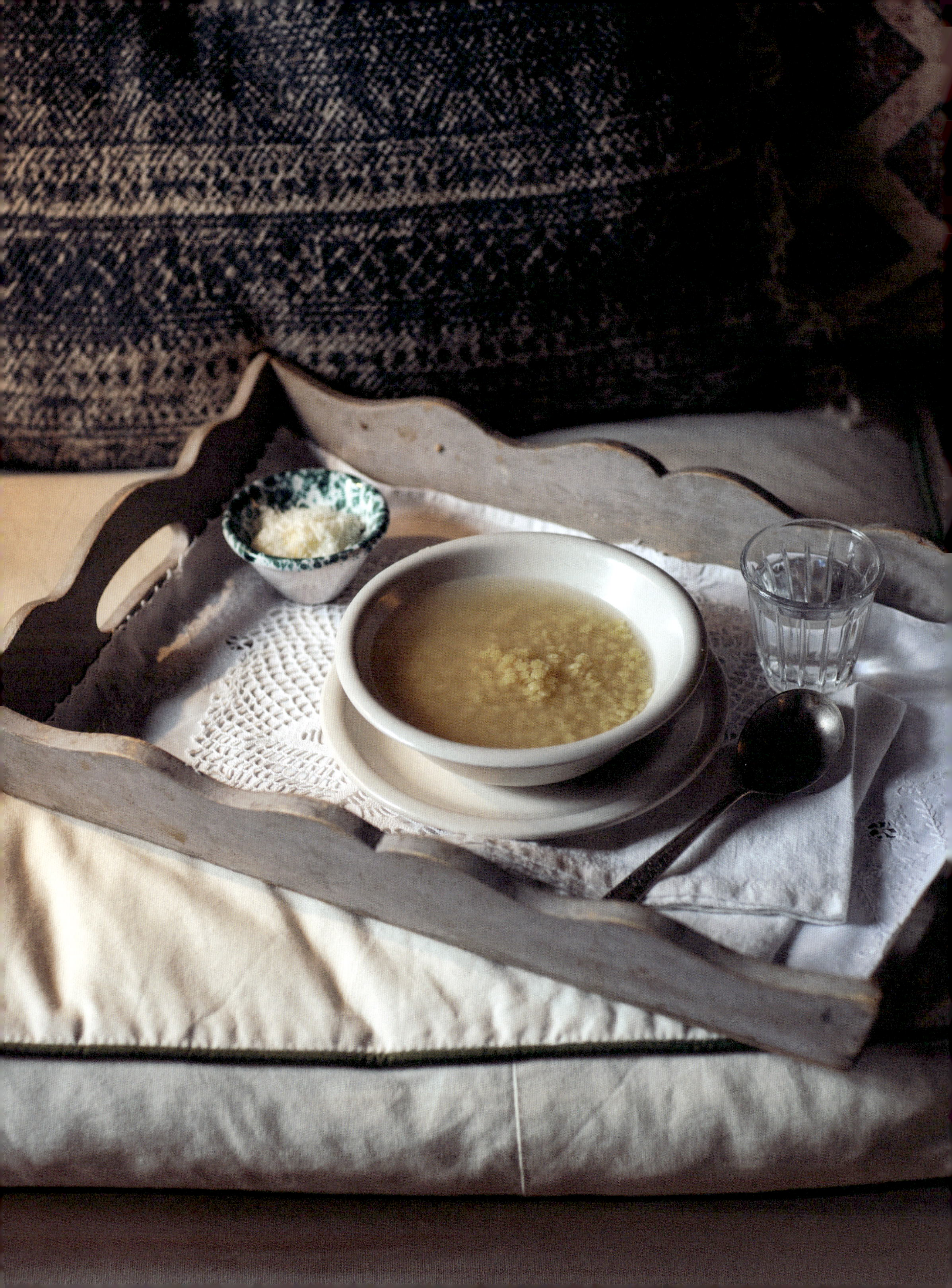

Pastina in brodo

Tiny pasta in broth

SERVES 4

1 litre (34 fl oz) Chicken & beef bone broth (page 73) or good chicken stock

200 g (7 oz) *pastina* of your choice; *stelline, filini* and *ditalini rigate* all work well

TO SERVE

grated parmesan

One of the humblest and most homely variations of a clear soup is *pastina in brodo* – mini pasta shapes such as *stelline* ('tiny stars'), *farfalline* (little butterflies) or *filini* (tiny spaghetti threads), cooked and served in broth. This is my ultimate comfort food, as it was what I was always fed as a child, both at home and at school, if I was feeling poorly. When left overnight with school friends or neighbours if my parents had to go away for a few days, we would be fed *pastina in brodo* topped with a few gratings of parmesan. So plain and yet so nourishing. For me, this simple family favourite is the taste of childhood winters and we still eat it often.

PREPARATION:– a few minutes
COOKING:– 5–8 minutes

Bring the stock to the boil in a saucepan. Once boiling, pour in the pasta, stir and cook as instructed on the packet. (Small pasta shapes usually take between 3 and 5 minutes.)

Ladle into individual bowls and serve sprinkled with a little parmesan.

NOTE:– If you don't have any ready-made broth handy, you can still make this soup using 1 Star stock cube dissolved in 1 litre (34 fl oz) water.

Malfatti in brodo

Mama's malfatti in broth

Malfatti are little dumplings made of ricotta and spinach. They are also known as *gnudi* or *nudi* ('naked') by dint of them being made the filling of a classic raviolo, but not being encased in pasta. I describe them as being poached and served in sage butter in my first book *A House Party in Tuscany*, but often on a cold winter's night I'll eat them this way instead – halving their size and serving them in a steaming bowl of broth topped with a little parmesan. *Malfatti in brodo* is a signature dish of my mother's, one she is now famous for among her friends in London, and they often ask her to make it – in particular her boyfriend, who refers to it as 'seduction soup'.

SERVES 4

large handful of fresh spinach

small handful of mint leaves

250 g (9 oz) ricotta, drained

3 tablespoons grated parmesan, plus extra to serve

generous grating of nutmeg

sea salt and freshly ground black pepper

1 organic egg

3 tablespoons '00' flour

1.2 litres (41 fl oz) Chicken & beef bone broth (page 73) or Vegetable stock (page 72)

PREPARATION:– 25 minutes
COOKING:– a few minutes

Wilt the spinach in a non-stick saucepan with a tablespoon of water. Once fully cooked, remove from the pan and squeeze and twist out any excess moisture from the spinach using a clean tea towel or paper towel. It's important to draw out all excess moisture. Very finely chop the spinach with the mint.

Place in a bowl with the ricotta and mix together with a fork. Add the parmesan, nutmeg, salt and black pepper, tasting and adjusting the seasoning as necessary. Mix in the egg, followed by the flour.

Lightly dust a clean surface with flour and flour your hands so the mixture doesn't stick. Next to you, have a couple of plates on which to place your *malfatti*.

Using a teaspoon, scoop up a small amount of the mixture to make a small round ball the size of a cherry. Gently drop this onto the floured surface, then roll it in a bit of flour, before picking it up and gently rolling it between the palms of your hands to make little cherry-sized *malfatti*. The mixture should make about 40 *malfatti* (10 per person). You can keep these in the fridge for up to 3 days (perhaps covered with an upturned bowl) before poaching them in the broth.

When you're ready to serve, place four bowls by the stove, ready to ladle the soup into.

Warm your broth in a large saucepan. Once beginning to bubble, reduce the heat to a simmer and start adding the *malfatti* in batches, being careful not to overcrowd the pan or they'll stick together. After about 1 minute, as each dumpling bobs to the surface, remove them using a slotted spoon, dividing them equally among the serving bowls.

Pour two ladlefuls of the broth into each bowl and serve sprinkled with a little parmesan.

> **VARIATIONS:–** Instead of using spinach in the *malfatti*, cavolo nero or silverbeet (Swiss chard) would also be delicious – as would fresh sage in place of mint. (For convenience you could also use thawed frozen spinach if fresh spinach isn't available, but be sure to squeeze all the liquid from it.)
>
> If you don't have any ready-made broth handy, use 1 Star stock cube dissolved in 1.2 litres (41 fl oz) water.

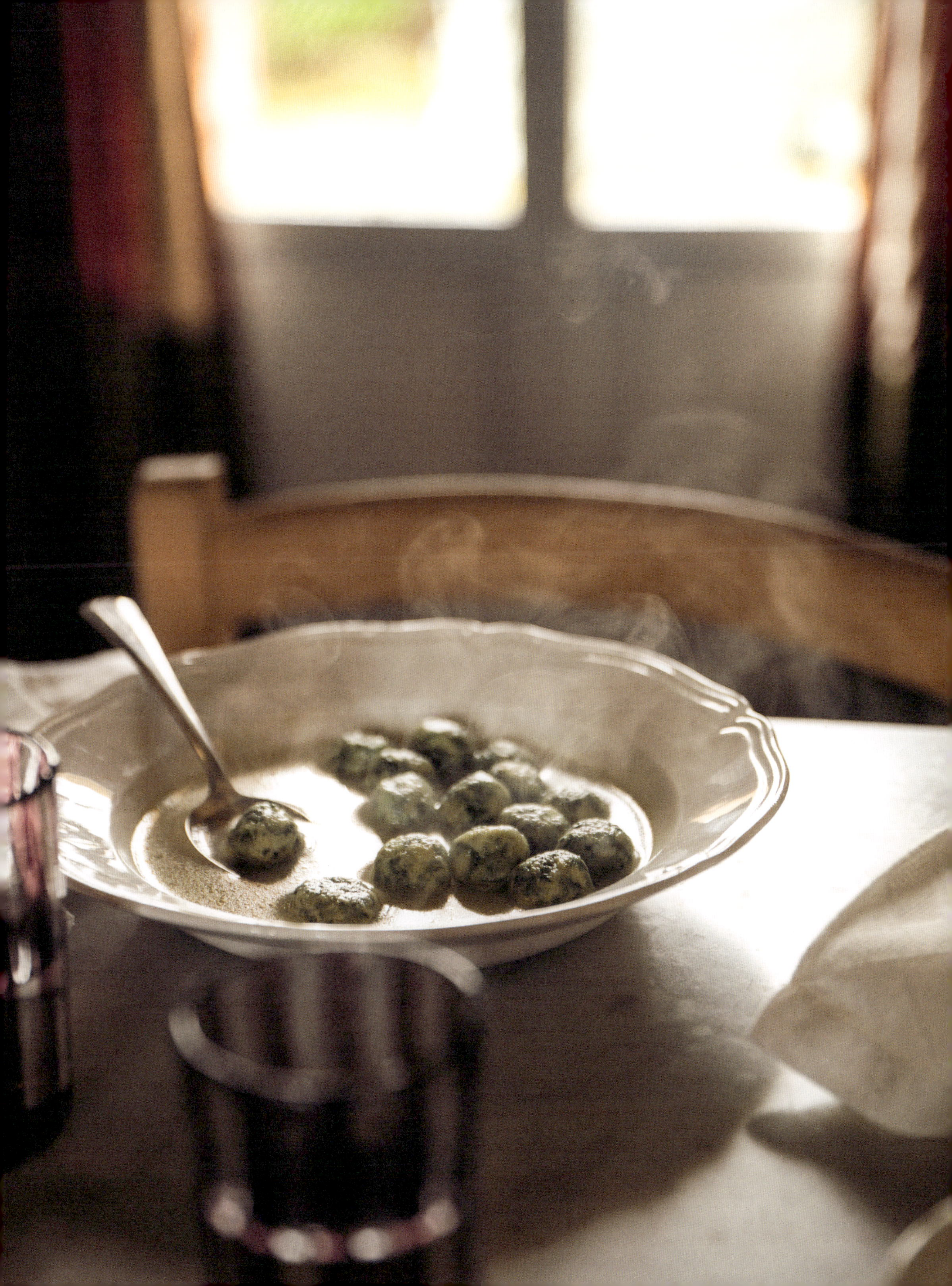

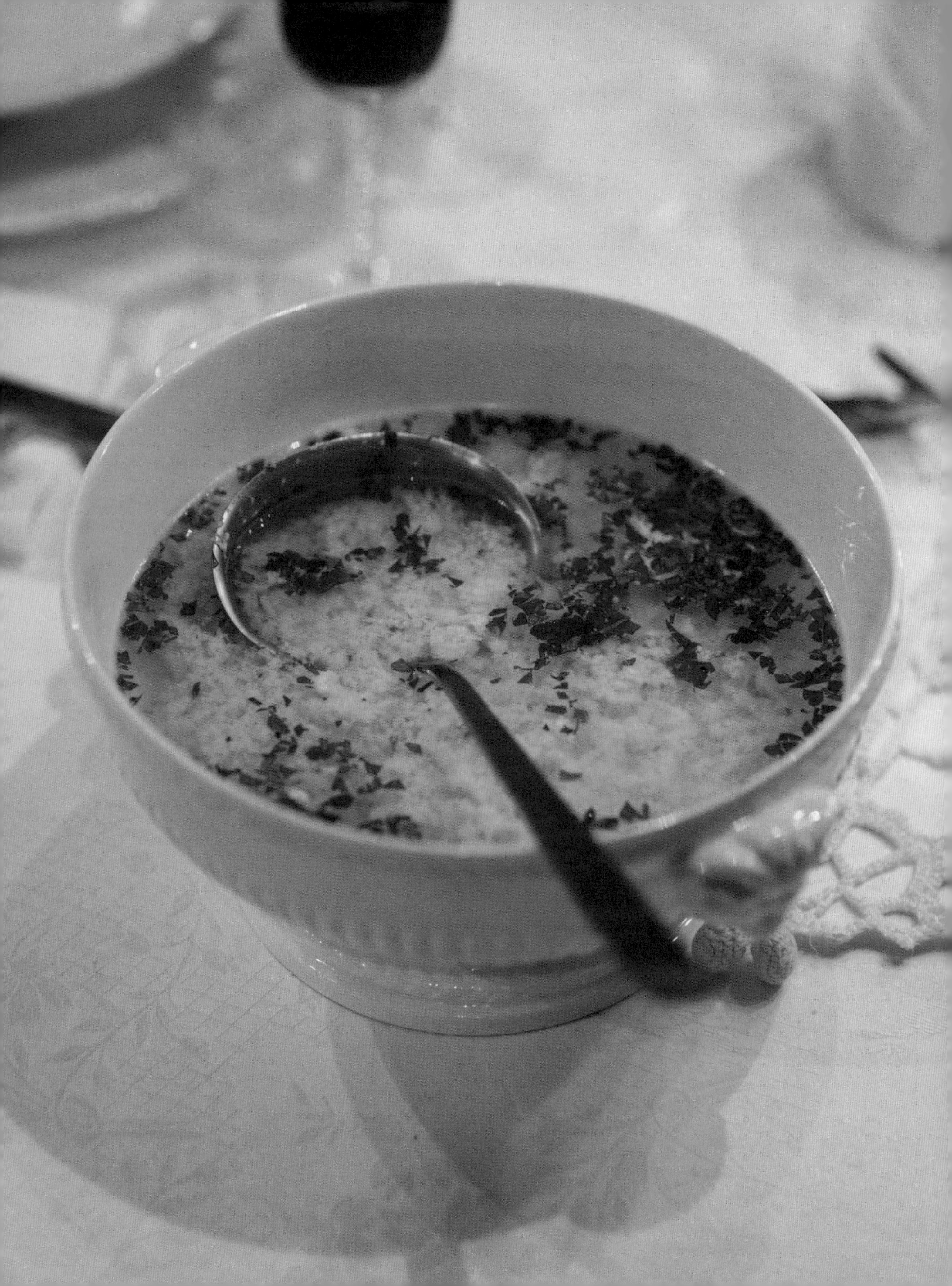

Stracciatella

Egg & parmesan 'shreds' in broth

SERVES 4

4 organic eggs

80 g (2¾ oz) grated parmesan

sea salt and freshly ground black pepper

handful of flat-leaf parsley, finely chopped

1.5–2 litres (51–68 fl oz) Chicken & beef bone broth (page 73) or Vegetable stock (page 72)

Another wonderful broth adornment my mother would make us was *stracciatella* – and these days it's a dish my friends will ring ahead and request I make when they're coming to stay on winter weekends. *Stracciatella* is a Roman dish which involves beating equal parts egg (one per person) and parmesan into the broth. Eggs and parmesan in broth may sound odd, but it is wonderful on a cold night with a piece of good bread to dunk in the soup. Warming, filling and indulgent thanks to the parmesan, it feels special and nutritious: the perfect comfort food.

PREPARATION:– a few minutes
COOKING:– a few minutes

Crack all the eggs into a bowl, then whisk with the parmesan. Add a pinch of salt, a few grinds of black pepper and the parsley.

Warm the broth in a large wide saucepan over a medium heat. Once steaming but not boiling, pour in the egg mixture from a height, stirring it in vigorously with a fork for chunkier pieces of egg, or a whisk for finer flakes of egg. (This is down to personal preference; mine is the former.)

Allow to start bubbling and cook for a further 2 minutes, then serve immediately.

NOTE:– If you don't have any ready-made broth handy, use 2 Star stock cubes dissolved in 1.5 L (51 fl oz) boiling water.

Minestrone di verdure

Vegetable minestrone

SERVES 4

3 carrots

1 large zucchini

a few cavolo nero leaves

a few leaves of silverbeet (Swiss chard) or white cabbage

2 potatoes, peeled

3 celery sticks

1 white onion

olive oil

sea salt

1 litre (34 fl oz) cold water or Vegetable stock (page 72)

½ teaspoon bicarbonate of soda (optional)

400 g (14 oz) tin cannellini beans, drained

1 parmesan rind (optional)

grated parmesan, to serve

A clear tasty liquid with lots of chopped vegetables bobbing about in it is one of my habitual orders at Ristorante La Torre, a wonderful family-run restaurant in the Crete Senesi. Vegetable soup may sound simple, but it truly is wonderful, and was the original base for the most famous of Tuscan soups, *ribollita*.

Literally meaning 're-boiled', *ribollita* (stale bread and vegetable stew) was originally devised as a way of using up the previous day's *minestrone di verdure* (vegetable soup) by recooking it with pieces of stale leftover bread. It's another fabulous example of how, when Tuscans come up with an ingenious way of using things up, it often becomes the more celebrated dish in itself. When I worked at the River Café in London, one of the head chefs, upon hearing I had grown up in Tuscany, remarked, 'Ah, where a soup is not a soup if you can't stand your spoon up in it', referring of course to our world-famous *ribollita*.

I love the fresh vegetable soup base below. To turn this into a classic *ribollita*, simply add a few torn-up slices of stale white bread (preferably sourdough, *casereccio* or Tuscan) halfway through the cooking time and serve with a few glugs of olive oil.

PREPARATION:– 15 minutes
COOKING:– 35 minutes

If your carrots are small, cut them into discs. If they are large, cut them in half lengthways down the middle, then cut them into half-moons. Do the same with the zucchini and set each aside in separate bowls.

Discard any tough stalks from the cavolo nero and the silverbeet or cabbage, then cut the leaves into strips about 1 cm (½ inch) wide. Cut the potatoes into 2 cm (¾ inch) chunks, the celery into 1 cm (½ inch) chunks, and very finely chop the onion.

In a large heavy-based saucepan (I use a cast-iron one), heat a couple of glugs of olive oil with a pinch of salt. Add all the vegetables except the zucchini and potatoes, pour the water over and add 2 teaspoons salt and the bicarbonate of soda, if using. Cover, turn the heat up high and wait for the liquid to come to the boil, which may take about 5 minutes.

Remove the lid and turn the heat right down. Add the zucchini, potatoes and drained cannellini beans, and the parmesan rind, if using. Leave to simmer for 20–30 minutes, until the vegetables are cooked and the broth is reduced and tasty.

Serve in shallow bowls with a hunk of bread, a little grated parmesan and a drizzle more olive oil.

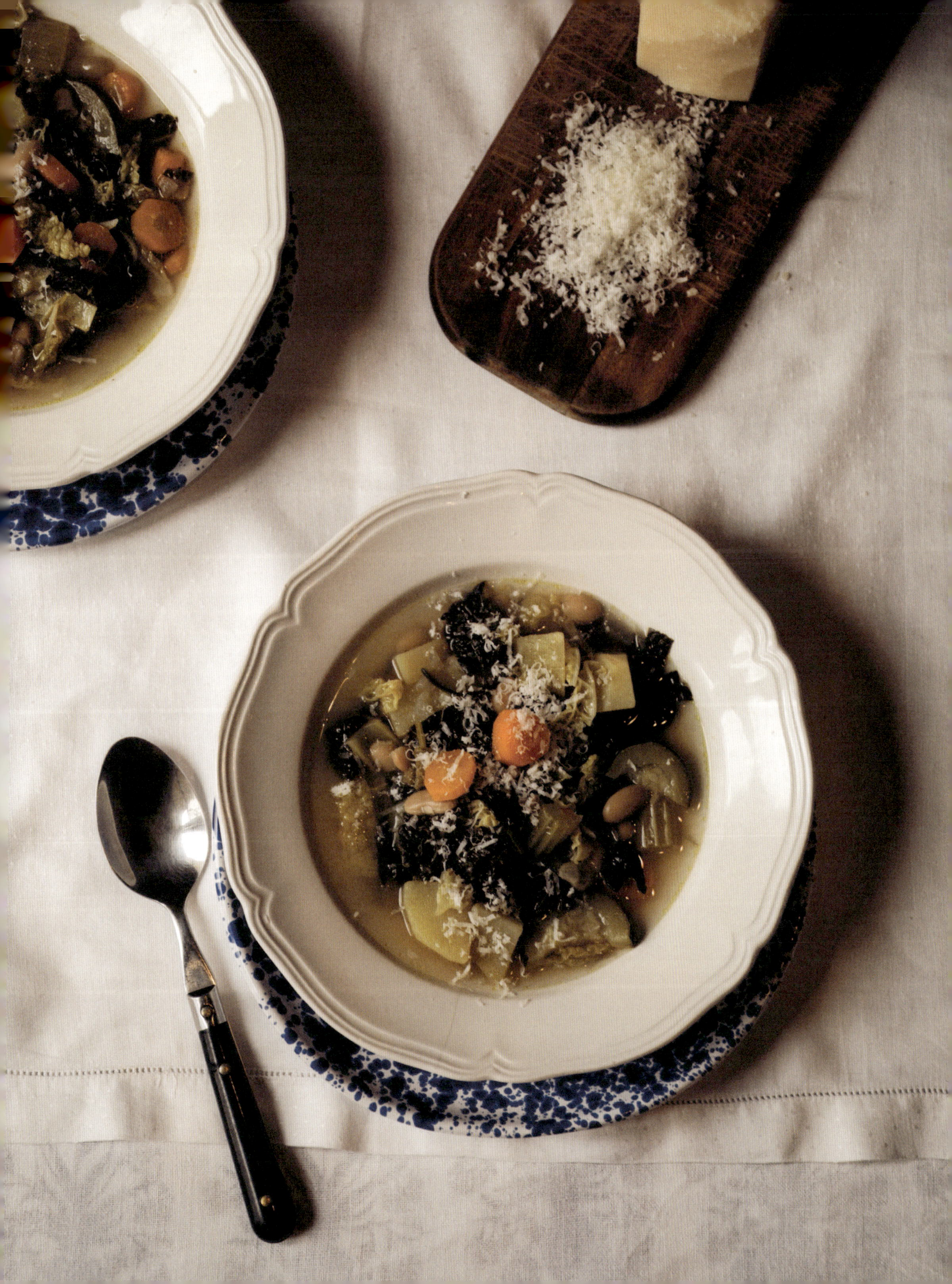

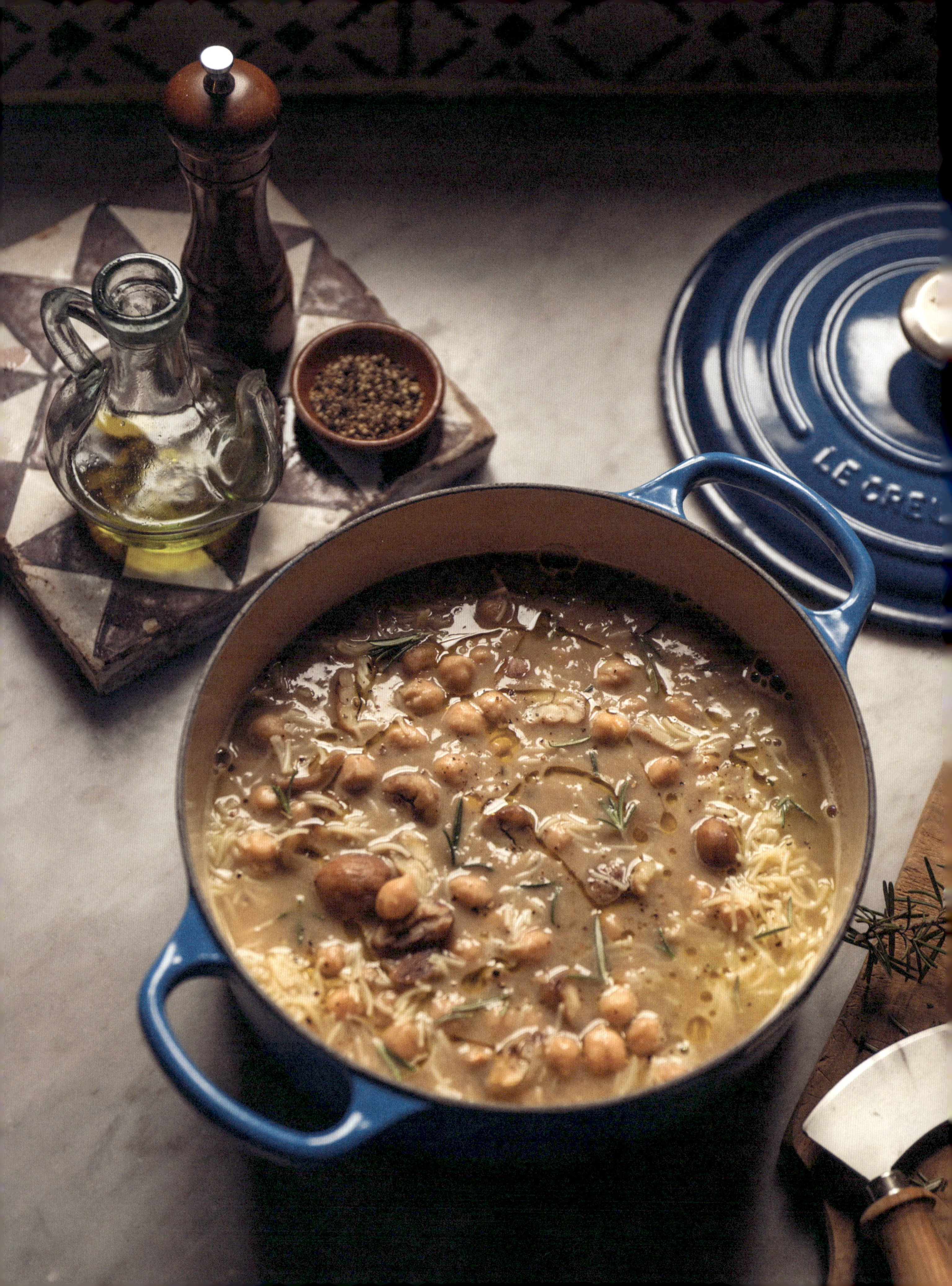

Zuppa etrusca

Etruscan chestnut & chickpea soup

SERVES 4

2 × 400 g (14 oz) tins or jars of giant chickpeas

2 × 180–200 g (6½–7 oz) packets whole cooked chestnuts

olive oil

1 red onion, finely diced

sea salt and freshly ground black pepper

1 garlic clove, crushed

3 rosemary sprigs, leaves picked and finely chopped

500 ml (17 fl oz) chicken stock or Vegetable stock (page 72)

two handfuls of pasta (optional)

TO SERVE

olive oil

grated parmesan

good crusty bread

My friend Niccolò introduced me to this dish. It's his favourite soup, and he loves it so much he buys jars of it from his old neighbouring farm in Chianti and eats it straight from the jar. I love how this dish brings together two quintessentially Tuscan ingredients, chestnuts and chickpeas, both of which have been grown around us at Arniano for thousands of years since the time of the ancient Etruscans. Traditional recipes call for soaking dried chickpeas and roasting the chestnuts, but for ease, I use ready-cooked chestnuts and tinned chickpeas, though of course you can soak and cook the chickpeas. If you do, retain the soaking water for the soup and substitute it for half the stock.

If you would like the dish to be even more substantial, add a couple of handfuls of pasta, such as *filini*, *ditalini*, broken-up spaghetti or, if you can get it, *gramigna* – small curled pasta tubes that are traditional in this soup but hard to find.

PREPARATION:– 10 minutes
COOKING:– 35 minutes

Drain the chickpeas, reserving their soaking liquid.

Very finely chop half the chestnuts. Split each of the remaining chestnuts in half and set aside.

In a heavy-based saucepan, heat a couple of glugs of olive oil with the onion and a pinch of salt. Cook for a few minutes, until the onion begins to look translucent. Add the garlic, rosemary and the finely chopped chestnuts and cook for another 2–3 minutes.

Stir in half the chickpeas, some salt, pepper and another glug of olive oil and cook for 5 minutes. Pour in the stock and the reserved chickpea liquid. Stir and leave to cook for 15–20 minutes, stirring occasionally.

Leave to cool a little, then transfer the soup to a blender and blitz until smooth. Return to the pan with another drizzle of olive oil, then taste and adjust the seasoning as necessary.

Stir in the chunky chestnut halves and the remaining chickpeas. (The soup freezes well at this stage, if making ahead, and will keep in the fridge ready to be reheated for up to 3 days.)

If using the pasta, add it to the soup with half a glass of water. Cook over a medium heat, stirring often, for about 5 minutes, until your pasta is well cooked.

Serve with a drizzle of olive oil, some grated parmesan and crusty bread.

Zuppa di farro

Nara's spelt & cannellini bean soup

SERVES 4

HERB OIL
2 rosemary sprigs
handful of sage
4 tablespoons olive oil

SOUP BASE
olive oil
1 large white onion, very finely chopped
sea salt
3 carrots, finely chopped
4 celery sticks, finely chopped
1 tablespoon tomato concentrate
2 × 400 g (14 oz) tins of cannellini beans, undrained (see note)
800 ml (27 fl oz) Chicken & beef bone broth (page 73), Vegetable stock (page 72) or stock of choice
100 g (3½ oz) spelt

TO SERVE
olive oil
grated parmesan

When I asked my friends at 'Nara's', our local trattoria in the village of Buonconvento, to show me how to make their *zuppa di farro*, which has been a favourite of mine since I was a child, they told me it was too simple to warrant a lesson and instead described the process, which I share with you below. The soup is a smooth blended bean and vegetable soup with little pieces of spelt floating in it, topped with olive oil and grated parmesan. They recommend using dried cannellini beans, but I often use tinned, so use whatever you have to hand and whatever your time allows. They do stress that this soup shouldn't be too tomatoey, but should be closer to 'the colour of a carrot once blended'. Don't cook the spelt in the soup as it's too thick, and the spelt will soak up all the liquid if the soup is left sitting too long.

I often make a batch of the soup base and freeze it, as it's great to warm through with a little stock to make a quick lunch.

PREPARATION:– 15 minutes
COOKING:– 45 minutes

To make the herb oil, place the rosemary and sage in a small saucepan and pour the olive oil over. Gently warm over a medium heat, but don't let the oil sizzle – switch off the heat as soon as you start seeing bubbles, immediately remove from the heat and set aside to infuse.

Drizzle a generous glug of olive oil into another saucepan. Add the onion, along with a pinch of salt, and turn the heat to medium. Cook gently for around 5 minutes, until the onion is translucent. Add the carrot and celery and cook for another 5 minutes, stirring occasionally.

Stir in the tomato concentrate and cook for a few more minutes. Add the tinned cannellini beans, along with their liquid. Stir together with another drizzle of olive oil and pinch of salt, then leave for another 3–5 minutes to amalgamate.

Stir in the stock and let it come to the boil, then turn the heat down and leave to simmer for 20 minutes.

In the meantime, cook the spelt in a small saucepan of boiling salted water for 25 minutes, or as instructed on the packet, until it is cooked but still retains a little bite. Drain, toss with some olive oil and set aside until serving.

When your soup is ready, let it cool for a few minutes before blending into a very smooth orange soup, the colour of a carrot. Taste to check the seasoning and adjust as necessary. Strain the herb oil and stir it through the soup. (The soup freezes well at this point, if making ahead.)

Ladle the hot soup into bowls, mix a quarter of the spelt through each and serve immediately. Drizzle with more olive oil and sprinkle with grated parmesan.

NOTE:– Instead of tinned cannellini beans, soak 200 g (7 oz) dried cannellini beans overnight in water with some sage and rosemary sprigs. Drain the beans and add them to the soup base once the vegetable or chicken stock has been added and brought to the boil. Leave to simmer in the broth for 1 hour while cooking the spelt.

VARIATION:– To make *pasta e fagioli*, omit the spelt and instead add more cannellini beans and a few handfuls of *stelline* pasta.

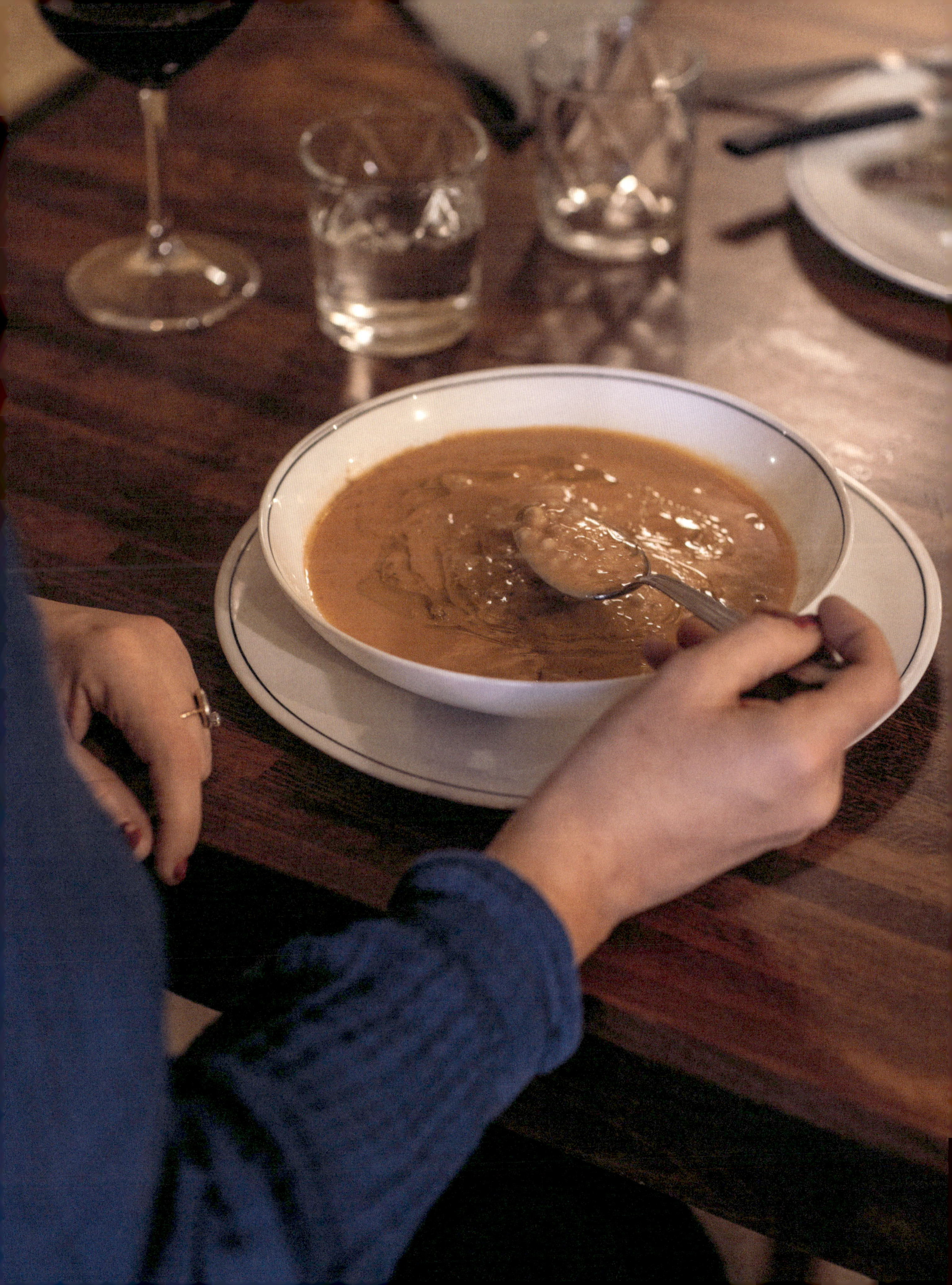

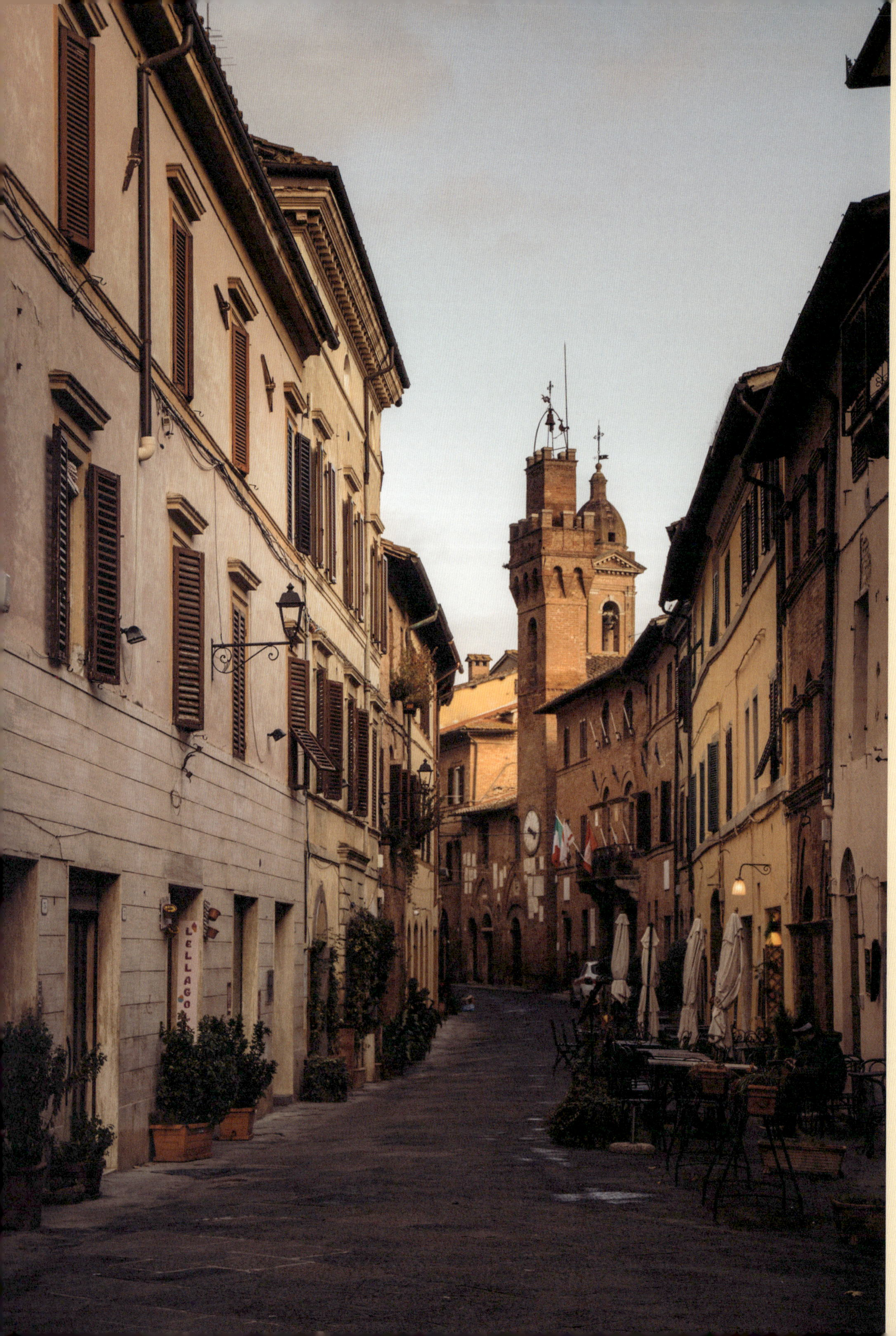

AROUND US AT ARNIANO

WHEN I MET my husband at a wedding in England and he asked me where I was from, I said I was from a village in southern Tuscany called Buonconvento, thinking he would have no idea where it was. As it happened, I was wrong. The previous month he had accumulated three speeding tickets from Buonconvento while competing in the Mille Miglia, a historic car race from Brescia to Rome that, for nearly every year since 1927, has been passing through Buonconvento – a small medieval town that sits on the Cassia, the ancient road north out of Rome to Etruria (Tuscany), which is still used today when heading from Tuscany down to Rome.

Unlike most famous Tuscan towns, Buonconvento is not on a hill, but down in a valley where the Ombrone and Arbia rivers intersect. As a consequence, it spends most mornings shrouded in fog, earning locals the nickname *ranocchi*, or frogs – creatures who like to be surrounded by mist in order to stay hydrated. It is a nickname they have eccentrically leant into by including an enormous neon-green cartoon of a smirking frog on their village flag. I spent a lot of my youth in Buonconvento, as the house I grew up in, Arniano, is only a ten-minute drive away. Buonconvento is where I went to school (until I was thirteen, when my parents realised I couldn't read or write English), where my sister and I went to ballet class, and where my mum's antiques shop was. And three times a week, to keep Mum company on her lunch break when the shop was shut, we would eat in the local trattoria, Da Mario – so Buonconvento really does feel like my home town. This isn't to say that it is a particular beauty. I wouldn't put it in my top ten places to visit for aesthetics in Italy, but home is home, and there is something special in having known the butcher, the baker and the barista for thirty-five years. And although the town itself is tiny and surrounded by ugly suburbs, it sits at the heart of one of Tuscany's most beautiful areas, with a huge array of wonderful things to see, do and eat.

It's unsurprising that people are attracted to the undulating hills and chalky white roads of Tuscany that surround us. Take the Cassia south and you head up the mountain towards Montalcino, famous for its breathtaking views and elegantly robust brunello wine. Just beyond is the Val d'Orcia, with Tuscany's cheese-making capital, Pienza, at its heart. To the east the windy road towards Asciano takes you through the Crete Senesi, an area now famous for white truffles, the craggy clay cliffs and fossils being a topographical reminder that this area was an underwater sea bed three million years ago. And while this area may not have changed

OPPOSITE:– Via Soccini, in the old town of Buonconvento – the street where my mum's shop was

87 AROUND US AT ARNIANO

physically in my lifetime, the economy has changed dramatically, evolving from being reliant solely on agriculture to embracing tourism, particularly for those seeking an authentic Tuscan experience, with the two industries now living side by side in happy symbiosis.

Tourism has really thrived around us. People now come specifically to learn about brunello wine, to help with the olive oil harvest, to gorge on pecorino cheese and to taste everything the land has to offer. When my parents moved from the Chianti region just outside Florence to this area between Siena and Montalcino in 1989, their friends were all horrified that they would go somewhere so far away, where no one ever ventured. When I was a child, we were a source of fascination as foreigners, known always as *gl'inglesi*, whereas now the community doesn't bat an eyelid at its variety of multicultural residents and visitors.

The main reason for this was the opening of an enormous five-star hotel in a hamlet named Castiglion del Bosco on the hill next to Montalcino – a hotel that has been voted the best not only in Italy, but in the world. Twenty years ago my parents were sceptical of the enormous resort and golf course being built by the Ferragamo family on the other side of the valley from Arniano, but all these years on, it's clear what a fabulous thing it has been for the community, having brought so many job opportunities to the area. Not least for my oldest school friend, Carolina, one of the cleverest people I know (she is a *dottoressa* of languages, speaking at least five). As one of Castiglion del Bosco's managing sommeliers and founder of its wine club, Carolina travels the world selling wines for the hotel, but is still based in her home town, a necessity for a woman who is part of an extended Italian family, the older members of whom need support.

Despite its recent success, and despite being in a now very popular part of southern Tuscany, Buonconvento has retained an authentic quality. People live here all year round, unlike smarter towns in the Chianti where everything is geared towards tourism. There is still an agricultural economy and community, historic industries being grain, spelt, pecorino cheese, timber, olive oil and, of course, wine production. The surrounding land is very fertile and blessed with access to lots of water, sitting at the intersection of two rivers – sometimes too much water when the rains come and the area floods. The town's name comes from *bonus conventus*, meaning the 'happy or fortunate community' who live in such an advantageous spot (although my friend William insists it means 'good with wind', a literal and wrong translation). As well as being on the Cassia, Buonconvento is also on the Via Francigena, the famous pilgrim's route from Canterbury to Rome, which perhaps also explains why many people I speak to have, remarkably, heard of it. Throughout history the town has been in a convenient and strategic spot for trade and passing commercial ventures, which is why in the 1300s locals deemed it sensible to protect themselves from passing invaders and began building the surrounding walls with its nine watchtowers, seven of which still stand.

Buonconvento's small but well-preserved centre is widely photographed. It has been named among the prettiest *borghi* (fortified hamlets) in Italy, which one might say is a stretch if you venture past the three streets of the old town, which centres around Via Soccini, a wide pedestrian street running north–south where the town hall is, where my mum had her antiques shop, and where you'll find the culinary institution Da Mario's, known locally as 'Nara's'. There is also a well-respected sacred art museum which is never open. Originally, Via Soccini was bookended by two portcullis gates with enormous wooden doors and adjoining watchtowers that were built to protect the town and were its only means of entrance. Sadly, the southern gate (Porta Romana) leading towards Rome was destroyed when the Germans retreated from the Allies in 1944 – along with many of the Liberty-era buildings that had popped up around the medieval centre in the late 1800s. The northern gate, which faces Siena (Porta Senese), is still there and is very impressive; it sits by the town theatre, where every year in June we would perform our ballet recitals, and films would be screened once a month (amazingly, you could still smoke in the cinema in the 1990s). Looking at Porta Senese, it's extraordinary to think of such an enormous structure being decimated at the other end of the street as recently as 1944. When I was a child, the war and fascism felt much more recent, as many of my classmates' grandparents were still alive, most of whom had had some sort of brush with Mussolini's regime and the war. Our school often organised field trips to hear these first-hand historical accounts, and one that sticks in my mind is when we visited a boy named Federico's grandfather, a local carpenter with seven fingers – three of them having been sacrificed to his trade – who told us about being conscripted as a very young man, and how he had several times actually seen the Duce in the flesh and saluted to him. After the fall of Mussolini, being an agricultural-based economy, Buonconvento and the surrounding area reacted by becoming a full-on Communist enclave, which it still is. The centre of all activity is the Bar Moderno, facing the ugly, modern piazza, its notice board topped with a hammer and sickle.

It's unsurprising that much of Buonconvento is so ugly, given so much of it was destroyed at the end of the war – though less explicable is the damage the commune inflicted in the early noughties by cutting down the ancient pine trees that lined the piazza, and tearing down the remaining Liberty-era buildings to make way for a hideous new hotel. The dramatic climax of the German retreat at Buonconvento is beautifully recounted by Iris Origo in her diary *War in the Val d'Orcia*, outlining the daily fears and deprivations in this corner of southern Tuscany during that time. She wrote this remarkable record at great personal danger to herself, hiding the pages in sacks she buried in the garden. This wasn't her only act of bravery: her home, La Foce, became a refuge for partisans, prisoners of war, orphans and Jewish children. In a moving scene she describes how she and all the children were standing in her now famous garden at Christmas in 1942, singing carols, when two German soldiers appeared. They abruptly stopped singing for fear the soldiers would discover that several of the Jewish children had forged papers. But instead, the soldiers asked them to carry on singing, as it reminded them of their own families back home. 'We came to hear the children sing,' they said.

Being on the Cassia, many famed sporting events pass through Buonconvento, including major cycling races such as L'Eroica, the Tour de France and Giro d'Italia, as well as various car rallies such as the Rally del Brunello and, of course, the Mille Miglia, all of which keep the town lively. Foodwise, this part of Tuscany is very fertile, and the rich soil yields good harvests. As well as vines and olive trees, the monks at Monte Oliveto Maggiore have been growing spelt and chickpeas here for five centuries, and in summer the surrounding fields are studded with bright yellow sunflowers prized for their seeds.

Buonconvento is where I do all my grocery shopping, as I know and trust the vendors. There is the family-run butcher, where the Orlandi brothers delight in handing you a business card featuring them topless in front of ageing beef carcasses and wielding some of their more alarming butchery equipment. Then there is the Tutta Frutta, the local greengrocer run by a couple in their seventies who are dedicated to providing an amazingly diverse array of seasonal fruit and veg. Three mornings a week, the husband drives in the dark to the wholesale market, so no wonder he is sometimes a little grumpy and has little patience for protestations about plastic bags. Next door is the bakery, Le Dolcezze di Nanni, which started in a side street by the railway station in the 1950s and has grown to command a large factory in the neighbouring village of Ponte d'Arbia. They now

OPPOSITE:– The Abbey of Sant'Antimo, a beautiful ancient church near Montalcino

have international fame, selling their amaretti biscuits and panforte abroad. I have seen their products in Whole Foods on High Street Kensington, amazed that the bakery from the Tuscan village I grew up in has made it as far as London.

Saturday mornings are particularly lively in Buonconvento as there is the travelling market, with the hustle and bustle of people coming to buy shoes, bedding, kitchenware and khaki hunting clothes (my father exclusively bought his trousers here, to my mother's dismay), as well as food. My preferred vegetable stall is run by a Sardinian family who provide very good local produce. Saturdays are also the one day of the week when I will buy fish inland, as the fish van has driven straight from the coast with fresh *vongole* (clams), *cozze* (mussels) and *branzino* (sea bass). And if one gets peckish, there is the deli truck selling freshly cooked porchetta, a whole roast suckling pig cooked for hours on a spit with lots of salt and herbs, served in delicious slices in a bread roll – a perfect midmorning snack while shopping.

But life in Buonconvento has certainly changed over the past decades, one big difference being that locals do not eat as much as they used to on their weekday lunch breaks. When we were children, my dad would take me or my sister to Nara's for lunch two or three times a week, mainly because our village school didn't have enough space to feed all the students on the same day, so there was a rota, half the school having lunch there two days a week, and the rest the other three days. Because of our age gap, my days never overlapped with Claudia's, so rather than do a forty-minute round trip to ferry one of us home and pick the other up, we had lunch at Nara's, which in those days was more than affordable. Run by three generations – from the ninety-year-old nonna and her daughters, both in their sixties, to their sons in their forties – the trattoria was always buzzing with builders and locals enjoying a very abundant working lunch consisting of antipasto, primo, secondo and dolce. But when Italy changed its currency from the lira to the euro in 2001, one consequence was a huge hike in the cost of eating out. Workmen became more likely to grab a sandwich at the bar than eat a three- or four-course meal at lunch. Nara and her mother have both passed away in recent years (the mother at the age of 101), but Anna, her sons and nephew are still running the restaurant, and she laments that it is now much quieter.

Up the road from Buonconvento is the famous winemaking town of Montalcino, a fortified medieval town high up on a mountain. Originally an Etruscan site, its walls date back to the 13th century. In 1555, when the city of Siena some 40 kilometres to the north came under siege from the Medici empire, Montalcino allowed Sienese leaders to take refuge in the town. Ever since, Montalcino has had a place of honour at the start of the historic procession that parades around Siena's central square for several hours ahead of the famous Palio horse race, with the first flag-throwers entering the square bearing banners in tribute to Montalcino.

Beyond Montalcino is the magical abbey of Sant'Antimo, which dates back to the time of Charlemagne and is surrounded by vineyards and ancient olive trees. Until a few years ago, the abbey was inhabited by French monks who were renowned for their Gregorian chant, which would be conducted by candlelight at midnight on Christmas Eve and which my parents would often take us to. The monks have now left and the abbey is run by a group of Mexican nuns who, alas, don't chant.

Back towards Asciano, about eight kilometres from Buonconvento, is another much larger living monastery, the abbey of Monte Oliveto Maggiore, home to some forty or so Benedictine monks whose cloisters feature some extraordinarily vivid 15th century frescoes. Situated on a promontory in the lunar landscape of the Crete Senesi, the abbey is surrounded on three sides by wooded ravines. The drive there from Buonconvento is a big part of the attraction, as it's such a lovely apparition that comes into view as you ascend the long and winding road up from the valley.

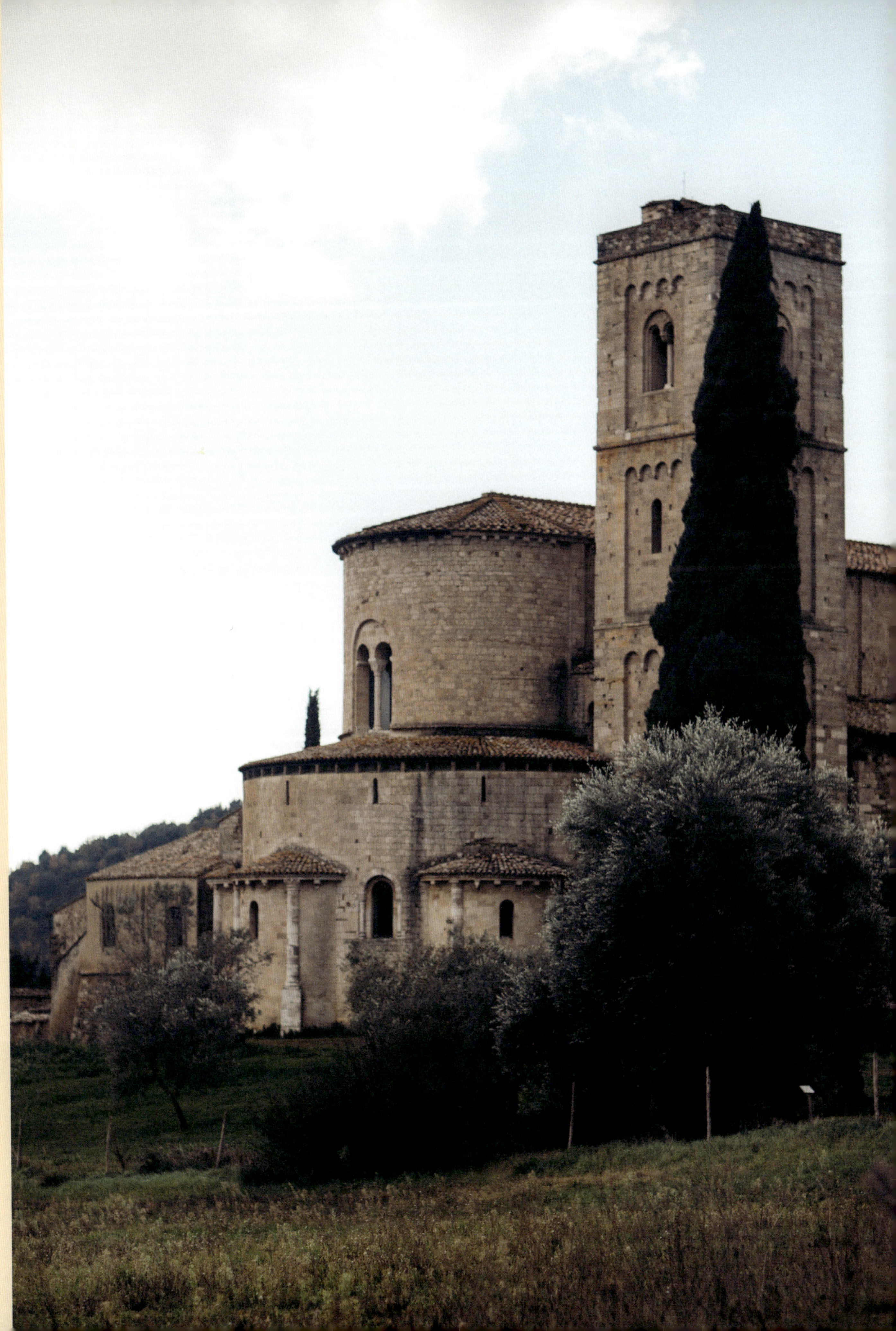

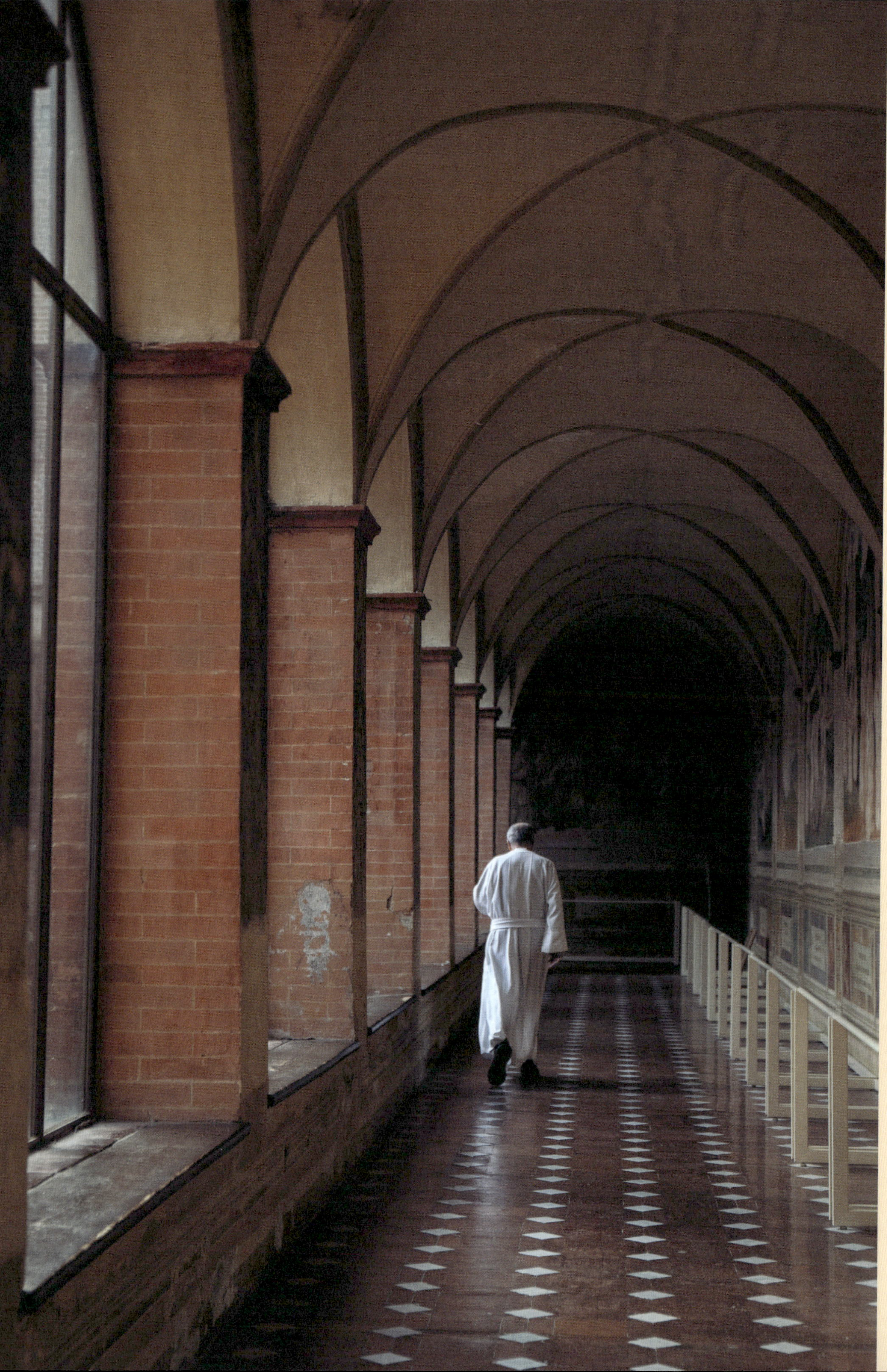

OPPOSITE:– The Great Cloister at the Abbey of Monte Oliveto Maggiore

The abbey was founded in 1319 by Saint Bernardo Tolomei, a member of a noble Sienese family who went to live as a hermit on the Tolomei estate in the Crete Senesi. Being so near the Via Francigena, he found himself hosting lots of pilgrims – and eventually, after experiencing a vision of Christ and the Virgin Mary surrounded by monks in white cassocks on the spot where the church now sits, he founded the abbey there. When the plague broke out in Siena in 1348, Tolomei left his post as abbot of Monte Oliveto Maggiore to help his dying brethren in his home town. He succumbed to the disease that same year and was later beatified in 1644 and canonised in 2003.

As you arrive at Monte Oliveto, you come to a medieval watchtower with a drawbridge that was designed to protect the abbey. You can walk across the drawbridge and pick your way down the steep path to the monastery on foot. Above the drawbridge, little terracotta statues of the Virgin Mary by Della Robbia sit above the entrance arches. The turret is also home to one of our best local restaurants, Ristorante La Torre, where one occasionally sees the white-cassocked monks watching the football or popping in for a coffee or amaro. I love combining lunch there with a visit to the monastery, which holds many treasures – in particular the great central cloister which is frescoed in panels depicting the most significant moments in the life of Saint Benedict. In 1495, the residing abbot asked Luca Signorelli to decorate the cloister, but Signorelli didn't complete the job as he was apparently offered more money to paint the frescoes in the cathedral in Orbetello, a fortified town in the neighbouring Tuscan province of Grosseto – and so the remaining frescoes were finished by Antonio Bazzi, known as Il Sodoma (a vindictive nickname given to him by fellow Renaissance artist Giorgio Vasari and which, unfortunately, stuck). It's possible to distinguish which panels are by which artist, as Sodoma usually included animals in his. In his panel titled 'How Benedict Mends the Crucible that is Broken', Sodoma included a self-portrait modelling himself as a rich merchant with badgers at his feet.

Similarly beautiful at Monte Oliveto are the pharmacy, library and the baroque church, which includes a choir stall made of inlaid wood depicting, in amazingly intricate detail, local landscapes and many animals.

When the monks are not praying, they are also excellent farmers, winemakers and gourmands. One of the three daily pillars of the ordinance, along with study of the word of God and choral prayer in the form of Gregorian chanting, is manual labour, which they put into practice on the swathes of land belonging to the abbey, growing olives for one of Tuscany's best olive oils, fields of spelt and chickpeas, as well as irises for saffron, which they have been growing for seven hundred years. (There are documents in the abbey's library detailing the production of wine, olive oil, chickpeas and spelt as far back as the 1300s, showing they have always used methods that minimally impact the land and take advantage of its natural fertility.) Don Andrea, who has been a monk at Monte Oliveto for twenty-five years and now heads all of their agricultural affairs, has revived the abbey's olive press, meaning they can press their own olives themselves. They are even investing in a honey extraction plant for use by the local community as well as the abbey. From their six hectares of vineyards they make good wines, one of which, their Monaco Rosso ('Red Monk'), in a blind tasting has been mistaken for brunello – though it can't be labelled as such as the vineyard doesn't sit within the boundary of Montalcino. The food the monks eat is dictated by the produce they harvest from their land, such as their Saffron 'speltotto', a dish of spelt cooked in the same way as risotto – using their own spelt, saffron, white wine and olive oil, the recipe for which they have kindly shared with me, and which you'll find on page 114.

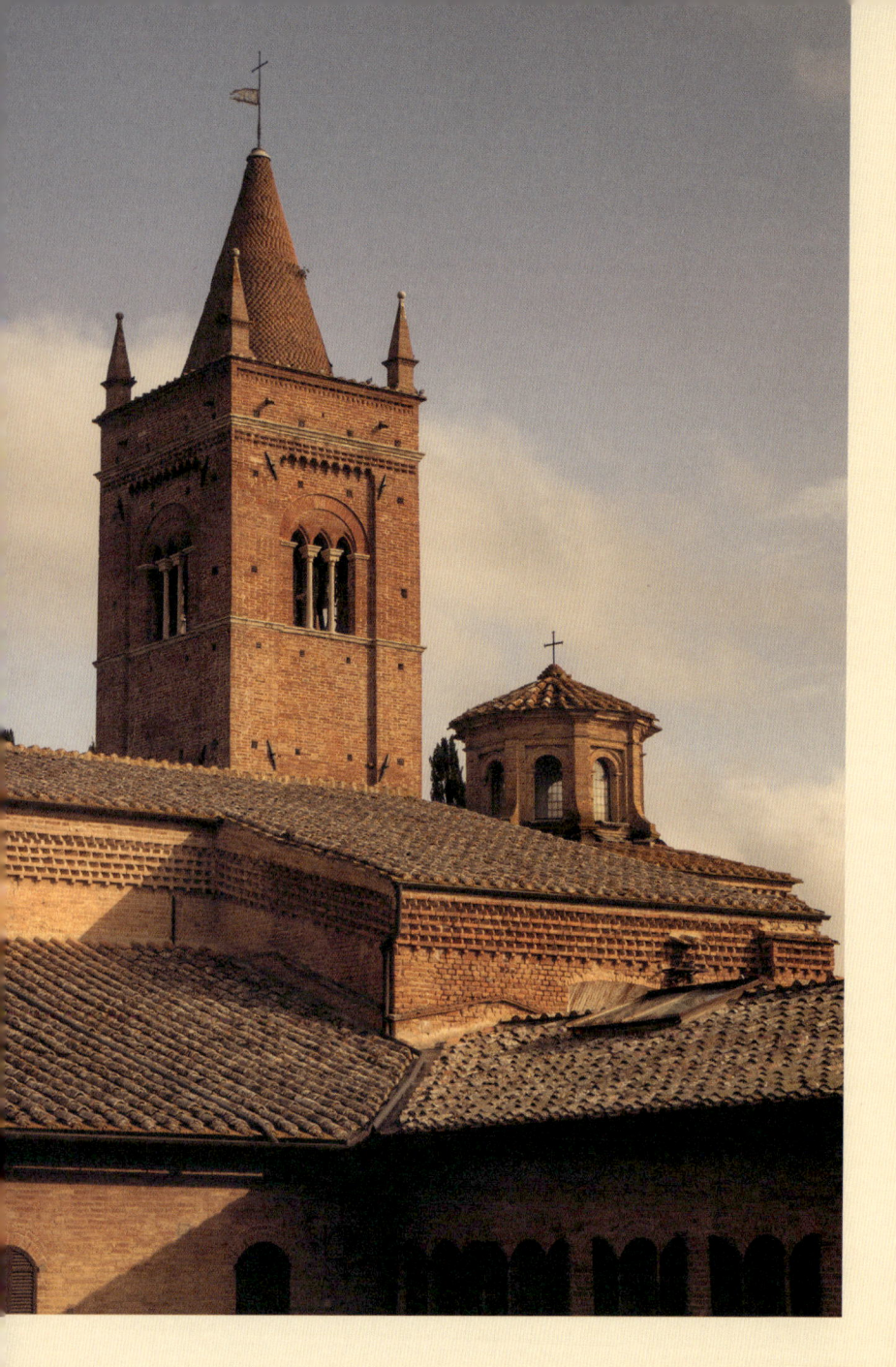

CLOCKWISE FROM TOP LEFT:–
Sunlight on the cloister at Monte Oliveto Maggiore; A corner of the great library with the original equipment used to make tinctures in the pharmacy and a 16th century painting of Madonna giving monastic dress to Saint Tolomei; Walking down the staircase from the library at the monastery; A photographer's studio in Via Soccini in Buonconvento – this was once my mum's antiques shop

AROUND US AT ARNIANO

BELOW:– Market day in Montalcino

OPPOSITE:– The drive to Castello Romitorio, a fabulous winery in Montalcino

Monte Oliveto is an atmospheric place to visit, particularly in the misty colder winter months when you're unlikely to bump into any other visitors and will have the whole cloister to yourself before wandering back up the hill for a hearty lunch at Ristorante La Torre.

Our area is also famous for cheese, specifically pecorino (*pecora* means 'sheep' in Italian). About a twenty minute drive from Montalcino is the perfect hilltop town of Pienza, whose main street is lined with cheese shops. Inside its cathedral is a startling demonstration of how buildings can move – built on the edge of a precipice, a crack pierces the marble floor from wall to wall, but has been stapled back together with heavy iron grips, which makes one feel as though the apse of the church is almost hanging off a cliff. From Pienza there are 360-degree views of southern Tuscany, including towards Monte Amiata, the long extinct volcano where I learned to ski with classmates from Buonconvento, and where our great family friend Beatrix now lives high up on the mountain in a town called Arcidosso, just below the mountain's three ski runs. At the top of the mountain is a giant iron cross, next to a tiny inn where they sell grilled plump sausages, polenta and carafes of Rosso di Montalcino to hungry skiers. I love standing in this spot on a crisp, cold, sunny day after a morning's skiing, looking down at the snowy slope and the valley beyond, knowing that Arniano and Buonconvento are down there, and so my own bed and a hot bath aren't too far away. This, I feel, is the southern boundary of our corner of Tuscany, a region so famous, and yet still so wild – and with so much to discover.

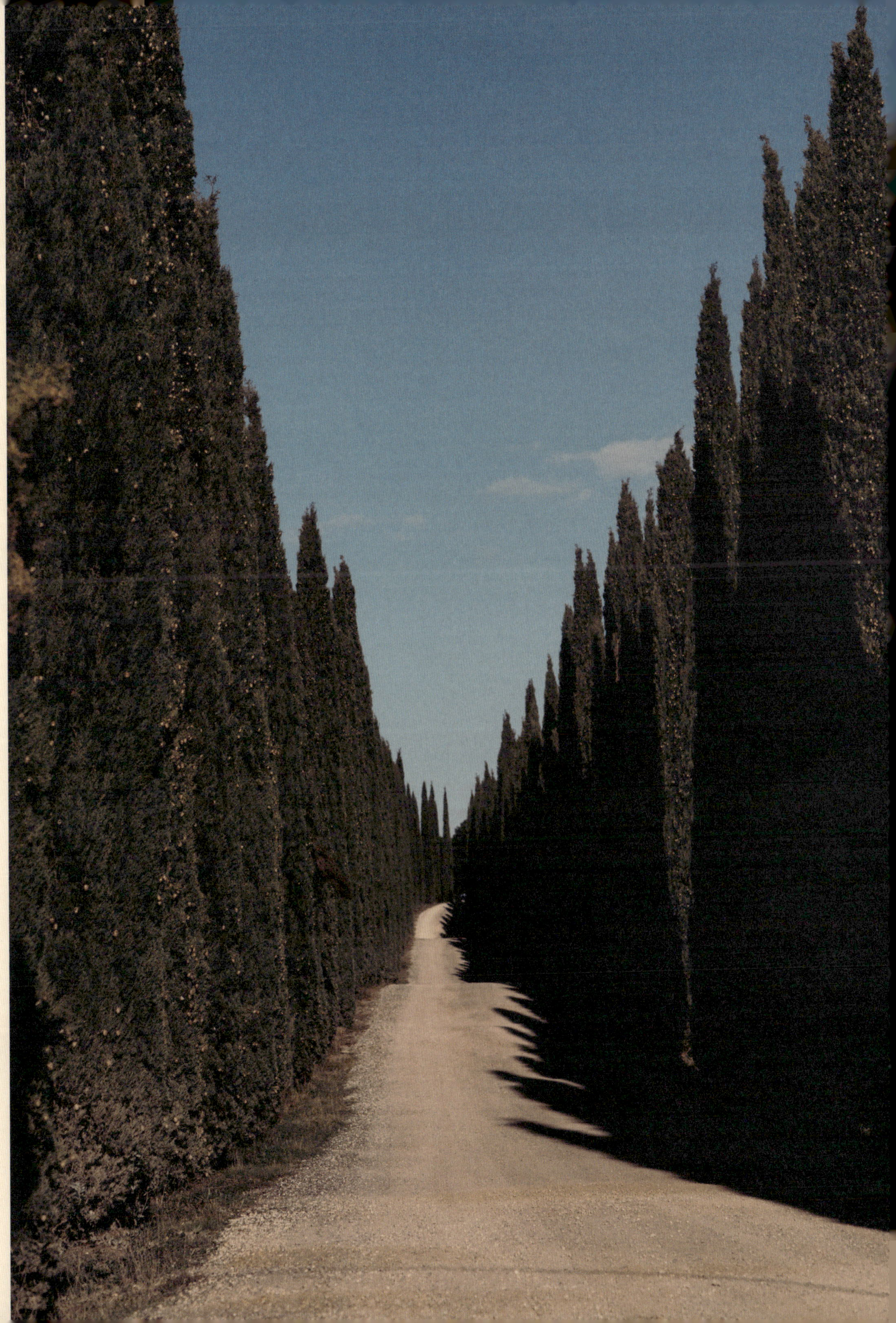

ABB·GEN·
SEXENNIVM·OLIVET·CONGREG·PAPE V·
QVAE
PRIMVM·SVFFRAGATORIBVS·CL·
ANNO·MDCXXVII·
MANIFESTA ĪSPIRAT·COEVNTIB·CŪCTIS
SE ILLI CONCREDIT
DEINDE
AB VRBANO VIII·PONT·MAX
FIDO VIRO MERITO CŌMENDATVR
MDCXXX·
REM NE OBTICEAM
BENE MVTVS LAPIS SVM POSITVS
D·ANGELO MARIA CANTONO
BONON·ABBATE
D·VICTORIO TESTA SENEN·
VIC GENERALIBVS·

PRIMI

PASTA & GRAINS

The *PRIMI* IS almost always my favourite section of any Italian menu, the one that gets me most excited and feeling most hungry. Traditionally in Italian cooking, a *primo* refers to a first course that is usually based on carbohydrates, to counterbalance a *secondo* which will normally comprise mostly protein. Eating habits have changed since I was a child, but in the 1990s when we would have lunch in our local trattoria, most people would still eat an antipasto followed by a bowl of thick soup or pasta, which then led on to a pork chop with a side of *fagioli al fiasco* (beans with olive oil and rosemary). This marathon would be finished off with a strong black coffee and a glass of vin santo (a local dessert wine) in which to dip a few *cantucci* (dry almond biscotti). Nowadays, it's unlikely that people will eat the full meal of antipasto, primo and secondo, but you can see the logic to how they are laid out.

In Tuscany, pasta sauces are hearty and often meaty, such as *pappardelle al cinghiale* (wild boar ragu), or the classic meat ragu, which was often on the menu when I visited my school friends' houses for lunch after morning classes. Ragu is a useful staple for any freezer or fridge as it can be used to dress pasta (page 116), top a 'lasagna' di polenta (page 119) or make classic lasagne. Bechamel also plays its part, not only in lasagne, but also to dress partially cooked pasta that is then baked in the oven to make *pasta al forno*, which we were served at least once a week when I was at school.

Many of the more traditional Tuscan pasta, rice and spelt recipes have been developed from necessity, to make the most of what's available or needs using up. Near us around Siena, pici is our traditional fresh pasta – a thick noodle-type spaghetti made of leftover bread flour and water, usually dressed in a garlicky tomato sauce known as *all'aglione* (*aglione* is the name for local elephant garlic) or with pecorino from nearby Pienza and black pepper (*cacio e pepe*). Around the famed wine region of Chianti, spaghetti *all'ubriacona* – also known as *alla Chiantigiana* – makes use of the gallons of *scarti* (leftovers) from the wineries to make a wine and pancetta sauce to dress spaghetti. Up around Monte Amiata, the mountain that dominates our view, people had limited access to wheat flour from the plains and so used local chestnuts that fell from the trees to make flour, which they used instead of traditional flour to make Chestnut gnocchi (see page 120).

Being carb heavy, pasta has always been a good cheap way for labourers to feed themselves, fill up for a hard day's work and be sated by something truly delicious. Pasta and rice are also fabulous vehicles for vegetables, and I find that with a few simple rules they give great scope for culinary creativity. For instance, I like to stir-fry brussels sprouts with garlic and chilli before tossing them through orecchiette, a perfect union of delicious greens and pasta – with a bit of pancetta thrown in for good measure (page 110). Or Tonnarelli with artichokes and prosciutto (page 109), a recipe devised by a friend of mine who owns a restaurant to use up the meat from the nub-end of a leg of prosciutto that is too fiddly to slice into silky slivers.

The following recipes offer a blend of old and new, very traditional presented alongside a few others I eat often, having followed some of the rules and mixed in a bit of imagination.

A FEW THOUGHTS ON PASTA

The most typical fresh pasta in Tuscany is pici, which is made simply with flour and water (no egg). The dough is rolled into thick long strips, more like noodles than spaghetti.

When buying any type of dried pasta, try to opt for the slightly more expensive brands that shape the pasta through bronze cutters, giving the pasta a rougher surface that allows sauces, oil and starchy water to adhere better. Cheaper brands are passed through a Teflon-coated cutter, making the pasta surface completely smooth, meaning there is nothing for the sauce to grip onto. I also always go for the packets where the pasta is pale yellow, rather than dark, as it will have been dried at a lower temperature for longer, meaning the cooking time will be more stable and reliable.

A few good rules of thumb when cooking dried pasta:

- Use a large pot with much more water than you think you need – this gives the pasta space to absorb the water, and to expand, without clumping together.
- Use much more salt in the water than you think you need. I normally add a fistful.
- Stir the pasta well at the beginning, again to help stop it sticking together.
- Cook the pasta for 1–2 minutes less than instructed on the packet. This means you can toss the pasta into the sauce and mix them together over the heat and it will be perfectly al dente once it gets to your plate.
- Always retain a mugful of the starchy pasta cooking water to help bind the pasta and sauce. Just add it a splash at a time if the pasta is looking dry – and don't dump the whole mug over it, to avoid flooding the pasta and making it watery. Add lots of extra grated parmesan if you do, to thicken it out again.
- Always remember that bossy old Italian truism – that it's the people who should wait for the pasta, not the pasta for the people. If you make sure everyone is sitting down before the pasta has finished cooking, they will be presented with the dish as it was intended. Hot and perfectly cooked, as opposed to coagulated, tepid and a bit sad.

Rigatoni al sugo finto

Rigatoni with 'fake' meat sauce

SERVES 4

2 white onions

3 carrots

4 celery sticks

handful of flat-leaf parsley

5 tablespoons olive oil, plus extra to serve

sea salt and freshly ground black pepper

½ glass red wine

2 tablespoons tomato concentrate

½ Star stock cube

500 g (1 lb 2 oz) rigatoni

2 tablespoons finely grated parmesan, plus extra to serve

Finto in Italian means 'fake', and this sugo is *finto* by dint of containing no meat at all. Instead, red wine is used to tint very finely chopped vegetables to give the impression of minced meat. In Florence it is also sometimes known as *sugo scappato* – *scappato* meaning 'escaped', the idea being that the meat has run away from the dish. I love *sugo finto* as it's wonderfully tasty and satisfying, made with inexpensive ingredients that cook down more quickly than a traditional ragu and come together to create something really special, and possibly even better than the original that it is trying to imitate.

PREPARATION:– 20 minutes
COOKING:– 1 hour

Very finely chop the onions, carrots, celery and parsley together so that the mixture resembles finely minced meat. You can carefully pulse each vegetable individually in a food processor, but make sure they don't get mushy. I prefer to chop them by hand.

Put the chopped vegetables straight into a large heavy-based saucepan with the olive oil and a pinch of salt. Leave to gently cook over a medium heat for about 5 minutes, stirring occasionally.

Once the onion starts to look translucent, pour in the wine. Leave to gently cook for 10 minutes while the wine reduces and the alcohol evaporates.

Stir in the tomato concentrate and, after a couple of minutes, add the stock cube and 500 ml (17 fl oz) water. Season with a generous pinch of salt and pepper and cook down without a lid on for about 30 minutes, until the liquid has reduced by half and you are left with a thick(ish) brown 'ragu'.

Bring a large saucepan of well-salted water to a rolling boil. Add the rigatoni, give it a good stir so that it doesn't stick together, and cook until al dente (check the packet instructions). Halfway through the cooking time, scoop out and reserve a mugful of the starchy pasta cooking water.

While the pasta is cooking, stir 2 tablespoons of parmesan through the ragu.

Drain the pasta, then toss it through the ragu with a few dribbles of the pasta cooking water. Add a little more if the pasta is looking dry or needs help mixing through the sauce.

Serve immediately, straight from the pan, with a drizzle more oil and a sprinkling of parmesan.

> **VARIATION:–** If you're feeling like some meat, rigatoni are also a delicious vehicle for a classic ragu (page 116) – simply substitute the *sugo finto* with the meaty version.

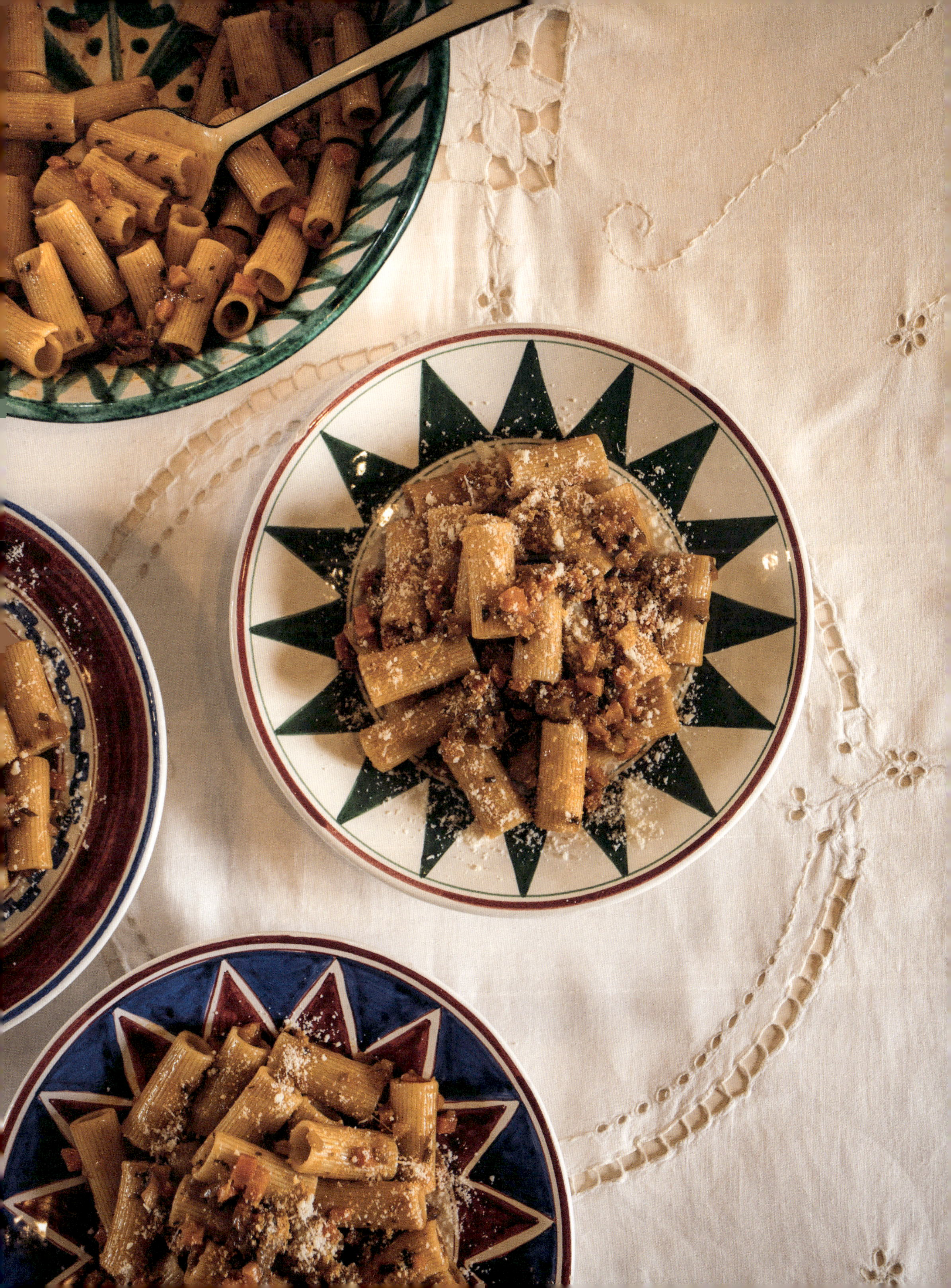

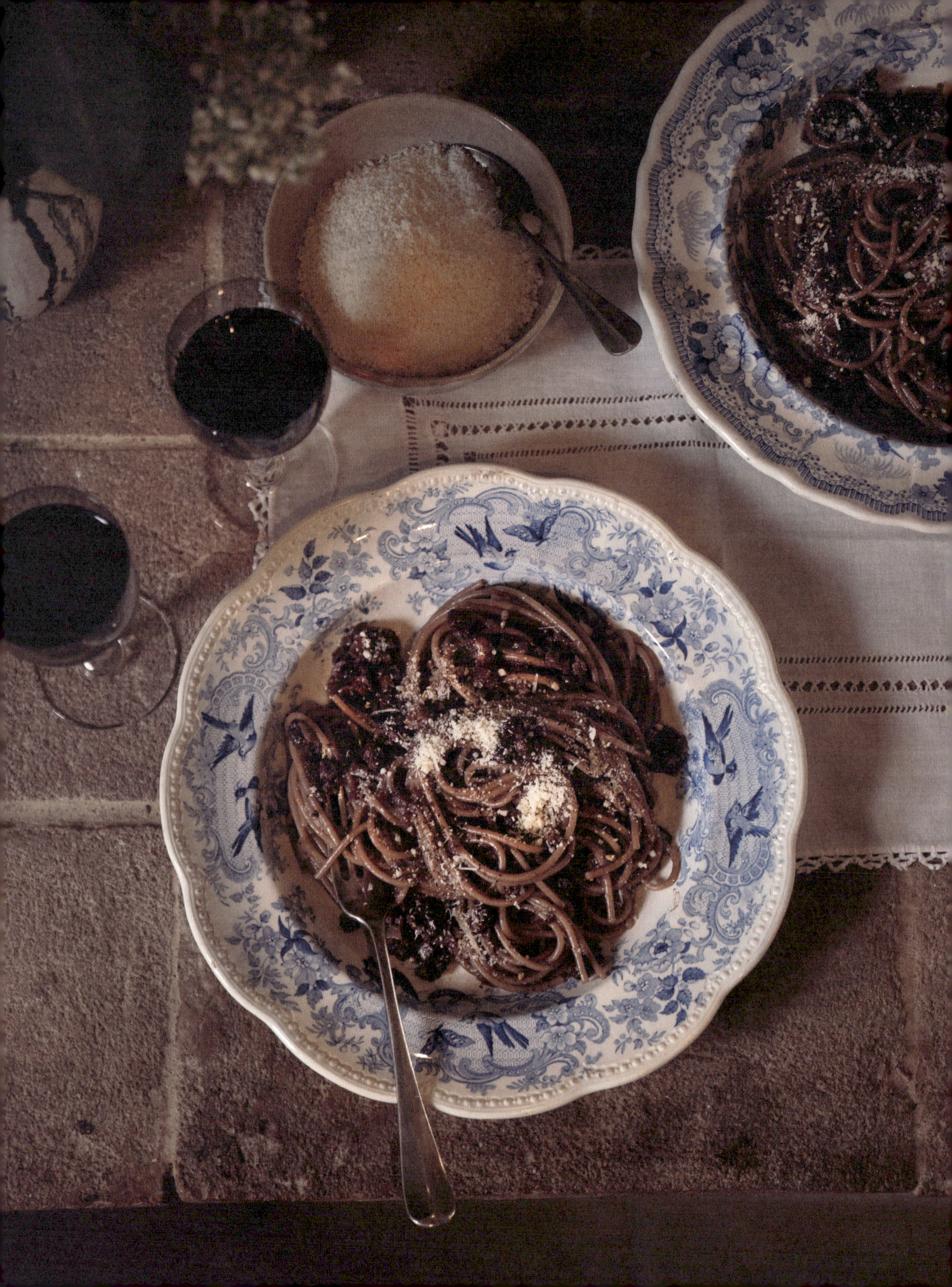

Spaghetti all'ubriacona

Drunkard's spaghetti

SERVES 4

1 white onion, finely chopped

100 g (3½ oz) unsmoked ready-diced pancetta, chopped

2 tablespoons olive oil, plus extra to serve

sea salt and freshly ground black pepper

1 bottle of chianti or any full-bodied red wine

400 g (14 oz) spaghetti

grated parmesan, to serve

Chianti is one of Italy's most emblematic wines, produced in the hills between Florence and Siena and protected by the symbol of the black cockerel that endorses every bottle of Chianti Classico. Winemaking is a huge part of Tuscan rural life, and having had access to lots of *scarti* (leftover wine), the wives of vineyard employees devised this local traditional dish, also known as *pasta alla Chiantigiana*. What is particularly wonderful about this dish is that it works well with wine that has been sitting around for a few days and you're desperate to get rid of. That wine that is no longer any good for drinking can be turned into a tasty meal by cooking it down with onions and pancetta and tossing it with pasta. Adding wine to the pasta cooking water also imparts some of its colour to the spaghetti. The recipe also works well with less wine if you only have half a bottle knocking around; the taste will just be more subtle.

PREPARATION:– 5 minutes
COOKING:– 15 minutes

Put the onion, pancetta and olive oil in a wide frying pan, large enough to hold all the spaghetti later. Cook on a gentle sizzle over a medium heat for about 5 minutes, until the onion becomes translucent and the pancetta opaque. Add a generous pinch of salt, black pepper and 2 glasses of red wine and leave to gently bubble over a medium heat.

Bring a large saucepan of well-salted water to a rolling boil. Add a fistful of salt and 2–3 glasses of red wine to the water. (If you happen to have another glass of wine left, add it to the pan of pasta sauce.)

Once the water has come back to a rolling boil, add the spaghetti. Once it has fully wilted down into the water, stir the spaghetti around so that the strands don't stick together. Halfway through the pasta cooking time (check the packet instructions), add a whole ladleful of the wine-stained pasta water to the sauce and turn up the heat – you want to keep the sauce quite liquid to be able to toss the spaghetti through it.

Once the spaghetti is al dente, use tongs to transfer the spaghetti to the frying pan and toss with the sauce, adding a little more of the reserved pasta cooking water if needed.

Serve immediately, sprinkled with parmesan and lots of black pepper.

Fusilloni con pesto al cavolo nero

Fussiloni with cavolo nero, walnut & pecorino pesto

Pesto is famously made using a lot of basil, which is at its best in summer, so I was excited to discover this winter version made using cavolo nero at Trattoria La Casalinga in Florence. It's a delicious dark green take on a summery classic for when the chilly nights are setting in and basil isn't at its best but 'black cabbages' are. I love this rich pesto and often make a jar of it when cavolo nero is in season to use over pasta, in a silky risotto or simply as a sauce for boiled potatoes or steamed vegetables. Andrea, the proprietor of Casalinga and grandson of the restaurant's founders, gave me the ultimate tip to keep the pesto vibrantly green: dunking the cavolo nero in iced water immediately after blanching. I always retain the cavolo cooking water to cook the pasta in to minimise washing up and to feel as though I am imbuing the pasta with some of the green goodness that might have been lost in the initial blanch. At Casalinga they use pecorino in their pesto, but you can use parmesan if you don't have pecorino to hand.

SERVES 4

500 g (1 lb 2 oz) fusilloni pasta (pappardelle is also delicious)

zest of 1 lemon

grated parmesan

sea salt

olive oil

PESTO

50 g (1¾ oz) walnuts or hazelnuts

1 bunch of cavolo nero

½ garlic clove, peeled

4 tablespoons olive oil

2 tablespoons finely grated pecorino or parmesan

sea salt

PREPARATION:— 5 minutes
COOKING:— 15 minutes

To make the pesto, spread the walnuts on a baking tray and lightly toast for 5 minutes in an oven preheated to 180°C (350°F) fan-forced. Remove from the oven and set aside to cool.

Fill a bowl with water and a few ice cubes to refresh the cavolo nero in after blanching. (You can skip the ice bath step, but your pesto will be much darker green rather than vibrant in colour.)

Bring a large pasta pot of well-salted water to a rolling boil. Strip the cavolo nero leaves from the stalks and either discard the stalks or reserve to use in a stock; you should have about 100 g (3½ oz) cavolo nero leaves. Blanch the cavolo nero with the garlic clove in the boiling water for 3 minutes if the leaves are small and tender, or 4 minutes if they seem particularly rubbery and tough. Once cooked, use tongs or a slotted spoon to transfer the cavolo nero to the ice bath for a few seconds, reserving the cooking water. Drain the cavolo nero thoroughly in a colander over the sink.

Transfer the cavolo to a blender and roughly chop for about a minute. With the motor still running, drizzle in the olive oil. Add the walnuts, cheese and a generous pinch of salt and keep chopping until smooth(ish) and green. Add 2 tablespoons of the cooking water and briefly blend.

Put the pesto in your pasta serving bowl.

Bring the pan of cavolo nero cooking water back to a rolling boil, adding more water if needed to fully submerge the pasta. Add the fusilloni, give it a good stir so that it doesn't stick together, and cook until al dente (check the packet instructions). Halfway through the pasta cooking time, stir 2 tablespoons of the pasta cooking water through the pesto to loosen it a little. Before draining the pasta, scoop out a mugful of the starchy pasta cooking water.

Drain the pasta and toss it through the pesto, using a little of the reserved cooking water to loosen the pesto if needed. Toss in the lemon zest, some parmesan, salt and a drizzle more olive oil.

Serve immediately.

> **NOTE:—** The pesto will keep in a clean jar or container in the fridge for up to 4 days; just drizzle a little olive oil over the top before sealing. It's delicious on toast, stirred through a plain risotto or drizzled over roast vegetables.

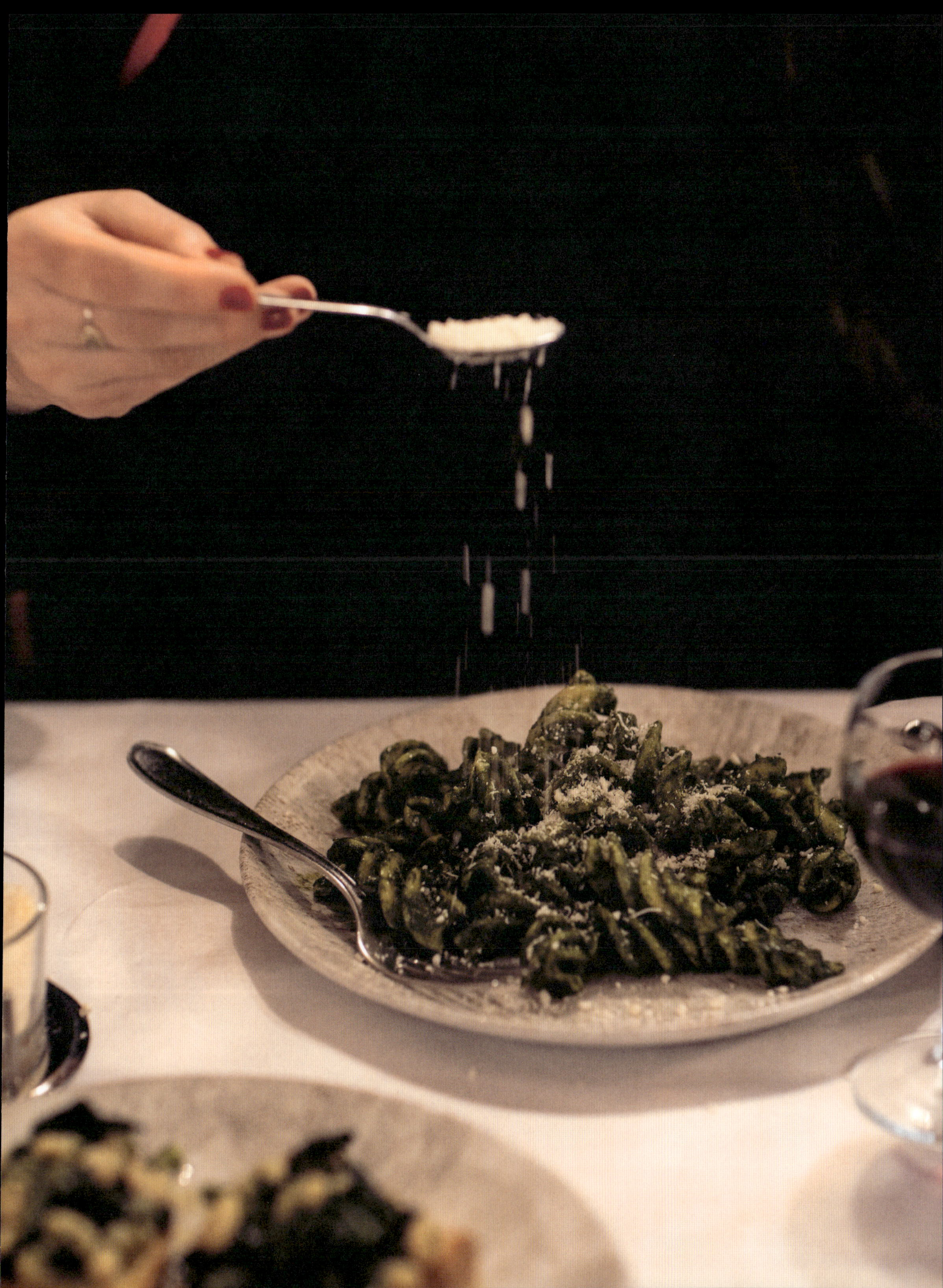

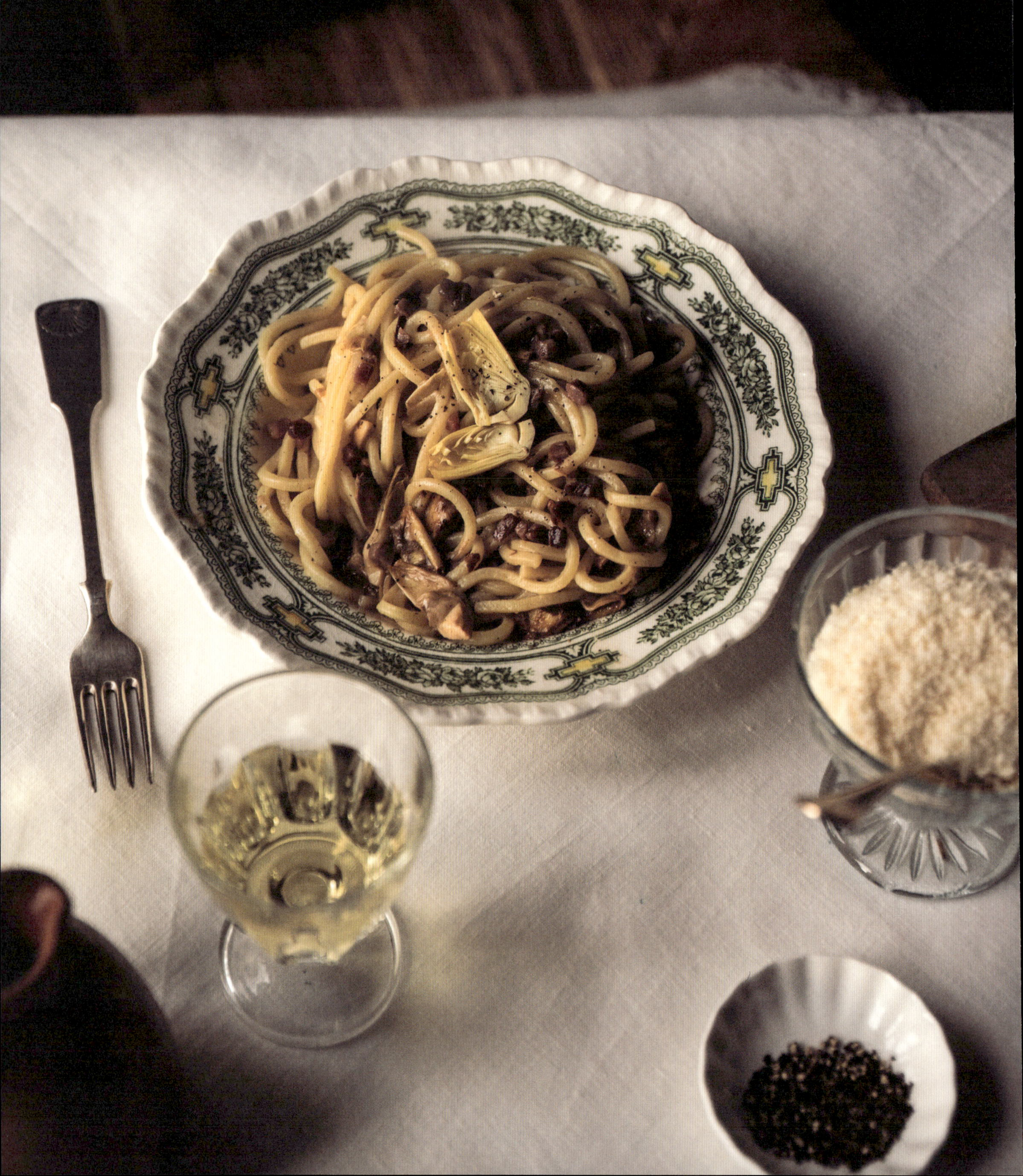

Tonnarelli con carciofi e prosciutto

Tonnarelli with artichokes & prosciutto

SERVES 4

200 g (7 oz) hunk of prosciutto di Parma, finely diced

olive oil

400 g (14 oz) jar of artichoke hearts

sea salt and freshly ground black pepper

2 glasses white wine or Prosecco

500 g (1 lb 2 oz) tonnarelli, linguine or spaghetti alla chitarra

50 g (1¾ oz) finely grated parmesan, plus extra to serve

You'll find this ingenious dish on the menu at Trattoria Cammillo in Florence on cold nights when artichokes are in season and they have reached the end of their leg of *prosciutto crudo* and can't make lovely thin velvety slices from it anymore. They take the end and chop it into tiny little bullets of prosciutto, which stud the pasta along with sautéed artichokes. If you can find fresh artichoke hearts, all the better, but I actually love this version with jarred artichokes as it's a quick store cupboard route to a deliciously hearty meal. You can use sliced or diced pancetta or prosciutto as well, which are more readily available than the end of a leg of ham.

PREPARATION:– 5 minutes
COOKING:– 25 minutes

In a wide frying pan, large enough to hold all the pasta later, fry the prosciutto with a drizzle of olive oil until crispy. Transfer to a bowl, keeping the pan handy.

Thoroughly drain the artichokes of all their oil in a colander set over a bowl for 5 minutes, then pat dry using paper towel. Transfer to a chopping board and roughly slice into chunks. If they still have their stems on, chop these into rounds.

Add another drizzle of olive oil to the prosciutto pan and fry the artichokes over a high heat with a grind of black pepper and pinch of salt for 5–8 minutes, until they get a little colour and look charred, turning occasionally. Pour in the wine, turn down the heat and simmer for 5 minutes, until the alcohol has evaporated.

Meanwhile, bring a large saucepan of well-salted water to a rolling boil. Add the pasta, give it a good stir so that it doesn't stick together, and cook until al dente (check the packet instructions). Halfway through the pasta cooking time, add a ladleful of the pasta water to the artichokes in the frying pan and leave to bubble away until the pasta is ready.

Keep a mugful of the pasta water. Using tongs, transfer the pasta to the frying pan and toss with the artichokes. Add a pinch of salt, some black pepper, the parmesan, a good glug of olive oil, plus a little of the pasta cooking water if needed, and toss again. Add the prosciutto and more black pepper.

Serve piping hot in shallow bowls, with a drizzle of olive oil and lots of parmesan.

Orecchiette con cavolo bruxelles e pancetta

Orecchiette with brussels sprouts & pancetta

SERVES 4

100 g (3½ oz) unsmoked pancetta, chopped

2 tablespoons olive oil, plus extra for the pancetta and to serve

350 g (12½ oz) brussels sprouts

sea salt and freshly ground black pepper

chilli flakes, to taste

3 garlic cloves, finely crushed or chopped

400 g (14 oz) orecchiette

1 tablespoon butter

2 tablespoons finely grated parmesan, plus extra to serve

More from Puglia than Tuscany, this is a dish I eat in the depths of winter when I'm craving pasta but also want to feel like I am eating something green. The garlicky stir-fried brussels sprouts are fabulous with any short pasta, and the pancetta provides a salty note, but you can of course leave it out if for a vegetarian meal.

PREPARATION:– 10 minutes
COOKING:– 20 minutes

In a wide frying pan, large enough to hold all the pasta later, fry the pancetta with a drizzle of olive oil until crispy. Transfer to a bowl, keeping the pan handy and letting it cool a little.

Slice the bottom off each brussels sprout and cut each sprout into quarters lengthways.

Heat the olive oil in the same pan, add all the sprouts and toss with some sea salt and chilli flakes. Spread the sprouts in one layer across the pan and leave to cook over a high heat for about 5 minutes so they get a little charred, making sure not to disturb them too much. After 5 minutes, turn the heat off and toss the garlic through the sprouts with another drizzle of olive oil and a pinch of salt.

Bring a large saucepan of well-salted water to a rolling boil. Add the pasta, give it a good stir so that it doesn't stick together, and cook until al dente (check the packet instructions). Halfway through the pasta cooking time, add a ladleful of the pasta water to the brussels sprouts, turn the heat back up and leave to bubble away until the pasta is ready.

Keeping a mugful of the pasta water, drain the pasta and add it to the pan with the brussels sprouts. Add a splash of the reserved pasta cooking water, along with the butter, parmesan and some black pepper and toss well. Add the pancetta and toss again, adding a bit more water if the pasta is looking dry.

Serve piping hot in shallow bowls, with a drizzle of olive oil and lots of parmesan.

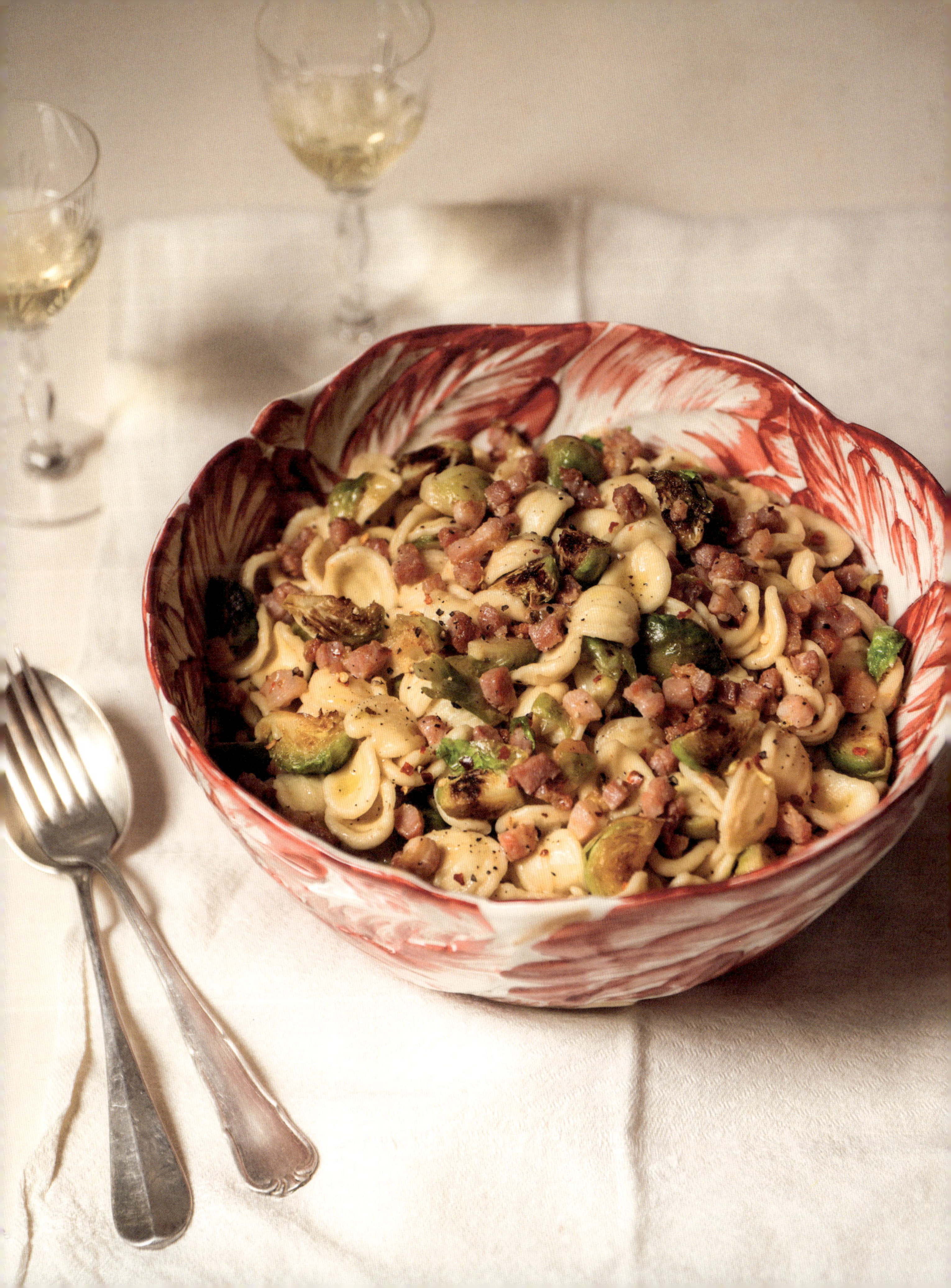

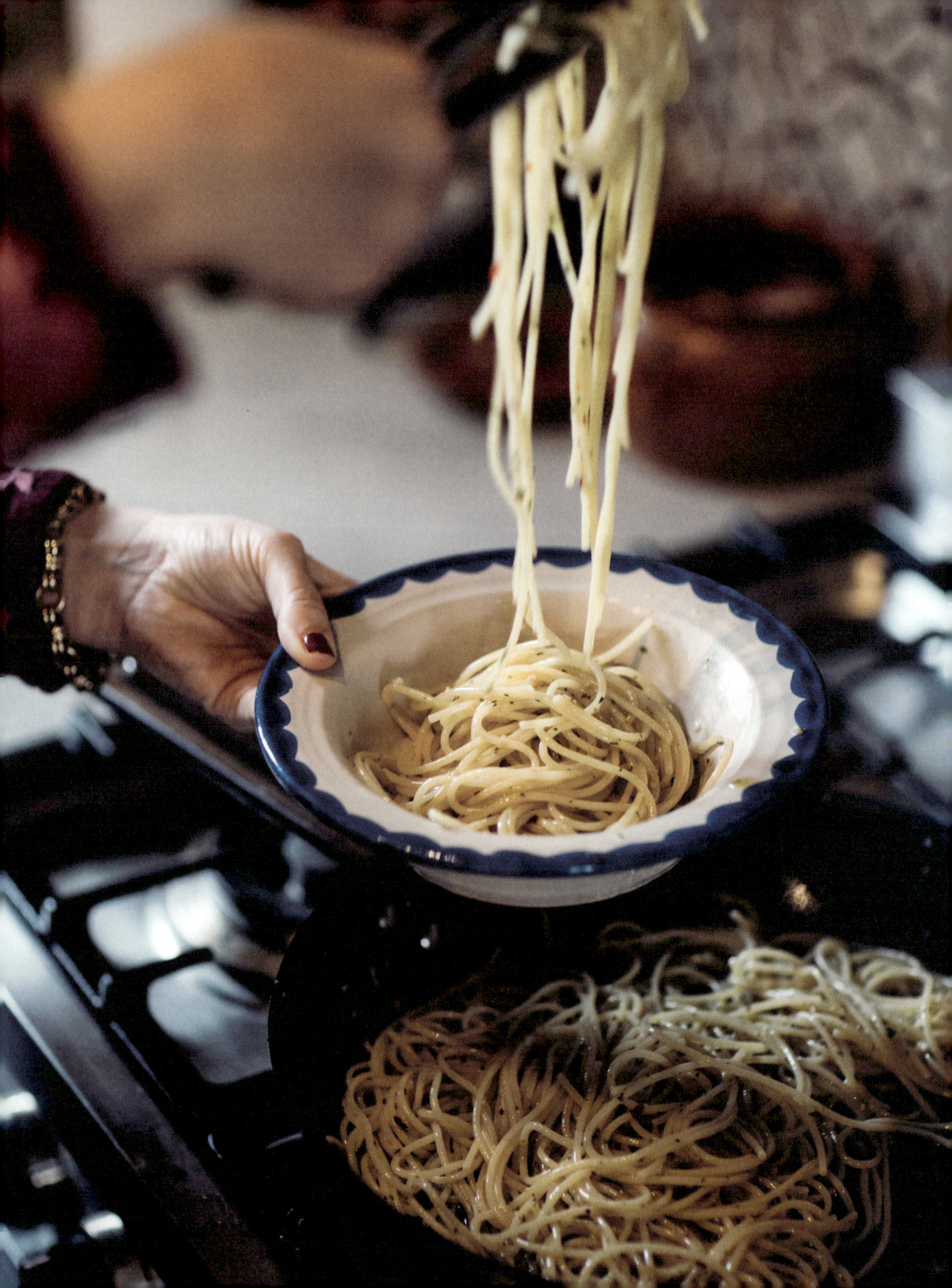

Spaghetti al rosmarino

Emergency rosemary & garlic spaghetti

SERVES 2

4 rosemary sprigs, leaves picked

4 tablespoons olive oil

4 garlic cloves, finely crushed or chopped

pinch of chilli flakes, or to taste

sea salt

300 g (10½ oz) spaghetti

grated parmesan, to serve

This is a Sienese recipe from our old family friend, Rossana. It's rather like an intensely herby version of a classic *aglio, olio, peperoncino*. It's perfect in an emergency, when you've just come home, want dinner in 10 minutes but don't have any food aside from pasta, olive oil, garlic and a few rosemary sprigs, either knocking around the fridge or snipped from a bush on your windowsill. The original recipe doesn't include chilli flakes, but I add a generous pinch as I find it adds another layer to the herby garlic flavour and keeps every mouthful interesting.

PREPARATION:– 5 minutes
COOKING:– 10 minutes

Bring a large saucepan of well-salted water to a rolling boil.

Meanwhile, very finely chop the rosemary leaves. In a wide frying pan, large enough to hold all the spaghetti later, gently heat the olive oil with the rosemary for a few minutes, allowing the rosemary to infuse into the oil; it shouldn't fry furiously or turn brown. Add the garlic, chilli and a generous pinch of sea salt and gently cook for a few more minutes.

Once the pan of water is at a galloping boil, add the spaghetti. Once it has fully wilted down into the water, stir the spaghetti around so that the strands don't stick together. Cook until al dente.

Halfway through the pasta cooking time (check the packet instructions), add two ladlefuls of the pasta cooking water to the rosemary mixture in the frying pan and turn up the heat to bring it up to a rolling boil. After 2–3 minutes, once it has reduced into an amalgamated liquid, switch off the heat.

Use tongs to transfer the spaghetti to the frying pan and toss with the rosemary and garlic sauce.

Serve immediately, with another drizzle of olive oil and lots of parmesan.

Il farrotto dei monaci

Saffron 'speltotto' from the monks of Monte Oliveto

SERVES 4

1 litre (34 fl oz) Vegetable stock (page 72) or Chicken & beef bone broth (page 73)

2 pinches of saffron strands, plus extra to serve (optional)

60 g (2 oz) unsalted butter

very good extra virgin olive oil

1 red onion, finely chopped

sea salt and freshly ground black pepper

500 g (1 lb 2 oz) spelt or pearl barley

1 glass of dry white wine, or any cooking wine

100 g (3½ oz) grated pecorino or parmesan, plus extra to serve

This recipe for spelt 'risotto' was given to me by the monks at our local abbey at Monte Oliveto Maggiore – a Benedictine monastery housing a wonderful cloister with beautiful frescoes depicting the life of Saint Benedict. In the 1950s, around 500 monks lived at the abbey; nowadays they number about forty, but they still farm the land surrounding the abbey, including 27 hectares (67 acres) of olives. They have been farming spelt here since the 14th century when the abbey was founded by Saint Bernardo Tolomei, and growing irises for saffron for almost as long. They also make white wine and a fabulous olive oil that has been voted one of the best in Tuscany. Don Andrea, who has been a monk at the monastery for over 25 years and heads the agricultural side of things, explains that this recipe, in which spelt is cooked in the manner of a risotto, was developed in direct response to the bounty around them. As Don Andrea proudly tells me, the only ingredients of this dish that they don't produce themselves are the butter and cheese.

Packed with nutrients, spelt is a grain with a delicious nutty flavour and pleasingly solid texture. This 'speltotto' is great as it requires much less continuous stirring than a traditional risotto, making it a bit more hands-off, but with equally good results.

PREPARATION:– 30 minutes
COOKING:– 35 minutes

Warm the stock and transfer a ladleful to a bowl or mug. Add the saffron strands and leave to soak for 30 minutes (or, for as long as it takes you to chop the onion, if you're pushed for time).

In a wide, heavy-based frying pan, melt a tablespoon of the butter with 3 tablespoons olive oil over a medium heat. Once the fat starts to sizzle, add the onion, along with a pinch of sea salt. Gently cook for 3–5 minutes, until the onion is translucent, stirring occasionally. Add the spelt and mix together thoroughly. Turn the heat up high and toast the spelt for about 2 minutes, stirring often. Reheat the stock over a medium heat and heat through, ready to be added to the spelt.

Stir in the wine and a pinch of sea salt. Leave over high heat until the alcohol has evaporated, stirring occasionally. Turn the heat down and leave until the spelt has absorbed all the liquid, stirring occasionally. Add the mug of saffrony stock, and two ladlefuls of the plain stock. Check and stir the spelt every so often, adding another ladleful of stock when it looks like it's drying out. Repeat this process for 20–25 minutes, until the spelt is cooked and most of the liquid has been absorbed. Don't worry if you don't use all the stock; if you run out of stock but feel the spelt is drying out, add a ladleful of water.

When the spelt is nearly cooked through, add the cheese and the rest of the butter. Stir until the butter and cheese have melted and amalgamated into the speltotto.

Try the spelt: it should be cooked, but still have a little bite. Adjust the seasoning as necessary.

Serve immediately, topped with a grind of black pepper, a little extra cheese, a drizzle more olive oil and a few pretty saffron strands if you so wish.

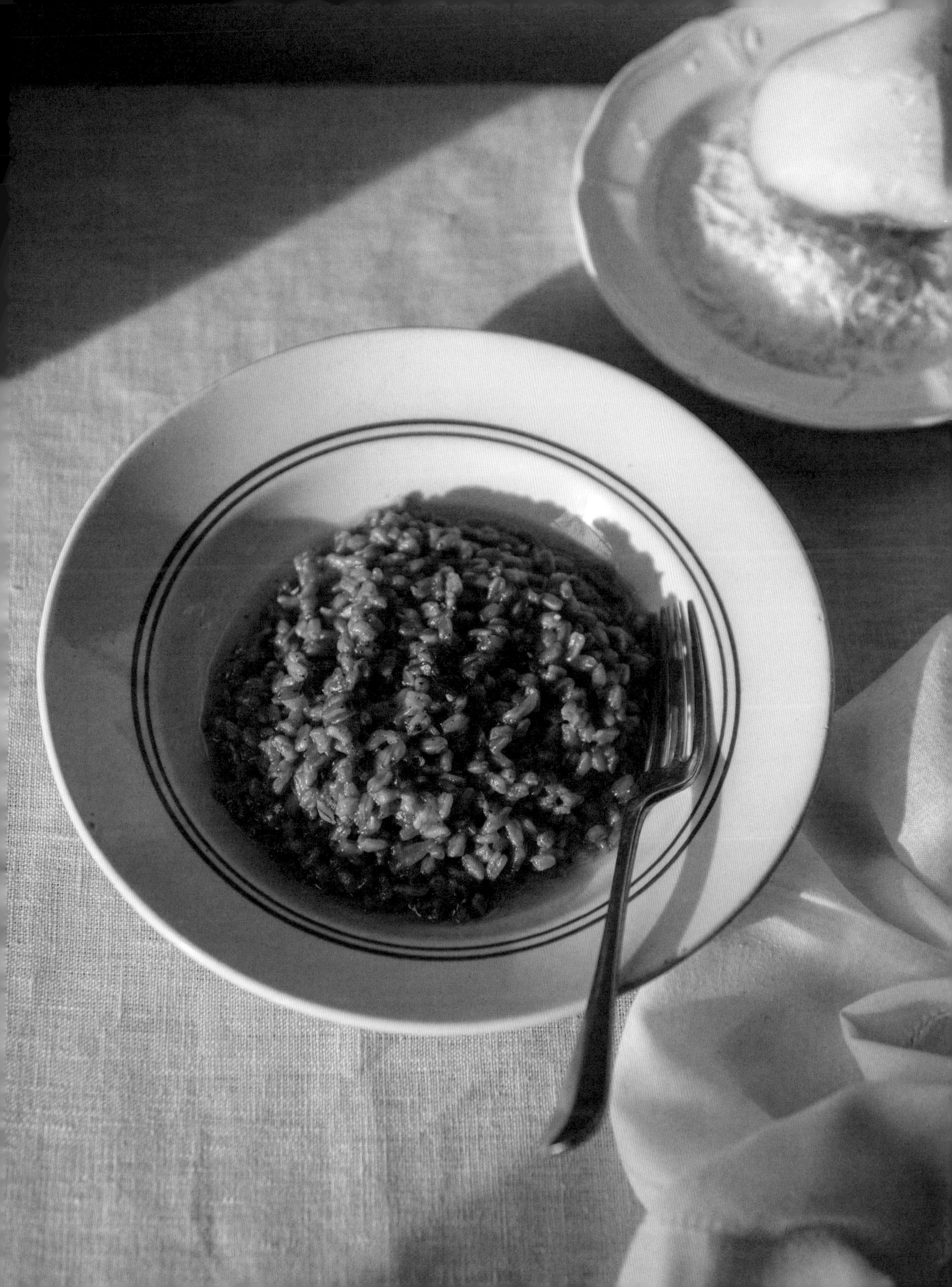

Penne al ragu

Penne bolognese

RAGU (SERVES 12)

5 tablespoons olive oil

2 rosemary sprigs, leaves picked and finely chopped

2 celery sticks, very finely chopped

1 red onion, very finely chopped

2 carrots, very finely chopped

sea salt and freshly ground black pepper

500 g (1 lb 2 oz) pork mince, or 5 organic pork sausages

500 g (1 lb 2 oz) beef mince

a few bay leaves

250 ml (8½ fl oz) red wine

250 ml (8½ fl oz) full-fat milk

400 g (14 oz) tin peeled plum tomatoes

1 teaspoon tomato concentrate

TO SERVE 4

400 g (14 oz) penne rigate

1 tablespoon olive oil

1 rosemary sprig

grated parmesan

Tuscany is a region of farmers and hunters, so ragu is a big part of the diet. It appears on menus in most restaurants and is made in most homes, often with the game shot during the hunting season – in particular wild boar, which is delicious, but difficult to get outside of Italy. Here is a more traditional recipe my school friends' mothers used to make for us for lunch after school.

Because of the long cooking time, it's worthwhile making a big batch of ragu and keeping some in the freezer for a quick tasty meal at the last minute. I'll often thaw some frozen ragu and use it on pasta, or pour it over cheesy polenta with a little bechamel to make a polenta 'lasagna' (page 119).

This ragu recipe makes enough to feed a crowd of 12. You'll only need about a third of it for this pasta dish, so freeze the remaining ragu in serving portions for a few more wonderful meals later on.

PREPARATION:– 20 minutes
COOKING:– 3 hours

First, make the ragu. Pour the olive oil into a large heavy-based saucepan (ideally a cast-iron one), add the rosemary and turn the heat to medium. Once sizzling, add the celery, onion and carrot, along with a generous pinch of sea salt, and cook for 10 minutes, stirring often.

Add the pork mince (or sausage meat, removed from the casings), breaking up the meat with the end of a wooden spoon. Once the pork is browned, add the beef mince and bay leaves. Brown together for about 10 minutes, stirring often. Initially the meat will start releasing liquid, but after 10 minutes the water will have evaporated, and the meat should start sizzling and frying again.

Stir in the wine and cook for 5 minutes, or until the alcohol has evaporated. Stir in the milk and leave to cook for a couple of minutes before adding the tomatoes and tomato concentrate. Half-fill the tomato tin with water, swirl it around to rinse off any extra tomato and pour it into the pan. Stir in some salt and black pepper and turn the heat down very low. Rest a wooden spoon over the pan and place a lid on top, so that the ragu is covered but steam can still escape.

Leave to gently cook for about 2 hours, checking and stirring every 15 minutes or so, and adding a splash of water or milk if the ragu is drying out.

The ragu is ready when it's reduced and thick. It will be delicious to eat immediately, but as with most stewed dishes, will be even better the next day.

TO MAKE PASTA WITH RAGU:–
Bring a large saucepan of well-salted water to a rolling boil. Add the pasta, give it a good stir so that it doesn't stick together, and cook until al dente (check the packet instructions).

Meanwhile, in a separate pan, heat the olive oil with the rosemary sprig. Stir in 300 g (10½ oz) of the ragu, adding a couple of tablespoons of the pasta cooking water halfway through the pasta cooking time.

Drain the pasta and toss with the ragu. Serve with parmesan.

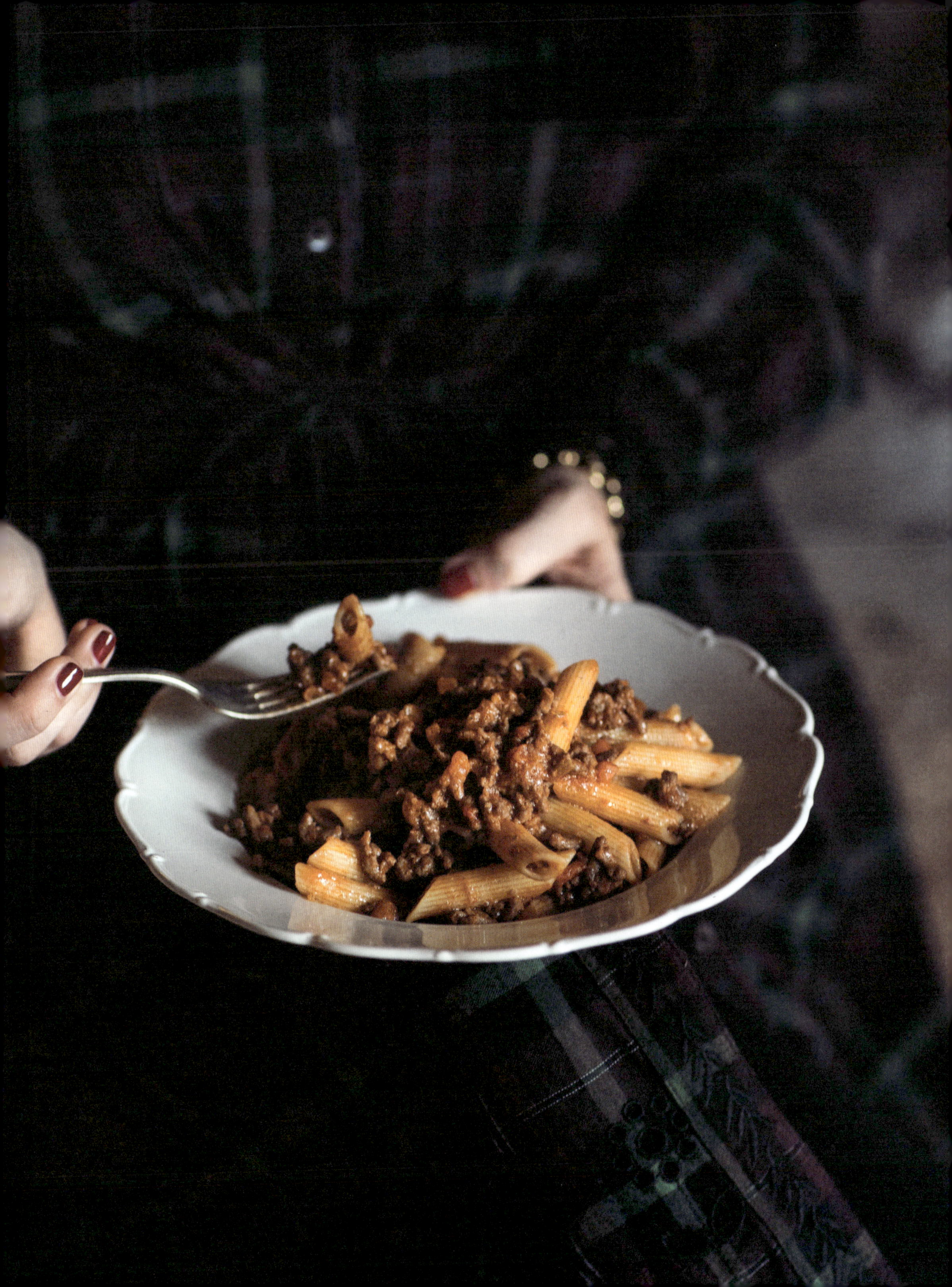

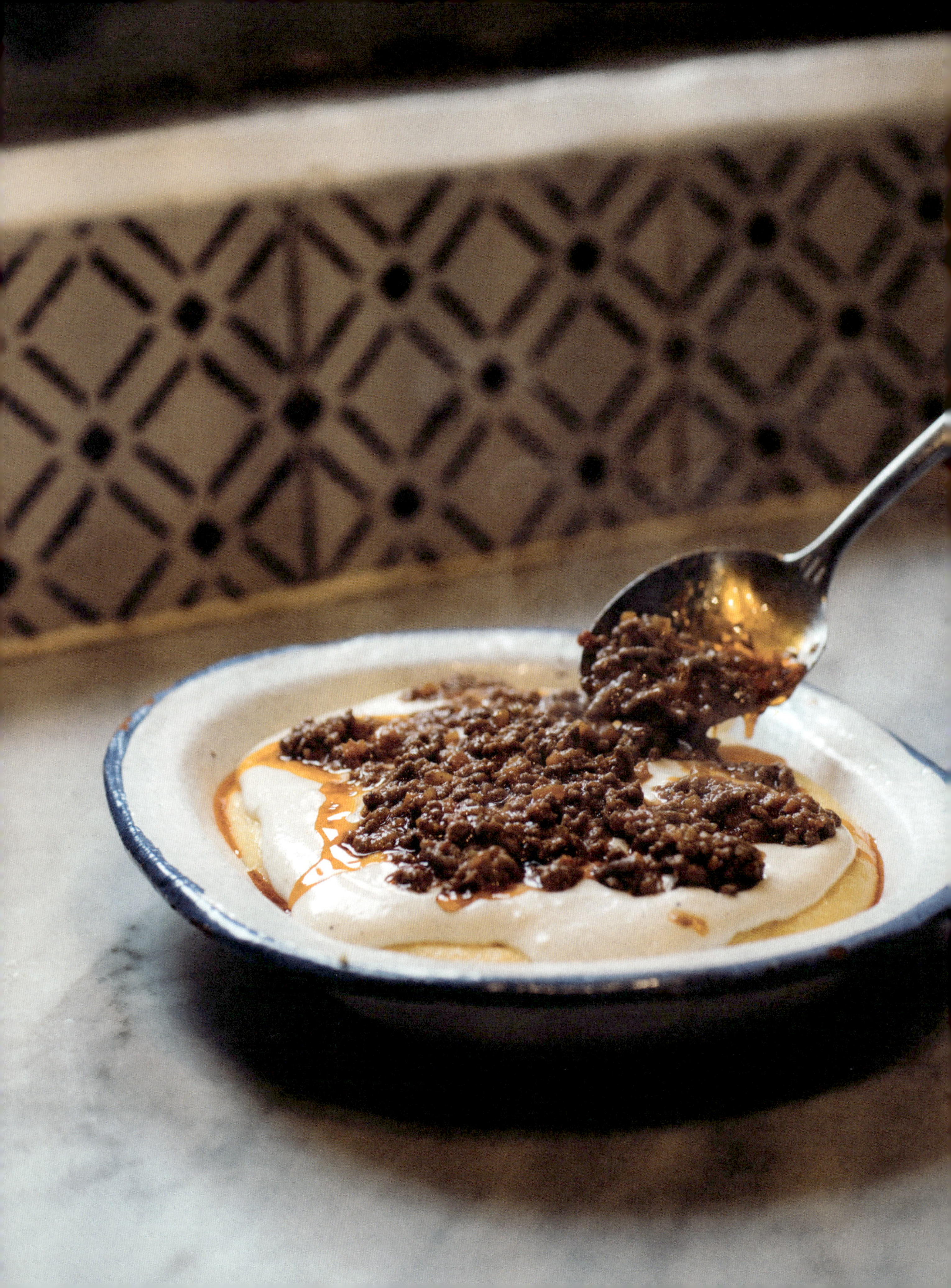

Polenta 'lasagna'

Polenta with bechamel & ragu

SERVES 4

500 g (1 lb 2 oz) ragu (page 116)

½ quantity of bechamel (page 144)

grated parmesan, to serve

POLENTA

150 g (5½ oz) instant polenta (or coarse cornmeal)

2 tablespoons olive oil

40 g (1½ oz) butter

50 g (1¾ oz) grated parmesan, plus extra to serve (optional)

Essentially a bowl of cheesy polenta topped with bechamel and a meat sauce, this is a dish that is served on cosy winter days. Our local trattoria, 'Nara's', always serves it on New Year's Day, knowing their diners might have sore heads and be in need of this culinary version of a hug. It has the main elements of a classic lasagne – the creamy bechamel and delicious meat sauce – but without the faff of making fresh pasta, and I find that the loose, cheesy polenta is a perfectly good vehicle for them. It is also possible to make this recipe gluten free by using cornflour in the bechamel. Our local *alimentari* (delicatessen) often sells this dish in room-temperature slices to be warmed up at home. I'm not mad on this, though, as I find that the polenta too stodgy if it isn't made and eaten immediately, and I miss the thin layers of pasta – whereas if the polenta is hot and loose, I love it.

COOKING & ASSEMBLING:– 20 minutes, if you have the ragu and bechamel ready

To make the polenta, bring 800 ml (27 fl oz) of well-salted water to a rolling boil in a large saucepan. Once boiling, slowly pour in the polenta from a height, stirring continuously with a whisk to remove any lumps. Stir in the same direction for a few minutes, then once the polenta begins to thicken, turn down the heat and add the olive oil. Stir continuously until the polenta is thick(ish) and cooked, which may take 5–10 minutes, depending on the brand. (I like my polenta a bit more loose and sloppy, rather than too dense, so I cook it with more liquid and for a shorter time.) Stir the butter and parmesan through.

Meanwhile, heat the ragu in a saucepan with a splash of water for 5 minutes, or until warmed through. If you made the bechamel ahead of time and it has become cold and thick, warm it in a pan with a splash of milk to help it loosen back up again.

Pour the polenta into a large serving bowl and leave for a minute or two to rest. Evenly spoon the hot bechamel over and dot the ragu across the top. Leave to rest for 5 minutes.

Put a big spoon in the bowl and allow people to help themselves, sprinkling with more parmesan if they like.

Gnocchi di castagne con burro e salvia

Chestnut gnocchi with butter & sage

SERVES 4

300 g (10½ oz) potatoes, peeled

a few gratings of nutmeg

sea salt and freshly ground black pepper

1 organic egg

100 g (3½ oz) chestnut flour, plus more for dusting

SAGE BUTTER

a few grinds of freshly ground black pepper

75 g (2¾ oz) butter

handful of sage leaves

TO FINISH

3 tablespoons grated parmesan, plus extra to serve

good olive oil

VARIATION:– For a heartier meal, dress the gnocchi in ragu (page 116) instead of sage butter.

NOTE:– You can wrap the gnocchi dough and leave it in the fridge for up to 2 days before shaping. The gnocchi also freeze well. There is no need to thaw them, as you can simply blanch them from frozen.

These unusual gnocchi are very quick to make, tasty and, as it happens, gluten free. The chestnut flour gives them a natural sweetness which is counterbalanced by the black pepper, sage and salt, so don't be shy on the seasoning. The trick is to keep their size uniform. I like my gnocchi quite small, but you can adjust the size to your taste, so long as they are all roughly the same size. They are also delicious dressed with ragu (page 116) instead of the sage butter.

PREPARATION:– 35 minutes
SHAPING:– 15 minutes
COOKING:– a few minutes

Bring a large saucepan of well-salted water to the boil. Add the potatoes and cook for 15 minutes, until they can be broken up with a fork. Drain and place in a large bowl.

Mash the potatoes well with a potato ricer, masher or fork. Season with the nutmeg, a generous pinch of salt and lots of grinds of black pepper. Leave to cool for a few minutes before cracking in the egg. Mix well with a fork.

Add a third of the chestnut flour and mix. Once amalgamated, add another third of the flour and mix until incorporated. Add the remaining flour and start kneading in the bowl. Once amalgamated and mixed into a rough dough, tip onto a surface lightly dusted with chestnut flour.

Knead together for a few minutes, until you have a uniform, well-mixed dough that you can form into a large loaf. There is no gluten in this mixture, so you don't need to knead it for as long as a traditional pasta or gnocchi dough; the chestnut dough will be quite loose and wet. (At this point you can wrap the dough and leave it in the fridge if you would rather shape the gnocchi later.)

Working on a large wooden chopping board, slice a handful of dough off and roll it into a log about 2 cm (¾ inch) thick. Use a knife to chop the dough into small equal-sized pieces. Dust with a little more chestnut flour and repeat with the remaining dough.

Bring a large saucepan of generously salted water to the boil.

Meanwhile, make the sage butter. In a wide frying pan large enough to hold all the gnocchi later, toast the black pepper in the dry pan for a few seconds before adding the butter and sage. Leave to melt over a medium heat, swirling the pan occasionally and allowing the sage to gently sizzle in the butter while the gnocchi cooks. Cook gently for 5 minutes, or until the butter browns a little, being careful not to burn it.

Once the water is at a galloping boil, add the gnocchi and stir. After about a minute, when they float to the surface, use a slotted spoon to transfer the gnocchi to the pan of sage butter. Toss to ensure all the gnocchi are well coated in the sauce, then fry for 3–5 minutes, tossing once or twice. Once the gnocchi have a little colour on them, switch off the heat then add the parmesan, a pinch of salt and a few more grinds of black pepper and toss again.

Serve immediately, with more grated parmesan, pepper and a drizzle of olive oil.

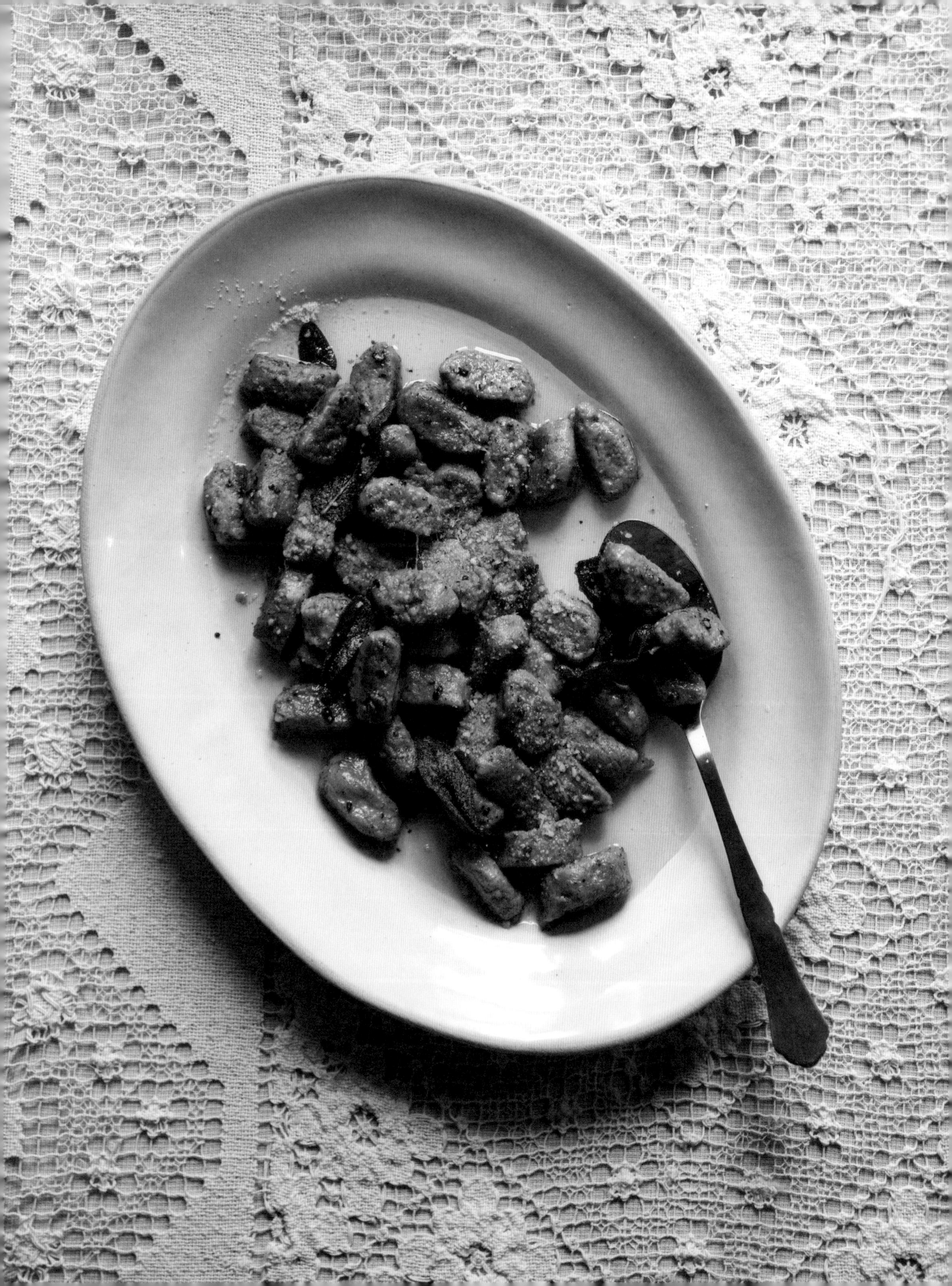

Pici Senesi

Sienese pici

MAKES ABOUT 800 G (1 LB 12 OZ)
SERVES 4

600 g (1 lb 5 oz) '00' flour or plain flour

300 ml (10 fl oz) tepid water

sea salt

1 tablespoon olive oil

200 g (7 oz) coarse semolina

Similar to spaghetti, but much thicker, these long thick Sienese pasta noodles always remind me of home and my childhood, and are a fabulous vehicle for hearty sauces such as the celebrated *cacio e pepe* ('cheese and pepper') and *ragu al cinghiale* (wild boar ragu).

Pici are quite tender, and don't have the chewy bite of orecchiette or more compact fresh pastas as they are traditionally made from finely milled '00' or '0' flour – the flour used in Tuscany to bake the traditional unsalted Tuscan bread. The flour left over from bread baking was used to make pici, and it was in this waste-not-want-not fashion that pici were invented.

Making pici for four is a joy and a fun thing to do together – but for any more diners it's a headache. When being shown to make pici by local culinary legend, Grazia, who cooks for festivals in our local village, Buonconvento, she told me about the nightmare of making pici for a hundred people without the pasta strands all sticking and clumping together. You need a huge amount of space to lay them out, so I stick to making them for a small number as it's still impressive but easy to throw together.

It's difficult to say exactly how much flour you will need, as it is slightly determined by whether the day is hot or cold, dry or humid. Locals say you need *la farina che prende* – 'the flour that it takes' – and it is true. By adding the water gradually, and mixing with your hands, you will see when the dough comes together into a mass that is possible to knead.

PREPARATION:– 10 minutes
KNEADING:– 15 minutes
RESTING:– 30 minutes
SHAPING:– 30 minutes

Tip the flour into a large bowl and make a well in the centre. (I wouldn't recommend doing this directly on your work bench as the water makes this dough more difficult to control than an egg-based pasta at this stage.) Fill the well with a splash of the water, two generous pinches of salt and the olive oil. With a fork, mix in the salt and olive oil and very gradually and gently start bringing the flour into the well from the sides. Pour in a little more water and, with a circular movement, keep gradually bringing in the flour, adding more water bit by bit until the dough has come together. You don't want it to be too wet, or the pici won't hold their shape, so don't add the water all at once.

Once the mixture has become a rough dough and no longer sticks to your fingers, tip it out onto a wooden surface and start kneading. (You might leave some flour behind in the bowl; this doesn't matter, as the amount that is absorbed depends on factors such as the temperature and humidity.) Knead for about 15 minutes, until you have a smooth dough. (You can also do this in a stand mixer with the dough hook attached.)

Shape the dough into an oval, like a loaf of bread, and lightly brush with olive oil to stop a crust forming. Leave to rest for at least 30 minutes, or under an upturned bowl in the fridge overnight. (You could also freeze it at this point before shaping.)

Dust a serving plate or baking tray with the semolina. Take the rested dough loaf and cut two or three slices off it, about 1 cm (½ inch) thick. Gently roll over these once or twice with a rolling pin, then cut them into long strips, about 1 cm (½ inch)

⟶ *Recipe continues*

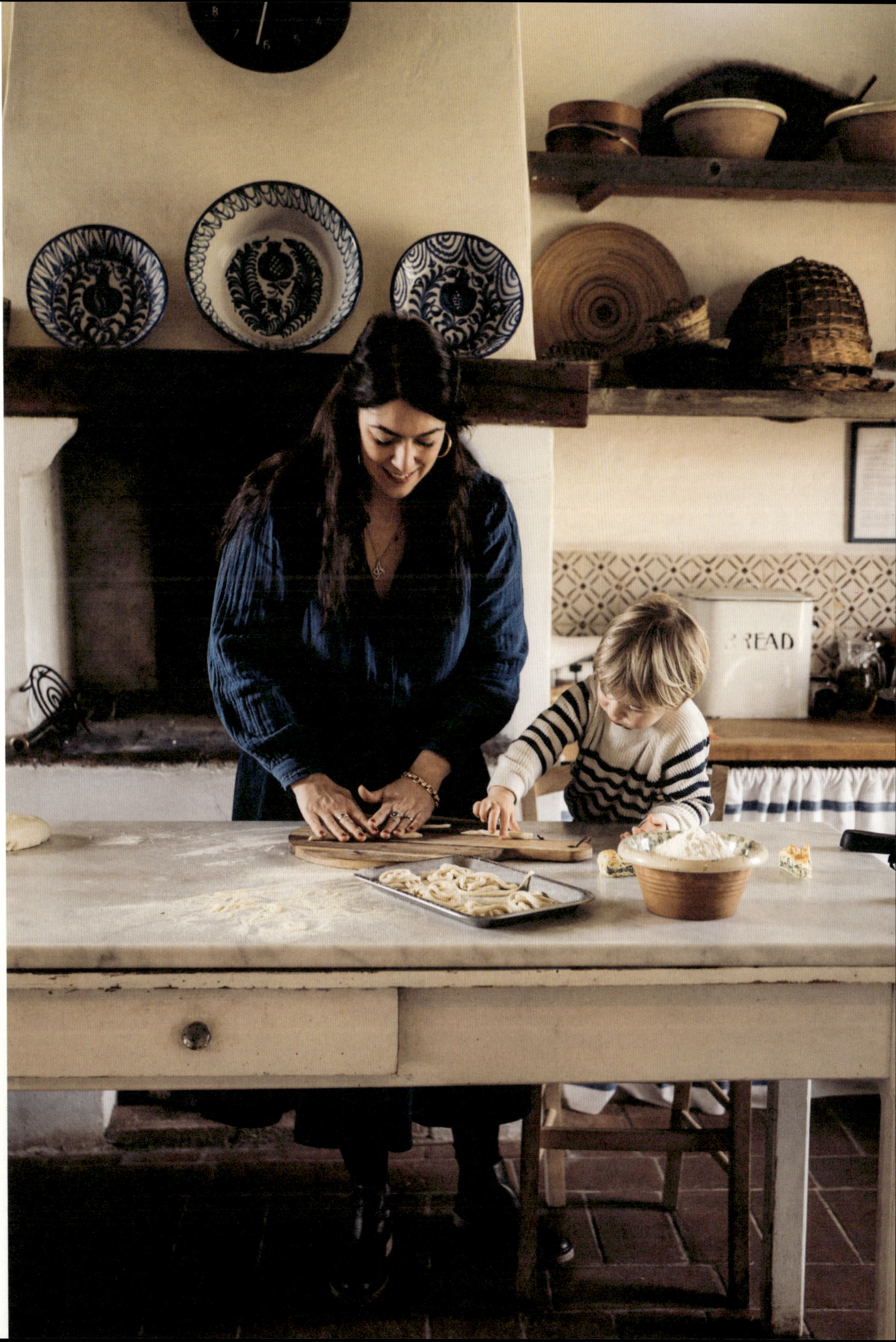
READ

wide. Using your hands, begin rolling one of the dough strips on an unfloured wooden board, by rolling the ends outwards to lengthen them, then moving to the middle and again gently stretching outwards to encourage the dough to stretch and lengthen. Eventually you should have a noodle about 20 cm (8 inch) long.

The beauty of pici is that they are all slightly different and imperfect, so don't worry if some end up thicker or thinner than others. Keep rolling out more dough strips, laying the shaped pici on the semolina-dusted tray as you go, tossing lightly to coat in the semolina, and loosely bringing a few pici together into nests on the tray as you work. Repeat until you have as many pici as you want, or you have used up all the dough.

Cover the tray of pici and keep in the fridge until ready to serve.

To cook the pici, bring a large saucepan of well-salted water to a rolling boil. Pour in the pici and give them a good stir so that the strands don't stick together. As soon as they come up to the surface, about 1–2 minutes, lift them out using tongs and toss your pici with your chosen sauce.

125

Pici all'aglione

Pici with garlicky tomato sauce

SERVES 4

4 elephant garlic cloves, or 3 regular garlic cloves

olive oil

sea salt

400 g (14 oz) tin peeled plum tomatoes

1 quantity of pici (page 122)

grated parmesan, to serve

This Tuscan recipe features aglione, the prized giant elephant garlic which grows in local valleys. In summer, aglione fresco ('fresh') is considered a delicacy, but the garlic is also sold year round as dried bulbs. It is much sweeter and milder than normal garlic, almost melting into the oil in this dish during gentle cooking. You can also use regular garlic here – just use a little less, so everyone doesn't get too garlicky.

PREPARATION:– a few minutes
COOKING:– 30 minutes

Peel the garlic cloves, slice them in half lengthways and remove the central green shoot. Using a garlic press, crush all the garlic into a small bowl. (You can also grate the garlic using a microplane.)

In a wide frying pan large enough to hold all the pici later, heat 3 tablespoons olive oil and add the crushed garlic and a pinch of salt. Over a low heat, very gently warm the garlic with the oil for about 5–7 minutes. You don't want the garlic to brown, just to very gently sizzle. Add the tomatoes and crush them using the end of a wooden spoon. Fill the tomato tin with water and swirl it around to get out all the remaining tomato, then pour it into the sauce with a generous pinch of salt.

Turn the heat up to medium and leave the sauce to bubble away for 20 minutes.

Meanwhile, bring a large saucepan of well-salted water to a rolling boil for the pici.

When your sauce is nearly ready, add the pici to the boiling water and give the pot a good stir so that the pasta strands don't stick together. As soon as they come up to the surface, about 1–2 minutes, lift them out using tongs and toss your pici through the garlicky sauce, adding a little of the pasta cooking water if needed to bring the dish together.

Serve immediately, with a drizzle more olive oil and a grating of parmesan.

Pici cacio e pepe

Pici with cheese & pepper sauce

SERVES 4

250 g (9 oz) pecorino romano, finely grated

1 tablespoon freshly ground black pepper

1 quantity of pici (page 122)

2 tablespoons unsalted butter

While *tonnarelli cacio e pepe* is a Roman dish, using a glossy sauce made with cheese, pepper and butter to dress Sienese pici has become typically Tuscan, and is something you'll see on many menus around us in southern Tuscany.

PREPARATION:– 5 minutes
COOKING:– 10 minutes

Bring a large saucepan of well-salted water to a rolling boil for the pici.

Put the pecorino in a bowl and have a fork to hand.

In a wide frying pan large enough to hold all the pici later, toast the black pepper for a minute or so over a medium heat, moving the pepper around the pan with a wooden spoon.

Add the pici to the boiling water and give it a good stir so that the strands don't stick together. After 1 minute, add two ladlefuls of the pasta cooking water to the pepper in the frying pan and leave to bubble over a medium heat.

Get another ladleful of the pasta cooking water and pour half into the bowl of grated pecorino, using the fork to amalgamate the water and cheese into a cream, adding more cooking water if needed.

Using tongs, transfer the pici to the frying pan. Add the butter and the creamy pecorino and toss well, adding a little more pasta cooking water if needed.

Serve immediately.

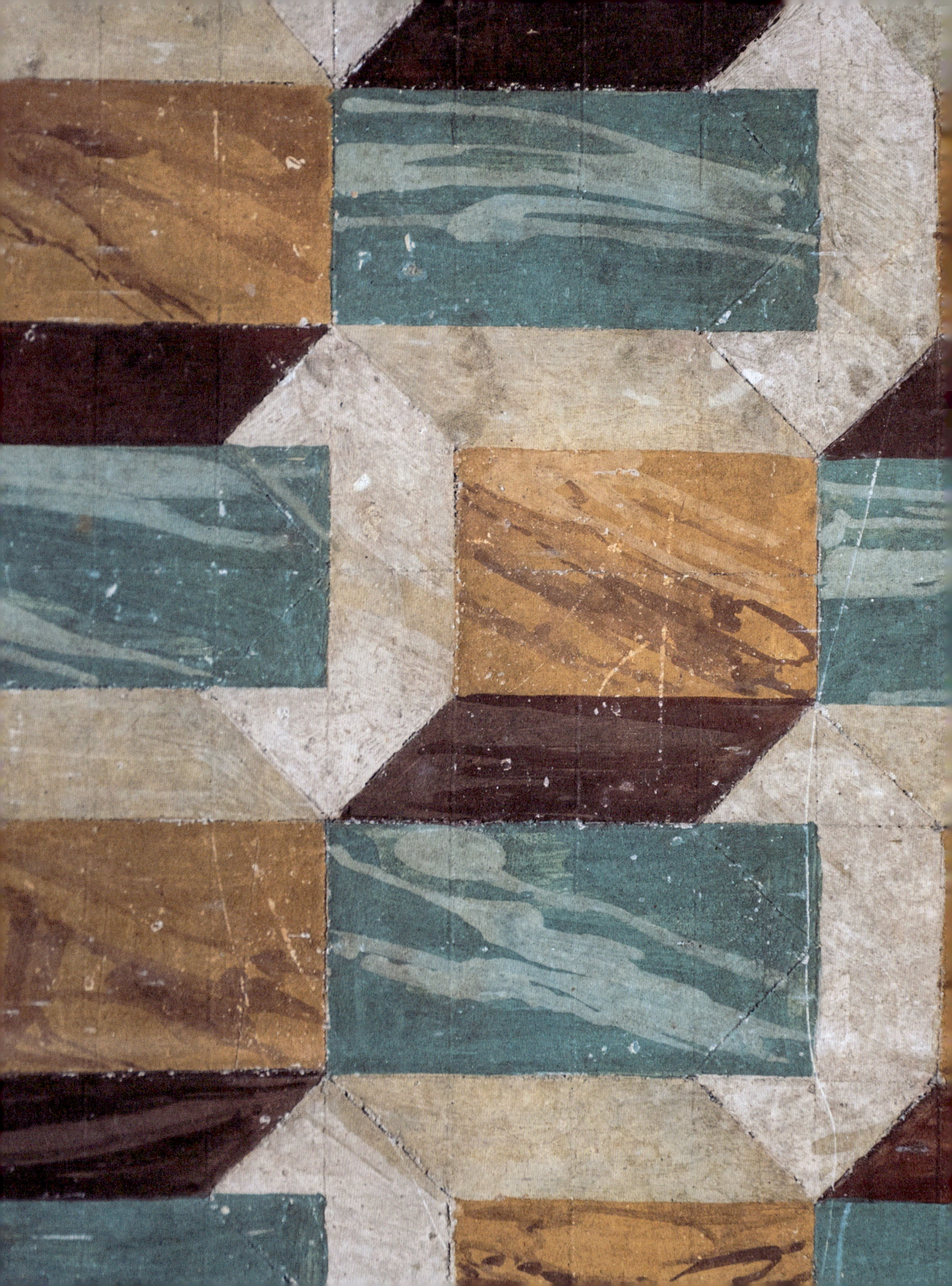

PIATTI DI MEZZO

VEGETARIAN MAINS

A WONDERFUL THING about the Italian language is that there is a whole host of terms which imbue a huge amount of nuance to very specific things. For instance, to *fare la scarpetta*, meaning to 'make a little shoe', is when you use a piece of bread to scoop up any remaining juices or sauce from your plate. There are several words for various types of soup which in English we would simply call, well, soup: *minestra* is soup with large pieces of chopped vegetables, fish or meat in it; a *zuppa* is a soup which has stale bread in it, coming from the word *inzuppare*, meaning to soak up; *brodo* refers to any broth-based soup; and *vellutata* is a 'velvety' soup that has been passed through a blender.

Piatti di mezzo is no different, literally meaning 'halfway dishes'. These are dishes with a starring role for a particular piece of veg, which aren't quite a meaty main, but are too substantial to constitute a *primo* or a *contorno*. In essence, they are a vegetarian *secondo* and would come as one's main dish in a meal, but the focus isn't on meat, as it is in so many traditional *secondi*.

These are the dishes I turn to on many a weeknight, when I don't fancy any meat and want to feed my family or friends something cosy and warming, frugal and vegetable based – though calling it a *piatto di mezzo* sounds infinitely more romantic than a 'veggie main'.

I especially love the vegetables that are available in winter, such as comforting cabbages, deliciously nutty artichokes and crunchy aniseedy fennel, so soft and mellow once cooked. Wherever I am in the world, I find seasonal produce a handy starting point for the all-important daily question – what shall I make for lunch? I also find that nature has a kind way of seeing us through the darker winter months with some of its more colourful leaves: radicchio varies from a deep fuchsia, through to an imperial purple and the palest pink; brassicas range from deep pond to the brightest brussels sprouts green.

One of the blessings of living in Tuscany is the access to amazing produce. The vegetables that are available here, whether home grown within the region or coming from other parts of Italy, are second to none, and there are plenty of dishes that celebrate the glories that are in season. Even if it is now possible to buy mint and raspberries in winter in the supermarket (which it wasn't when I was a child), it is very difficult to shop any other way than seasonally. It dictates what one eats, and how one eats it, and with what – and as nature has a lovely way of hinting at what should be eaten with what, the maxim 'what grows together goes together' is an enduring truism.

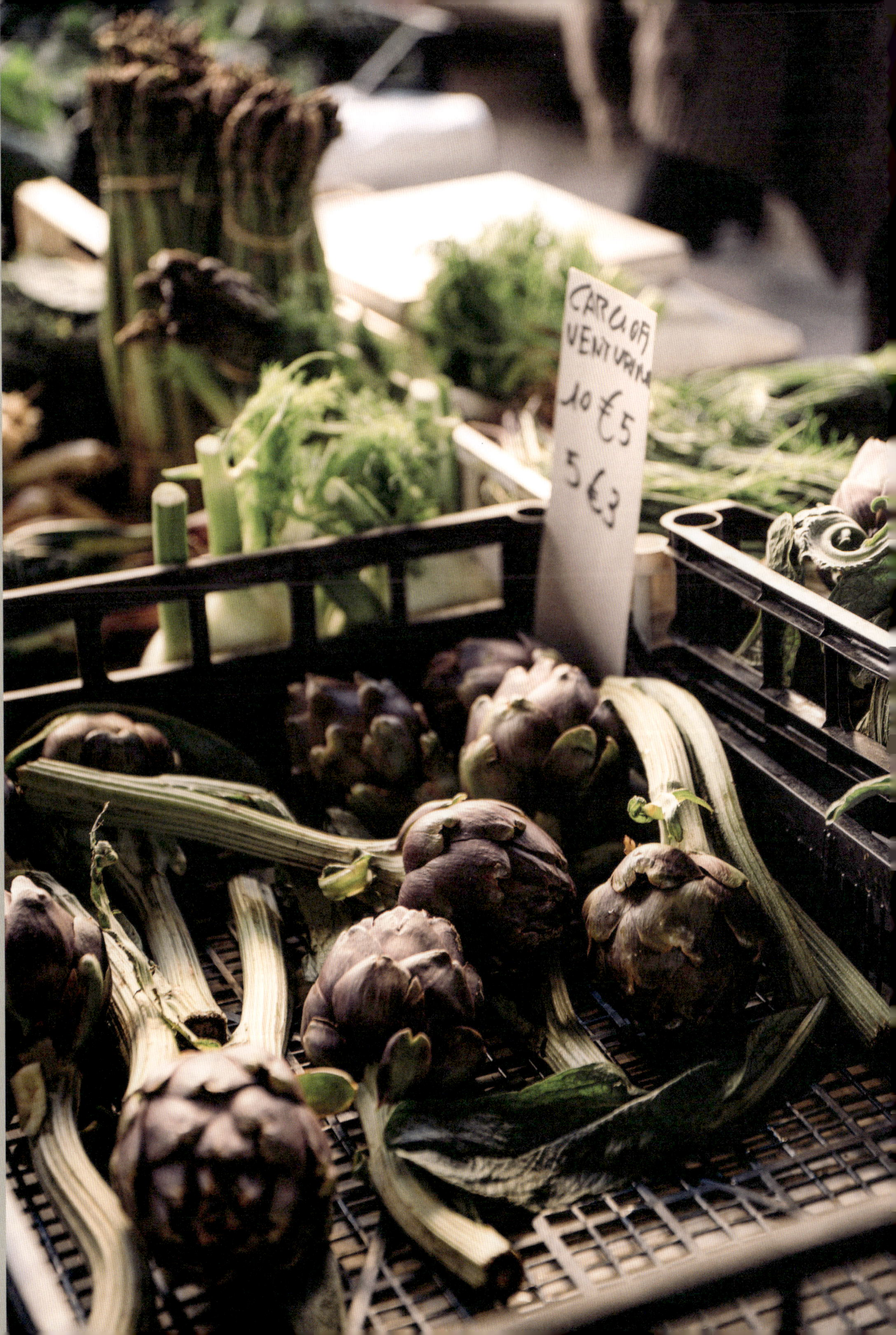
10 €5
5 €3

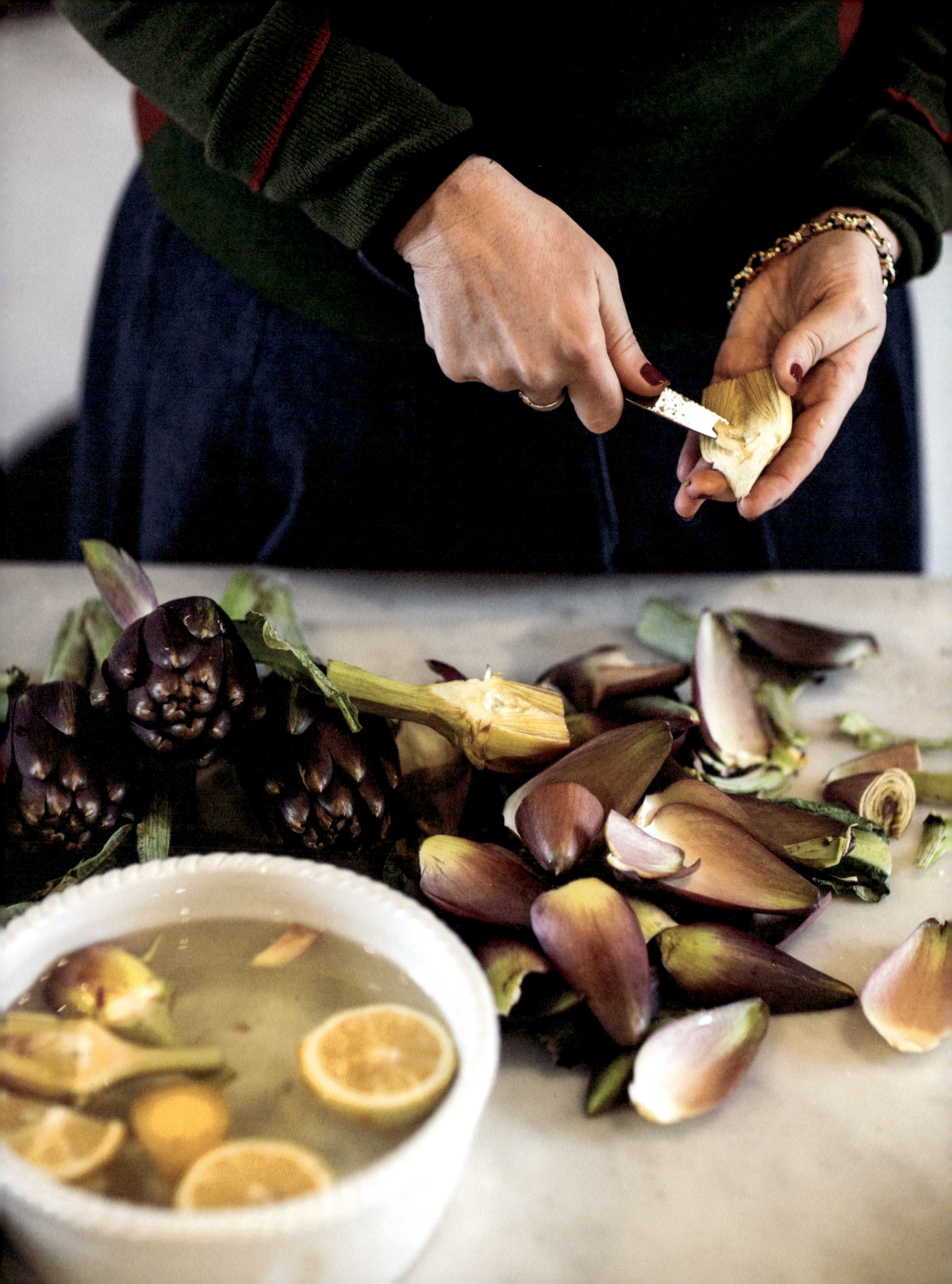

Frittata di carciofi

Artichoke frittata

SERVES 4

2 organic eggs

sea salt and freshly ground black pepper

2 Sardinian spiky artichokes or globe artichoke hearts

juice of ½ lemon

40 g (1½ oz) butter

2 tablespoons olive oil

20 g (¾ oz) grated parmesan

It was at Trattoria Cammillo that I fell in love with frittatas, for the simple reason that they make them incredibly thin and very large, almost the size of a pizza, so that they are just holding together whatever seasonal vegetable is being served. I asked one of the chefs his trick and how many eggs he used, thinking it must be at least four – and he smiled and said, 'Just two in a very wide pan'. From then on, I have always made frittatas this way. *Frittata di carciofi* is my favourite as the artichoke's nutty and earthy flavour goes beautifully with the richness of the cheese, butter and eggs.

This dish serves one as a main, or two as a starter or as part of a wider feast on a cold night.

PREPARATION:– 20 minutes
COOKING:– 15 minutes

Crack the eggs into a bowl, season well with salt and black pepper and beat with a fork.

To prepare the artichokes, tear off the tough outer leaves (the ones that feel woody and that your digestive system won't be up to) until you get to the thinner, more tender leaves. Cut the stem of the artichoke about 3 cm (1¼ inches) from the base. Using a potato peeler, peel away the dark green outer layer until you come to the light green flesh, then peel away any remaining woody bits from the base of the artichoke where the stems meet the leaves. Quarter the artichoke lengthways and remove the hairy 'choke' with a paring knife, then thinly slice each artichoke piece again into quarters lengthways, so you have thin pieces of artichoke. Place in a bowl and squeeze the lemon juice over them.

In a wide frying pan, melt half the butter with the olive oil over a medium heat. Pick up the pan and swirl it around so that the fat goes up the sides of the pan, to stop the egg sticking later.

Once sizzling, add the artichokes. Season well with salt and black pepper and toss with the oil and butter. Cook over a medium heat for 10 minutes, tossing occasionally, until the artichokes darken and slump and have a little colour. Add the rest of the butter and swirl it around the pan. Flatten the artichokes out with a wooden spoon so they are evenly distributed in one layer over the bottom of the frying pan.

Pour the beaten eggs over, then gently pick up the pan and swirl it to allow the egg to evenly coat the artichokes. Cook without stirring for 2–3 minutes. Once the egg starts to look opaque at the bottom, sprinkle the grated parmesan over. Leave for a minute or two until the top has slightly set and the cheese has started to melt.

Using a spatula, gently ease the frittata onto a serving plate, cheese side up. Sprinkle with more pepper and serve immediately, either on its own, or with a Cabbage, apple & walnut salad (page 202).

I porri di babbo al forno

Dada's baked leeks in bechamel

SERVES 4

6 leeks

sea salt and freshly ground black pepper

½ **quantity of bechamel sauce (page 144)**

4 tablespoons grated parmesan

pinch of chilli flakes (optional)

This is a really delicious thing to throw together on a cold winter's night. Whenever my mum, the cook of our home, was away and my dad was in charge of feeding me and my sister, we ate a lot of what was known as 'nursery food': scrambled eggs on toast, sausages grilled on the fire in the kitchen, shepherd's pie – and, when he discovered the UHT ready-made bechamel sauce that you can buy in supermarkets here in Italy, leeks baked in the oven in bechamel and topped with parmesan. It was, of course, a winner with us kids, being both cheesy and hot. We would eat it with toasted bread doused in new-season olive oil and sea salt.

I love this on those evenings when I'm not in the mood to make anything elaborate, and often make it as a side dish if I'm having friends over – or just enjoy it on its own with toast by the fire, as I used to with my dad and sister, possibly in front of a movie, a consummate cosy evening in that always makes me think of my dad.

Nowadays I make my own bechamel as I don't find it at all strenuous, but if you see the UHT stuff and are in a hurry, give it a go. We never complained that my dad hadn't made his.

PREPARATION:– 10 minutes
COOKING:– 30 minutes

Preheat the oven to 180°C (350°F) fan-forced.

Prepare the leeks by chopping off the tough dark green section of the leaves at the top and removing the tough outer layer. (Give them a good rinse and they'll be great to use in a vegetable, chicken or meat broth.)

Slice the leeks into discs about 2 cm (¾ inch) thick, down to the root, placing them in an ovenproof dish large enough to hold all the leek slices in one layer as you go. Season well with salt and black pepper and cover in the bechamel. Finish by sprinkling with the parmesan and some chilli flakes if using.

Bake for 25 minutes, or until the bechamel is bubbling and the top is browned.

Remove from the oven and leave to rest for 5 minutes or so before serving.

DELICIOUS WITH:– Cabbage, apple & walnut salad (page 202), Cavolo nero tossed 'in the pan' (page 197), Claudia's chestnut & mushroom 'peposo' (page 140).

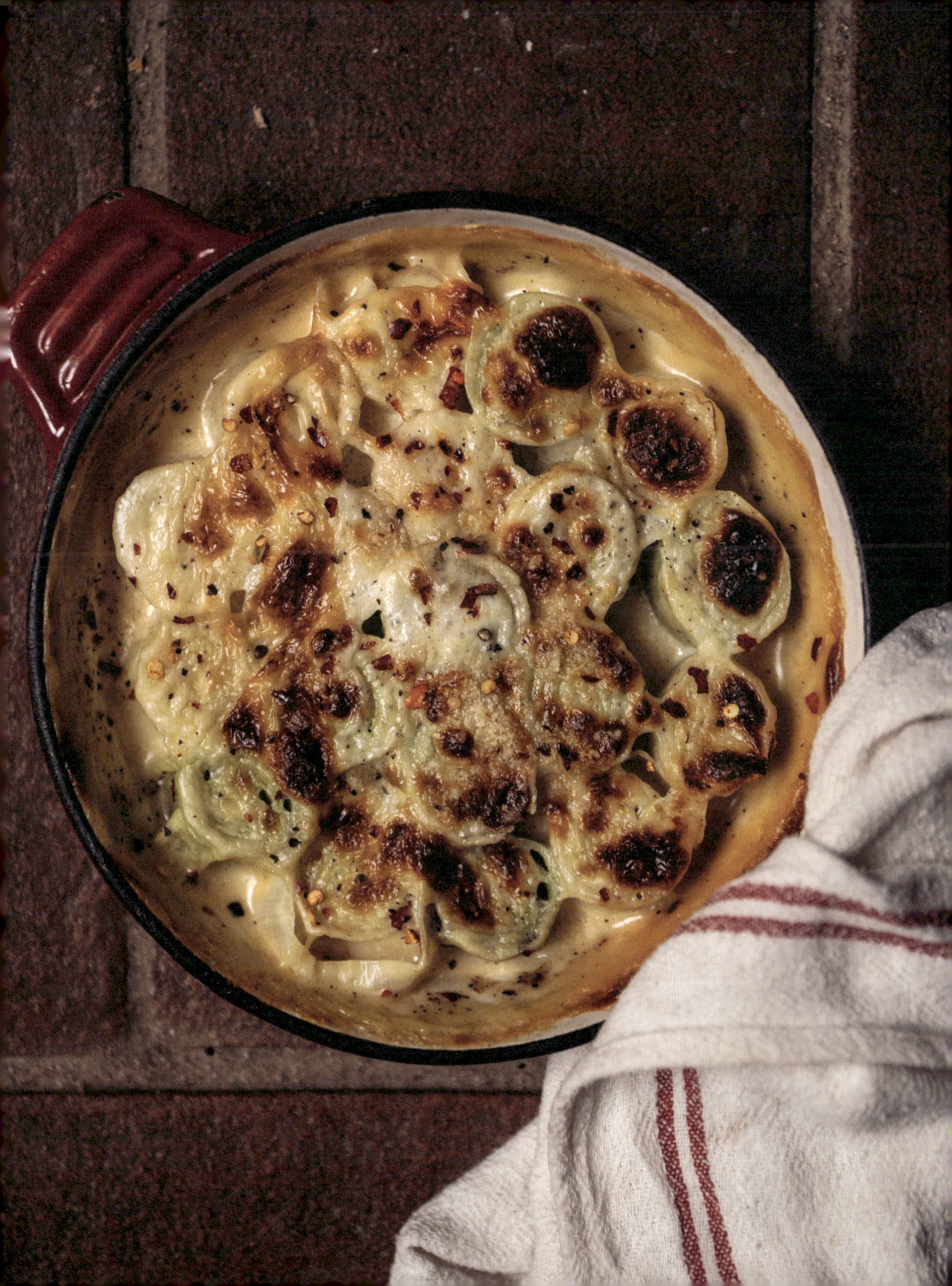

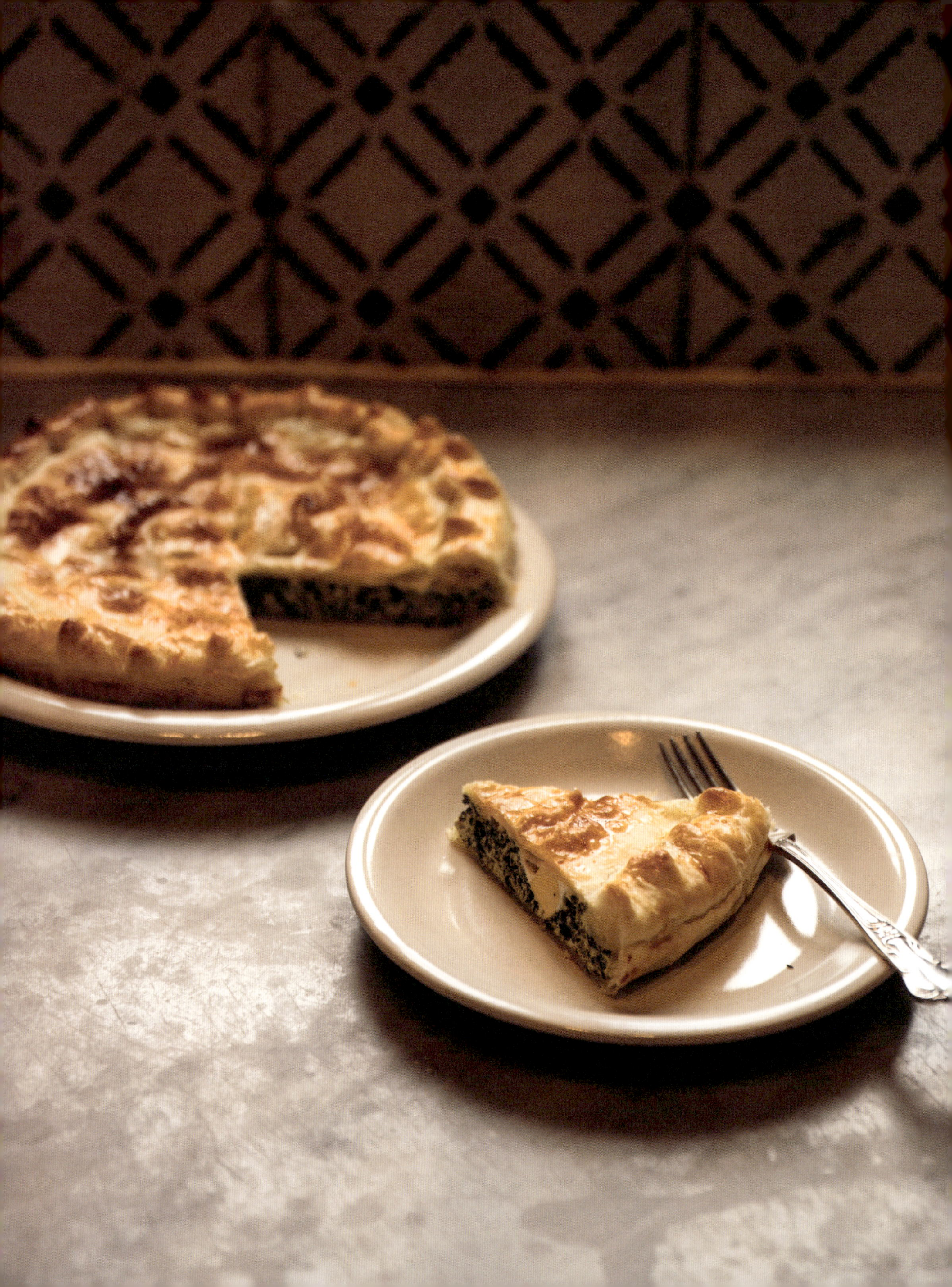

Torta salata

Sage, spinach & quail egg pie

SERVES 4

2 sheets frozen ready-rolled puff pastry

1 organic egg, lightly beaten

1 heaped tablespoon grated parmesan

FOR THE FILLING

250 g (9 oz) frozen spinach, thawed, or 400 g (14 oz) fresh spinach

large handful of sage leaves, about 20 g (¾ oz), finely chopped

small handful of flat-leaf parsley, finely chopped

250 g (9 oz) fresh ricotta, drained

2 organic eggs

60 g (2 oz) grated parmesan

½ whole nutmeg, grated

½ teaspoon chilli flakes, or to taste

sea salt and freshly ground black pepper

7 quail eggs

> **VARIATION:–** Mix a few chopped anchovy fillets into the filling before spooning it into the pastry case.

Torta salata, or savoury pie, is a mainstay for on-the-go eating in bars in Tuscany and is also served in slices as an *aperitivo* or as a starter for dinner. I love it as it's stuffed with aromatic greens, is really quite versatile as you can use any greens you like in the mixture, and any leftovers are also great at room temperature the next day. If you add whole raw eggs into the mixture, this pie would become a *torta pasqualina*, the famous savoury Easter pie. I love adding quail eggs to the mix as they are smaller and less dominant than a chicken's egg. It's super easy and just requires making little indentations in the filling with a teaspoon and cracking an egg into each to add a mini hard-boiled egg surprise.

PREPARATION:– 40 minutes
COOKING:– 30 minutes

About 20 minutes before starting the recipe, take the puff pastry out of the freezer so that it thaws enough to be rolled out.

Grease a 25 cm (10 inch) tart or cake tin and line the bottom with baking parchment. Roll out one sheet of the puff pastry and gently transfer it to the tin. Trim off the excess pastry with a sharp knife, brush the pastry with some of the egg wash and prick the bottom all over with a fork. Put the tin in the freezer for at least 20 minutes. (I often leave an egg-washed pastry case in the freezer for emergencies and quick last-minute dinners, then simply fill and bake the pastry case from frozen. It will keep in the freezer for a few weeks.)

Preheat the oven to 190°C (375°F) fan-forced.

Meanwhile, make the filling. If using thawed spinach, wrap it in a clean tea towel and wring out as much moisture as possible. Transfer to a colander in the sink and again squeeze out as much water as possible, either with your hands or by placing a small plate on the spinach and pressing down hard.

If using fresh spinach, wilt the leaves with a splash of water in a deep, wide saucepan over a medium heat, gently tossing with tongs as they cook down. (If there isn't space for all the spinach initially, add it in batches.) After a few minutes, once the spinach is bright green and has wilted into a manageable amount, wring out the water by placing the spinach in a colander as described above. (Don't wring it out hot in a tea towel as the tea towel will split.) Set aside until cool enough to handle, then roughly chop.

Place the spinach in a bowl with the sage, parsley and drained ricotta. Mix in the organic eggs, parmesan, nutmeg and chilli flakes and season with salt and black pepper.

Retrieve the pastry case from the freezer and add the filling, smoothing out and levelling it using the back of a spoon. Use a teaspoon to make seven little indentations in the filling at regular intervals, then crack a quail egg into each one. Sprinkle with the heaped tablespoon of parmesan and lay the second pastry sheet over the top. Trim the excess pastry, then pinch the bottom and top pastry layers together with your fingers all the way round the pie. Brush the top with more egg wash and cut four airholes into the pastry lid to allow steam to escape.

Bake for 30 minutes, or until the filling has puffed up and the pastry top is nicely browned. Leave to rest for a few minutes before slicing.

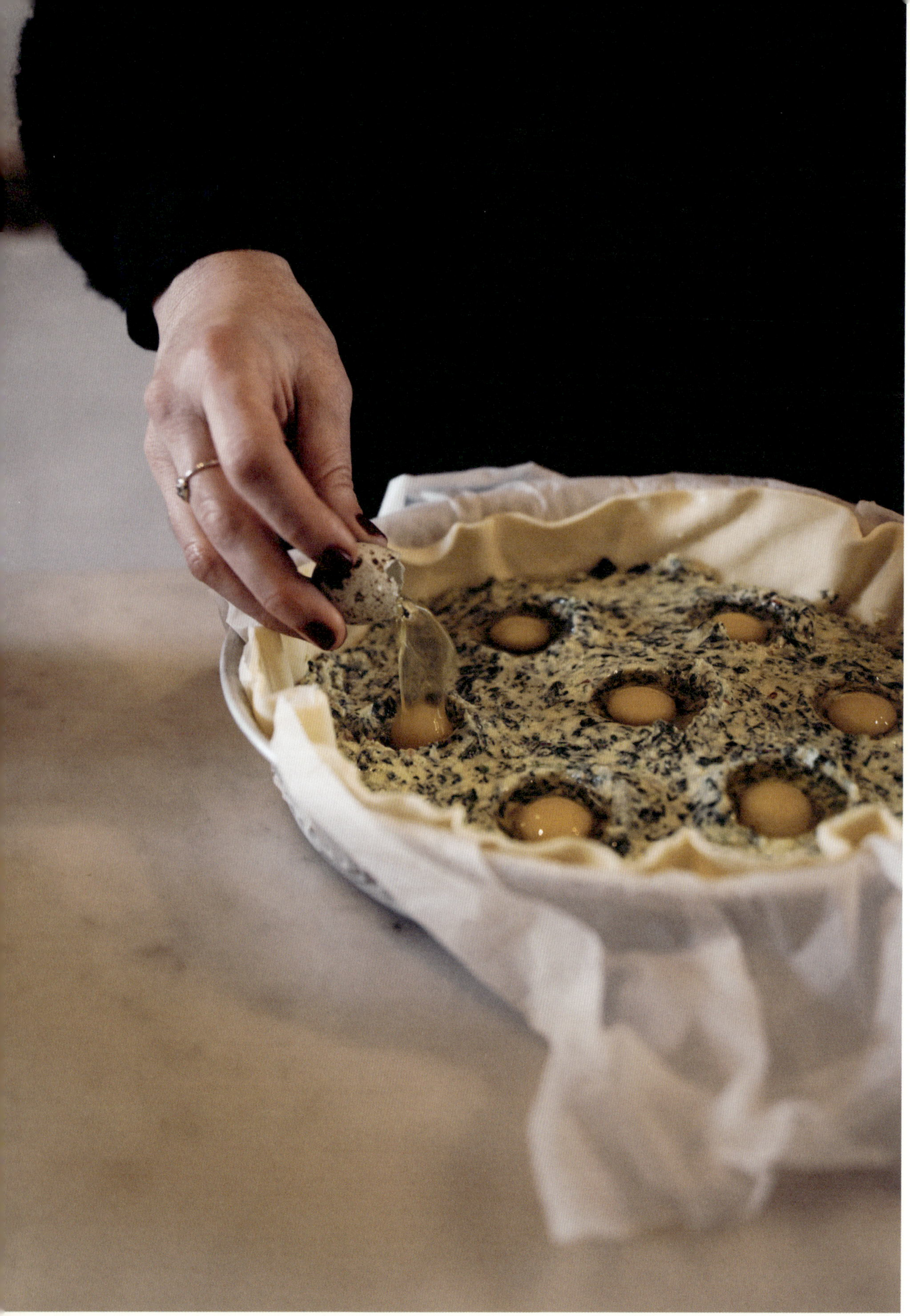

PIATTI DI MEZZO

Il 'peposo' di Claudia

Claudia's chestnut & mushroom 'peposo'

SERVES 4

olive oil

½ red onion, finely diced

sea salt

500 g (1 lb 2 oz) button mushrooms, sliced in half lengthways

large handful of thyme sprigs, leaves picked

1 teaspoon plain flour

3 garlic cloves, finely crushed or chopped

2 teaspoons freshly ground black pepper

2 packets of pre-cooked chestnuts

1 tablespoon tomato concentrate

a few bay leaves

½ bottle robust chianti or any red wine

300 ml (10 fl oz) Vegetable stock (page 72) or water

finely chopped flat-leaf parsley, to serve

My sister, Claudia, has long been a vegetarian. This has always been for environmental reasons rather than not loving the taste of meat. Having grown up in Tuscany, it is a great sacrifice for her to give up things like prosciutto, salami, pancetta and her favourite: penne with ragu from our local trattoria, 'Nara's'. She loved this last dish so much, in fact, that she became famous for her habitual childhood order of *'Penne al ragu con extra ragu'*, which would solicit an extra bowl of ragu for her to douse her already well-dressed pasta in. It was an eccentricity our father was particularly amused by. To give herself something equally delicious to eat when we make a warming *peposo* on a wintery night, she adapted a stew from Riverford Organic Farmers – an amazing organic vegetable farm in the UK who share wonderful ways to cook with their produce – using some of Tuscany's own finest offerings: mushrooms, chestnuts and red wine. Claudia upped the pepper and cooks the stew as you would a traditional *peposo* (page 176), and we all now often prefer this lighter vegetarian version to the meaty original.

PREPARATION:– 5 minutes
COOKING:– 1 hour

Preheat the oven to 180°C (350°F) fan-forced.

In a flameproof casserole dish, heat 3 tablespoons olive oil with the onion and a pinch of salt. Cook over a medium heat for about 5 minutes, until translucent.

Toss in the mushrooms and thyme and leave to get a little colour for 5–7 minutes, stirring occasionally. Add the flour, garlic and a pinch more salt. Mix together and stir-fry for 3 minutes, then stir in the pepper, chestnuts, tomato concentrate and bay leaves and cook for a minute or so. Pour in the wine and cook for about 10 minutes, until the alcohol has evaporated.

Add the stock or water and bring to the boil over a medium heat. Put the lid on, transfer to the oven and bake for 35 minutes, checking once or twice and topping up with a splash more wine if the pan is drying out. The stew is ready when the sauce has reduced down by a third, and the mushrooms are cooked but still retain a little bite.

Remove from the oven and serve straight from the dish, sprinkled with some flat-leaf parsley.

DELICIOUS WITH:– This vegetarian stew is fabulous with polenta (page 119) or Garlicky rosemary cannellini beans (page 198) and Greens tossed 'in the pan' (page 197).

VARIATIONS:– For something supremely good and greedy, try Claudia's brilliant idea of turning this into a pie. Simply roll out a sheet of puff pastry, cut a steam hole in the centre, brush with beaten egg and lie the pastry flat in the fridge while you cook the mushroom *peposo*, removing the stew from the oven 5 minutes early. Lay the pastry over the dish and bake for a further 20 minutes, until the pastry is flaky and brown.

You can also use the mushroom peposo instead of ragu in the *Penne al ragu* on page 116 and the polenta 'lasagna' on page 119 to make those dishes vegetarian.

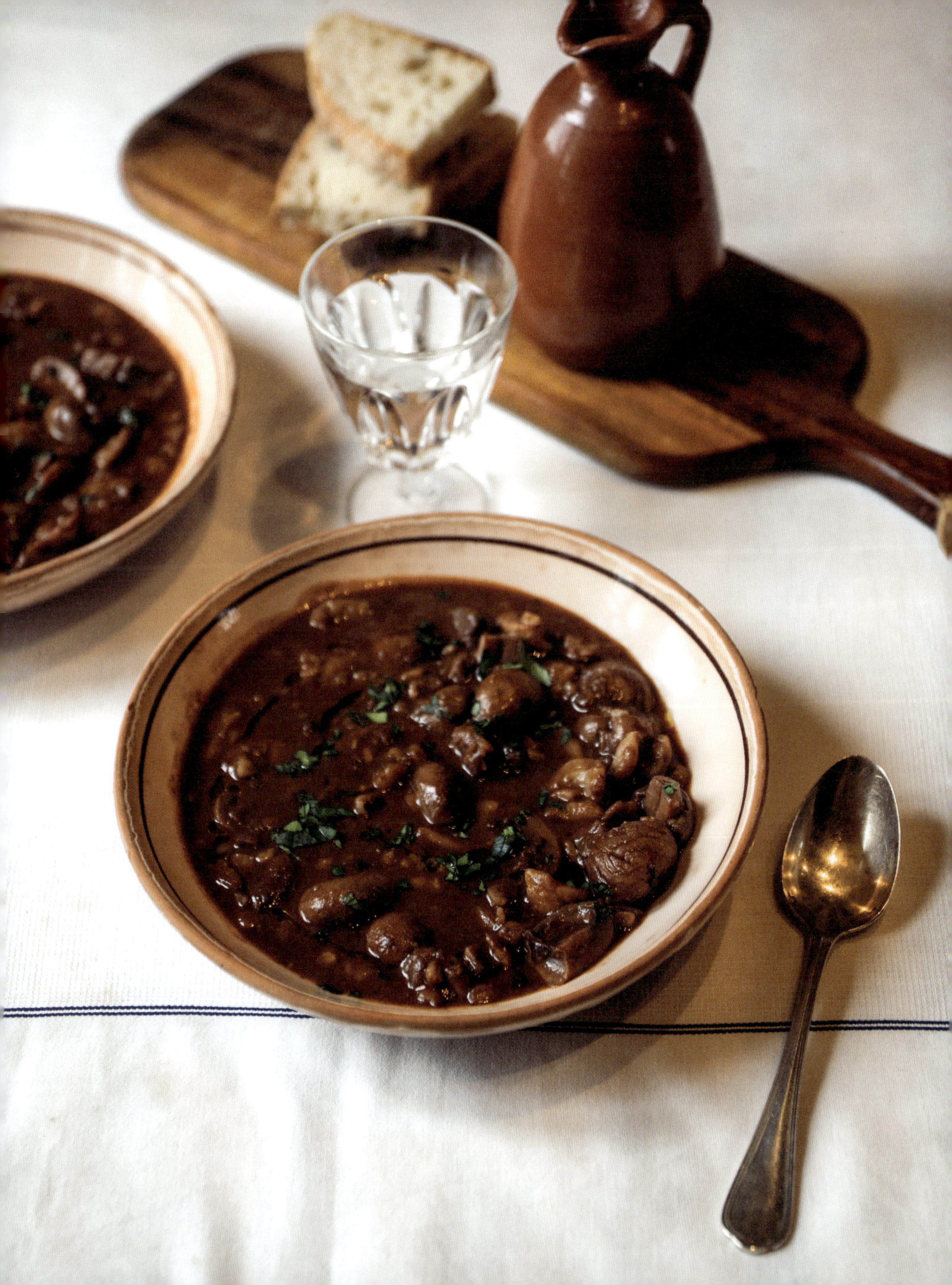

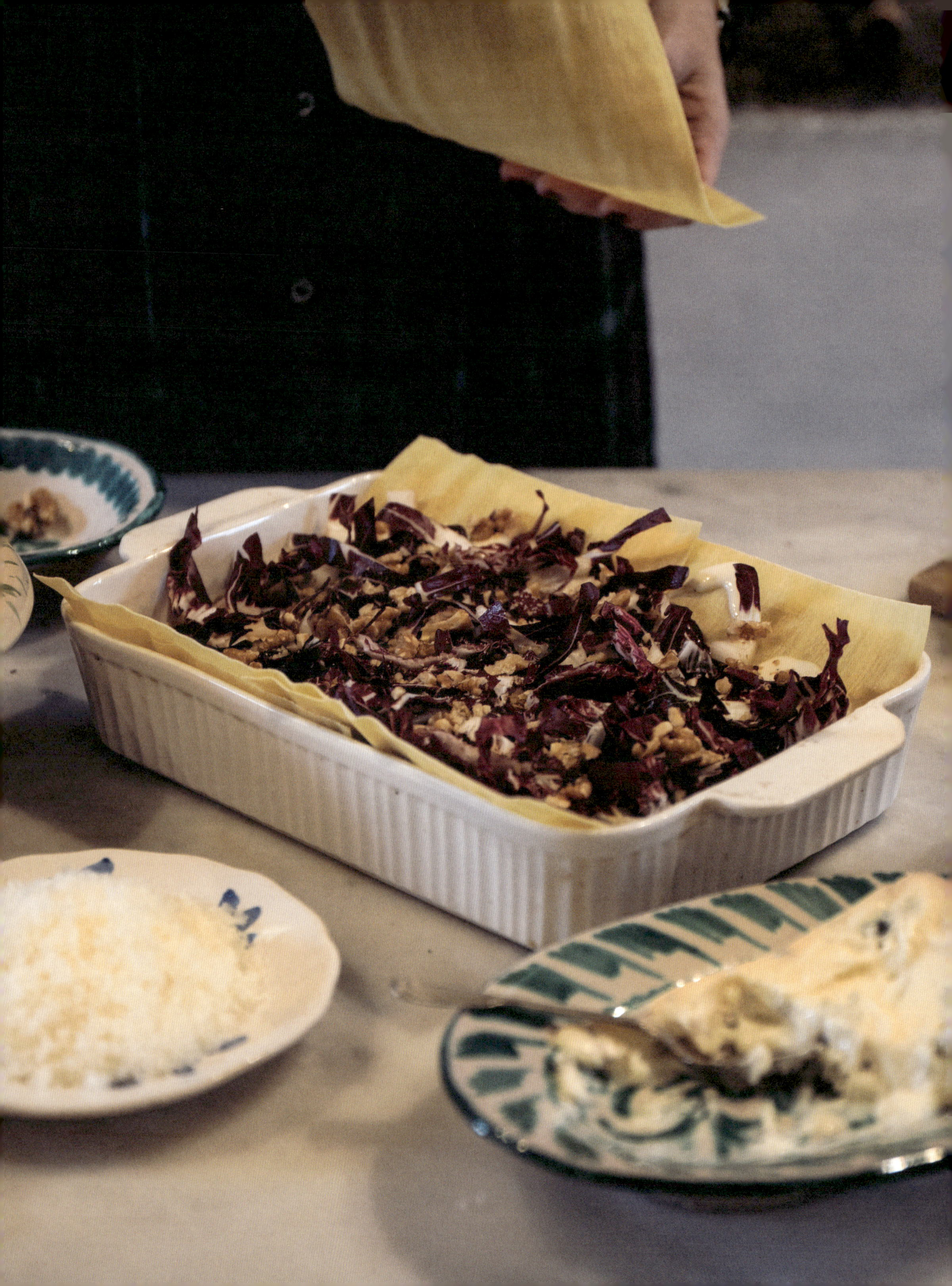

Lasagne di radicchio, gorgonzola e noci

'Good time' radicchio, gorgonzola & walnut lasagne

SERVES 4

1 large head of red radicchio

500 ml (17 fl oz) double cream

sea salt and freshly ground black pepper

½ whole nutmeg, grated

70 g (2½ oz) finely grated parmesan

6 fresh lasagne sheets

3 handfuls of hazelnuts or walnuts, roughly chopped

200 g (7 oz) gorgonzola

I first had this dish at my friend Janet's beautiful winery in Montalcino, called Tenuta Buon Tempo ('buon tempo' means 'good time'). The vineyard sits on the other side of Montalcino from us at Arniano, so it is always exciting to see the countryside from a different perspective. Aside from being a nice spot to visit, it is apparently one of the best spots for growing Sangiovese grapes to make the best brunello as it's high up but sunny. Janet served this radicchio, walnut and gorgonzola lasagne in individual little dishes. I loved its combination of flavours, particularly when paired with a glass of the winery's excellent brunello.

I have made a large version here for ease, but if you have little wide ramekins and the mood takes you, just make very sweet little individual servings and bake them for half the amount of time. It sounds like a very rich dish, but it's really mainly salad with a little cream and cheese. I would serve it on a cold day with nothing more than a peppery salad, or a vinegary Cabbage, apple & walnut salad (page 202).

PREPARATION:– 15 minutes
COOKING:– 35 minutes

Preheat the oven to 180°C (350°F) fan-forced.

Remove any sad outer leaves from the radicchio. Slice the head in half and place them cut side down on a chopping board. Cut the radicchio halves into wide ribbons, avoiding the woody stalk end.

In a bowl, mix the cream with a few pinches of salt, black pepper, the nutmeg and half the grated parmesan.

In an ovenproof dish, lay out two sheets of lasagne next to each other, overlapping them a little to come up the sides of the dish a bit. Spoon over a third of the seasoned cream and drape over half the radicchio leaves. Sprinkle with half the walnuts, then use a teaspoon to dot about a third of the gorgonzola evenly over the radicchio. Repeat with another layer of lasagne sheets, cream, radicchio, walnuts and gorgonzola. Top with the final two lasagne sheets, then the last third of the cream. Crumble the last of the gorgonzola over and sprinkle with the remaining parmesan.

Bake for 30–35 minutes, until the top is bubbling and golden. Remove from the oven and leave to rest for 5 minutes before serving.

> **NOTE:–** I always use fresh lasagne sheets from the fresh pasta section at the supermarket for this dish. If you can only find dried lasagne sheets in boxes, I recommend blanching them in salted boiling water for 1–2 minutes before assembling, so you can drape them in the baking dish and they don't have a weird texture.

Finocchi, pasta e besciamella al forno

Baked fennel & pasta with bechamel

SERVES 4

butter, for greasing

grated parmesan, for sprinkling

2 large fennel bulbs

300 g (10½ oz) conchiglie, mezzi rigatoni, rigatoni or any short pasta

BECHAMEL

600 ml (20½ fl oz) full-fat milk

sea salt and freshly ground black pepper

50 g (1¾ oz) butter

50 g (1¾ oz) '00' flour

40 g (1½ oz) grated parmesan

½ whole nutmeg, grated

1 teaspoon dijon mustard

DELICIOUS WITH:— Greens tossed 'in the pan' (page 197), Cabbage, apple & walnut salad (page 202).

At school in Buonconvento, for lunch we would often be given *pasta al forno*, parboiled pasta that was dressed either in bechamel or tomato sauce and baked in the oven with lots of parmesan on top. That was always a good day, as it's exactly what you want to eat as a seven-year-old. It's still one of my ultimate comfort foods, but nowadays I like to smuggle in some veg and a slightly more grown-up flavour by adding lots of fennel and some mustard.

PREPARATION:— 15 minutes
COOKING:— 45 minutes, plus resting time

To make the bechamel, pour the milk into a saucepan with two pinches of salt and a few grinds of black pepper. Set over a high heat, and as soon as the edge starts bubbling, remove from the heat.

In a separate saucepan, melt the butter over a medium heat. When it starts bubbling, gradually add the flour, a tablespoon at a time, stirring as you go with a wooden spoon. You want the flour and butter to amalgamate and sizzle into a paste, known as a roux (the mixture of butter and flour used to thicken sauces). Once the paste starts coming away from the sides of the pan, add a ladleful of the hot milk.

Remove the roux from the heat and stir together until smooth, gradually adding more milk once the previous batch has been mixed through, stirring constantly. (To avoid a lumpy bechamel, make sure that the mixture is completely smooth before adding more milk.) Add the parmesan, nutmeg, more black pepper and a good pinch of salt.

Once you have added all the milk, place the pan back over a medium heat and use a whisk to stir while the bechamel thickens over the heat. After a few minutes, once you have a thick, creamy sauce, your bechamel is done. Stir the mustard through.

(If you're making the bechamel ahead of time, cover it with plastic wrap; before using, simply heat it with a splash more milk and it will loosen up again.)

When you're ready to assemble the dish, preheat the oven to 180°C (350°F) fan-forced. Rub a little butter around a roasting tin large enough to hold all the pasta and fennel, then line with a little grated parmesan.

Slice off the woody base of each fennel bulb and remove any woody tops, as well as the outer layer if it is very thick and tough. Slice the bulbs in half lengthways, then place on a chopping board, cut side down, and cut across into 1 cm (½ inch) wide pieces.

Bring a large saucepan of well-salted water to a rolling boil, then add the pasta and fennel and boil for 5 minutes.

Using a slotted spoon, transfer the pasta and fennel to the roasting tin; don't worry about bringing a splash of the pasta cooking water with it. Add half a ladleful of the pasta water to the pan, then pour the bechamel over the mixture and toss well, making sure the pasta is completely coated in the sauce. Cover liberally with more grated parmesan.

Bake for 30–40 minutes, until the sauce is bubbling and the top is browned. Remove from the oven and leave to rest for 5 minutes before serving.

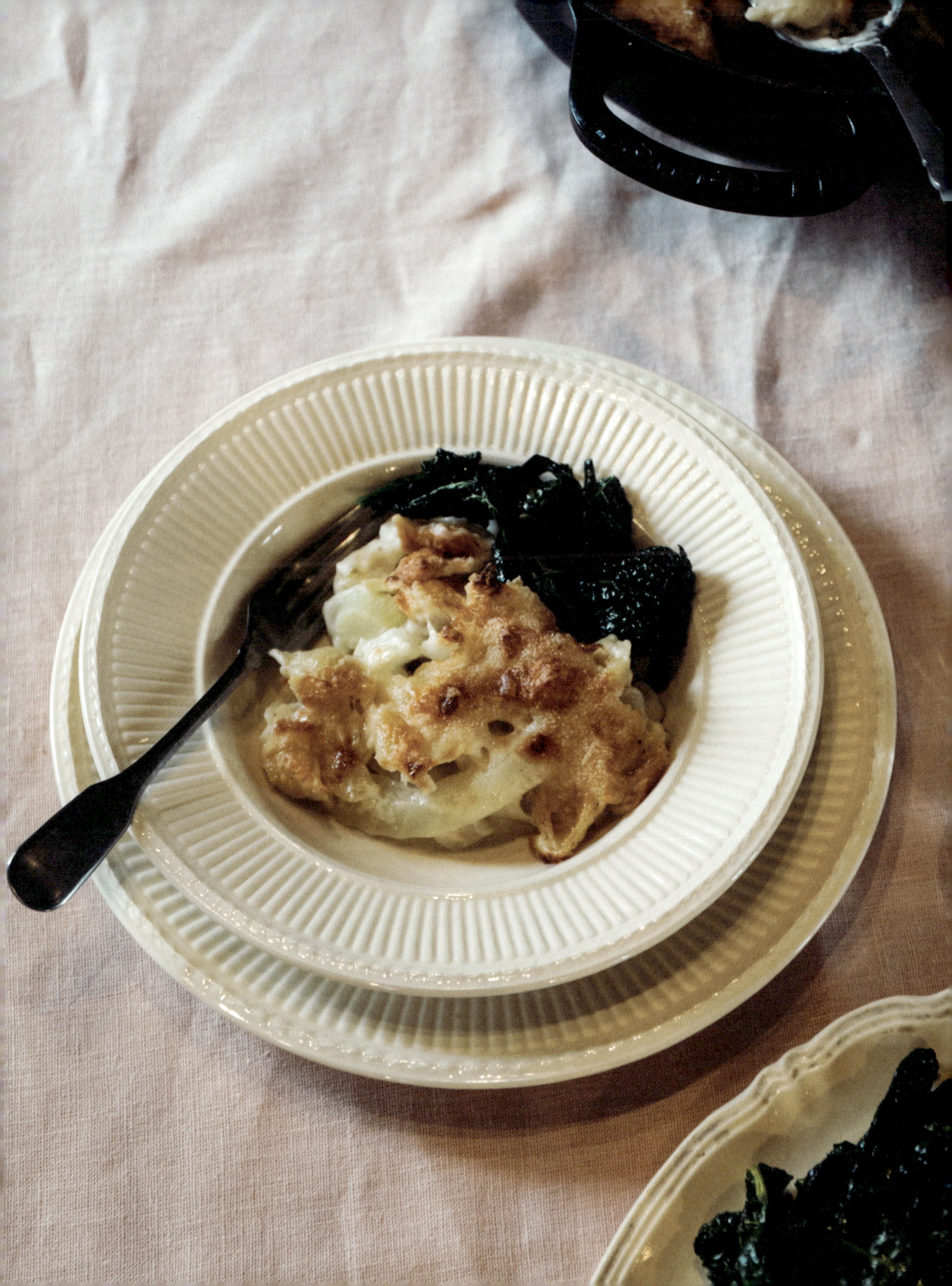

146

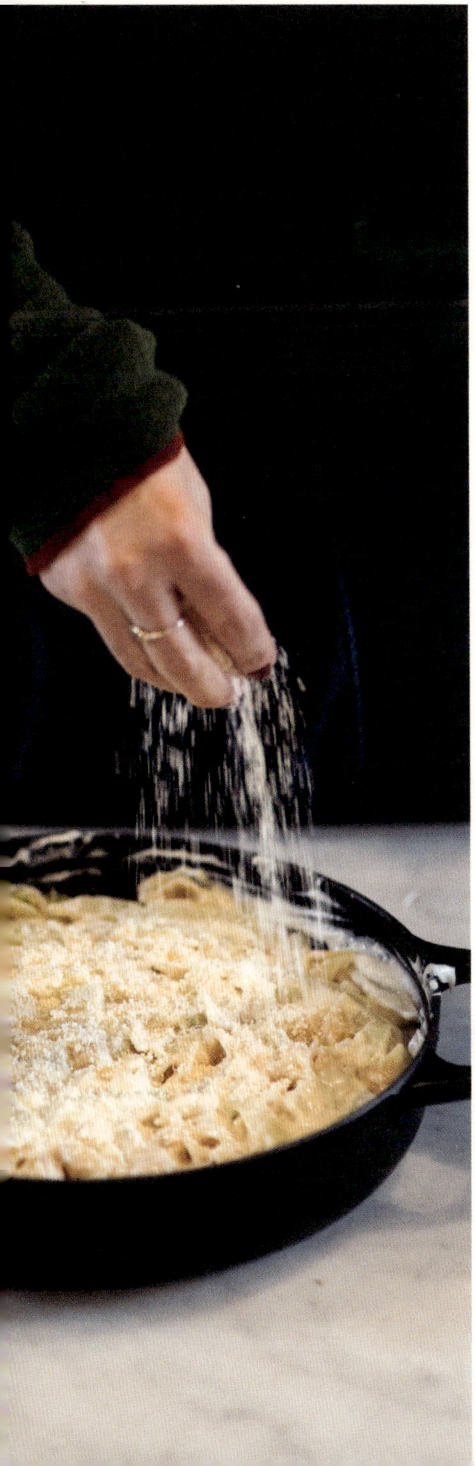

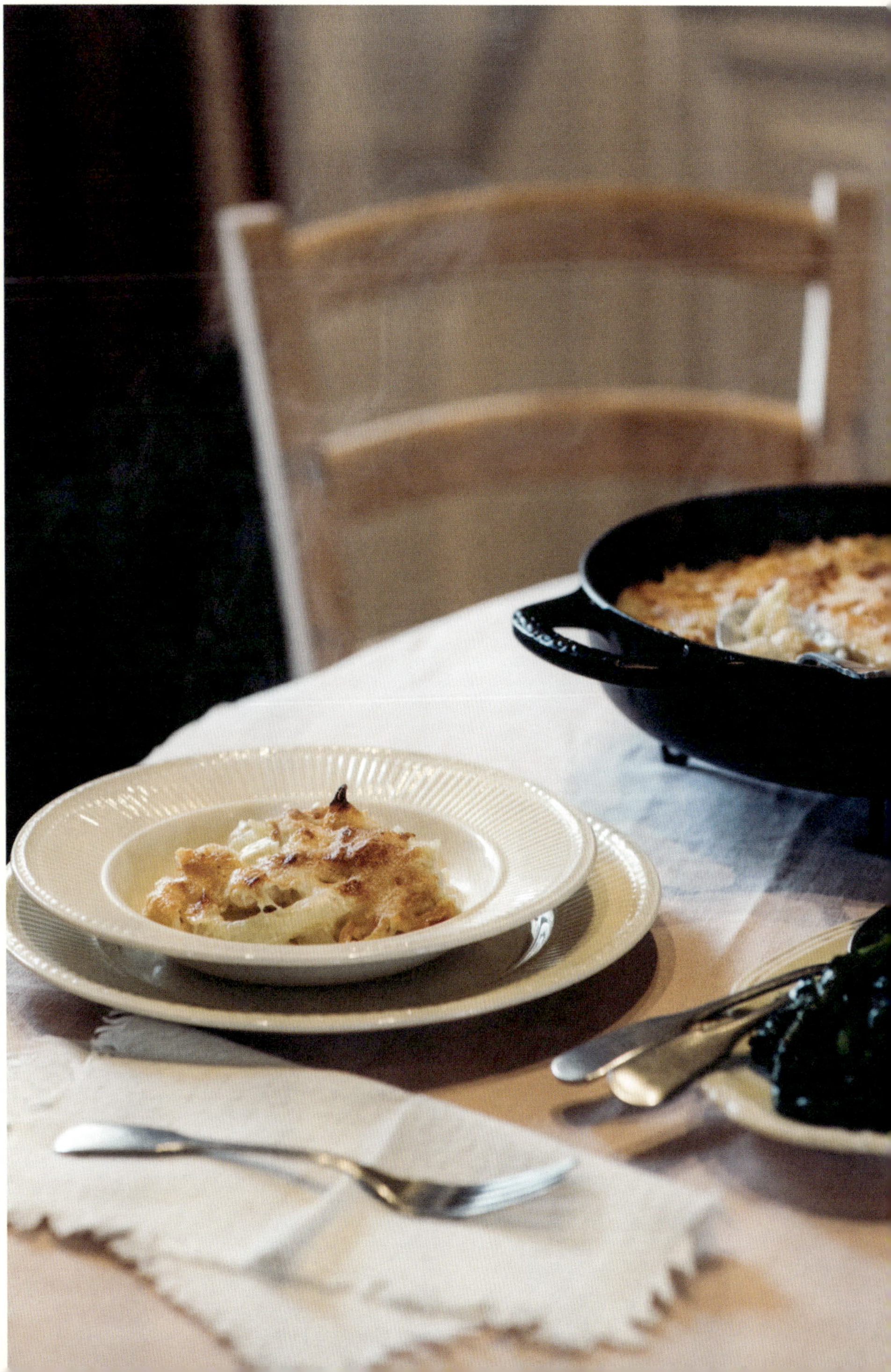

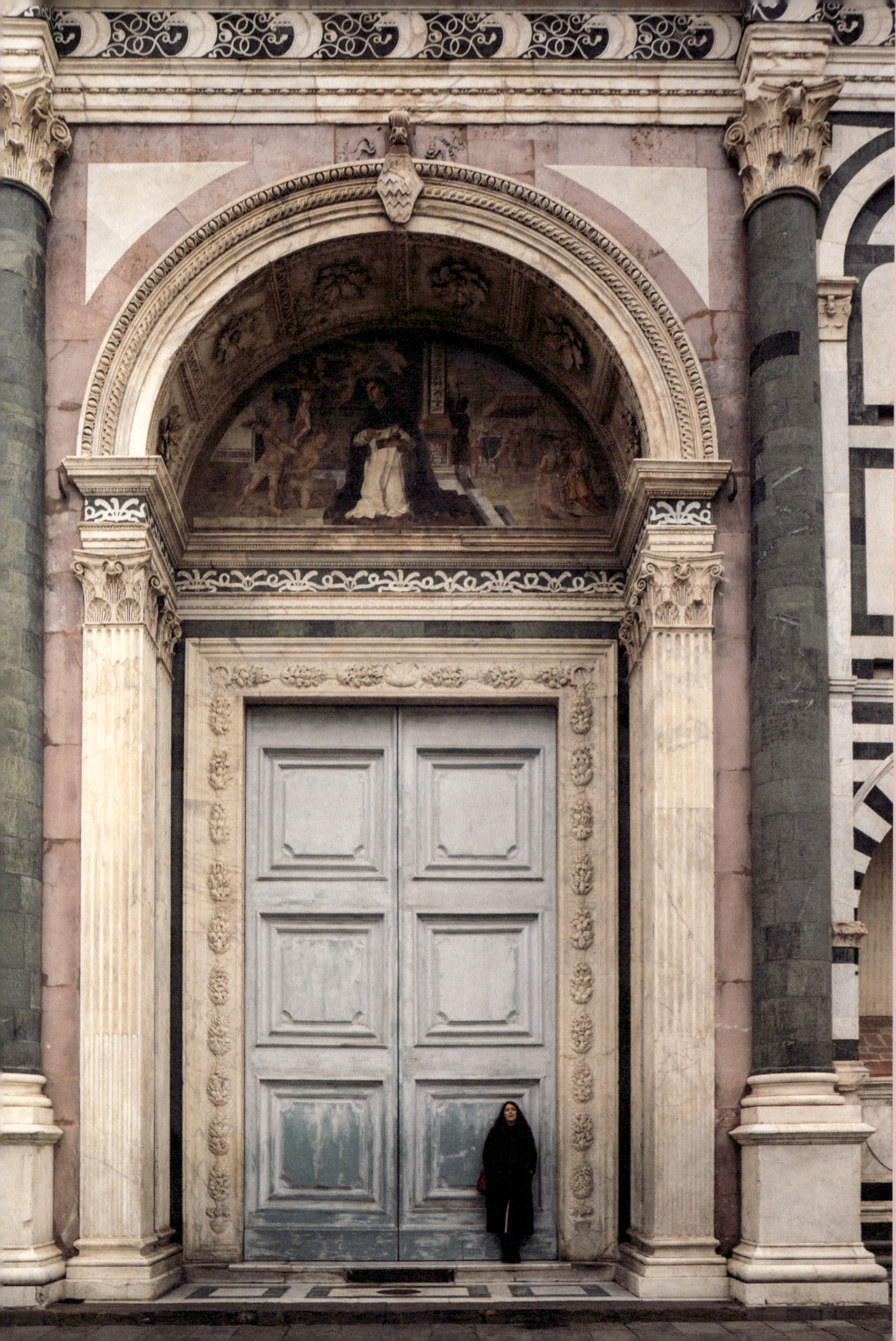

FLORENCE

WHEN I THINK of Florence, it is of the cacophony of church bells that accompanies my morning coffee every day at 8.30 am sharp. The flat where I live with my husband, Matthew, and son, Milo, is across the road from the River Arno, on the top floor of an old palazzo in the city centre. It snakes around an internal courtyard, meaning there are windows everywhere pouring in light and the sound of church bells from every corner. This makes up for the hike up the hundred stairs from the street (there's no lift).

Our road is narrow and busy, with the Ponte Vecchio at one end and the even more beautiful Ponte Santa Trinita at the other. The best time to step out is early in the morning before the tourists have had their breakfast. This is when you see a city lived in, with locals drinking their coffees at the bar, shopping at the market stalls in Piazza Santo Spirito and generally going about their errands. Early is also the time to visit the many treasures of Florence – if you brave the Uffizi Galleries in busier months, I would not consider walking through the doors more than two minutes after opening at 8.15 am.

Winter is a moment of respite in this, one of the most visited cities in the world. It's when I like to remind myself of the many treasures I live among, and will nip into a gallery or museum on the way to lunch to see a painting or fresco. Visiting churches is particularly rewarding in Florence as they house some of the city's most beautiful objects. At either end of the Piazza Pitti are two such churches. The Chiesa di San Felice, at the south end, contains a wonderful fresco of *San Felice reviving San Massimo*, started by Giovanni da San Giovanni and finished by Volterrano in 1636, with a fabulous wintery landscape in the background. To the north, sandwiched between the Piazza Pitti and the Ponte Vecchio, is Santa Felicita, home to Pontormo's *Deposition from the Cross*, an exquisite painting well worth a visit, especially if you come furnished with a one-euro coin to put in the meter, which then resplendently illuminates the altarpiece. I often prefer these little bursts of beauty in situ rather than the overwhelming cacophony of visual stimulation offered by wonderful museums such as the Uffizi.

When I do visit the more well-known sites, it tends to be in winter: from November to March, the city becomes quieter, allowing you to wander through churches such as San Marco, Santa Croce or Santa Maria Novella in relative quietude. It is the best time to visit the Brancacci Chapel, where you can see Masaccio's Adam and Eve being expelled from Paradise – the first known depiction in the history of art in which the banished couple appear to have some misgivings about their new reality.

Being in a valley, surrounded by a mountain range and with a river running through it, Florence in the hotter months can reach dizzying temperatures.

OPPOSITE:— In front of the central door of the facade into Santa Maria Novella

FOLLOWING LEFT:— The statue of *Winter* by Taddeo Landini which stands on one of the south corners of Ponte Santa Trinita

FOLLOWING RIGHT:— Milo and me bumping into our friend Betty at the Thursday morning flower market in Piazza della Repubblica

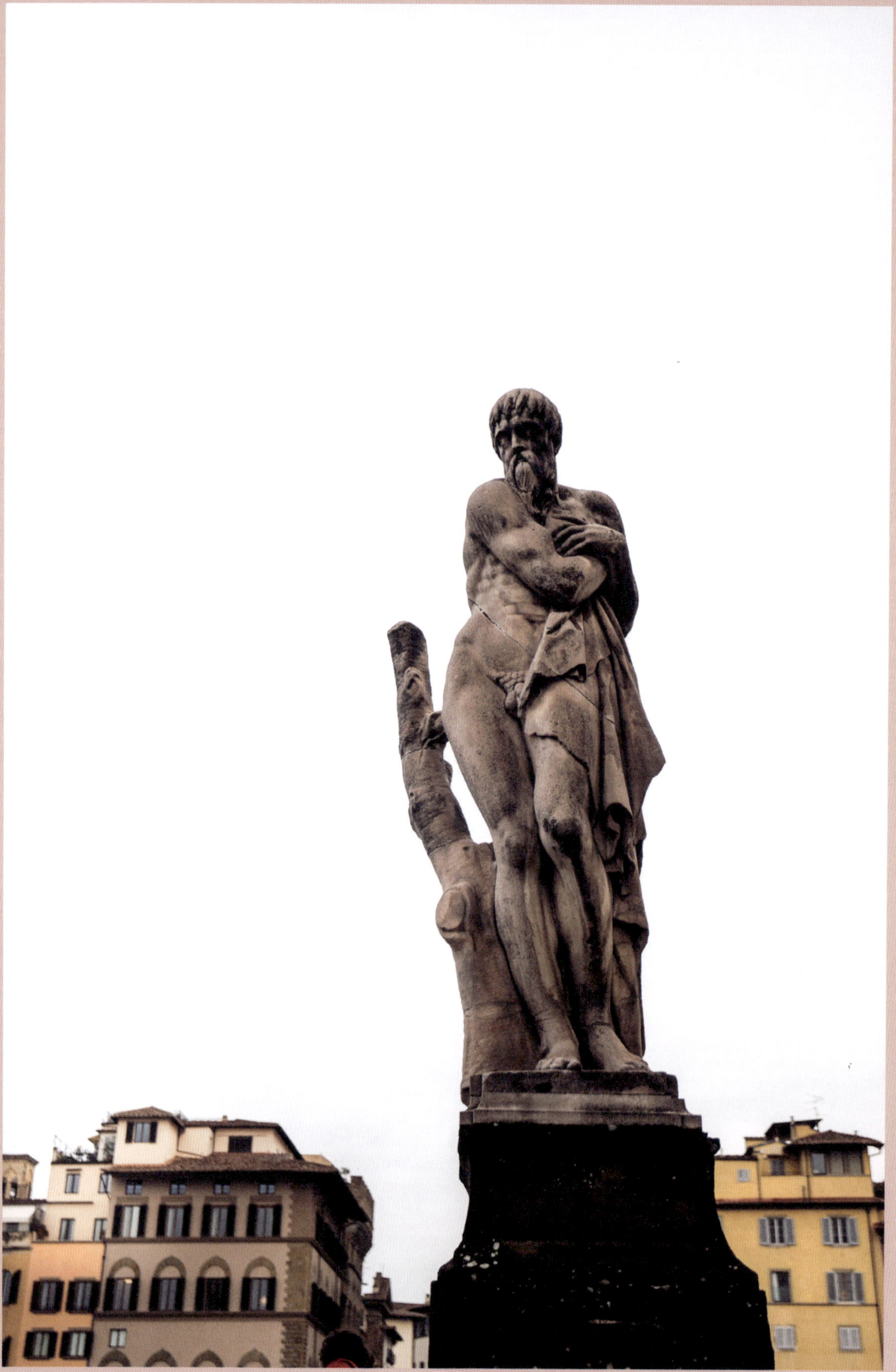

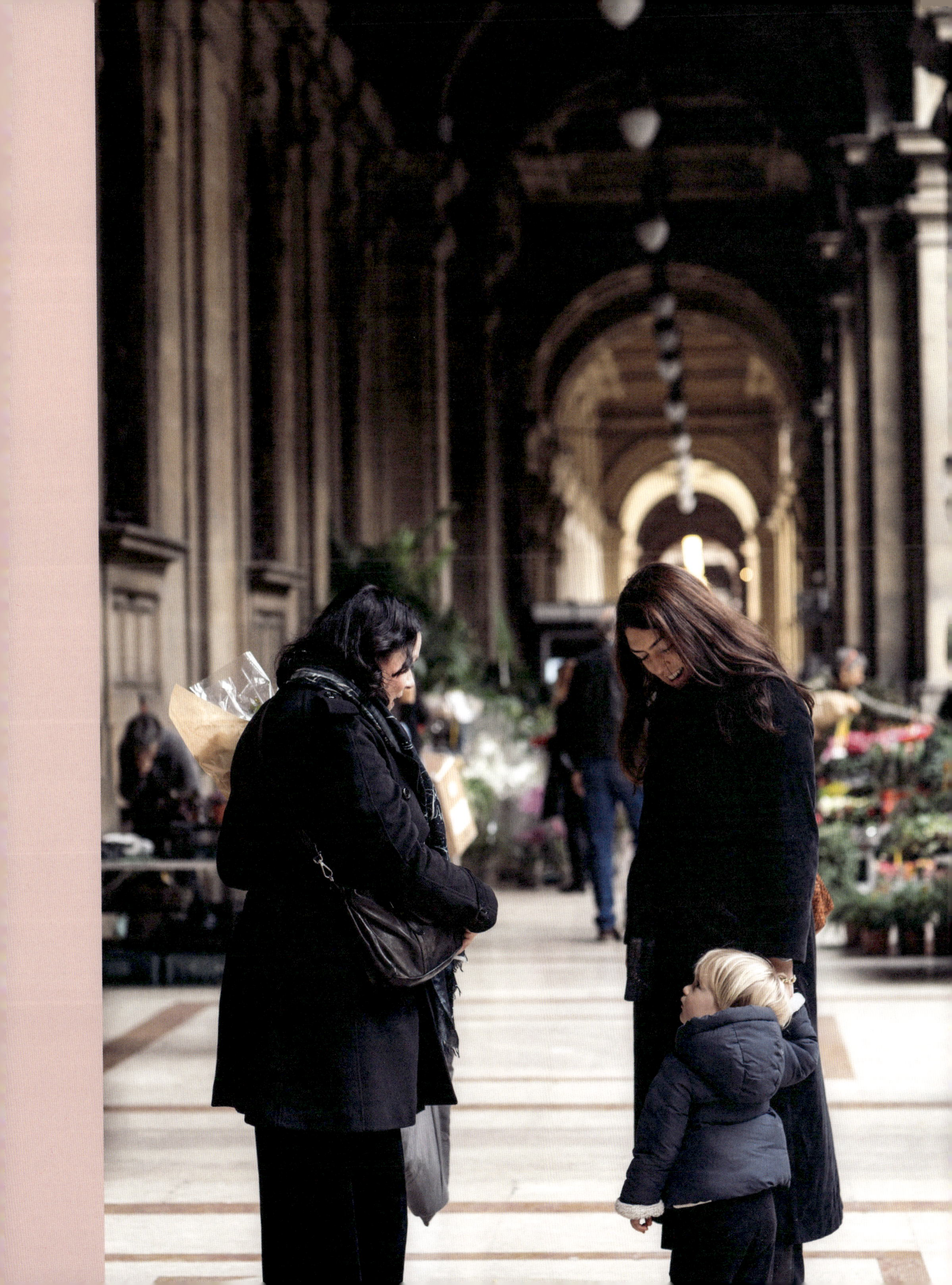

Conversely, in winter, icy winds whip through the city from the Pistoia Mountains. The arrival of the cold is welcome; it feels as though the city is being reclaimed. One moves back inside to eat, and cosy trattorias provide shelter from grey, drizzly days. One joy when days are clear and cold is crossing Ponte Santa Trinita and looking down the river towards the mountains to see if they are flecked white with snow. This is always a moment of temptation: you know that if you hop in the car you could be skiing in Abetone within 90 minutes. My husband, mother and godmother, Emma, had one such conversation over dinner one night when I was away, and when I rang the next morning all three were on a chairlift heading for the top of the slopes.

Winter or not, early in the morning is the only time to visit famous places like Rivoire, the glamorous bar on Piazza Signoria where you can get everything from coffee, pastries and intricate chocolates to cocktails, all served to you by white-coated waiters. Being opposite the Loggia dei Lanzi, with its eleven classical statues, Rivoire has always been popular with tourists. Mis-time your visit and you may be surrounded by a busload of cruise-shippers looking confused and harassed. I once went half an hour later than usual and got stuck behind an order for 27 cappuccinos. But living in a famously beautiful city with lots of visitors is all about learning to share the spaces and using them at different times. At 8 am you will find yourself surrounded by Florentines, usually loudly exchanging their recipes for *lampredotto* (stewed tripe) while the white-coated barmen make their coffee. Legend has it that Rivoire is the birthplace of the negroni cocktail, and they do still make the best; its colour is a pale muted red rather than the vivid vermillion of most negronis whose makers are too heavy-handed on the Campari.

While I love nipping into Rivoire on a Thursday morning when I visit the weekly flower market in the covered gallery running off Piazza della Repubblica, my usual haunt for my morning coffee is a tiny, narrow little place called Caffe Melloni on Via de' Bardi. It is family run and very friendly, with a whole little world going on each morning. There are no tables, just a couple of bar stools, so it is very much geared towards locals looking for a quick breakfast on their feet. They have a wonderful array of tempting pastries, sandwiches and *schiacciata* (Tuscan focaccia), as well as freshly squeezed blood orange juice and anything stronger you may desire, and it's where one catches up with the man from the garage, the brother and sister who run the dry cleaners and the lady from the post office, all chasing down something delicious to start their day. When we first moved to Florence, the barman was a famously grumpy old Florentine who made a mean coffee and sang very loudly as he worked; he has since retired and the staff behind the bar are now entirely female, with the owners' daughters having taken over.

This is what tends to make a good Florentine bar or restaurant – that many of them are still family run, making them lively and fun. These are the places I like to seek out, where the owners' deep involvement means there is a strong pride in the food they are making and how they serve it. The longest-running and most successful are those that are unapologetically unbending to the fads of globalisation and tourism. Caffe Melloni, for instance, still closes every day for the family to have lunch from 1 to 2 pm, an hour when you might think a passing customer might like a sandwich themselves. Fabulous restaurants such as Alla Vecchia Bettola on the south side of the city, famous for their *penne alla Vecchia Bettola* (tomato and vodka pasta), were founded in response to the standardisation of 'Italian food' in the 1970s. Rebelling against tourists arriving and asking for pizza or spaghetti with meatballs in a city famous for its grilled and roasted meats, vegetables and beans, Florentine trattorias such as the Vecchia Bettola decided to specifically celebrate Tuscan and Florentine dishes: *crostini neri* (Crostini with chicken liver pate, page 62), *coniglio fritto con carciofi* (fried rabbit and artichokes), *arista di maiale* (roast herb-infused pork loin), *bistecca alla Fiorentina* (Florentine steak, page 166) and *fagioli al fiasco* (cannellini beans in olive oil). Still today, their food is hardy, tasty and happy-making.

Andrea, the proprietor of another wonderful family-run trattoria – Casalinga, by Piazza Santo Spirito – tells me he would rather leave spaghetti carbonara to his colleagues in Rome, saying, 'What has carbonara got to do with Florentine food?' The word *casalinga* means 'housewife' or 'homey/homemade', and was the name given to the restaurant by Andrea's father when they opened their doors more than sixty years ago in 1963. In his eighties, and still prepping fresh sage for service at a table in the corner early in the morning, using a pair of scissors to snip the leaves from the stems, he tells me the name has kept their feet firmly on the ground and reminded them to stick to what they know: delicious, uncomplicated Florentine fare (see page 106 for their pasta with cavolo nero pesto).

The unbending nature of Florentines when it comes to food is perfectly summed up by another favourite restaurant, Osteria Vini e Vecchi Sapori, off Piazza Signoria. When we first moved to Florence in 2016, we spent a few months living in a one-room studio apartment on Via dei Pandolfini, and every day on my way to work I would walk past this tiny but intriguing-looking restaurant that was always full. The phone seemed always to be engaged – and curiously, the door always locked – making it impossible to book a table. Eventually, we one day managed to wave at the locked glass door long enough that a man in glasses opened it to see what we wanted. Tommaso, now a firm friend, explained that whenever they are super busy, which is all the time, they take the phone off the hook and lock the door until the change of tables at 9 pm so they can get on with the business of service. This means you have an hour's window between 11 am and midday to call or drop in to book a table. Despite the difficulty of booking, the food and atmosphere really are worth it. Their menu is always varied and interesting and features some of the best fried artichokes, *bistecca Fiorentina* and pastas I've ever eaten. And on each menu is a list clarifying what they will not serve: 'NO pizza, NO cappuccino, NO ice, NO spritz, NO ketchup.' Which always reminds me of the rather passive-aggressive but fabulous response of another place we love, Trattoria del Carmine, to a British friend who asked the waiter for butter, rather than olive oil, to spread on a piece of bread. The waiter didn't say no but instead brought the butter, in a one-kilo catering block, still in its wrapping, and dumped it unceremoniously on the table. These are just some examples of why it's best not to bring your own habits, preconceptions or sideways requests to Florence when it comes to food and drink. Just let them do what they do best – which is to present you with simple fare, executed perfectly, alongside a restorative glass of chianti.

I have always spent time in Florence, as it was only an hour and a half's drive from our home south of Siena, and being the capital of Tuscany was the nearest 'big city' (or whatever you call a town with a population under half a million). Sometimes, to my great chagrin, I would be dragged around the antiques shops and markets while my mum hunted for treasures for her store in our local village of Buonconvento. On any such morning, she would cleverly make my sister and me think that it was our idea to go to Florence for an ice cream and a glamorous lunch in one of my parents' favourite restaurants. But soon we would be groaning with boredom and dragging our feet as we sat in yet another bric-a-brac shop while our mother negotiated heatedly with the proprietor as to the value of an old brass bed or painted cabinet. While these memories are vivid, it was as an adult that I really came to know Florence, when my husband and I moved to the city in 2016, ostensibly for a few months. We told our landlady that we'd need the flat for a year at most – yet here we still are, nine years on.

CLOCKWISE FROM TOP:—
The wood carver's workshop at Castorina 1895; The view from the top of Paretaio in the private garden of my friends Violet and Savannah; Artwork at Trattoria Cammillo; Walking out of my favourite spot for coffee on Via de' Bardi

FLORENCE

OPPOSITE:– A panel by Liesl Brewseter in the studio at San Francesco

Florence held an enormous glamour for my sister and me as children, as it was where our parents had met and fallen in love. In the 1970s, my father worked at the British Institute on the river, on Lungarno Guicciardini. (*Lungarni* is the name given to the boulevards along the river, literally meaning 'along the Arno'.) He lived in a flat on Via Guicciardini, leading away from the Piazza Pitti, round the corner from where we now live, a flat where he apparently had notoriously wild parties. My sister and I also loved Florence as it was where our best friends, Violet and Savannah, lived in a real-life Italian version of *The Secret Garden*. 'San Francesco', as we called their home, is in a rambling walled garden to the south of the city containing the old convent of San Francesco di Paola, various outbuildings (Violet and Savannah's house was in the old *aia*, or dry store), and the hillock of Paretaio – at the top of which is a woodland glade overlooking the most perfect private view of Florence's skyline. Their parents, Adam and Cloe, were two of my parents' dearest friends. Cloe's family had owned San Francesco since 1874. Her great-grandfather, the sculptor Adolf von Hildebrand, first saw it when walking up towards Bellosguardo, (the hill adjoining Paretaio and aptly named 'beautiful sight'), to take in the views of Florence, immediately deciding he must buy it and house his studio there. The sculptures he created in what is still called 'The Studio' are still dotted around the garden and under the *loggia* of the main house.

From the moment he bought it, San Francesco was at the centre of the social set that was to become known as the 'romantic exiles'. Florence was so full of foreign – and in particular, English – settlers in the late 19th century (about 30,000 of Florence's population of 200,000) that locals called all foreigners *inglesi*, whatever their nationality. Successive generations at San Francesco have all been artistic. Hildebrand's daughter, Lisl, created an art school on the ground floor of the house, and her daughter Cloclo – Cloe's mother – was a prolific painter, whose dreamy landscapes of Greece and Italy are vivid in my memory, as they hang all around the property. I have always loved her use of colour, applied with the same technique of traditional fresco painting to canvas, imbuing her works with a rich and romantic quality. Cloclo's protectiveness of her work was almost comical – she refused to sell a painting unless the prospective buyer had a good enough reason for wanting it. As a result, most of her work is still owned by the family.

Cloclo married Willy Peploe, son of the Scottish colourist Samuel Peploe, and Cloe's elder siblings, Mark and Clare, were both celebrated filmmakers. In her film *Grandmother's Footsteps*, Violet and Savannah's cousin, Lola Peploe, beautifully tells the wonderfully romantic and artistic story of Cloclo and San Francesco, highlighting the tensions Cloclo felt between creativity and motherhood. The magic of San Francesco for us as children was that, being a secret walled garden within a city, it was possible for me, my sister, Violet and Savannah to scamper off and 'go on adventures' for hours without our parents needing to worry about us. We would climb to the top of Paretaio, and in front of the uninterrupted skyline of Florence, dominated by the sight of Brunelleschi's dome and the wispy impression of the Pistoia Mountains beyond, play hide and seek and swing from trees while our parents had long lunches in Cloe and Adam's courtyard at the foot of the hill.

As I've grown older, I feel now that the Arno gives the city much of its magic. Whenever I visit friends lucky enough to have windows looking onto the river, I am mesmerised by the shimmering of the water at night, the lights of the city reflected in its surface. For the first five years that my husband and I lived in Florence, I worked for a very fabulous soap brand called Ortigia, in a building along one of the *lungarni*, and my commute took me each day on a seven-minute walk along the river via Caffe Melloni for a coffee. I never stopped being amazed at being able to gaze out at the Uffizi across the water as I plodded along. My boss back then was, and still is, a great friend, and we would spend cosy winter evenings

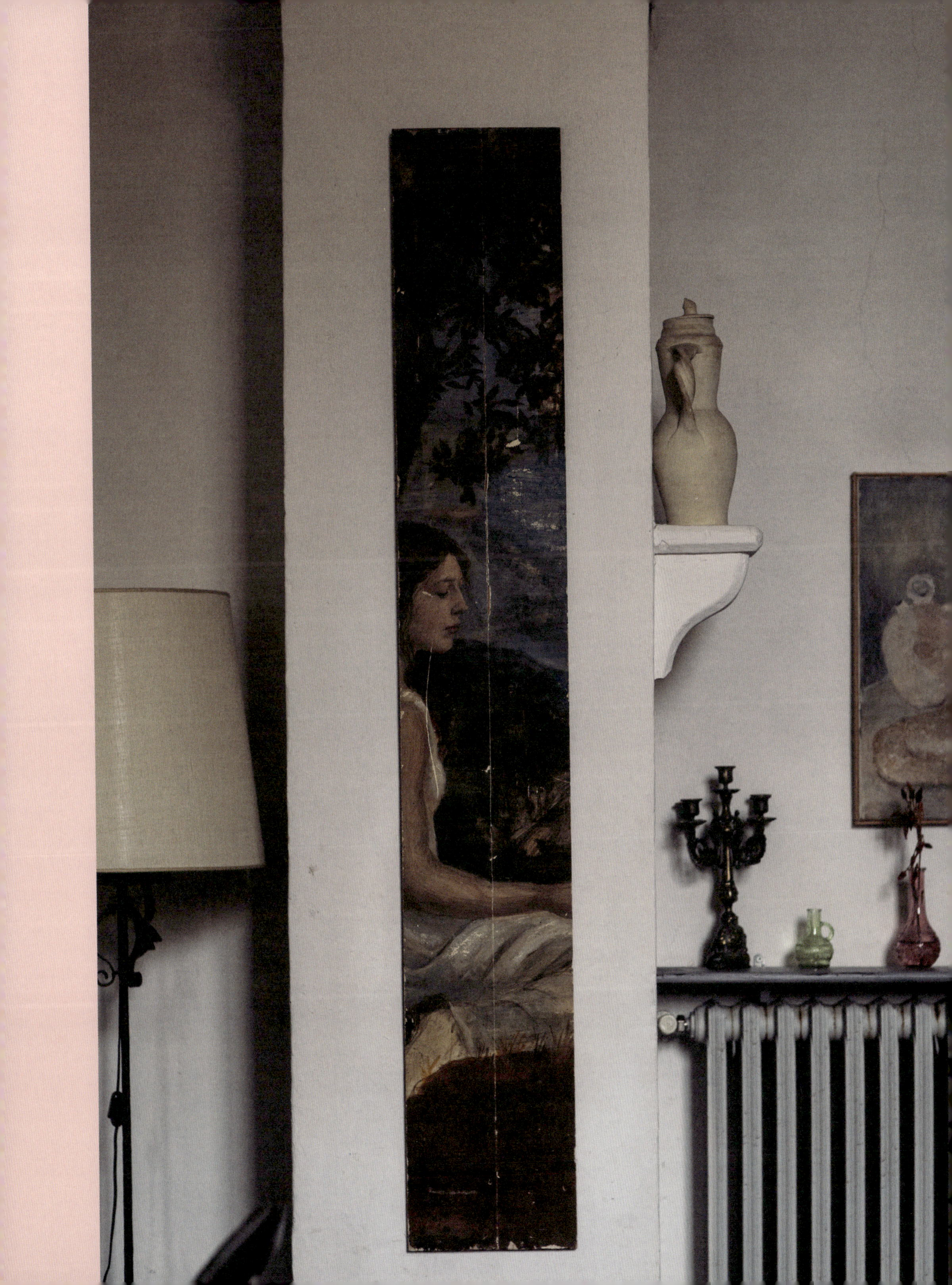

in her drawing room watching old black-and-white films in front of the fire with the reflected light from the water dancing on the ceiling. She has since moved, but those evenings in her flat on the water are indelibly marked in my memory, in particular one night when a friend of hers had driven down from northern Italy and brought with him a hamper full of black truffles he had foraged. We spent a lovely evening eating buttery scrambled eggs with obscene quantities of shaved black truffle as we gossiped and sipped on glasses of wine. It is moments like these, which one feels wouldn't happen anywhere else, that make winter nights in Tuscany something to cherish rather than dread.

Aside from adding a touch of magic, the river is the 'dividing line' between the city of Florence and Oltrarno ('beyond the Arno'), the neighbourhood where we live. Until the second half of the 20th century, people would talk about going 'into town' if they were crossing the river north, or 'leaving town' if they crossed the river to Santo Spirito, our local church and piazza. Oltrarno is the part of Florence that I love most, as it has an easy laid-back feeling and less of the hustle and bustle of the more famous spots north of the river. It's a joy to buy food from the farmers' stalls in Piazza Santo Spirito, or to drink a coffee with Brunelleschi's wonderfully original Basilica facade as a backdrop.

Santo Spirito is a busy pedestrianised square, where the young meet to have an *aperitivo* in the many bars, and it seems incomprehensible that it was at any time not considered to be a part of Florence. My friend Chiara tells me that when her grandfather opened the Oltrarno culinary institution Trattoria Cammillo in 1942, it was from the rubble of the Second World War. They worried that their original location by the Ponte Vecchio was too far from 'town' to be a success, as smart Florentines lived north of the river. But Florentines will go a long way for good food, and after the retreating Germans blew up the entire Ponte Vecchio area to prevent the Allies crossing in 1944, Chiara's parents reopened at their current location one bridge up by Ponte Santa Trinita, where they have been serving old-world, white-tablecloth glamour ever since. Amusingly, Chiara tells me that in her parents' day clients would often still complain bitterly about them being in the wrong part of town where it was impossible to park, and so would often opt to go to the other glamorous hotspot, Harry's Bar, which was north of the river on Lungarno Vespucci. This included my parents, who often chose to go there when they drove up to town so they could park outside. Harry's Bar has since moved, but when it was still in its old premises, the idea that it was far from Cammillo was comical, as it was only an eight-minute walk between the two restaurants.

Our nearest bridge is, aside from the Ponte Vecchio, possibly the most revered in Florence. Commissioned by Cosimo I de' Medici, as so much of the city was, Ponte Santa Trinita was designed by Bartolomeo Ammannati, with some parts attributed to Michelangelo. It consists of three extremely elegant elliptical arches, said to be the oldest of their kind. The road of the bridge is still made up of stone blocks, and at each of its four corners stands a 17th century sculpture representing each of the four seasons. Florentines have a particular love of this bridge, and its bombing by the Germans was one of the more traumatic losses during the Second World War. The morning after the bombardments that destroyed it and all the bridges of Florence, aside from the Ponte Vecchio (apparently spared by order of Hitler), the art historian Ugo Procacci, as he watched the celebratory cries of 'Viva l'Italia!', inwardly mourned an Italy that could no longer boast the Ponte Santa Trinita.

Rebuilding the bridge was a labour of love, completed in 1958. The four statues representing the seasons were fished out of the Arno riverbed during the works, but Primavera – Spring – was missing her head, which was assumed to have been looted and sold abroad. The architect Luigi Bellini offered an enormous cash reward for anyone who could track down the missing head, and photos

FOLLOWING:– The Ponte Vecchio from Ponte alle Grazie

of Primavera's face ended up on the covers of the national press with the headline 'Have you seen this woman?!'. Thankfully it was found washed up on the banks of the river a few miles out of town in 1961, so the restoration of Ponte Santa Trinita could finally be completed. One wonders if the tourists posing on its edge to get a photo of themselves with the Ponte Vecchio in the background know of its history, and of the love that went into restoring its beauty for the city of Florence to erase the memory of the devastation of those dark years.

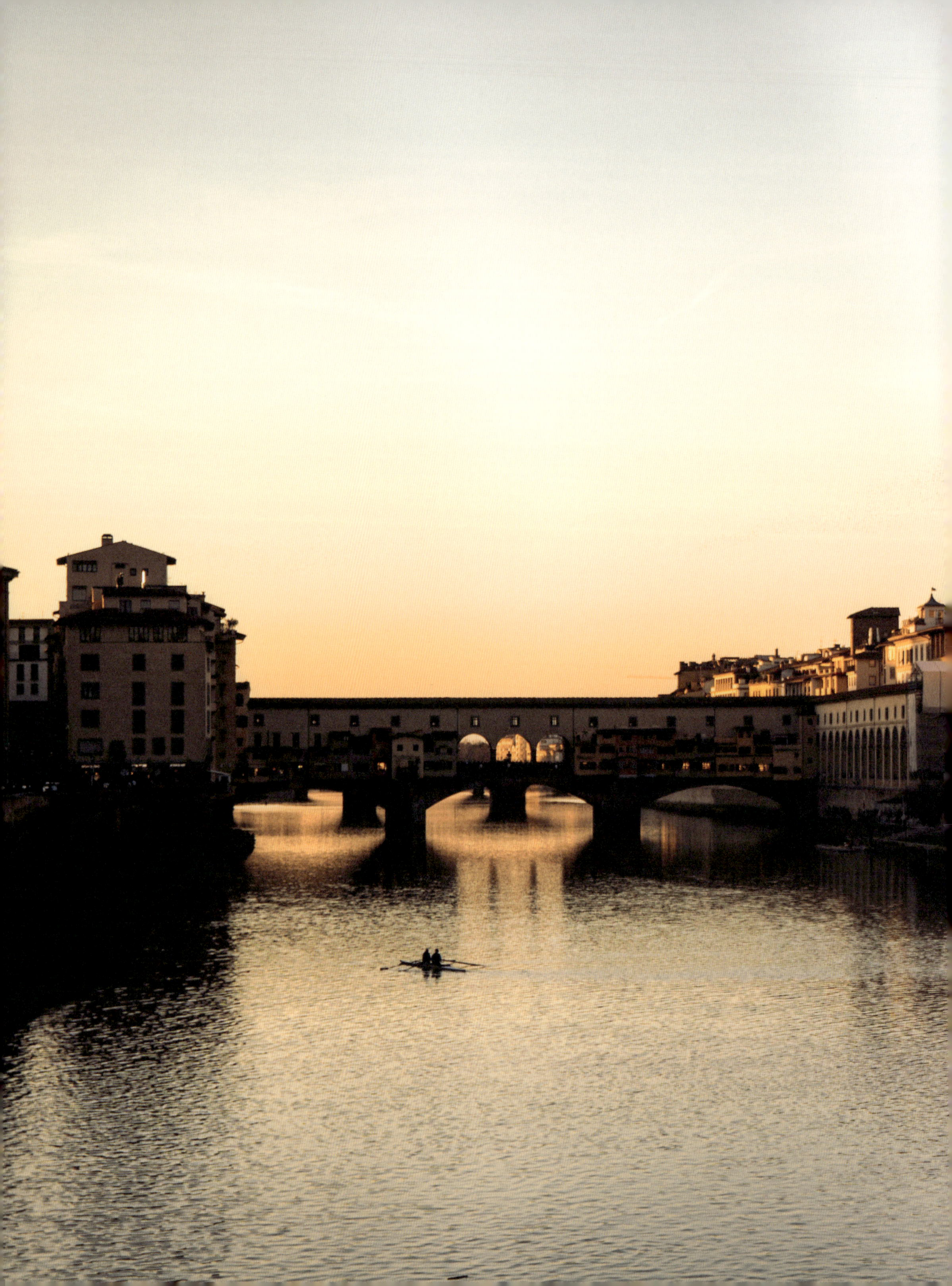

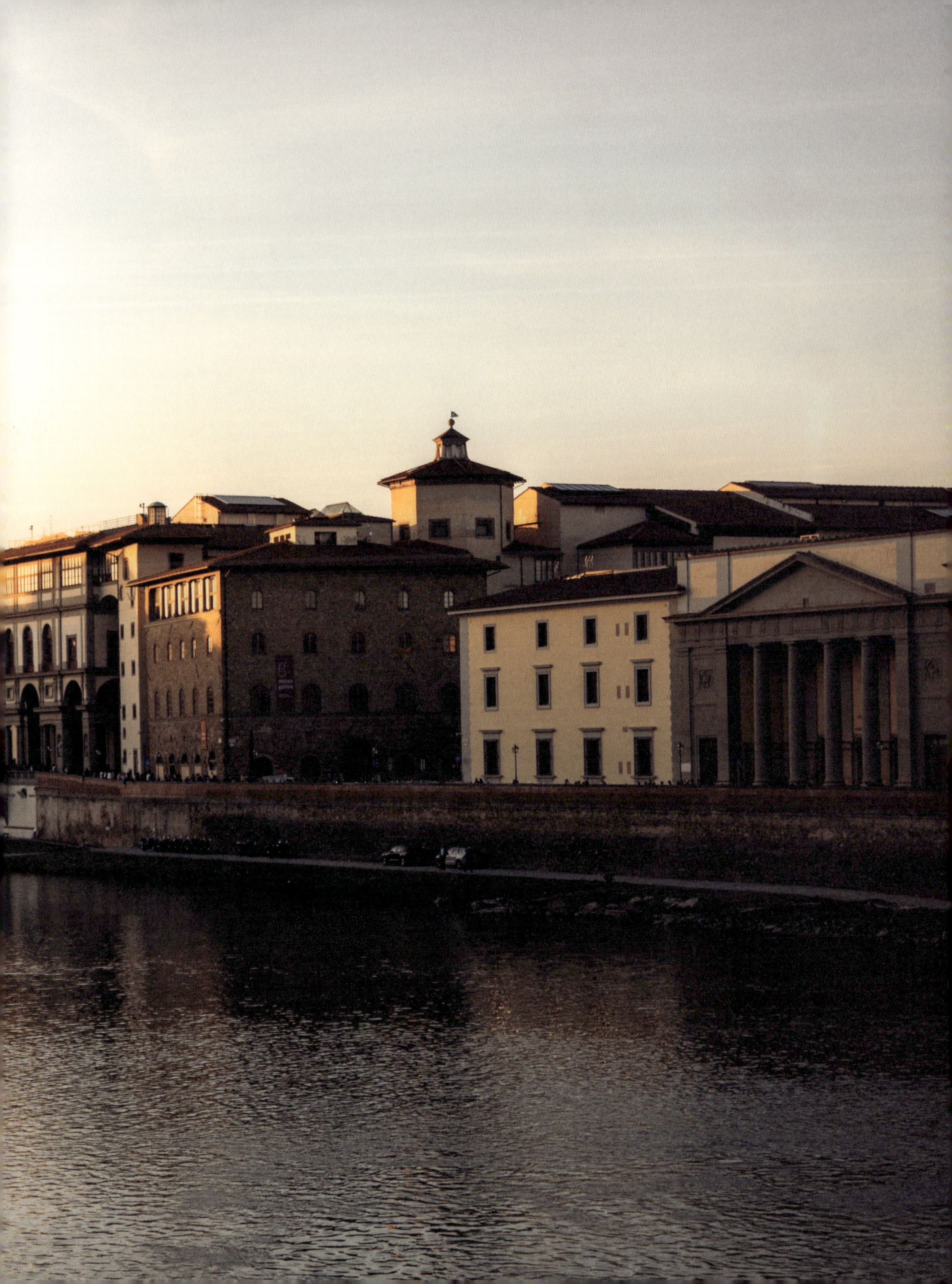

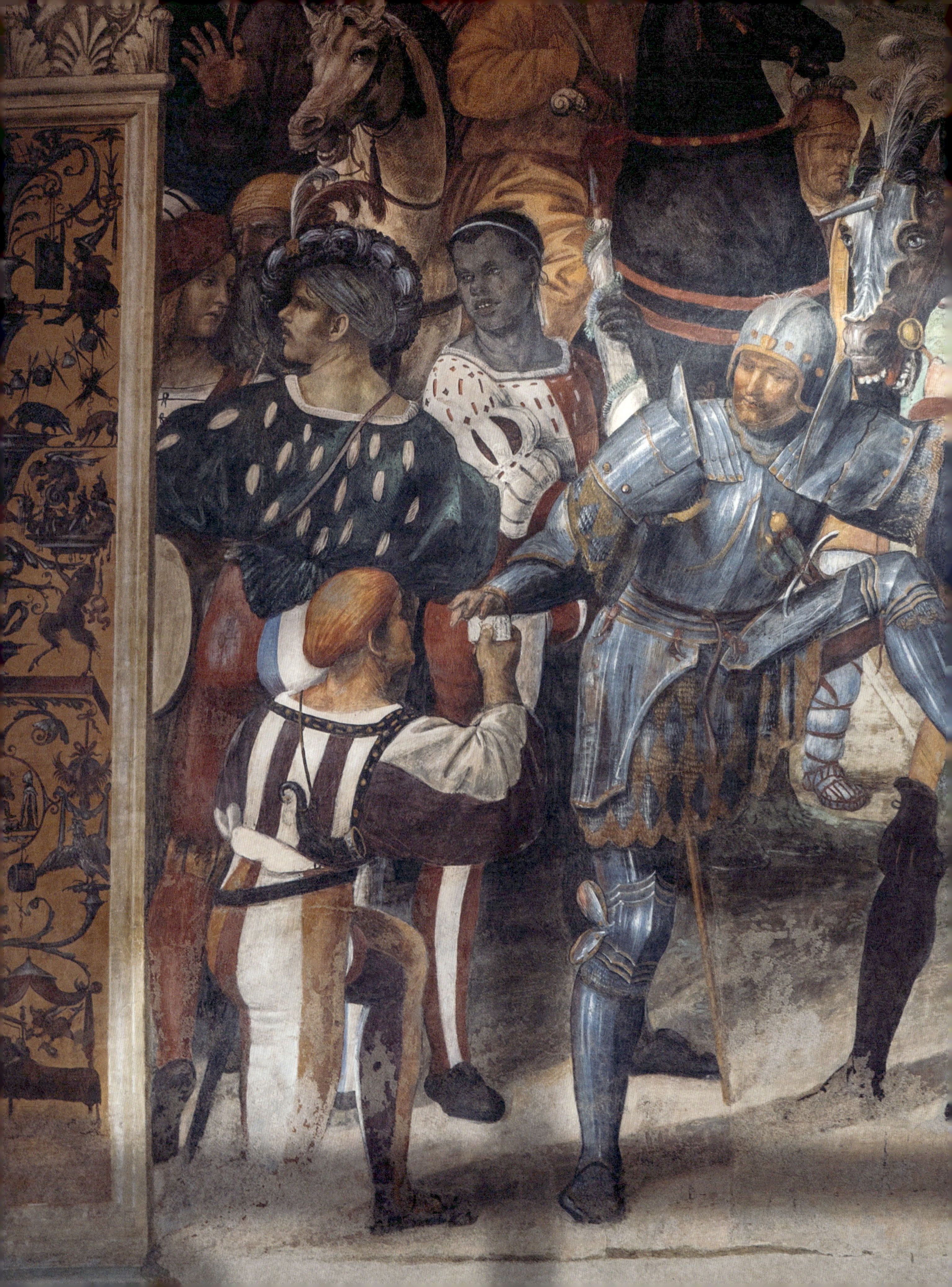

SECONDI DI CARNE

MEATY MAINS

Tuscan cuisine is a carnivore's delight: plump Italian sausages, T-bone steaks 'four fingers high', spatchcocked chickens and long whole pieces of pork ribs sizzling on a grill over an open fire are all classic staples. It's a celebratory, generous sort of cooking which is meant to be shared with friends and loved ones. Served alongside a simple plate of *fagioli al fiasco* (cannellini beans dressed in oil and rosemary) and perhaps some unsalted Tuscan bread, this represents Tuscan fare at its best – the simple cooking of quality ingredients, with very little done to them.

A historically rural region whose economy was mainly based on farming, Tuscany has always raised some of Italy's most prized livestock, such as the famous enormous white Chianina ox used to make the best *bistecca alla fiorentina* (Florentine T-bone steaks), and Cinta Senese pork, one of the oldest breeds in Italy, whose black-and-white striped form can be seen in a 1300s painting by Lorenzetti in Siena's town hall. Its meat makes some of the best prosciutto, as well as one of my favourite dishes, *arista di maiale* (page 170), which is a herby simply roasted pork loin. Throughout history, meat in Tuscany has been prepared in extremely varied ways, veering from the incredibly simple – a fabulous piece of beef cooked rare with no oil or salt over fire, such as *bistecca alla fiorentina* (page 166) – to the terrifyingly imaginative, like the Florentine *cibrèo*, a stew popular with the Medici family, made of the wattle, beak, liver, heart, testicles and cockscomb of a cockerel.

Usually when meaty mains involve a sauce or are stewed, it was to disguise the fact that the meat was a cheap cut or slightly past its prime. Historically, nothing was ever wasted. *Polpettone*, or meatloaf, was originally a way to use up the previous day's *lesso* (boiled meats), while *peposo*, a rich dark beef stew simmered for hours in a kiln with lots of red wine and black pepper, was a way to cook off and mask the taste of dodgier pieces of beef.

All throughout Tuscany, locals still eat and adore nose-to-tail dishes which many visitors find challenging. In Florence there are queues at stands selling *lampredotto* – the stewed fourth stomach of a cow or veal, sliced up and served in a bread roll topped with salsa verde. Of course, this frugal art of using every part of the animal originally came from want and necessity, but even now these dishes are beloved in their own right and are enjoyed every day.

When I was a child in the 1990s, the area surrounding Arniano was still very rural and tourism hadn't yet arrived in that part of Tuscany. As the main industry was farming, we were always very close to where our food came from. Most of my classmates were the children of farmers so play dates were usually at their family farms, where we would feed their sheep, whose milk would be turned into pecorino cheese, and go and see the pigs in their pens. The local butcher's farm is only a few kilometres away from their shop in Buonconvento, meaning one knows where their meat is produced. When I was five, my parents shared a couple of pigs with a neighbour who was a farmer, and when slaughter day came, we all went to their house. My mother asked the farmer's mother to keep an eye on me and my sister, who was a toddler, and to on no account bring us to the nearby outhouses that would serve as the abattoir, as we were too young to witness the slaughter. The farmer's mother thought this was ridiculous – and as soon as my mum left she marched us over to the outbuilding where the pigs were being killed. I can still remember the rivers of blood, the iron-y smell of blood, and our friends – the pigs – cut in half hanging from the ceiling. My sister and I were quite upset initially, but within a few hours we were helping to make sausages and turning the handle on the machine to make salami and were very happy.

I tell this story not to put you off eating meat, but to highlight that, even if you don't like the more challenging cuts that are prepared in Tuscany, there is a great respect for the animal, which calls for it to be used in its entirety. I bear this in mind when I shop by trying to opt for only good-quality, farm-reared organic cuts, as I would much rather eat expensive meat only every so often than cheap battery or cage-reared every day.

In this chapter I've brought together some of the region's classic – and less daunting – meaty mains, or *secondi*, which are best enjoyed on a cosy winter's night.

Bistecca alla fiorentina

Florentine steak

SERVES 4

1–1.5 kg (2 lb 3 oz–3 lb 5 oz) T-bone or porterhouse steak

flaky sea salt

good-quality olive oil

Fuoco nobile (noble fire) and *carne* (meat): these are supposed to be the only two elements in cooking a true *bistecca alla fiorentina*, possibly the most emblematic of all Tuscan dishes. The 'noble fire' comes from cooking the meat over coals made exclusively from oak, burned down until the embers are covered in a white dusting of ash, which is when the coal is at its hottest. The meat is served only one way – rare – and many a restaurant in Tuscany will have a sign on their wall stating that if customers would like their *fiorentina* cooked any way other than rare, they should order something else.

This symbol of Tuscan cooking is a T-bone steak from a mature Chianina ox, cut at least 'three fingers' high from the rear loin area. The 'T' is flanked by the tender fillet on one side and the flavoursome sirloin on the other. For the meat to be as tender and delicious as possible, I'm told it's essential that the animal has had a happy life and been free to roam the fields. Due to the genetic make-up of Chianina cattle, the meat itself isn't fatty, but lean, tender and tasty, the fat being wrapped around the outer layer of the cut, meaning the meat doesn't oxidise during the all-important hanging (at least 25 days), so the meat fibres break down and tenderise even more.

These steaks are serious and expensive. They are sold by the gram and weigh at least 1 kg (2 lb 3 oz), making them a dish for sharing. Usually the waiter will tell you the weight of each available steak – often bringing them out to show you – and you'll make your selection based on how many of you will be partaking and how hungry you are.

Tradition calls that the steak not be salted before cooking, and that it be served simply with a plate of cannellini beans or maybe a roast potato. Our friend Matteo, who has opened one of the best steakhouses in Florence, Regina Bistecca, adopts a slightly more French stance, serving side dishes such as creamed spinach and fries alongside their very excellent steak. If you have *bistecca* twenty times at Regina, you are presented with your own steak knife engraved with your name, which they keep at the restaurant for you and bring out for you whenever you visit.

Opposite is my method for cooking a *fiorentina* at home. The best method is a gentle cooking on the barbecue, but for those moments when it has not been possible to conjure up the *fuoco nobile* (any Tuscans please stop reading now), I also give the option for using a non-stick pan. Just remember that the pan will cook the steak twice as quickly as on the grill. It won't get that distinctive smoky flavour, and the fat won't have melted away as it would over the fire, but it will be delicious nonetheless.

I am also assuming that outside of Italy you may not be able to find a *fiorentina*, so the timings below are based on a T-bone or porterhouse steak that is maybe two fingers high. If you manage to find one that is three fingers high, cook it for 8 minutes on its flat sides rather than 6 minutes.

And remember, you never salt a *fiorentina* before cooking – only afterwards.

PREPARATION:– the time to get your fire ready
COOKING:– 18 minutes, plus 10 minutes resting

Remove the steak from the fridge 3 hours before cooking to allow it to come up to room temperature. Cover with a clean tea towel until ready to cook.

Light a barbecue using high-quality coal (don't use firelighters as they will impart their taste to the meat). Stack a loose pile of charcoal with a well at its centre and place a few sheets of twisted-up newspaper in the well. Once they are burning, put another small piece of coal on top of the well. Leave the fire to catch and burn down until the embers are white-hot and look like they are coated in ash.

Alternatively, heat a large, heavy-based non-stick frying pan until it's searing hot, then cook the steak as described below, but halve the timings, as the heat is more intense than over the fire.

On the barbecue or non-stick pan, stand the steak vertically on the bone for 1–2 minutes, to allow the meat to start gently warming without cooking too intensely. Still standing it vertically, put the steak on the fat side for 2 minutes, not allowing the fat to burn.

Now put the steak on one of the flat sides for 6 minutes. Using a big pair of barbecue tongs, flip the steak over and leave on the other side for 6 minutes. Finally, stand the steak on the bone end again for 1–2 minutes, to allow all the juices to gently redistribute themselves.

Remove from the heat, cover loosely with foil and leave to rest for 10 minutes.

Slice the meat along the bone to release the fillet and sirloin pieces, then slice into 2 cm (¾ inch) wide strips away from the longest bone. Reassemble the slices around the bone on a serving plate or chopping board. Sprinkle liberally with flaky sea salt and drizzle with good-quality olive oil. Bring to the table and help yourselves.

DELICIOUS WITH:— Tuscan roast potatoes (page 199), Garlicky rosemary cannellini beans (page 198), Florentine peas with ham (page 191), Cabbage, apple & walnut salad (page 202), Greens tossed 'in the pan' (page 197), Roasted baby onions (page 194), Dada's baked leeks in bechamel (page 134).

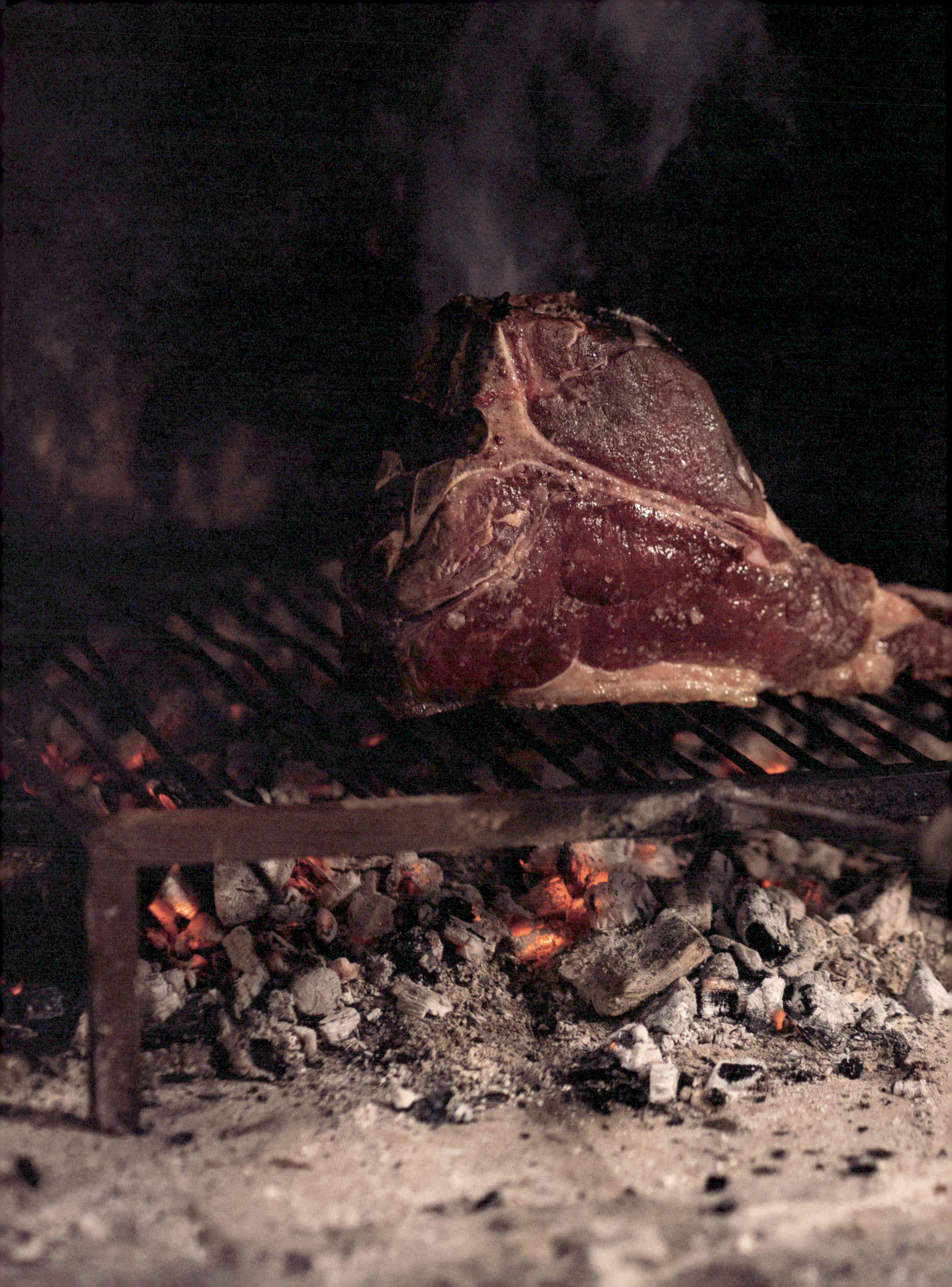

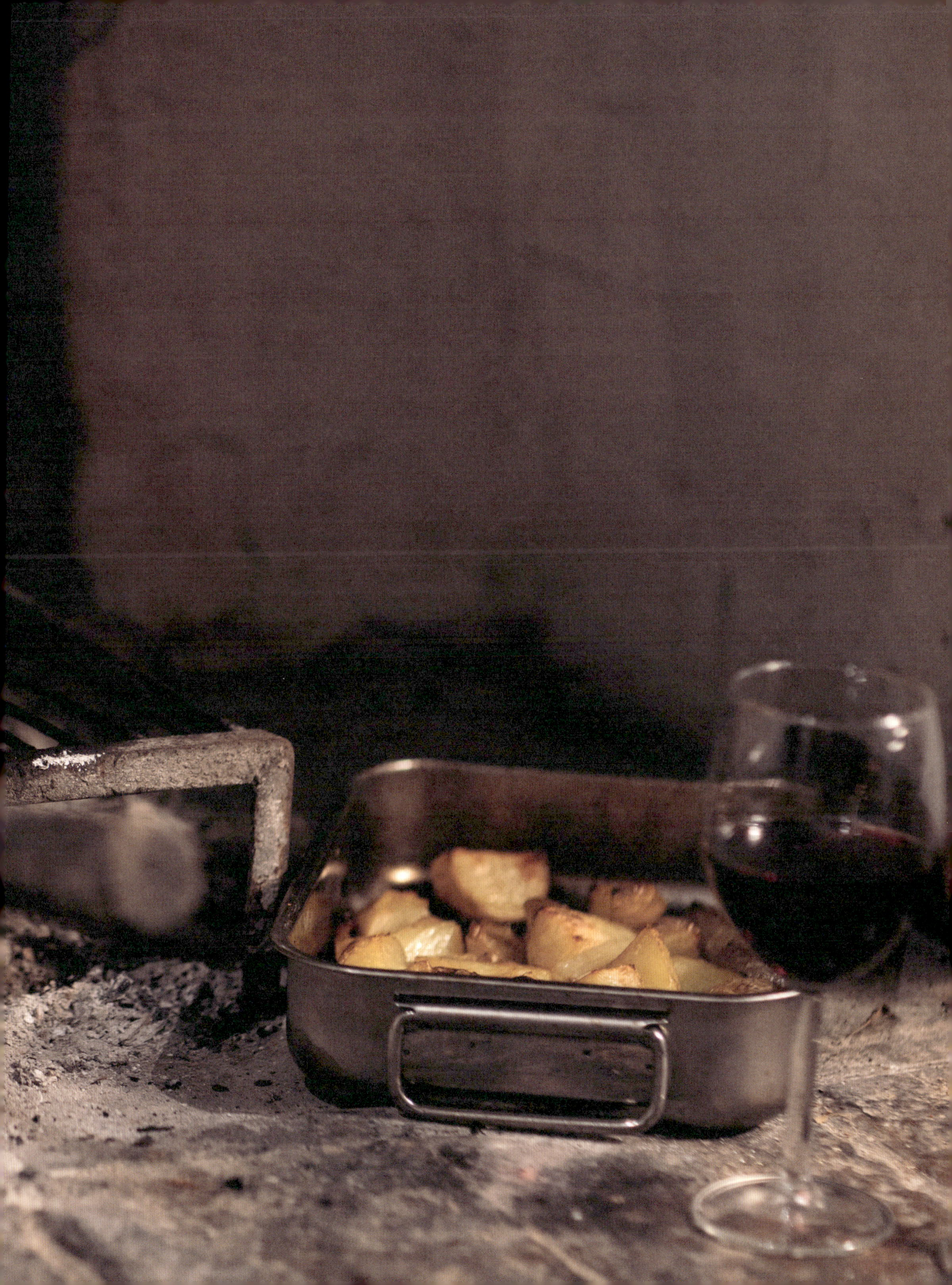

Arista di maiale con patate

Herby roast pork loin with potatoes

SERVES 4

600–800 g (1 lb 5 oz–1 lb 12 oz) organic pork loin, boneless and rindless if possible

sea salt and freshly ground black pepper

2 whole garlic cloves, lightly crushed with the side of a knife

sage leaves

4 tablespoons olive oil

1 kg (2 lb 3 oz) waxy potatoes, peeled and cut into 3 cm (1¾ inch) chunks, about the size of a ping pong ball

FOR THE STUFFING

4 garlic cloves, finely crushed or chopped

a few rosemary sprigs, leaves picked and finely chopped

large handful of sage leaves, finely chopped

DELICIOUS WITH:—
Greens tossed 'in the pan' (page 197), which I always make with savoy cabbage and lots of chilli to accompany the roast pork – though cavolo nero is also delicious. For something fresh, a Cabbage, apple & walnut salad (page 202) is great, as is A very good green salad (page 189).

Roast pork loin is one of the most typical and popular *secondi* in Tuscany. Legend has it that its name, *arista*, dates back to medieval times when a group of passing Greek monks exclaimed 'aristos!' (the best) when being served a plate of this dish in Florence. Locals assumed this was what the cut was called in Greek, and for whatever reason, the name stuck. *Arista* is the *secondo* I most order when I eat out, as the meat is incredibly tasty, and the potatoes cooked in the same pan with the herby cooking juices and oil are the perfect accompaniment. It is also alleged by many a local doctor to be the leanest (and therefore most healthy) cut of meat you can eat. I also love that it can be made in one pan and served with something simple, such as a radicchio salad.

In Italy, pork loin is sold without the rind unless it is being cooked on the spit for porchetta. Outside of Italy it can be hard to get rindless pork loin, so I have outlined below how to prepare pork loin if you would like it to come with crackling.

PREPARATION:— 20 minutes
COOKING:— 1 hour 15 minutes, plus resting time

Remove the pork loin from the fridge (and any packaging) about 1 hour before cooking to come up to room temperature. Season all over with salt.

Preheat the oven to 250°C (480°F) fan-forced, or as high as it will go.

In a small bowl, combine the stuffing ingredients and season with a generous pinch of salt and black pepper.

Use a long thin knife to pierce the end of the pork loin to make a hole through the centre. Make another hole at the other end and try to meet the other hole in the middle. You can use the end of a wooden spoon to burrow in, making the hole a little wider. Fill the cavity with the stuffing. I do this by standing the pork loin on one end and stuffing half the herb mixture in the hole, pushing it further down the cavity with my fingers, and then turning the loin the other way and stuffing the other end of the pork with the remaining herb mixture until compactly stuffed.

If the joint comes with its rind for crackling, score the fat on top of the pork in a crisscross fashion. (This isn't necessary if the joint is rindless.)

Pat the top of the pork dry with paper towel and rub with a couple of generous pinches of salt. Place the pork in a large roasting tin, on top of the two whole garlic cloves and a few sage leaves. Pour the olive oil over the pork. Roast for 20 minutes, then remove from the oven.

Turn the oven down to 180°C (350°F). Add the potatoes to the pan, toss in the hot oil and season well with salt. Roast for another 45 minutes, or until the fat on top of the pork is dark brown and the potatoes are browned.

Remove the pan from the oven. Carefully transfer the pork to a plate or chopping board and leave to rest under a piece of foil. Return the potatoes to the oven for 10 minutes to crisp up while the meat rests.

After 10 minutes, slice the meat as thinly as you can and arrange on a serving dish. Drizzle all the cooking juices over the pork and serve with the potatoes.

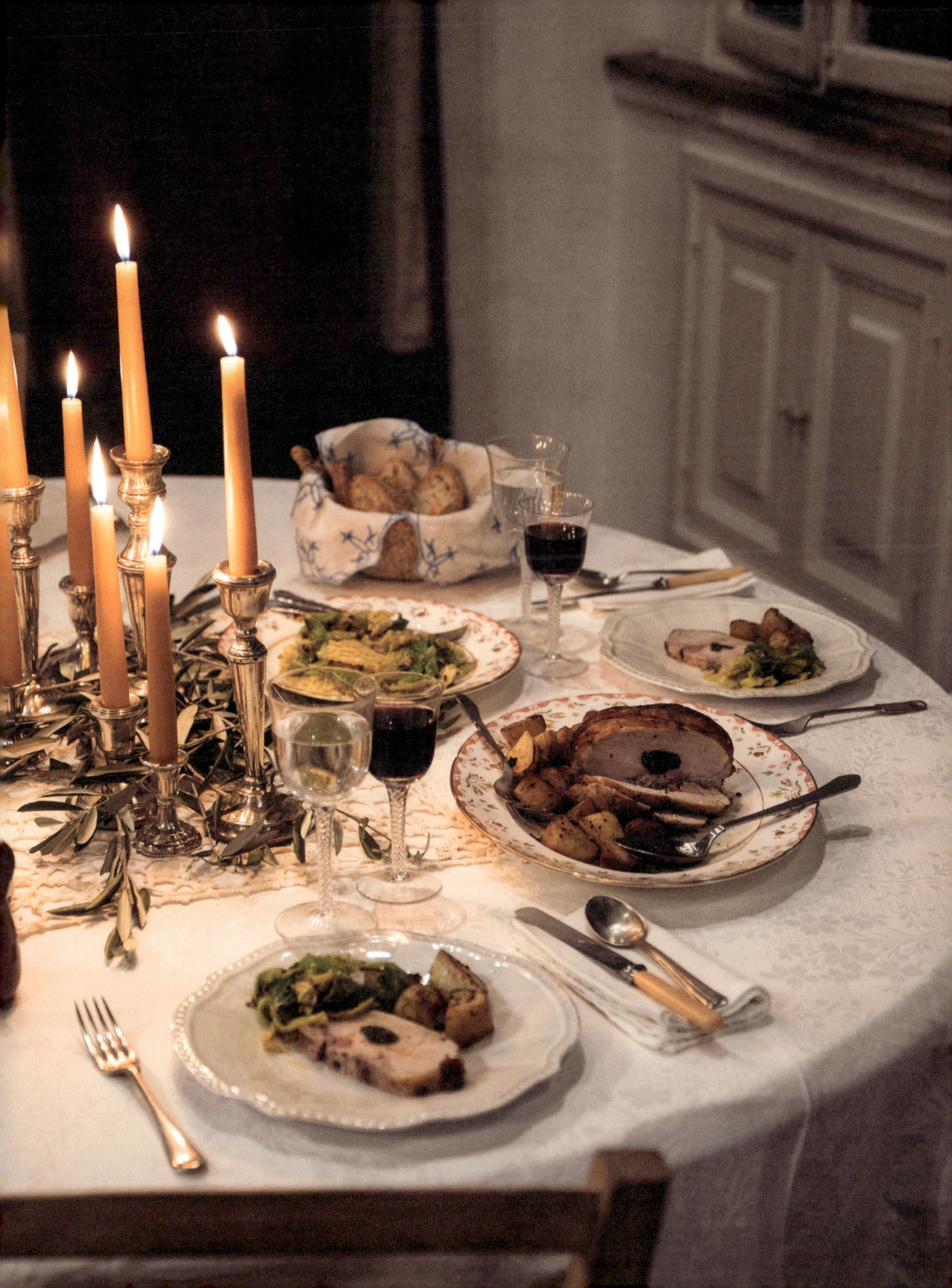

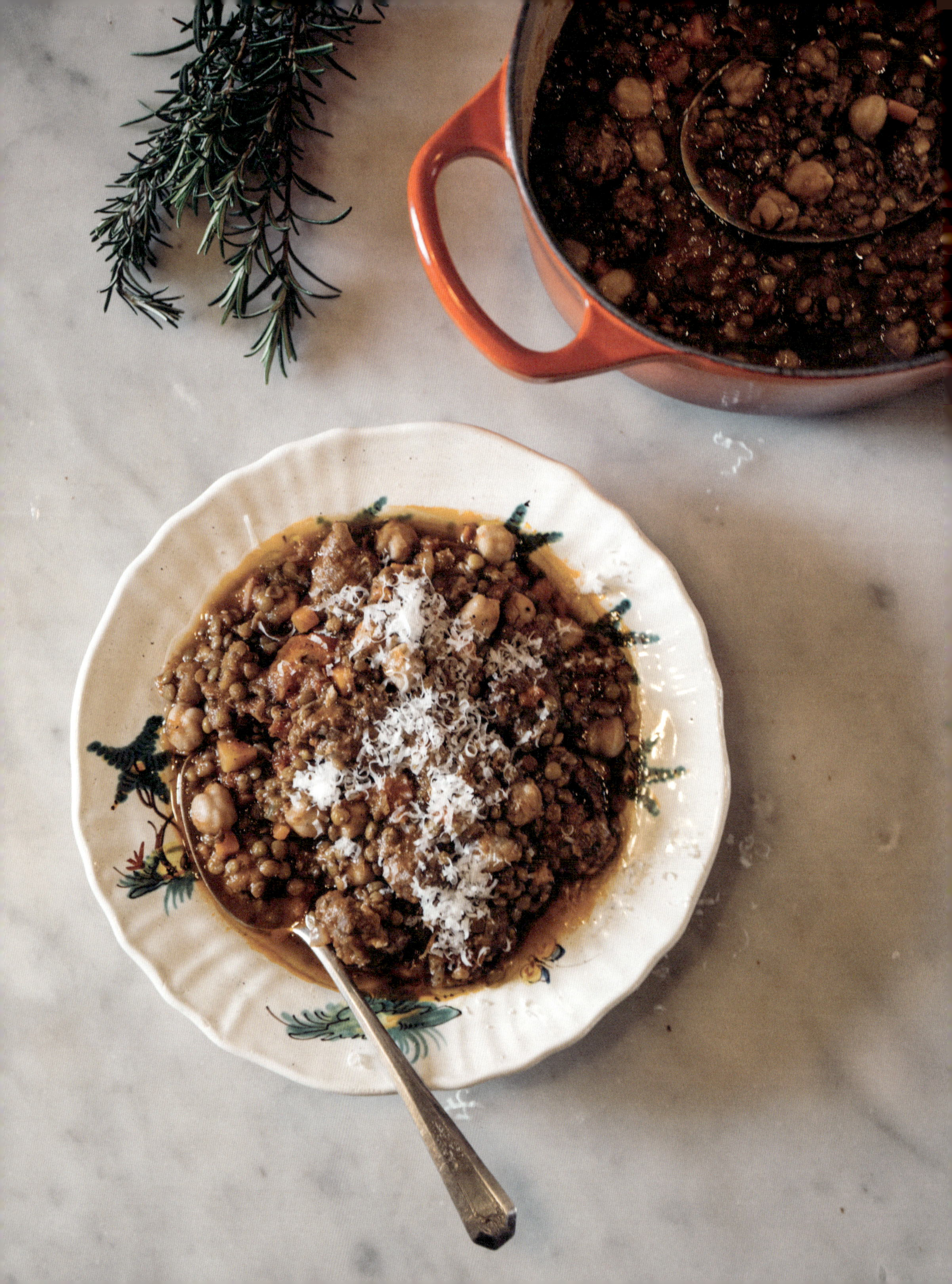

Salsicce, ceci e lenticchie

Sausage, lentil & chickpea stew

SERVES 4

6 large organic pork sausages

olive oil

1 onion (red, golden or white all fine), finely diced

sea salt and freshly ground black pepper

1 garlic clove, grated

1 carrot, finely chopped

1 celery stick, finely chopped

a few rosemary sprigs, leaves picked and finely chopped

1 glass red wine

1 teaspoon tomato concentrate

pinch of chilli flakes (optional)

200 ml (7 fl oz) water or stock

400 g (14 oz) tin peeled plum tomatoes

200 g (7 oz) small black or green dried lentils

2 × 400 g (14 oz) tins giant chickpeas

TO SERVE

finely chopped flat-leaf parsley

grated parmesan

olive oil

Lentils are traditionally eaten on New Year's Eve in Italy as they are supposed to bring prosperity, wealth and luck for the coming year. They are usually paired with cotechino – an Emilian sausage made primarily of pork rind, which requires very long, gentle cooking.

This is a quicker version which adds chickpeas and tinned tomatoes. If you can find plump Italian sausages with a thick grain, they will hold together well, but any good-quality sausages without too much heavy flavouring will do. Just buy the best you can find and afford. I cook dried lentils in the sauce as I usually have these to hand, but you could also use pre-cooked or tinned lentils if you're short of time – simply shorten the cooking time by 10 minutes and add the precooked chickpeas at the same time.

Eaten piping hot from a bowl and topped with a light dusting of parmesan and a drizzle of olive oil, this is comfort food at its best.

PREPARATION:– 10 minutes
COOKING:– 1 hour

Remove the skins from the sausages. In a heavy-based frying pan, heat a few glugs of olive oil until sizzling. Add the sausages, breaking each up into four large chunks with the end of a wooden spoon, and brown over a medium–high heat for 3–5 minutes, until they have a little colour – don't worry if they break into smaller pieces. If they release lots of liquid, wait for this to evaporate and then brown. Remove from the pan using a slotted spoon and set aside.

Turn down the heat and add the onion to the pan, along with a pinch of salt; there should be plenty of fat in the pan from the sausages. Leave to cook for 2 minutes, stirring occasionally. Stir in the garlic, carrot, celery and rosemary and leave to gently cook for 5 minutes. If the sausage fat starts catching or browning the veg too much, stir in a splash of the wine to deglaze the pan and stop them burning.

Add the sausages back to the pan with the wine, tomato concentrate and chilli flakes, if using. Use a wooden spoon to scrape up any bits sticking to the bottom of the pan, then leave the alcohol to evaporate for 5 minutes.

Stir in the water or stock, along with the tinned tomatoes. Fill the empty tomato tin with water, swirl it around and pour the tomatoey water into the pan, adding a generous pinch of salt. Break up the tomatoes with the end of a wooden spoon. Stir in the lentils and leave to cook for 10 minutes, stirring occasionally.

Open the tins of chickpeas and empty the contents into the stew. Stir together, then leave to gently bubble over a low heat, uncovered, for another 20–25 minutes. If the pan looks like it is drying out, stir in a splash more wine or water. The stew is ready when it is thick and rich and the lentils are completely cooked.

Taste and adjust the seasoning as necessary. Serve piping hot, with a sprinkling of parsley, a grating of parmesan and a drizzle more olive oil.

Il timballo di Grazia

Grazia's radicchio, sausage & rice timballo

SERVES 4

300 g (10½ oz) risotto rice

1 litre (34 fl oz) chicken stock, approximately

1 red onion

sea salt and freshly ground black pepper

olive oil

3 thick organic Tuscan pork sausages

½ head of radicchio, sliced into fine ribbons

pinch of chilli flakes

60 g (2 oz) butter

100 g (3½ oz) grated parmesan

FOR THE CHEESE SAUCE

200 ml (7 fl oz) single (pure) cream

200 g (7 oz) finely grated parmesan (you could also use gruyere)

a few gratings of nutmeg

sea salt and freshly ground black pepper

Grazia is something of a legend around Arniano, famed as one of the best local cooks of traditional dishes of southern Tuscany. When I was a child, she always cooked at the *sagre* (feasts) of Buonconvento, but in true Italian style, she retired when she had grandchildren to fulfil her new role as *nonna*. She did come out of retirement to cater for the wedding of my oldest friend, Carolina, preparing this fabulously opulent and celebratory dish – a rice timballo studded with radicchio and sausage and topped with a creamy cheese sauce.

Use the best-quality sausages you can buy for this dish. If you can only get small thin ones, add an extra sausage to the filling.

PREPARATION:– 20 minutes
COOKING:– 45 minutes, plus resting time

Put the rice in a wide, deep saucepan, ideally one with a lid. Pour in enough stock to cover the rice by about 2 cm (¾ inch). Chop the onion in half and add an onion half to the rice, plus a few pinches of salt. Cover the pan (with foil, if necessary) and set over a medium heat. Leave to cook and steam without removing the lid for 12–13 minutes.

In the meantime, finely dice the remaining onion and place in a frying pan with a good glug of olive oil and a pinch of salt. Leave to cook over a medium heat for 5 minutes, or until the onion is translucent. Remove the sausages from their casings and add the meat to the pan, using a wooden spoon to break it up into coarse chunks. Cook, stirring now and then, for about 5 minutes, until well browned; if the meat releases any liquid, just let it evaporate. Add the radicchio and cook, stirring often, until the radicchio has wilted. Season to taste with black pepper and chilli flakes, then set aside while the rice finishes cooking.

Check the rice: it should still be a little al dente, but not chalky, and all the liquid should have been absorbed; add a splash more liquid if it's drying out but still needs cooking. Once the rice is cooked, discard the onion half and add the sausage mixture. Stir in the butter and parmesan well, so they melt into the hot rice, then season as needed with more pepper and salt. Let the rice cool a little while you prepare your mould/s.

You can serve the rice in individual portions in little moulds, or in one large one – a ring mould, cake tin, or whatever you have to hand, really. Lightly butter the mould/s, spoon the rice in until half full, and then, with your hands, really push the rice down into the mould/s to make sure it is well compacted, so the rice doesn't collapse when unmoulded. Fill the rest of the mould with rice and press down again with your hands so it's really packed in.

Let the rice set for at least 20 minutes, or in the fridge for up to 2 days before reheating and serving.

When you're ready to serve, place the mould/s in an oven preheated to 160°C (315°F) fan-forced. Bake small timbales for 10 minutes, or a large timbale for 15 minutes.

While the rice is reheating, make the cheese sauce. Put the cream in a small saucepan over a medium heat and stir in the grated cheese, nutmeg and a pinch of salt and pepper, seasoning to taste.

Remove the timbale/s from the oven and rest for 5–10 minutes, so the butter and cheese bind the rice together and the mixture doesn't collapse when unmoulded.

To release the timbale/s, place your serving plate securely over each mould and invert the rice onto the plate. Remove the mould and you should be left with a lovely mound of shaped rice. Drizzle the cheesy sauce over and serve immediately.

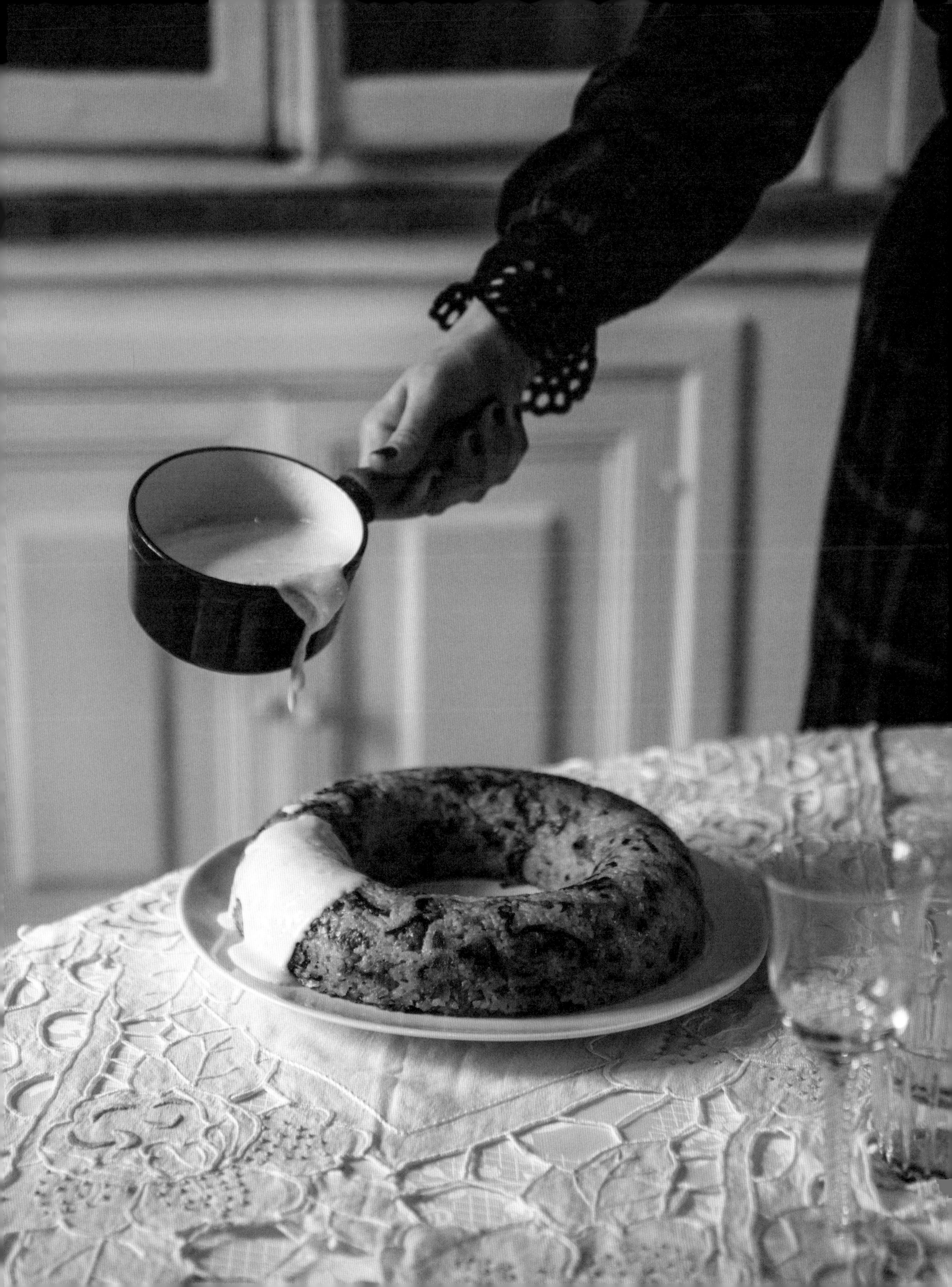

Peposo al fornaciaio

Black pepper stew

SERVES 4

1 kg (2 lb 3 oz) braising beef, chuck, neck or shin (choose a piece with a high fat content)

2 tablespoons black peppercorns

½ teaspoon freshly ground black pepper

sea salt

12 garlic cloves, peeled

1 tablespoon tomato concentrate

1 rosemary sprig

handful of sage leaves

a few bay leaves

2 bottles robust chianti red wine

1 tablespoon olive oil

A simple thick, dark beef stew made with lots of black pepper, *peposo* heralds from Impruneta, a small town just south of Florence where my parents lived and farmed just before I was born, and which has always been known for its *fornaciai* – potters who produced some of the region's finest terracotta and ceramics. *Peposo* was developed by the kilnsmen to cook a tasty meal and mask any slightly suspect bits of meat by covering it in gallons of cheap local chianti wine and leaving it to cook down in the hot kilns for hours. Legend has it that when Renaissance architect Filippo Brunelleschi was building Florence's magnificent cathedral, he would go to Impruneta to visit the terracotta makers and their kilns to choose some construction materials. He saw them each day eating a rich meaty stew and, having tried it, suggested that it would be elevated to dizzying heights with the addition of black pepper, which was very expensive at the time. Brunelleschi understood the power of feeding his troops, and set up several food stands around the construction site of Florence's cathedral, all of them serving *peposo*.

Aside from needing a long cooking time, *peposo* is one of the most hands-off recipes you could imagine. It's important to make this dish in a heavy-based saucepan, if possible. Traditionally they used terracotta, to withstand the long slow cooking, and so the bottom of the stew didn't burn. I use a cast-iron casserole dish, but if you're using a standard saucepan, just make sure you check it often.

They would not have originally used olive oil in the dish, but I like to add a drizzle at the start of the cooking to seal the meat.

This is one of those dishes that is even better the next day.

PREPARATION:– 15 minutes, plus marinating time
COOKING:– 3 hours

Cut the beef into 4 cm (1½ inch) chunks. Any intensely tough bits of fat can be trimmed, but remember that the fat is what will make the meat tender after several hours of cooking, so don't get rid of too much.

Place the beef in a non-reactive bowl large enough to hold all the ingredients. Add the black peppercorns, ground pepper and a few generous pinches of salt and mix together with your hands. Add the garlic cloves, tomato concentrate and herbs, pour the wine over, then cover and leave to marinate at room temperature for 1 hour (or even overnight in the fridge – just remember to take it out a couple of hours before you begin cooking).

When you're ready to cook, heat the olive oil in a heavy cast-iron casserole dish. Use a slotted spoon to fish the meat out of the marinade, into the pan. Seal for 3–5 minutes, turning the meat over every so often with a wooden spoon; no need for the meat to be completely browned. Pour in the marinade liquid (including all the aromatics) and turn the heat down low.

Leave to simmer, uncovered, for 3 hours, checking every 20 minutes or so to make sure the pan isn't drying out. If it is, add a glass of water or stock. Keep a particularly close eye in the last half hour in case the pan is burning on the bottom.

At the end of 3 hours, the peposo should be dark and the wine reduced almost completely to a thick dark sauce.

Serve hot, spooned over some buttery polenta, or with Garlicky rosemary cannellini beans (page 198) and greens. Or a stale piece of bread, as the ancient Tuscans would have done.

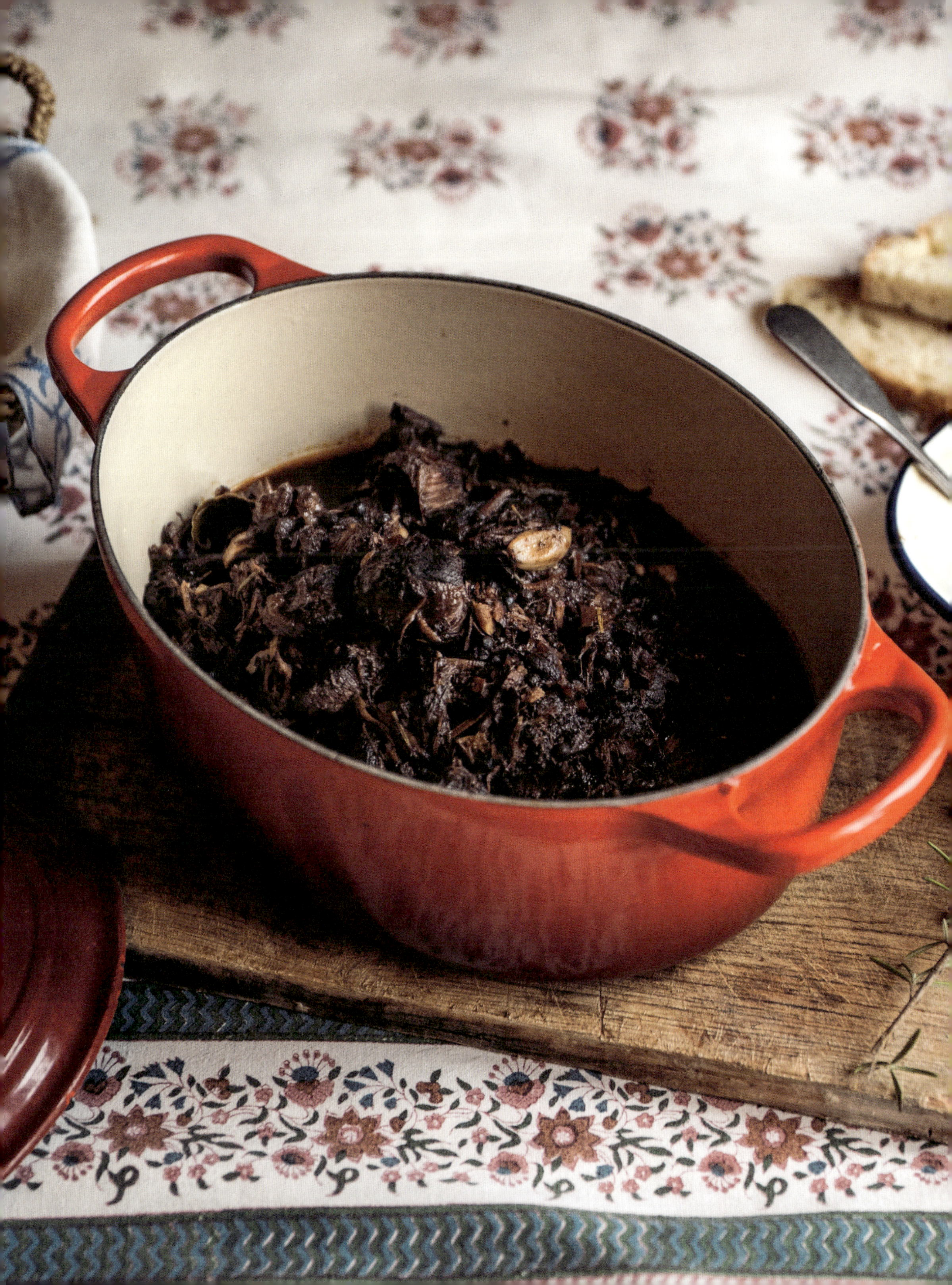

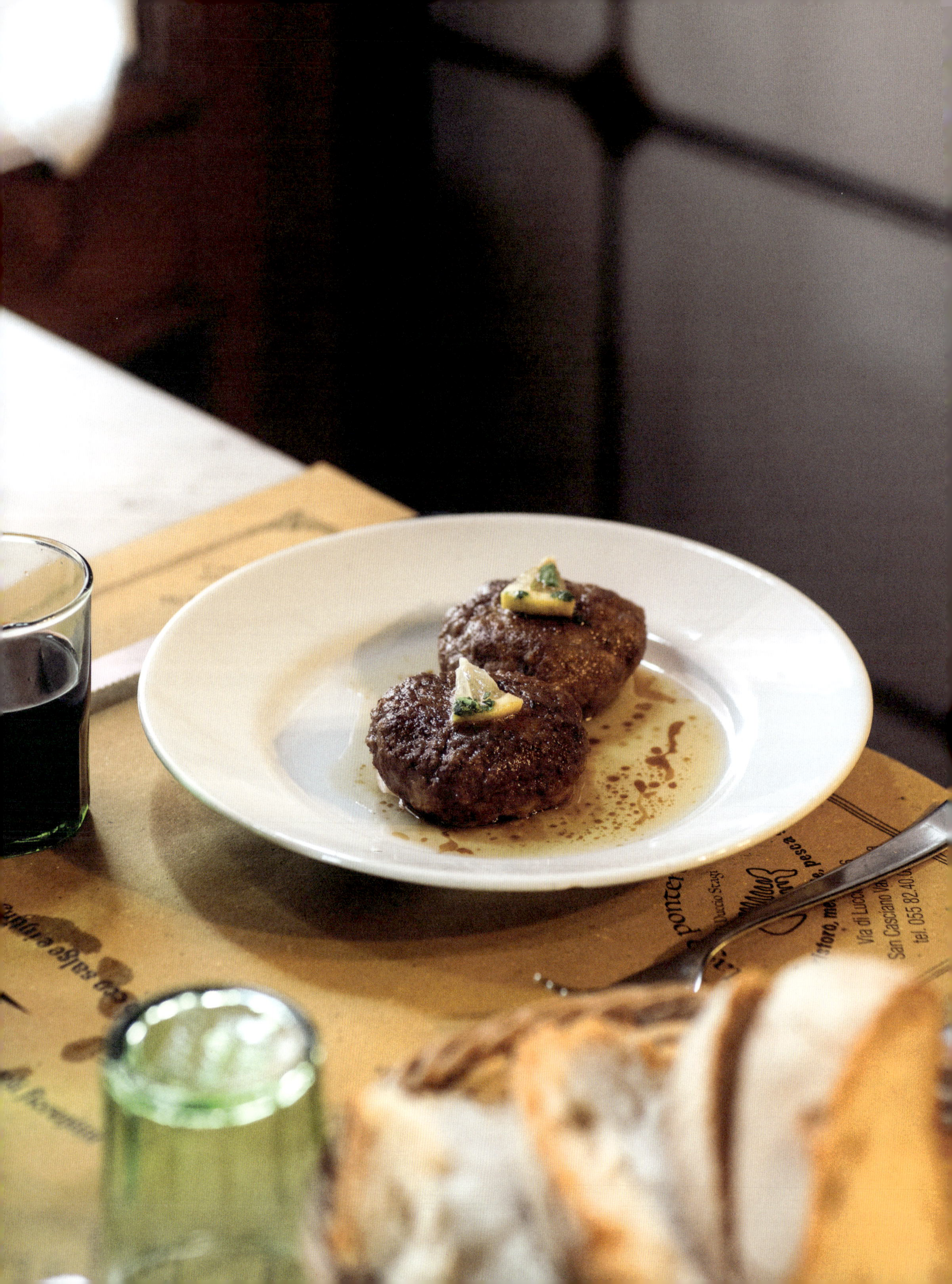

Polpette al limone

Lemony meatballs

SERVES 4

1–2 slices white bread (about 50 g/1¾ oz), crusts removed

50 ml (1¾ fl oz) warm full-fat milk

plain flour, for dusting

500 g (1 lb 2 oz) beef mince (or a mix of pork and beef)

zest of 2 lemons

juice of 1 lemon

4 tablespoons grated Grana Padano

sea salt and freshly ground black pepper

1 organic egg

olive oil

1 tablespoon butter

100 ml (3½ fl oz) water or chicken stock

3 lemon slices, about 5 mm (¼ inch) thick, cut into quarters to make triangles

---

DELICIOUS WITH:—
Garlicky rosemary cannellini beans (page 198), Tuscan roast potatoes (page 199), Greens tossed 'in the pan' (page 297) with garlic and chilli.

Lemony meatballs are something I always order if I see it on the menu at one of my favourite Florentine restaurants, Alla Vecchia Bettola, who have kindly shared their recipe with me here. Meatballs are quite common in Italian cuisine, originating long ago with the arrival of merchant spice traders – probably from Persia, who would have brought the idea of kofta with them. The famous early 20th century food writer Pellegrino Artusi begins his recipe for *polpette* by saying he would never be so pretentious as to try to teach anyone to make meatballs, as everyone knows perfectly well how to make them. But after some experience, I would entirely disagree: I have been trying to recreate this particular restaurant's perfectly lemony, soft yet compact meatballs for over three years now, never quite achieving their deliciously soft texture until they told me their secret – very plain, crustless white sliced bread soaked in warm milk (or microwaved for 1 minute). Swapping this for breadcrumbs has made all the difference.

Another bonus is that you can shape these meatballs a day ahead, leave them in the fridge, then simply bake them in about 20 minutes if you have guests. Their citrusy, light and meaty texture is always a hit, and perfect for a cosy evening meal.

PREPARATION:— 30 minutes, plus chilling time
COOKING:— 35 minutes

Place the bread in a bowl, pour the milk over and leave for 10 minutes. Once a little soaked, stir with a spoon until the bread and milk are fully amalgamated.

Dust a plate with plain flour to dip the meatballs into.

In a large bowl, mix the mince with the lemon zest, lemon juice, grated cheese and a generous pinch of salt and black pepper. Add the bread and milk and mix with your hands. Crack in the egg, add another generous amount of seasoning and mix together really well. Cover and leave to set in the fridge for 20 minutes, or even overnight, to make them much easier to shape.

Preheat the oven to 180°C (350°F) fan-forced.

Pick up enough mince to make a sphere the size of a golf ball. Roll between your hands into a compact ball, then flatten slightly between your palms. Roll each meatball in the flour, making sure they are well coated. Shake off any excess flour and set aside on a chopping board or plate.

In an ovenproof frying pan, heat a glug of olive oil over a medium heat. Working in batches, seal the meatballs on both sides for 1–2 minutes each, transferring them to a plate as you go. Don't have the heat too high, and don't get too much colour on them – we want the meatballs to be tender rather than crunchy.

Once all the meatballs are browned, melt the butter in the frying pan and stir well to deglaze and loosen all the meaty bits. Mix in the water or stock, scraping up anything left on the bottom of the pan. Return the meatballs to the pan and top each meatball with a little lemon wedge.

Put the pan in the oven and bake the meatballs for 15–20 minutes, until they are sizzling and the cooking liquid is bubbling.

Serve hot, with liberal amounts of the lemony cooking liquid.

Il polpettone di Carolina

Carolina's meatloaf

SERVES 4

500 g (1 lb 2 oz) beef mince, organic if possible

2 organic eggs

handful of chopped flat-leaf parsley, plus extra to serve

2 garlic cloves, grated

4 tablespoons breadcrumbs

big handful of grated parmesan or Grana Padano

sea salt and freshly ground black pepper

FOR THE SAUCE

olive oil

1 onion, finely chopped

1 carrot, finely chopped

a few thyme sprigs, leaves picked

1 garlic clove, grated

1 glass red wine

2 × 400 g (14 oz) tins of peeled plum tomatoes

400 g (14 oz) tin butter or cannellini beans, drained

A mainstay of Tuscan cooking, *polpettone* – meatloaf – was historically a way to use up precious leftovers from the previous day's *lesso* (boiled meats), but is nowadays a dish in itself made with good minced beef. This is the *polpettone* that my friend Carolina's mother used to make and now Carolina makes – an easy one-pot wonder I absolutely love. They sometimes stuff their *polpettone*, flattening out the meatloaf mixture on baking parchment and adding maybe two slices of ham and either four cubes of provolone or cheddar cheese or two peeled boiled eggs. I like this plainer version, but feel free to play around with fillings.

PREPARATION:– 15 minutes
COOKING:– 1 hour, plus resting time

Put the beef in a large bowl and use the end of a wooden spoon or your hands to break up the meat. Crack the eggs in and mix together. Add the parsley, garlic, breadcrumbs, grated cheese and a generous amount of salt and black pepper. Bring together either with your hands or a spoon, not working the mixture too much, or the *polpettone* will be quite dense when cooked.

Tip the mixture onto a large piece of baking parchment. If you are making a plain *polpettone*, lift the sides of the parchment and roll the *polpettone* into a log, patting the ends to smooth them out. (If you are putting fillings inside, flatten the meat, lay the ham across the centre, arrange the cheese or egg on top, then roll the meat into a log around the filling.) Once you're happy with the shape, roll the baking parchment around the *polpettone*. Transfer to the fridge while you prepare the sauce (or even overnight if you prefer).

Heat a few glugs of olive oil in a flameproof casserole dish, then add the onion, carrot, thyme leaves and a pinch of salt. Stir and leave to sweat over a medium heat for about 5 minutes, then stir in the garlic and cook for a few more minutes.

Pour in the wine, turn the heat up to high, then leave the alcohol to evaporate for 5 minutes. Stir in the tinned tomatoes and a generous pinch of salt, breaking up the whole tomatoes with the end of a wooden spoon. Half-fill each tomato tin with water, swirl it around and pour the tomatoey water into the dish, stirring it in. Cook, uncovered, over a medium heat for 10 minutes.

Meanwhile, preheat the oven to 180°C (350°F) fan-forced.

Unwrap the *polpettone* and place it in the dish, on top of the sauce. Ladle or spoon some of the sauce over the meatloaf, then transfer to the oven and bake for 15 minutes.

Turn the oven down to 160°C (315°F) and bake the meatloaf for another 25 minutes.

Add the beans to the pan and stir them through the tomato sauce. Bake for a further 15 minutes.

Remove the meatloaf from the oven and leave to rest for 10 minutes or so, before serving in slices topped with the sauce, beans and an extra sprinkling of parsley.

> **DELICIOUS WITH:–** Greens tossed 'in the pan' (page 197) with garlic and chilli.

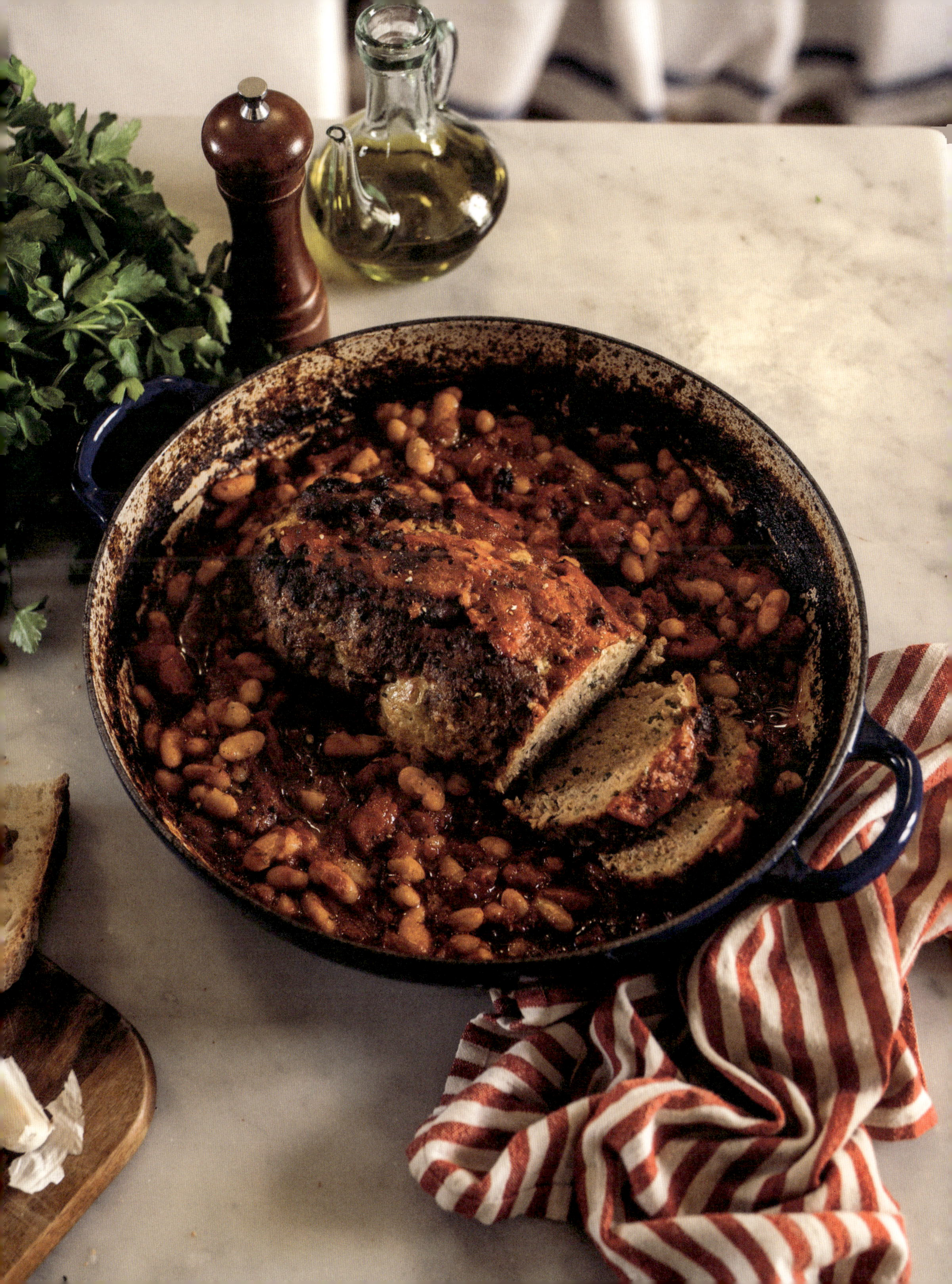

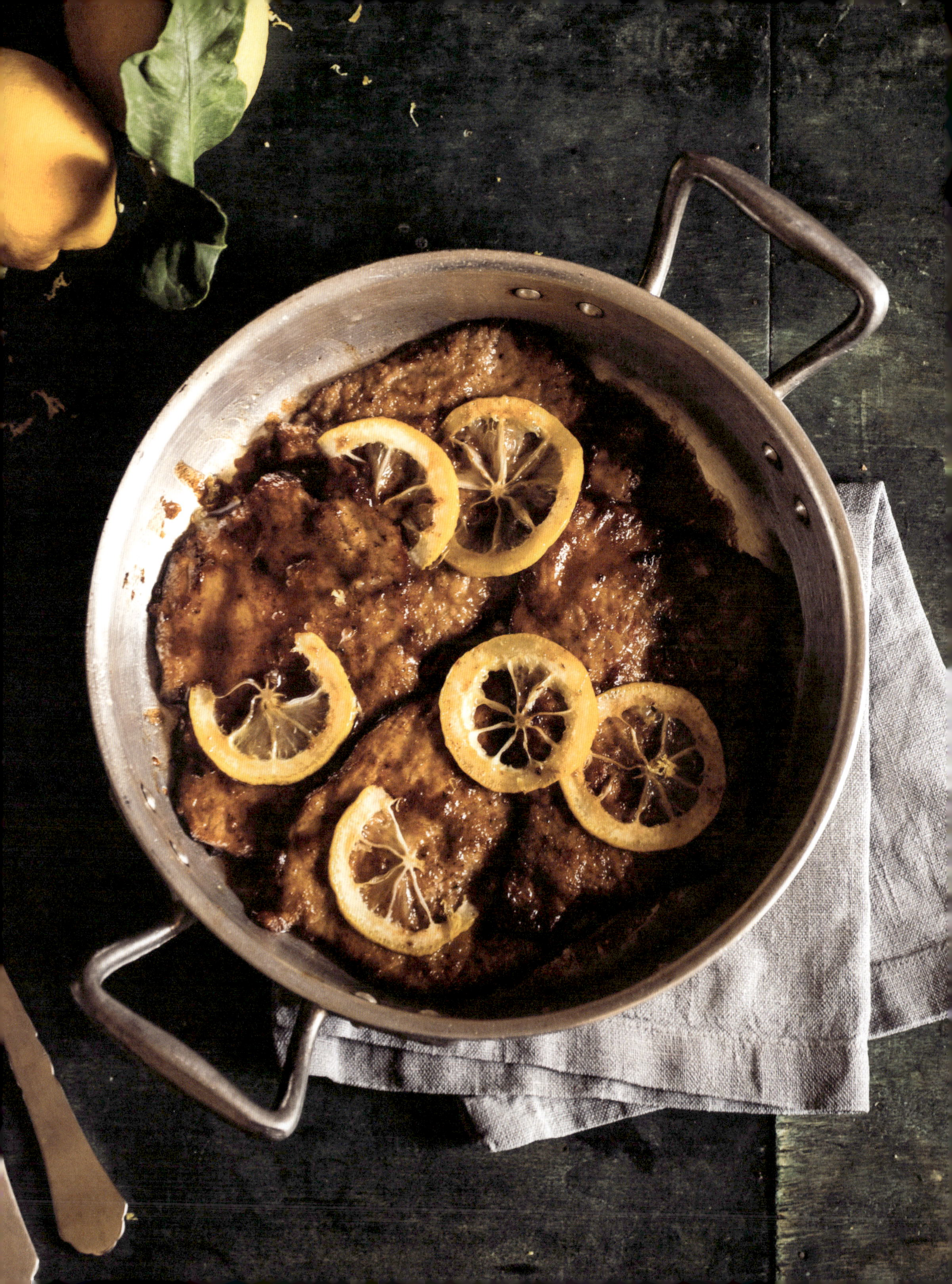

Scaloppine al limone

Lemony escalopes

SERVES 4

plain flour, for dusting

4 veal or lean beef escalopes

sea salt and freshly ground black pepper

2 tablespoons olive oil

1 tablespoon unsalted butter

1 glass white wine

juice and zest of 1 lemon

4–6 thinly sliced discs of lemon

In Tuscany, *scaloppine* is a classic and popular dish both at home and when dining out. My friend Carolina's grandmother would often make it for us 'al limone' if I went to her place for lunch after school. It is the dish I am most likely to order if I see it on a restaurant menu as it is rich, delicious and aromatic – it's also a fairly safe bet if you're in an unknown eatery.

I love making this dish at home as it is tasty and very quick to throw together. The escalopes also reheat really nicely if you want to prepare them ahead of time.

PREPARATION:– 15 minutes
COOKING:– 15 minutes

Cover a dinner plate in a thick layer of flour.

Tenderise each escalope by placing it on a clean chopping board and lightly bashing across it with a rolling pin, then flipping it over and repeating on the other side.

Season each escalope with salt and black pepper. Dip each one in the flour to lightly coat, shaking off any excess, and transfer to a separate plate.

In a wide frying pan, heat the olive oil and butter and swirl around the pan to make sure the base is entirely covered in a little fat. Once hot, fry the lemon slices for 1 minute on each side so they get a little colour, then transfer to a plate. Add the escalopes to the pan and sear for 1 minute on each side, until lightly golden. (If searing in batches, add a teaspoon more butter and drizzle of olive oil in between.)

Return all the veal to the pan, turn down the heat and pour in the wine and lemon juice. Sprinkle with the lemon zest, season with salt and black pepper and leave to bubble for about 5 minutes, until the sauce is reduced and a little thickened.

Remove from the heat and serve.

DELICIOUS WITH:– Tuscan roast potatoes (page 199) and A very good green salad (page 189).

Pollo ai carciofi

Chicken with artichokes

SERVES 4

1 organic chicken, about 1.5–2 kg (3 lb 5 oz–4 lb 6 oz), cut into pieces, or a mix of thighs and drumsticks

2 tablespoons white wine vinegar

olive oil

sea salt and freshly ground black pepper

2 garlic cloves, crushed

4 Sardinian spiky artichokes

1 lemon, halved

2 glasses white wine

handful of roughly chopped flat-leaf parsley

DELICIOUS WITH:— This dish goes well with something as simple as a Cabbage, apple & walnut salad (page 202). If you want a more substantial meal, it's fab with Tuscan roast potatoes (page 199) and Roasted baby onions (page 194) or Dada's baked leeks in bechamel (page 134).

This is a variation on a local classic, rabbit with artichokes. I love rabbit – it's cooked often and in lots of delicious ways around us, but I find it hard to get outside of Italy, so I have substituted it with chicken. This dish calls for fresh artichokes, which may sound daunting to prepare, but the process is quite meditative and not too laborious once you have the hang of it. At a pinch you could use jarred artichoke hearts, though you would need to drain them thoroughly and pat them well with paper towel to remove any excess oil before tipping them directly into the pan after you've browned the chicken, then searing them briefly before adding the chicken back in.

PREPARATION:– 20 minutes, plus marinating time
BROWNING & ROASTING:– 50 minutes

Remove the chicken from the fridge at least 1 hour before cooking to come up to room temperature.

Trim off any excess skin or gristly bits, then place in a shallow dish large enough to hold all the chicken. Pour the vinegar and a generous glug of olive oil over and toss, making sure all the chicken pieces are well coated. Add a good pinch of salt, along with the garlic, and toss again. Leave to marinate for 1 hour out of the fridge, or even covered overnight in the fridge.

Prepare the artichokes as instructed in the Artichoke frittata recipe on page 133, cutting them into quarters once you've removed the hairy choke, then placing them in a bowl and squeezing the lemon juice over them. Set aside.

When you're ready to cook, preheat the oven to 180°C (350°F) fan-forced.

Drizzle about 1 tablespoon olive oil into an ovenproof frying pan or flameproof casserole dish. Working in batches and starting skin side down, brown the chicken pieces on all sides, using tongs to turn them over, taking care as the fat will render and spit as it begins to sizzle. Once each piece of chicken is nicely golden, return it to the marinade dish.

Add the artichokes to the pan and fry over a medium heat until lightly browned on both sides, seasoning well with salt and black pepper.

Return the chicken to the pan, with all its marinating juices, mixing well. Pour the wine over and leave to evaporate for 3–5 minutes.

Cover the pan, then transfer to the oven and bake for 20 minutes.

Remove the pan from the oven. Carefully tip the pan to one side and, using a serving spoon, scoop up some of the juices and pour them back over the chicken. Bake, uncovered, for another 10 minutes, or until the chicken is browned and cooked through.

Top with the chopped parsley and serve immediately.

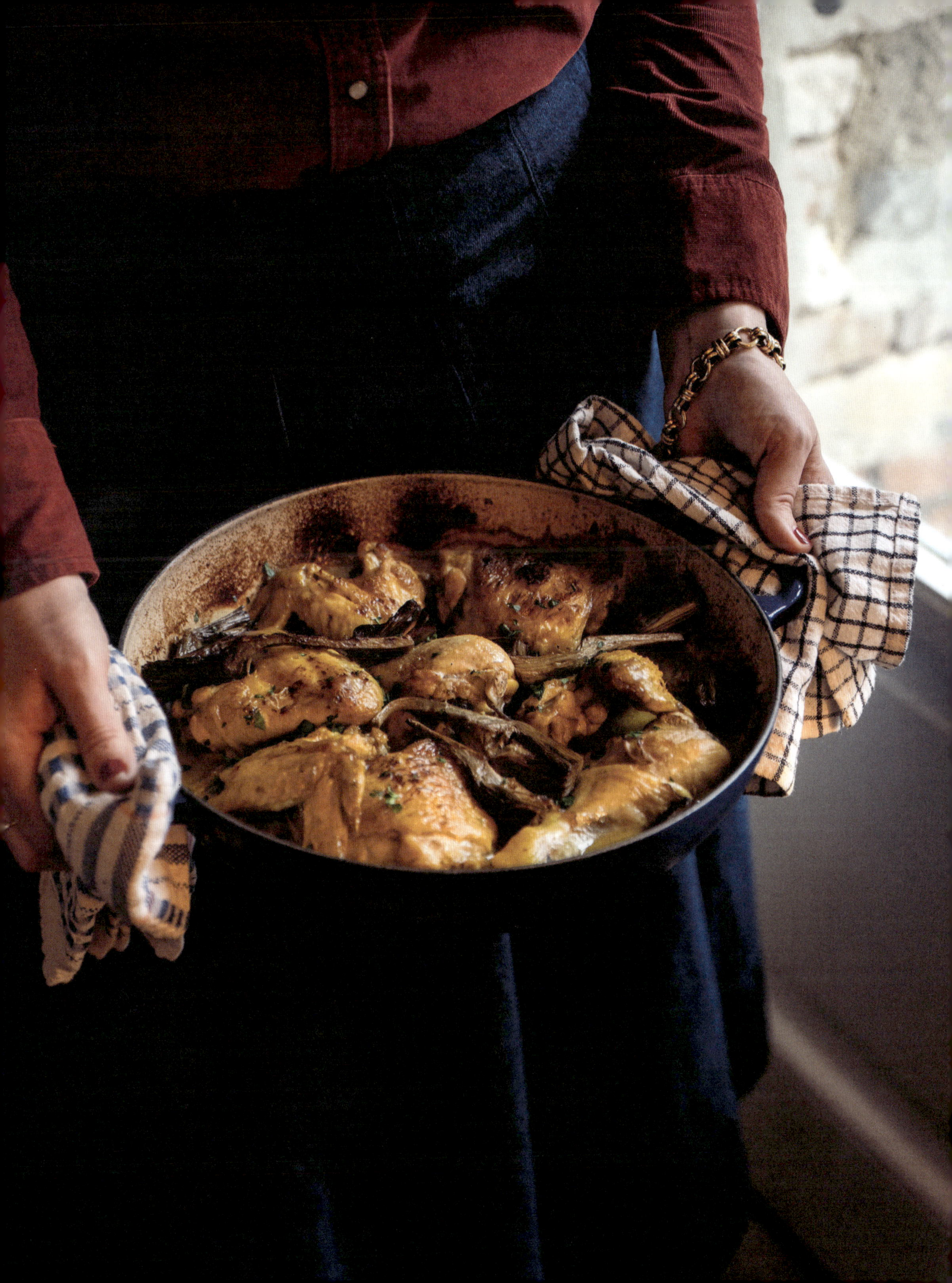

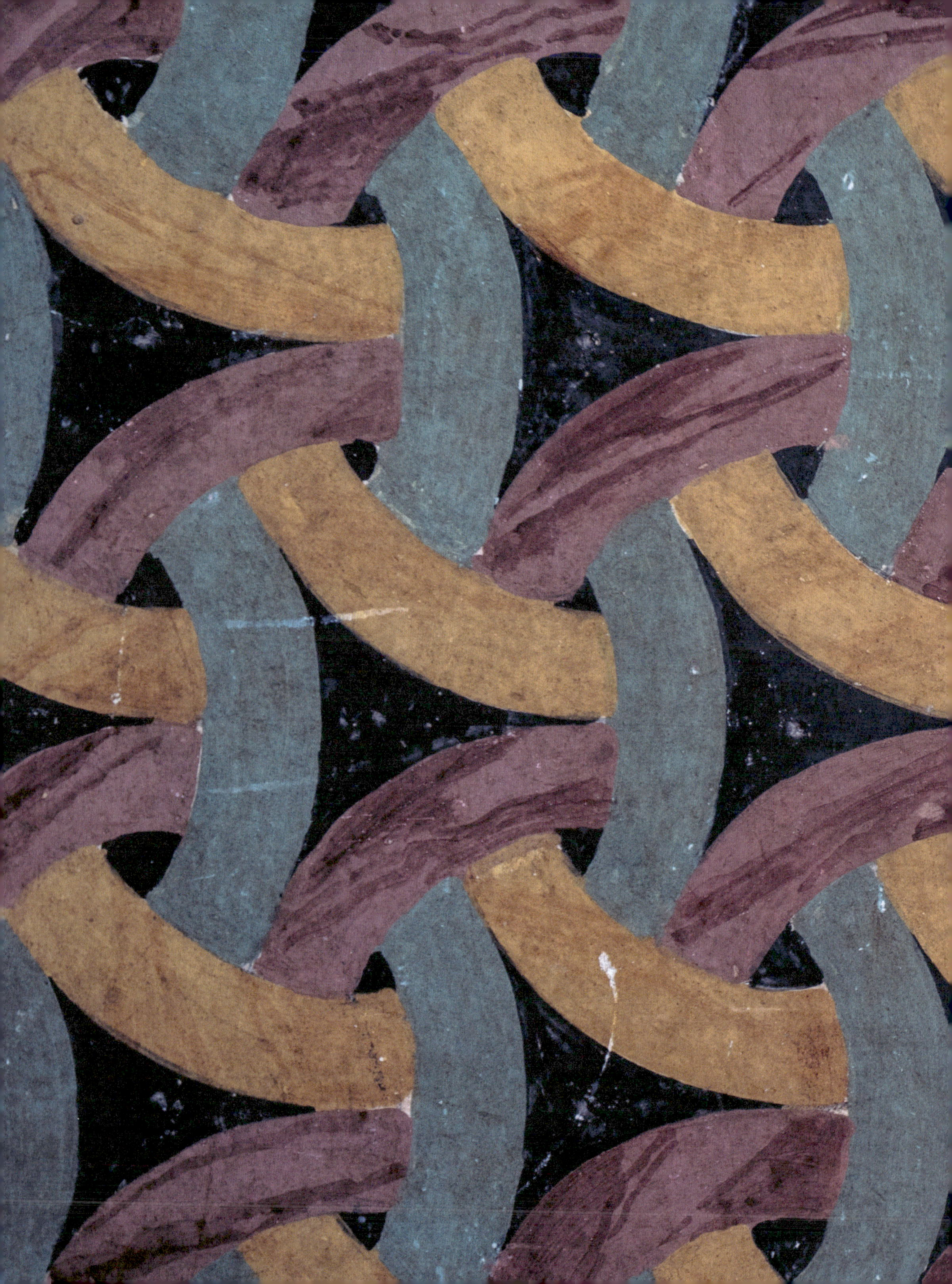

CONTORNI

SIDES

Due to one's usually having had an *aperitivo*, antipasto and possibly a *primo* by the time the *secondo* comes around, Tuscan cuisine usually calls for meaty mains to be served simply and on their own, sometimes with a few green salad leaves to prettify the plate or perhaps a dish of white beans.

When in a restaurant, the *contorni* – side dishes – is often the section of the menu I am most interested in, as it's where you'll usually find a seasonal vegetable celebrated in various ways – a crisp radicchio or artichoke salad with shavings of parmesan, or *carciofi trifolati* (sautéed artichokes with garlic and parsley), leading me to order a *contorno* as a starter.

However, the stalwarts of *contorni Toscani* are ubiquitous year round: simple *patate al forno* (very salty and delicious roast potatoes); *fagioli al fiasco* (slow-braised rosemary-infused cannellini beans dressed in very good olive oil); *bietole* (chard) or *spinaci* (spinach) cooked in *padella* ('in the pan') with a little garlic and a whole chilli, and served at room temperature dressed with olive oil and sea salt.

My usual preference is a roast potato and some greens, but if you order more than one *contorno* per person the waiter will usually look at you as though you're mad, as it's bound to be too much food. But I like the feasting feel of lots of things to put on one's plate, so will always flout tradition and make several side dishes whenever I am cooking from this book.

ANTIPASTI THAT COULD ALSO BE USED AS A SIDE:–

FENNEL IN LEMONY ANCHOVY SAUCE (page 54) – This would be delicious with Herby roast pork loin (page 170), Florentine steak (page 166), Chicken with artichokes (page 184) or Sage, spinach & quail egg pie.

BAKED PORCINI WITH CHEESE, HONEY AND THYME (page 57) – Wonderful with Lemony escalopes (page 183), Chicken with artichokes (page 184).

OTHER DISHES THAT COULD ALSO BE USED AS A SIDE:–

BUTTERY POLENTA – Make the polenta as described on page 119 and serve with Chicken with artichokes (page 184), Black pepper stew (page 176) or Claudia's chestnut & mushroom 'peposo' (page 140).

SAUSAGE, LENTIL & CHICKPEA STEW (page 173) – Omit the sausages and the stew would be a delicious accompaniment to Herby roast pork loin (page 170), Chicken with artichokes (page 184), Black pepper stew (page 176), Claudia's chestnut & mushroom 'peposo' (page 140), Dada's baked leeks in bechamel (page 134) or Sage, spinach & quail egg pie (page 137).

DADA'S BAKED LEEKS IN BECHAMEL (page 134) – A hearty, cheesy dish to go with Herby roast pork loin (page 170), Black pepper stew (page 176) or Chicken with artichokes (page 184) or even a Florentine steak (page 166).

Cooked contorni are almost always served at room temperature, though of course you can break this rule if you prefer your veg piping hot.

A VERY GOOD GREEN SALAD

Insalata verde

1 head of lettuce of your choice, leaves separated

1 handful of lamb's lettuce (optional)

1 teaspoon fine sea salt

1 tablespoon white wine vinegar

3 tablespoons very good olive oil

If you've ever asked yourself why salads in Italy are so flavoursome, the answer is well distributed salt – and lots of it. When she needs to *condire* (dress) a salad, I've seen my friend Chiara put about a teaspoon of fine salt in a tablespoon, cover this in white wine vinegar and then whisk the two together in the spoon with a fork to allow the salt to dissolve, and so coat the salad leaves really well. It's only at this point that any olive oil is added, as it would otherwise prevent the salt dissolving.

This is a rough recipe for a very good Tuscan green salad to go with most things.

PREPARATION:– 5–10 minutes

Wash and thoroughly dry your salad leaves and place in a salad bowl.

Put the salt and vinegar in a small glass. Use a fork to agitate the salt and encourage it to dissolve, then leave it for a few minutes. Once you can no longer see any salt granules, tip the mixture over the salad and toss thoroughly.

Drizzle with the olive oil and toss again. Serve immediately.

> **DELICIOUS WITH:–** This salad is wonderful with most things. You'll see it pictured on page 167 with Florentine steak.

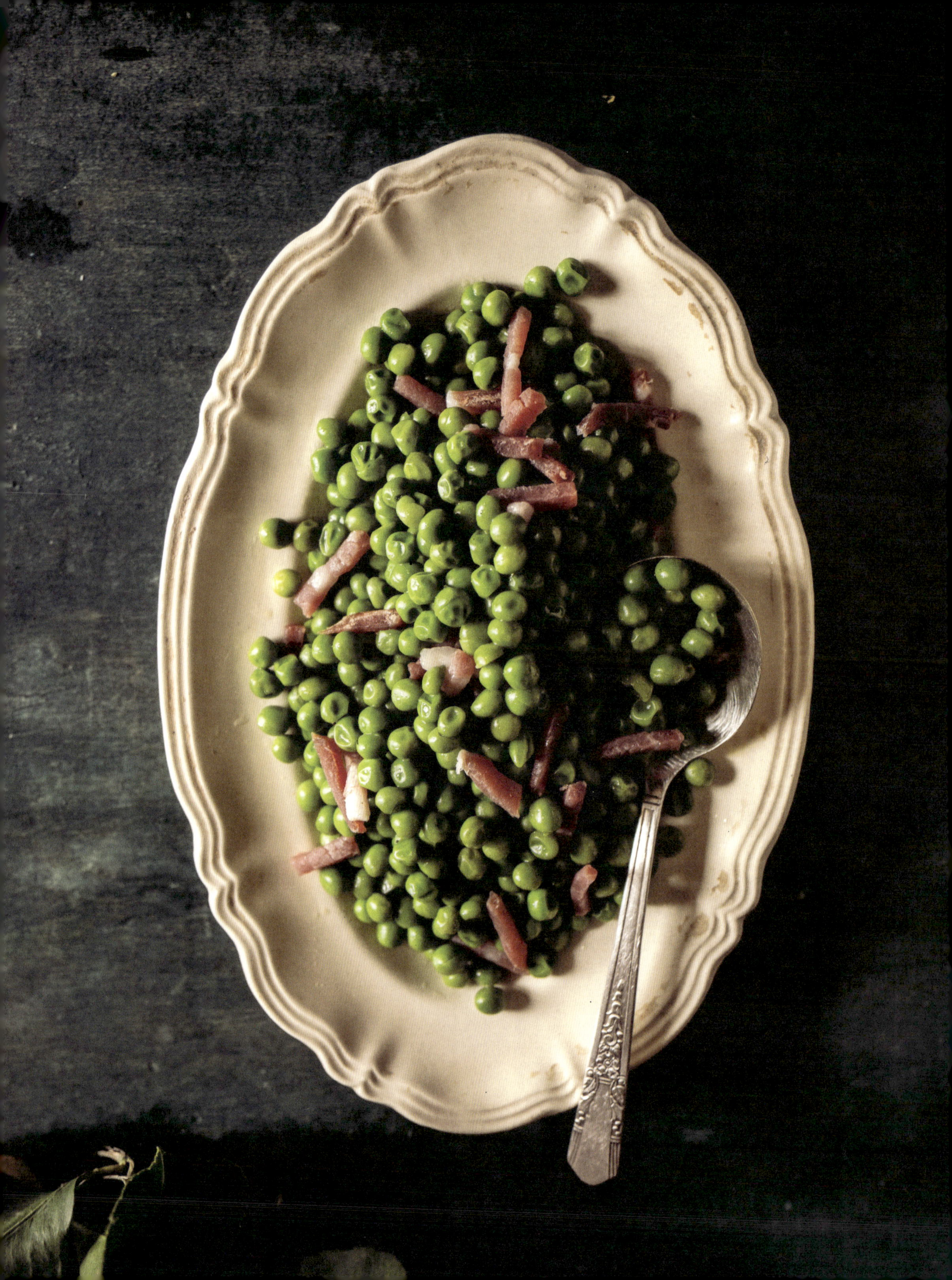

Piselli alla fiorentina

Florentine peas with ham

SERVES 4

400 g (14 oz) frozen peas

4 tablespoons olive oil

2 garlic cloves, peeled and lightly crushed with the side of a knife

1 teaspoon caster sugar

olive oil

sea salt and freshly ground black pepper

60 g (2 oz) prosciutto di Parma, very finely diced

This is a typical side dish in Florence, at its most delicious in spring when peas are having their short season, but it is made year round with frozen peas as well. It's a wonderful combination of sweet and savoury as the peas' natural sweetness is enhanced with a tiny bit of sugar, which goes very well with the salty prosciutto.

PREPARATION:– 10 minutes
COOKING:– 20 minutes

Put the frozen peas (don't thaw them) in a wide frying pan with the garlic, sugar, olive oil and a generous pinch of salt and grind of black pepper.

Pour in just enough water to cover the peas, turn the heat up to medium and allow to warm through very slowly. Once hot and slightly bubbling, leave to slowly simmer for 10 minutes.

Switch the heat off and leave the peas to cool a little for 10 minutes or so.

Stir the prosciutto through and serve hot, or at room temperature.

Carciofi trifolati

Artichokes with parsley & garlic

SERVES 4

1 lemon

6 Sardinian spiky artichokes

olive oil

1 garlic clove, peeled and lightly crushed with the edge of a knife

sea salt and freshly ground black pepper

1 small handful of flat-leaf parsley leaves, finely chopped

Trifolare in Italian means to cook a thinly sliced seasonal vegetable in a frying pan over a lively flame with olive oil and garlic, finished off with chopped flat-leaf parsley. In winter, cooking fresh artichokes in this way gives you a wonderful side dish for simply grilled or roasted meat or fish. I also love treating this as a *piatto di mezzo* ('halfway dish') and having it as my main alongside a hunk of good pecorino and fresh bread doused in olive oil.

PREPARATION:– 25 minutes
COOKING:– 20 minutes

Fill a bowl with cold water, squeeze the juice of half the lemon into it and drop the half lemon shell into the water. Prepare the artichokes as described in the Chicken with artichokes recipe on page 184. As you chop the stems and remove the hairy chokes, rub the cut surfaces with the other lemon half and drop the artichoke pieces into the lemony water, to stop them turning brown. You can leave the artichokes in the lemony water in the fridge for up to a day if you want to prepare this step ahead of time.

In a wide frying pan with a lid, heat a few glugs of olive oil with the garlic clove and a pinch of salt. Once sizzling, turn the garlic clove over. Using a slotted spoon, transfer the artichoke pieces to the pan, retaining their lemony soaking water.

Cook over a lively flame for 5 minutes, stirring occasionally. Once the artichokes have a little colour, add two ladlefuls of their lemony soaking water and a generous pinch of salt and black pepper. Partially cover with the lid, turn down the heat and simmer for 15 minutes, until you can easily pierce the artichokes with the tip of a knife.

Stir the parsley through, transfer to a plate and serve either hot, or at room temperature. These are also very good the next day.

DELICIOUS WITH:–
Good bread and cheese,
Lemony escalopes (page 183),
Florentine steak (page 166).

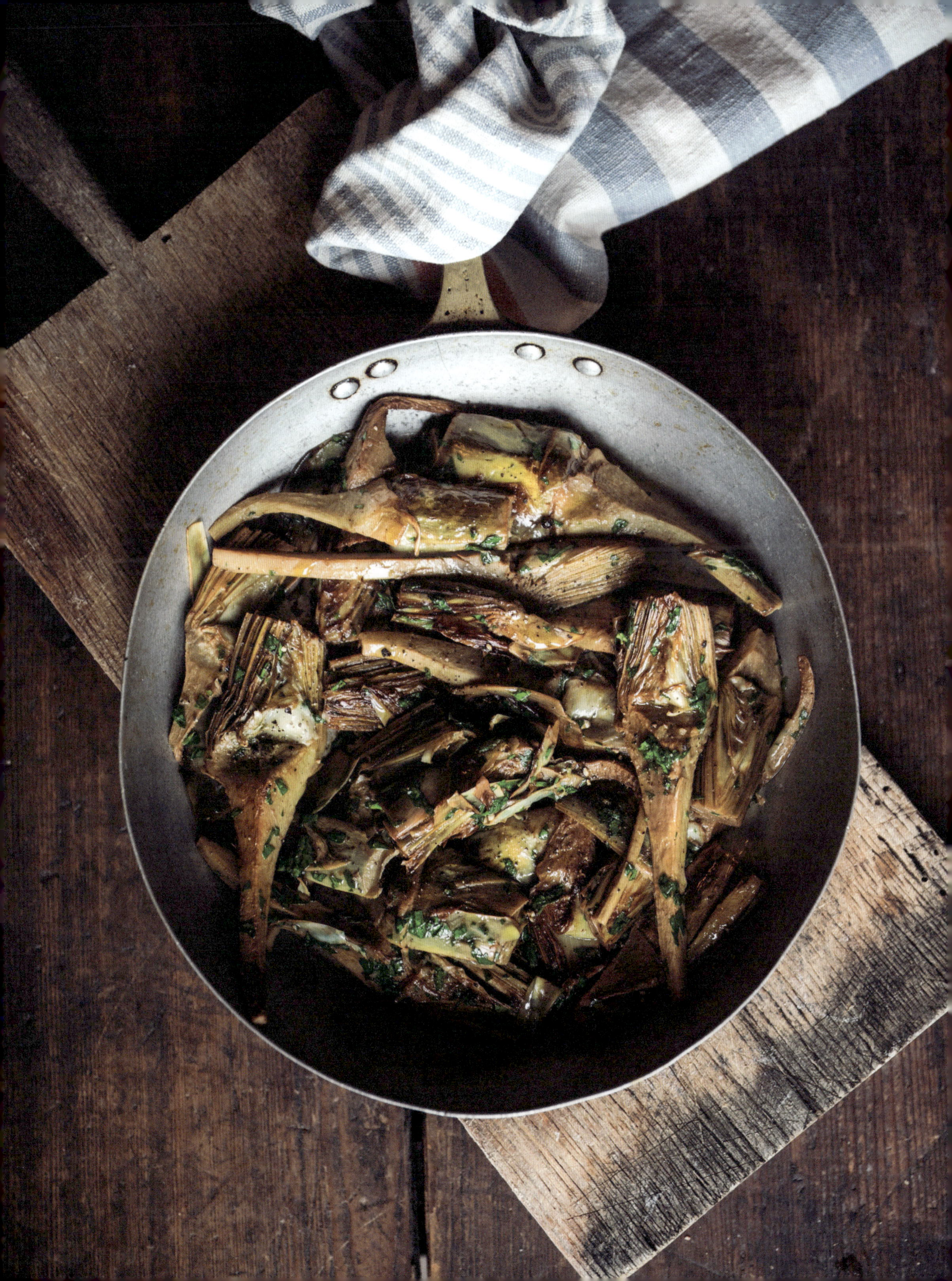

Cipolline al forno

Roasted baby onions

SERVES 4

400 g (14 oz) baby onions or golden shallots

olive oil

sea salt

1 glass white wine

In Italy it is possible to buy small baby onions ready-skinned, making this a supremely easy side dish to pull together quickly. Unfortunately, these are harder to get outside of Italy, so you'll need to peel your own baby onions or shallots, making it a slightly longer process. It's well worth it, however, for these *agrodolce* (sweet and sour) treats, which go so well with most centrepiece dishes.

PREPARATION:– 10 minutes (even less if you find ready-peeled onions)
COOKING:– 35 minutes

Preheat the oven to 200°C (400°F) fan-forced. (If you happen to be baking another dish in the oven at the same time at a lower heat, don't worry too much, as these onions are pretty forgiving – just roast them a little longer than instructed below.)

Peel the onions of their outer layer, keeping them whole. Toss them in a roasting tin with a good glug of olive oil and several generous pinches of salt. Roast for 10–15 minutes, until the onions get a little colour.

Remove the roasting tin from the oven, toss the onions a few times and pour the wine over them. Roast for a further 20 minutes, or until the onions are soft and browned and the wine has almost completely reduced away.

Serve hot, alongside your main dish.

DELICIOUS WITH:– Herby roast pork loin (page 170), Black pepper stew (page 176), Claudia's chestnut & mushroom 'peposo' (page 140), Lemony meatballs (page 179), Carolina's meatloaf (page 180).

Finocchi al forno

Baked fennel with chilli & parmesan

SERVES 4

2–3 fennel bulbs

1 garlic clove, finely crushed or chopped

½ teaspoon chilli flakes, or to taste

sea salt and freshly ground black pepper

olive oil

1 tablespoon unsalted butter

a hunk of parmesan

I love baked fennel. Its aniseed-y tones are mellowed out by long cooking and their texture and mild flavour are wonderful when paired with cheese. This dish is a great accompaniment to most meaty mains, but I'll also often eat it on its own, maybe with a salad, on a winter's night if I'm by myself or just with my family.

PREPARATION:– 10 minutes
COOKING:– 25 minutes

Preheat the oven to 180°C (350°F) fan-forced.

Bring a large saucepan of well-salted water to a rolling boil.

Slice off the woody base of each fennel bulb. Remove any woody tops, and the outer layer if it is very thick and tough, so you are left with the tender core. (If your fennel is small, you may not need to remove a layer.)

Slice the fennel bulbs in half lengthways and place cut side down on a chopping board. Slice lengthways into wedges.

Add the fennel to the pan of boiling water and blanch for 5 minutes, then drain well in a colander.

Transfer to an ovenproof dish and toss with the garlic, chilli flakes and a generous pinch of salt and black pepper. Drizzle with olive oil and toss again. Dot the butter over the fennel, then grate the parmesan in a generous, even layer over the fennel.

Bake for 20 minutes, until the top is bubbling and golden.

DELICIOUS WITH:– Herby roast pork loin (page 170), Carolina's meatloaf (page 180), Lemony meatballs (page 179), Lemony escalopes (page 183), Black pepper stew (page 176), Florentine steak (page 166), or simply on its own with A very good green salad (page 189).

VARIATIONS:– Turn this into a gratin by pouring 200 ml (7 fl oz) double cream over the fennel before you grate the parmesan over the top. I sometimes also sprinkle on 2 tablespoons breadcrumbs for extra texture. You can also play around with spices by adding ½ teaspoon ground turmeric, or a pinch of grated nutmeg, which is particularly delicious if you are making a creamy gratin.

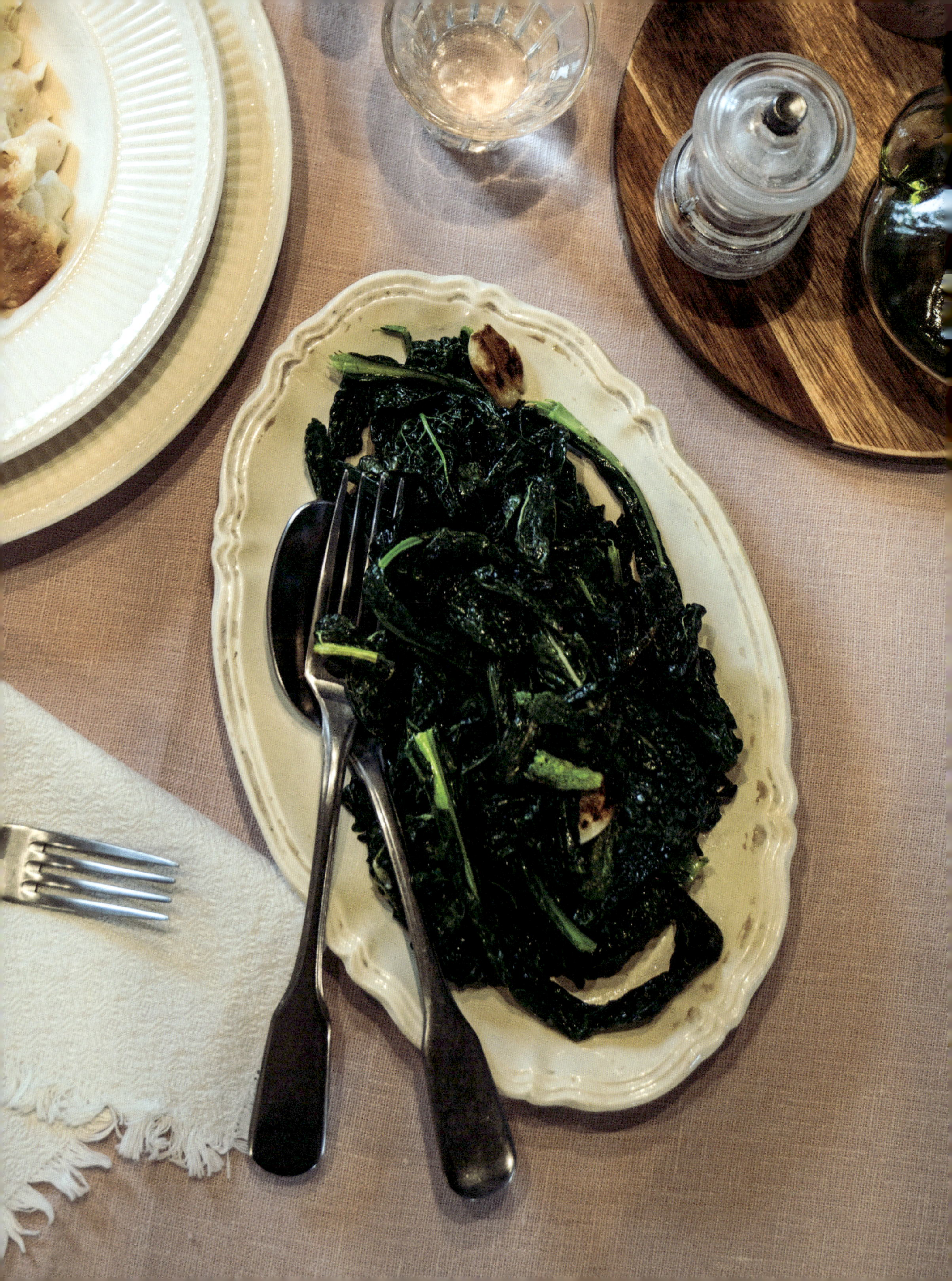

Verdure saltate in padella

Greens tossed 'in the pan'

SERVES 4

good-quality olive oil

2 garlic cloves, peeled and lightly crushed with the side of a knife

pinch of chilli flakes, or 1 small dried chilli

sea salt and freshly ground black pepper

CHOOSE YOUR VEGETABLE

1 big bunch, ½ head or about 400 g (14 oz), of any of the following:
- broccoli, cut into florets
- cavolo nero, leaves removed from stalks
- cabbage (white, sweetheart, savoy)
- chard (silverbeet/Swiss chard)
- spinach leaves
- brussels sprouts, bottoms trimmed

Spinach or any leafy greens such as chard (*bietole*), blanched and then finished in a frying pan with a whole clove of garlic, olive oil and chilli, is a very common side dish on any Tuscan menu and goes perfectly with a Florentine steak (page 166), roast chicken or *tagliata di manzo* (sliced steak). I also find this a fabulous way to prepare most green vegetables, and often cook them this way. Softer ones can be cooked straight in the pan with a couple of tablespoons of water, while tougher veg just need to be blanched in boiling salted water for a few minutes before tossing in the pan.

PREPARATION:– 5–10 minutes
COOKING:– 5–10 minutes

Prepare your chosen vegetable. If using broccoli, cavolo nero or particularly tough savoy cabbage, blanch these in a saucepan of boiling salted water for 3 minutes. Drain and set aside, after slicing the cavolo nero or cabbage leaves into ribbons about 2 cm (¾ inch) wide.

If using chard or spinach, slice into ribbons about 2 cm (¾ inch) wide. If using white or sweetheart cabbage (or a tender savoy cabbage), slice in half lengthways, then slice across into ribbons. If using brussels sprouts, either cut these in half or into ribbons. Set aside.

Put a wide frying pan, preferably one with a lid, over a medium heat. Add three glugs of olive oil, the garlic cloves and chilli. Leave to heat for a minute or so, then add the sliced greens – the oil should sizzle when you add the vegetables. Stir-fry for a couple of minutes, adding a generous pinch of salt and some black pepper. Add 4 tablespoons of water and another drizzle of olive oil, turn down the heat, then cover and cook for 3–5 minutes.

Remove the lid from the pan, give the vegetables a stir and let the liquid evaporate for a few minutes, stirring often. Once the liquid has completely reduced and the greens are cooked through, taste and adjust the seasoning as necessary. Some leave the garlic in the greens; I discard it at this point.

Transfer to a serving plate and serve hot or at room temperature, drizzled with a little more olive oil.

DELICIOUS WITH:– Savoy cabbage tossed in the pan is fabulous with Lemony meatballs (pictured on page 171), Garlicky rosemary cannellini beans (page 198), Black pepper stew (page 176). I also love it with extra chilli alongside Herby roast pork loin (page 170).

Cavolo nero tossed in the pan is wonderful served alongside Baked fennel & pasta with bechamel (page 144), Herby roast pork loin or any of the recipes in the Piatti di Mezzo and Secondi di Carne chapter.

Brussels sprouts tossed in the pan is lovely as a side to Herby roast pork loin (page 170).

Fagioli al rosmarino e aglio

Garlicky rosemary cannellini beans

SERVES 4

5 tablespoons olive oil

2 rosemary sprigs, finely chopped

2 × 400 g (14 oz) tins cannellini beans

2 garlic cloves, finely crushed or chopped

sea salt and freshly ground black pepper

Fagioli al fiasco are so synonymous with Tuscany that elsewhere around Italy, Tuscans are known as *mangiafagioli* or bean eaters. A fiasco is a sturdy glass decanter in which beans were traditionally braised overnight over a very low heat with some garlic and rosemary sprigs. Even when using more modern appliances such as a saucepan, the key to *fagioli al fiasco* is to cook the dried beans over a heat so low that the beans are never agitated – never at a rolling boil.

When I'm short on time and haven't remembered to soak dried beans overnight, this method below is how I get deliciously oily rosemary beans. I love this recipe as it's incredibly tasty and very quick to prepare.

PREPARATION:– 20 minutes
COOKING:– 5–10 minutes

Put the olive oil and finely chopped rosemary in a frying pan over a medium heat. Once the oil starts sizzling, switch the heat off and leave to infuse for 15 minutes.

Drain the cannellini beans and rinse under cold running water.

Switch the oil back on and stir in the crushed garlic. Leave the oil to warm up again over a medium heat, then cook for 2–3 minutes.

Stir in the beans and a few generous pinches of salt and black pepper, mixing well. Leave to heat through for a few minutes, adding a drizzle more oil if the beans are looking dry.

Serve piping hot.

DELICIOUS WITH:– Claudia's chestnut & mushroom 'peposo' (page 140), Black pepper stew (page 176), Lemony meatballs (page 179), Herby roast pork loin (page 170).

Patate al forno

Tuscan roast potatoes

SERVES 4

1 kg (2 lb 3 oz) waxy potatoes
olive oil
fine sea salt

Patate al forno are, along with beans, one of the most ubiquitous sides in Tuscany. Their salty, soft, carby texture is the perfect accompaniment to the region's hardier meatier fare. I love them as they don't need peeling or parboiling – simply chop them into small pieces, season with indecent amounts of salt and shove into a hot oven.

PREPARATION:– 15 minutes
COOKING:– 45 minutes to 1 hour

Preheat the oven to 190°C (375°F) fan-forced.

Run the potatoes under cold running water to make sure they are clean. Cut into halves if the potatoes are small, or quarters if medium sized. If the potatoes are large, cut them into sixths by slicing in half lengthways and then across. You want the chopped pieces to be about the size of a ping pong ball.

Place in a roasting tin large enough for all the potatoes to sit in a single layer, without being too crowded. Drizzle with three good glugs of olive oil, season liberally with fine salt and toss.

Roast for 45 minutes to 1 hour, tossing halfway during baking, until browned and cooked through.

Serve immediately.

DELICIOUS WITH:– Lemony escalopes (page 183), Black pepper stew (page 176), Lemony meatballs (page 179), Greens tossed 'in the pan' (page 197), Carolina's meatloaf (page 180), Chicken with artichokes (page 184).

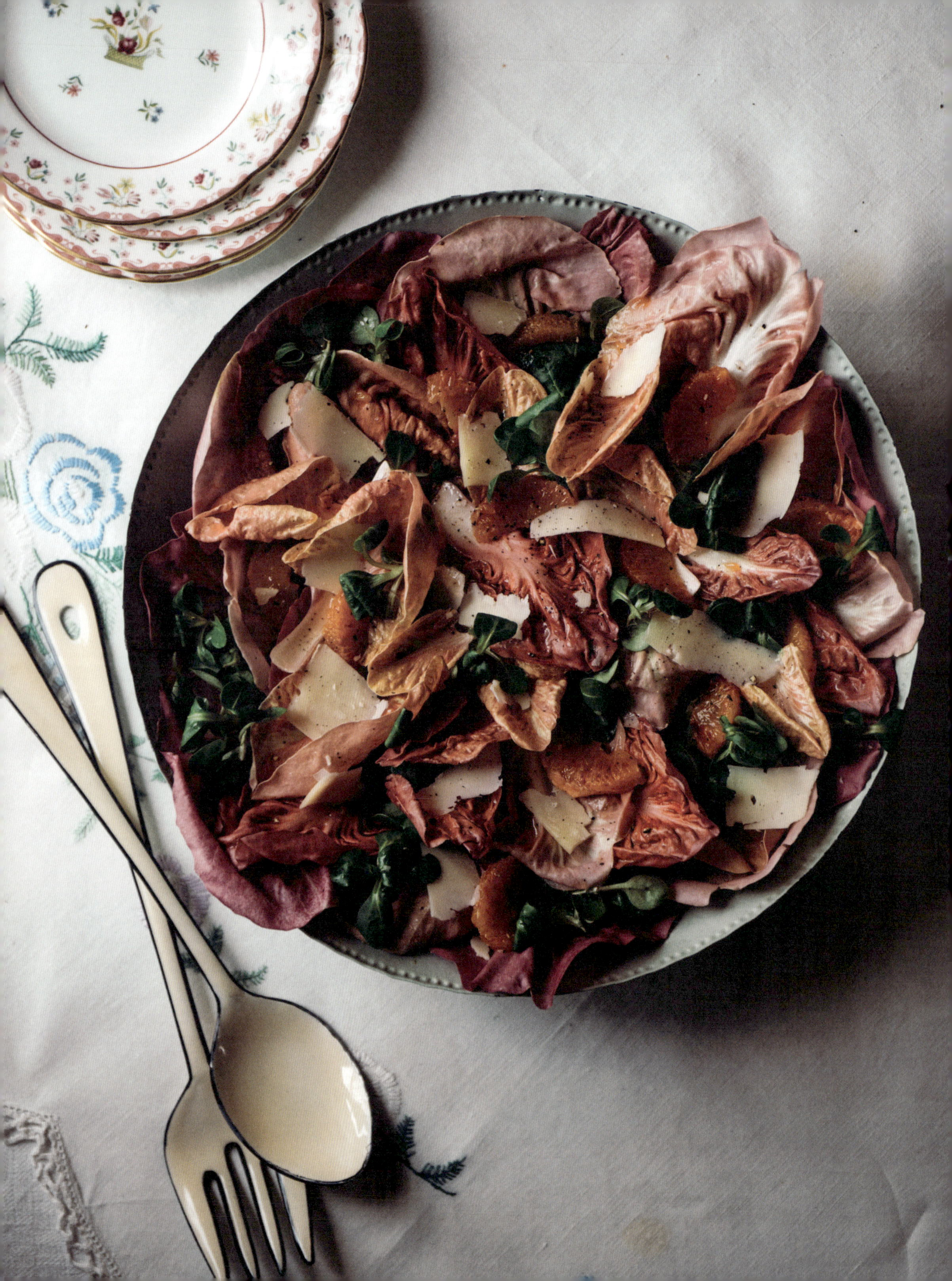

Insalata di radicchio e arance rosse

Pink radicchio & blood orange salad

SERVES 4

2 heads of pink radicchio

large handful of lamb's lettuce or watercress

hunk of aged pecorino or parmesan (manchego or comté would also work well)

1 blood orange

3 tablespoons olive oil

juice of ½ lemon

sea salt

I love how the colder months send us bright pops of colour just when we need cheering up, blood orange and pink radicchio being two of my favourites. This salad is a celebration of these vibrant ingredients and is also a great combination of flavours. If you can't find a blood orange, you can simply use a regular one – in fact, this salad is also delicious with no orange at all.

PREPARATION:– a few minutes
ASSEMBLING:– a few minutes

Clean and carefully dry all the salad leaves, keeping them as intact as possible. Mix together in a serving bowl, ready to dress.

Using a potato peeler, shave shards off the hunk of cheese until you have a nice handful of shaved cheese.

When ready to serve, peel the orange, removing all the white pith, then slice into segments and arrange over the salad. Pour the olive oil and lemon juice over the salad, add a generous pinch of salt and toss well.

Add the cheese, toss again and serve.

Insalata di verza cappuccio, mela e noci

Cabbage, apple & walnut salad

SERVES 4

3 handfuls of walnuts, pecans or almonds

2 tablespoons white wine vinegar

sea salt and freshly ground black pepper

4 tablespoons olive oil

1 teaspoon runny honey

½ head of white cabbage

1 firm apple

A fresh, crisp accompaniment to lots of hearty winter dishes. If you'd like to serve this salad as a starter or a main, add a few tablespoons of gooey gorgonzola.

PREPARATION:– 10 minutes
COOKING:– a few minutes

Preheat the oven to 180°C (350°F) fan-forced.

Spread the nuts in a roasting tin and bake for 5 minutes. Remove from the oven and set aside to cool completely.

Pour the vinegar into a small jug, add ½ teaspoon salt and stir until dissolved. Add the olive oil, honey and lots of black pepper and stir vigorously until well combined.

Slice the cabbage into thin ribbons and place in a large salad bowl.

Just before serving the salad, peel and core the apple and cut into thin slices or wedges. Add to the cabbage and toss together with the nuts, dressing and another generous pinch of salt.

Toss again, taste and adjust the seasoning as necessary. Serve immediately.

VARIATION:– This salad would also be lovely with Castelfranco radicchio leaves, or a mixture of red radicchio, Castelfranco and white cabbage.

DELICIOUS WITH:– Saffron 'speltotto' (page 114), Sage, spinach & quail egg pie (page 137), Dada's baked leeks in bechamel (page 134), Baked fennel & pasta with bechamel (page 144), Grazia's radicchio, sausage & rice timballo (page 174), Chicken with artichokes (page 184).

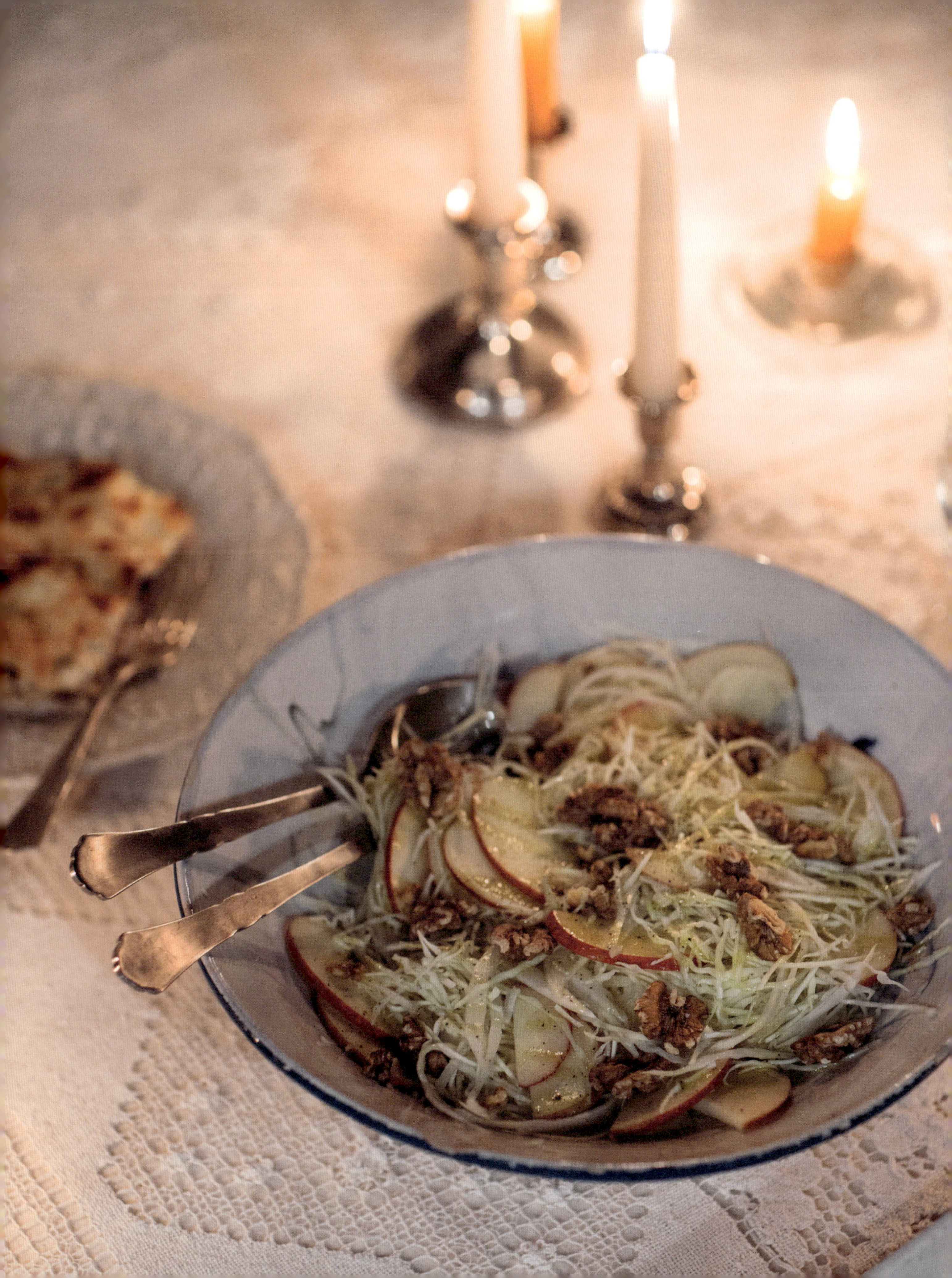

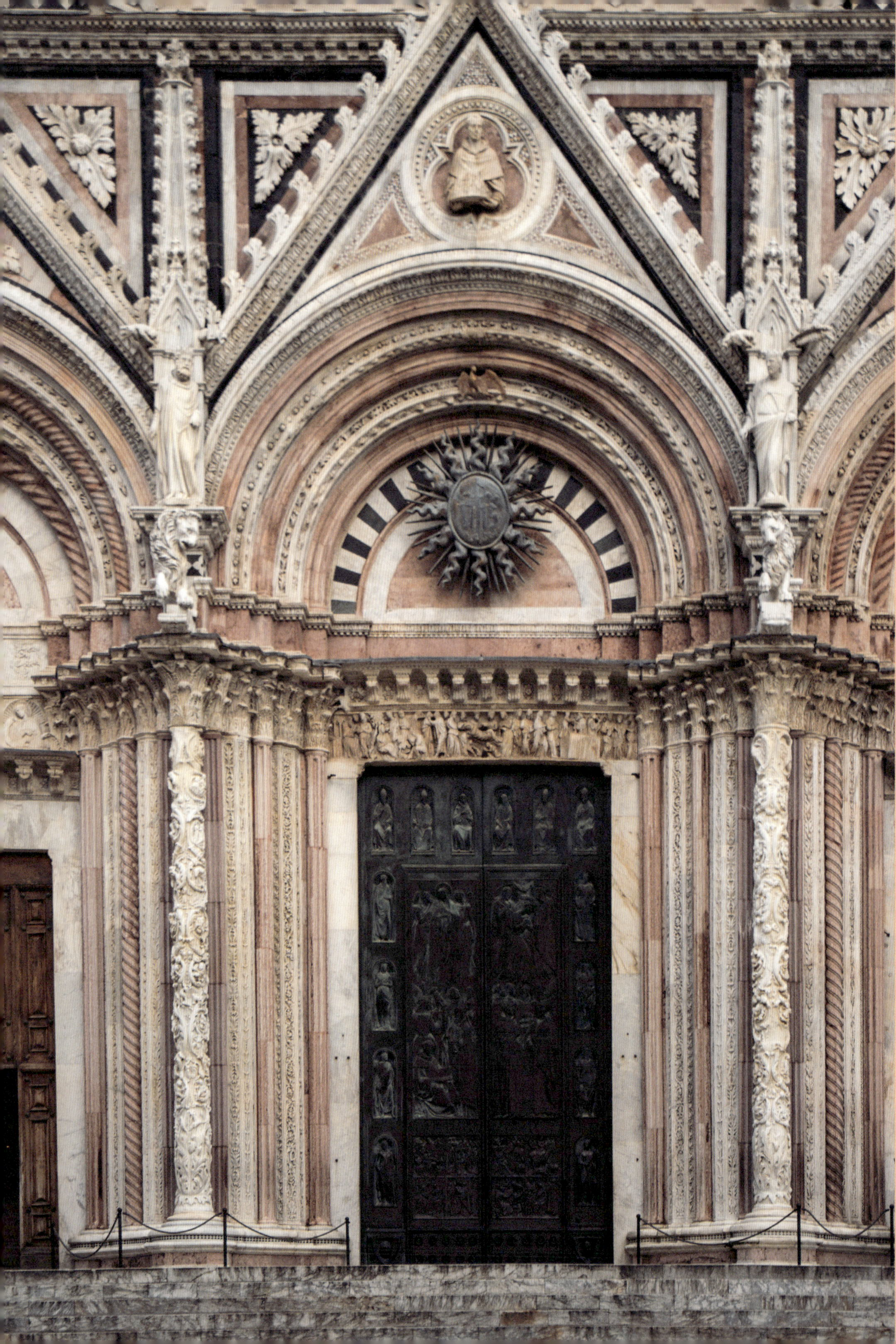

SIENA

FOR SUCH A small place, the perfect medieval city of Siena, a fortified hilltop town in the centre of Tuscany, holds many moments of excitement. No matter how many times you visit, there are several corners of such beauty that they cause you to stop in your tracks.

In Siena, it is necessary to abandon your car on the outskirts of the ancient city walls and continue into the centre on foot. We would always drive in from the west and head to 'Lo Stadio', the carpark that snakes around the city's football stadium. The Stadio was my parents' preferred parking option as it sits atop one of Siena's three hills, so you begin to pick your way through the city's narrow dusky orange-bricked streets from above, descending towards the city's main square – the 'Campo' (Piazza del Campo) – and don't have to huff and puff until the necessary uphill return to the car. Driving round the old walls towards the stadium also takes you past the most glorious view of Siena's highest point, on which the city's majestic cathedral stands. One doesn't have to be Sienese to concede that this cathedral, the Duomo di Siena, is one of the most magnificent in Italy. Its black-and-white striped form rising up out of the higgledy-piggledy terracotta-coloured buildings, all with green shutters, is a lovely thing to behold.

Today, Siena is home to about 60,000 people, and it is possible to cross the centre from north to south in about half an hour, though this might be a strenuous thirty minutes as you walk up and down the various hilly backstreets. Despite its tiny size, it is stuffed with wonderful architecture, paintings, pageantry and history. Next to the entrance to the Stadio sits the Basilica of San Domenico – another beautiful building, its exterior less lavishly adorned than the cathedral's – where you can, if you so wish, visit the relics of one of Italy's two patron saints, Caterina of Siena, in the form of her mummified head and thumb. Things become less gruesome as you continue towards Via Banchi di Sopra, Siena's main shopping street, where you'll pass Palazzo Salimbeni, home to the world's oldest bank – Monte dei Paschi di Siena, founded in 1472 – and Bar Nannini, the famous *pasticceria* that makes some of the town's most delicious *ricciarelli* (soft almond biscuits) and panforte.

Just beyond this point, one descends a steep flight of stairs into Vicolo San Pietro, a small alley leading down through an arch, into the Campo – the city's scallop-shaped piazza around which one of the world's most dramatic horse races, the Palio, takes place twice every summer. To me, the Campo is one of the most beautiful man-made outdoor spaces there is, the tall medieval buildings giving the impression of being in a film set. From Vicolo San Pietro, the square sweeps down towards Palazzo Pubblico, with the city's famous clocktower – the elegant and majestic Torre del Mangia – rising out of its castellated top. When I was a child my parents would often make us walk the 87 metres to the top of the tower, an activity I loathed as I hate heights. The spiral internal staircase is only one person wide, so if you encounter oncoming traffic in the form of other visitors descending the stairs, it becomes quite a manoeuvre to get past one another safely. Of course,

OPPOSITE:– The central west-facing door at Siena Cathedral

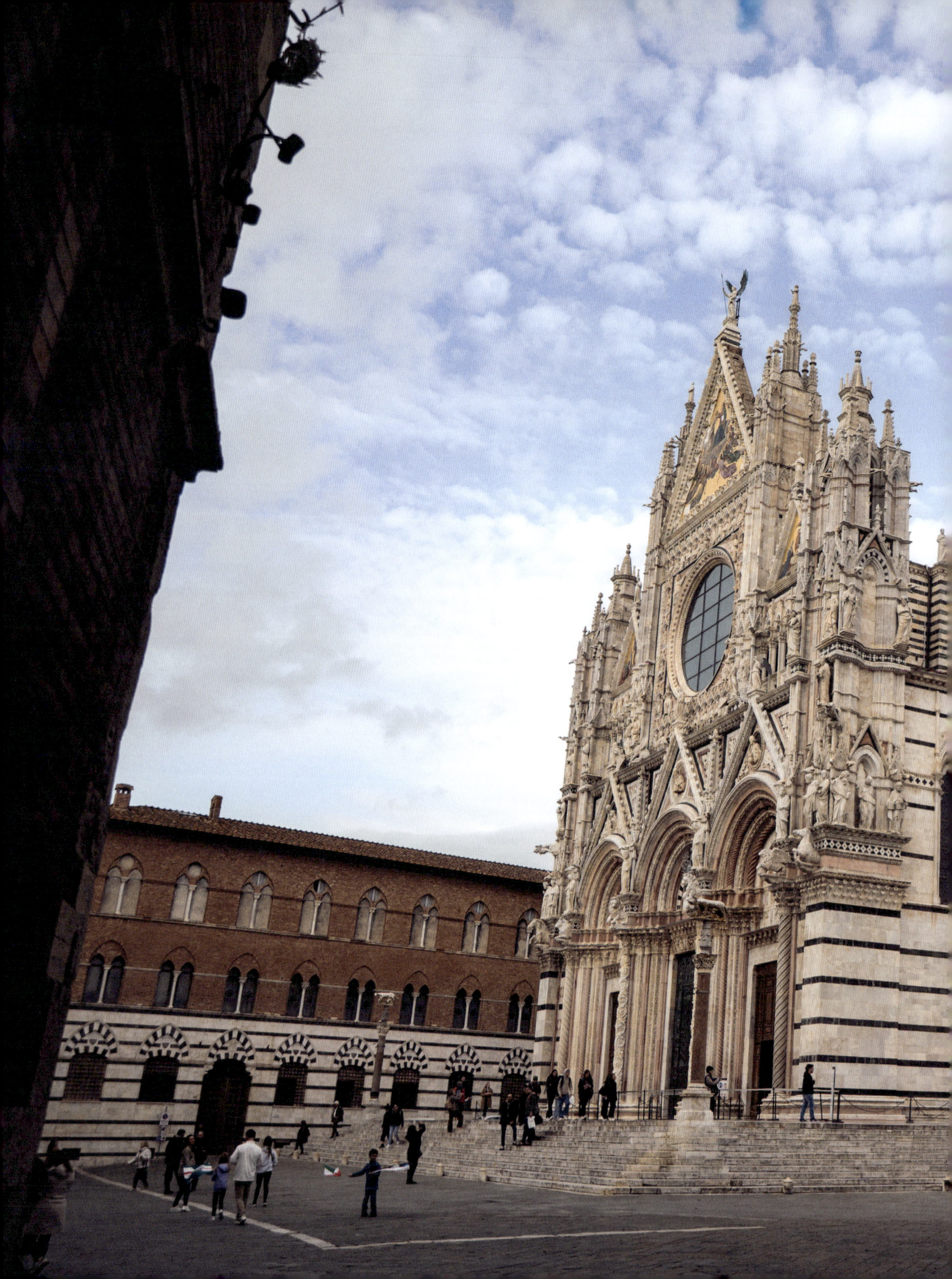

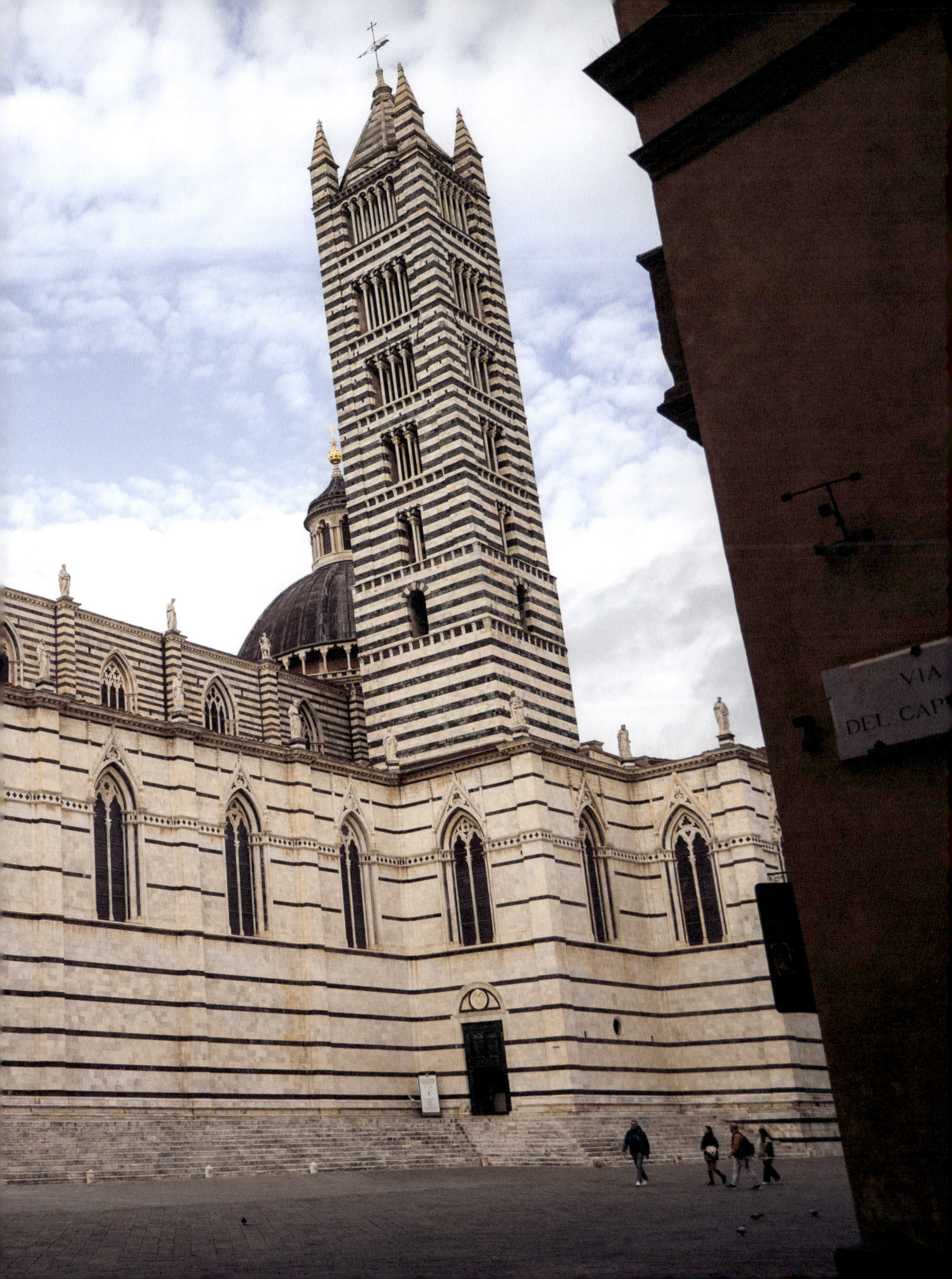
VIA
DEL CAP

PREVIOUS:– Siena Cathedral

when one reaches the top and looks out across the Tuscan hills and the rooftops of Siena, the terrifying journey becomes worth it as you are presented with a fairly staggering view.

As the capital of the province of Siena, in which our local village sits, the city of Siena was our nearest major population centre when I was growing up, and is where we had to go to do any family admin: to enlist in school, to register my mum's antiques shop, and where my parents had to take the accountancy and bookkeeping exams necessary to open a shop. Going to Siena was always exciting, mainly because, as children and adolescents, it was where we could buy CDs and DVDs, spending our pocket money on singles or box sets which had been released several months earlier in England. We also loved it as the frisson in the air from the Palio – the bareback horse race held twice a year around Piazza del Campo – can be felt year-round. Even in darkest winter, with the race still months away, you can hear youngsters from the city's seventeen *contrade* (districts) practising their drum rolls for the parades. My sister and I would sometimes bring our scooters and race down the steepest parts of the square, pretending to be the horses as we hurtled and bumped along the flagstones, or we'd buy flags of our favourite *contrade* – Bruco ('Caterpillar') for my sister, Nicchio ('Scallop shell') for me – and run around the Campo waving them as our parents sipped glasses of wine at Bar Il Palio. I too now love to sit in that same spot outside the bar, sipping a Campari spritz while looking out onto the square as the sun passes overhead and light and shadows move across the Palazzo Pubblico and Torre del Mangia.

Just off the square is Siena's best restaurant, Osteria Le Logge, where my father always used to go whenever he was in town, and where dinner tables after the Palio races are at a premium. His great friend Mirco is still the proprietor and, while the food is a bit fancy for my tastes, the dining room is pretty and cosy, like the backstreet in which the restaurant sits. In Siena I like to keep it simple, as there is a tendency for the trattorias and restaurants on the main thoroughfares to try to be clever with traditional Sienese food, which rather defeats the point of its famed simplicity. I always much preferred going to the pizzeria in the corner of the Campo, Il Bandierino ('The Little Flag'), for a straightforward margherita, until they too jumped on the 'fancy' bandwagon and started bringing an amuse-bouche before one's pizza. Nowadays I keep my time on the square strictly to *aperitivo* hour, venturing into the small-fronted yet cavernous restaurants in the backstreets to feast on simple 'real' food, such as the city's famous thick noodles, known as pici – either in a *ragu al cinghiale* (wild boar), or in a *cacio e pepe* (cheese and black pepper) made with pecorino from the Crete Senesi near Arniano. It is in the backstreets that you will find authentic places such as the tiny Osteria Nonna Gina, where the menu is handwritten and photocopied onto brown paper in a reassuringly no-frills approach.

Siena is a city which is at its most romantic in winter. Summer feels electric as tensions build before the Palio, but it is also crowded, hot, and because it is necessary to go everywhere on foot, rather sticky. In winter, Siena's extraordinary colours and proportions are at their best in the crisp frosty air. Little stalls set up in the Campo selling roasted chestnuts and the many delicious fried sweets the city is famous for: *frittelle di castagne* or *frittelle di riso* (chestnut or rice fritters), dusted in shimmering white sugar and handed to you in brown paper to soak up any excess grease. Visiting Siena was always a particular treat on Boxing Day when we were young as we begged our parents to take us to the open-air ice-skating rink that would be set up for the festive season and to eat *frittelle* in the square. In exchange we had to agree to go to the cathedral to light a candle for loved ones, which back then felt like a chore, but now is a great pleasure, as there is nothing I love more than wandering into the Duomo. Its scale is all at once enormous and compact, smaller than the cathedral in Florence, yet somehow all the more overwhelming in its beauty with its black-and-white striped columns and blue star-studded cupolas. Every small detail of the cathedral's interior feels like a unique masterpiece, right down to the hexagonal crescent-moon tiles lining the floor of the Piccolomini Library in the left-hand nave of the church. Beautiful details are a feature throughout Siena; it is a city which was planned with meticulous intent. Torre del Mangia, for instance, was built to be the same height as the width of Piazza del Campo, the subtle symmetry making the square all the more pleasing to behold, even if the beholder isn't exactly sure why.

Standing at the top of Torre del Mangia looking down at the Campo, at its compact size and tight corners, reminds one of the madness of the Palio, Siena's bareback horse race which takes place in the Campo twice every summer. However bonkers it might seem to outsiders, this isn't mere pageantry, but a historic tradition dating back to the 13th century that sits at the heart of the community and is a personal passion for every single citizen, most of whom will have been baptised into their *contrada* (district Palio team) at birth. It is an event by the Sienese for the Sienese, and they really couldn't be less interested whether tourists attend or not.

Confusingly, the race is run twice a year, on 2 July and 16 August. Both races are completely independent from each other, and neither is supposed to be more important than the other, though there is more gravitas to winning the August Palio, as the winning jockey and horse are carried into the city's cathedral by celebrating crowds – an honour not afforded to the winner of the July Palio. The race takes its name from the race's trophy, 'Il Palio', which itself derives from the Latin word *pallium*, meaning 'drape' – the prize being a silk banner hand-painted with an image of the Madonna by a contemporary artist for each race. The fanatical desire of every local is for their *contrada* to win this flag in order to triumphantly parade it through the streets and hang it in their home church. The various ancient enmities and alliances between the different *contrade* add political intrigue and intricacy to the race – further complicated by the fact that the jockeys have no allegiance whatsoever to the *contrada* they happen to be racing for. They are hired hands, mercenaries, who are entirely corruptible and liable to bribery from other parties. For this reason, 48 hours before the race, jockeys are forced to hand in their phones and are escorted by security at all times, including to the toilet, so they can't collude with anyone outside of their *contrada*. However, collude they do – in full view of spectators on the track. As the ten participating *contrade* line up on the starting line, you see the jockeys circling one another and talking in hurried whispers, offering large sums on behalf of the *contrada* they are running for to persuade an ally to fall back to better their own chances – or, more often, to knobble or block a rival. Those jockeys who do accept money to botch their own chances best be careful, as the moment the race is over, they will almost certainly be set upon by supporters of the *contrada* they have betrayed. My mother remembers sitting on the finish line and seeing one such turncoat desperately clambering over the heads of the crowds to escape the furious and rather menacing *contraioli* who were trying to get their hands on him.

The most comfortable and expensive way to watch the Palio is from a flat with windows looking onto the square. About 5000 people watch it for free standing in the square's centre, closed in three hours before the start to watch the parade and race. This is jolly and fun, though in the full July and August sun with no shade, it can feel like quite a long afternoon. The race itself only lasts 90 seconds, the time it takes for the horses to gallop around the square three times, but the preceding parade takes almost four hours, and the lining-up of the horses as the jockeys cut their deals can also take hours. The third way to watch the race is to sit in the stands surrounding the square. These stands possibly have the best view and are where you see most of the action. When I was twenty, my dad and I were invited by his friend Marco to join him in the stands. As we were sitting glued to the race,

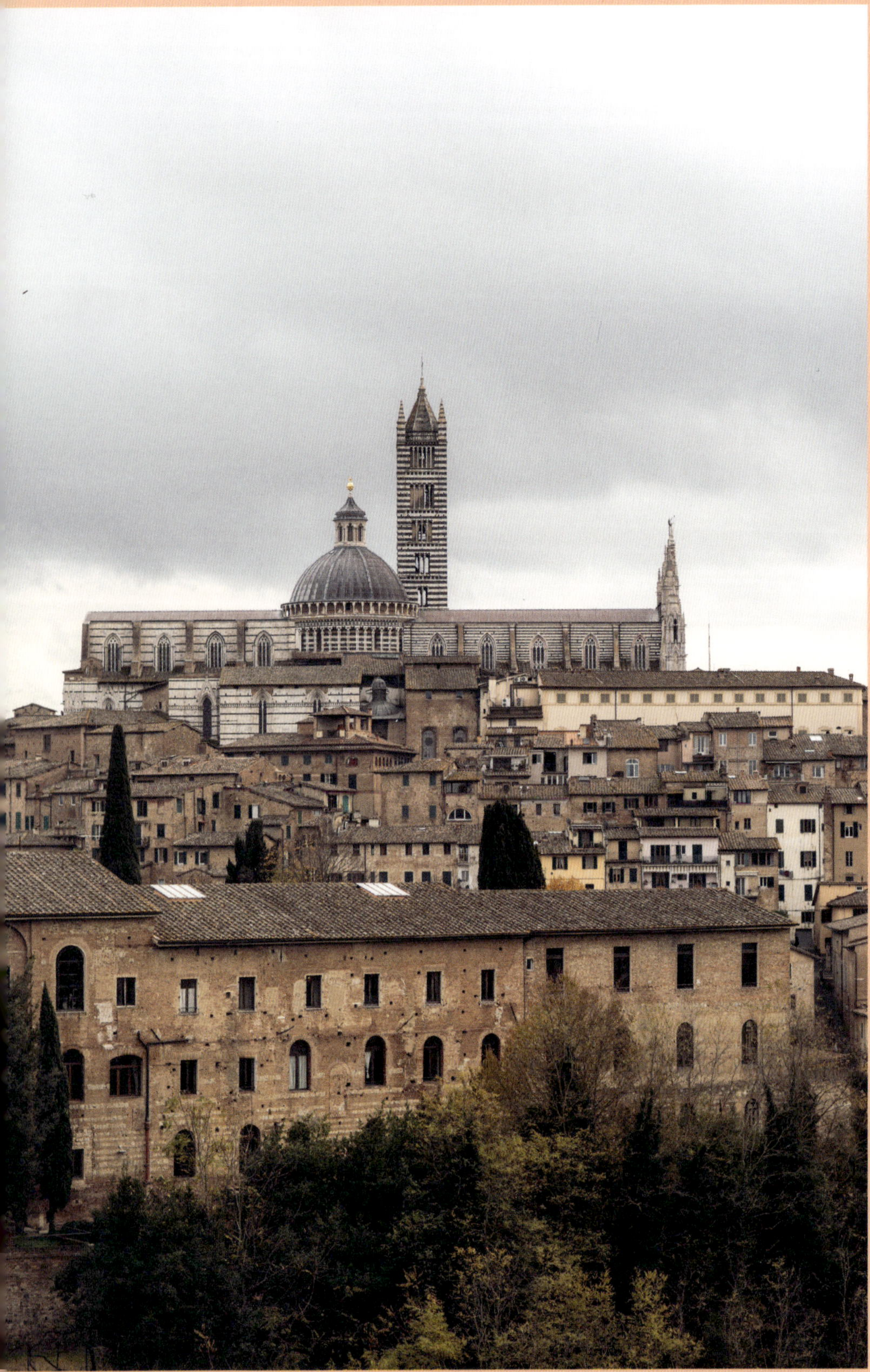

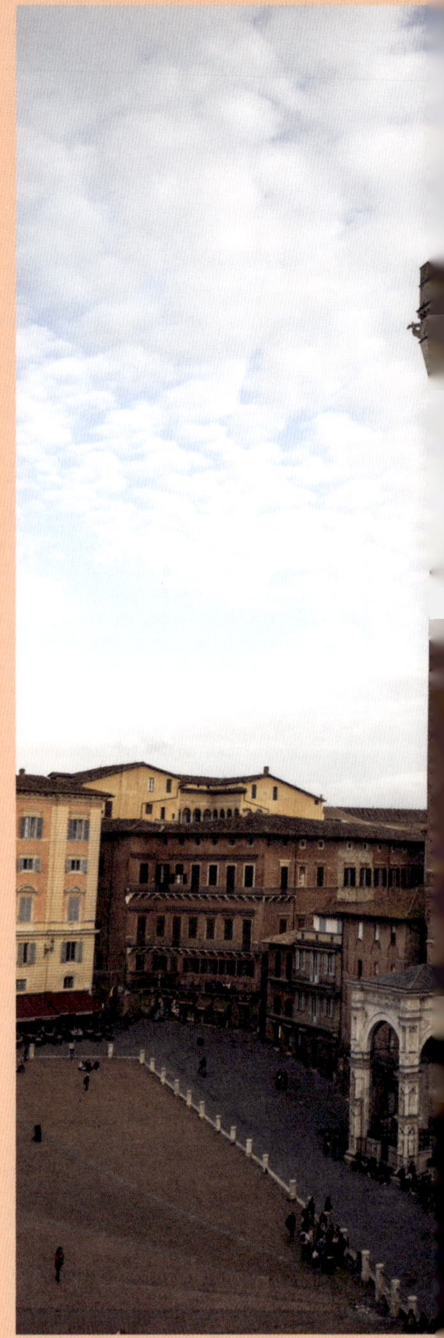

CLOCKWISE FROM TOP LEFT:—
My favourite view of Siena Cathedral;
Torre al Mangia from the private apartment
of my friend Rossella ; Menus at an enoteca;
Palio prints at Osteria Nonna Gina

211   SIENA

we didn't notice that one of the jockeys grabbed another by the leg as they came thundering down the track towards us, managing to flip him off his horse and into the lap of the man sitting directly in front of us. This is the thing about the Palio: it is intensely controlled, while also being fairly lawless. It is the only horse race in the world where a riderless horse can win, so long as their bridle sits in place on their head.

More recently, Marco invited me back to join him in the stands with my husband, Matthew. As we picked our way through the crowded backstreets towards the square, our excitement grew as every official who looked at our tickets widened their eyes and exclaimed what great seats we had. When we sat down in the front row, we realised that the safety barrier in front of us was half a foot higher than it was anywhere else. A local recommended that, when the horses began galloping towards our corner, we should stand up. 'As a show of support?' asked our friend Tom hopefully. 'No,' laughed the man, 'because this is one of the tightest corners and the horses usually hit the barriers pretty hard, so you'll get a few bad bruises on your knees if you don't stand up!' This was frightening and thrilling in equal measure when thinking of the ten racehorses that would soon be thundering towards us at breakneck speed.

Aside from the madness of Palio days, Siena is a quiet, sleepy sort of place where everyone knows everyone. A lawyer friend stopped practising law when she moved here from Florence, as she felt it would be too awkward acting as opposing counsel to someone she would inevitably know. Having never been developed or over-expanded, the city feels quite close to the surrounding countryside. Piazza del Campo means 'the square of the field', and Siena's lands have always been rich and fertile, which is a huge part of why Siena has somehow, more than elsewhere, retained that frugal and simple cuisine which celebrates above all its quality ingredients. Chianina beef from Val di Chiana is cooked simply over coals or roasted, as are the famous local Cinta Senese pigs, depicted in paintings as far back as the 1300s. Sienese antipasti have always been simple, even more so than in Florence, and usually consist of a plate of salumi (cold cuts) and cheeses from the Crete Senesi, all of which are salty and fatty and perfect with a glass of Chianti Classico from Siena's north, or a Rosso di Montalcino from the south, to cut through their richness. Sienese desserts sound frugal as they hark back to medieval times, but are in fact fruity and satisfying to eat – such as panforte, a baked mixture of nuts, candied fruits, honey and spices (or lots of black pepper in the case of *panpepato*). Or *ricciarelli*, the soft almond biscuits that came to the city through Arab influences centuries ago via passing traders and Sicilian migrants. And, of course, brittle, dry *cantucci* (almond biscotti), served alongside a small glass of sweet amber-coloured vin santo ('saintly wine'), a dessert wine mentioned in the 11th century writings of Boccaccio. All of this hearty fare suits Siena's winter and makes for some of the city's best dishes, retaining the sense of a rugged, tavern-like cuisine of the Middle Ages.

Siena has always been Tuscany's second most important city after Florence, and the fierce competition between the two, which sit only about 60 kilometres apart, dates back centuries. Eight hundred years on, the Sienese still talk about the Battle of Montaperti (1260) in which they decimated invading Florentine forces. In the 1100s, Siena threw off its feudal oligarchy and established itself as a Republic, becoming a vibrant and influential city state run by a complicated system of magistrates and nine councillors whose power is reflected in the scalloped shape of Piazza del Campo, with the scallop divided into nine segments, one for each councillor. In 1226 the city began construction of its beautiful cathedral, a gargantuan task that would take over 170 years to complete. Requiring huge amounts of money, skill and resources, such a project was not something a city undertook unless it was at the peak of its economic and cultural powers. The fact

FOLLOWING:– Piazza del Campo

that Florence wouldn't begin building its own world-famous cathedral until almost a century later shows that at that time, Siena was at least as powerful, if not more so, than Tuscany's modern-day capital.

The rivalry with Florence has helped the city of Siena, throughout history, to fiercely and proudly retain its distinct character and feel. The construction of Siena's cathedral over almost two centuries is a fabulous example of how these two cities vied for supremacy in the region, and how size was what mattered in the exhibition of wealth and power in the Middle Ages. The Duomo di Siena was, and is, a masterpiece, and was the largest in Tuscany for a time – though when it later emerged that a new cathedral in Florence was destined to be even larger than Siena's, it was decided to add a new south-facing wing, which would extend the length of Siena's cathedral to 140 metres, making it the largest in Europe and therefore at that point, the world. The extension took nine years, and workers had almost finished vaulting the roof when the works were brought to a screeching halt in 1348 by the Black Death, which killed over half of Siena's population. Interestingly, part of the skeleton of the abandoned 'Duomo Nuovo' still stands and has become part of the fabric of the square surrounding the cathedral. Today you can climb to the top of what would have been the new south-facing facade and look out across the Sienese countryside, contemplating the massive nature of these works, and what trauma the city must have suffered in order to leave them unfinished.

Dusky orange is the predominant colour when you pick your way through the streets of Siena or walk into Piazza del Campo. All the buildings are made of the terracotta-coloured bricks that were the area's most readily available material, leading to the name of the colour – Burnt Siena. The surrounding earth, right up to us at Arniano, is rich in clay, a very inexpensive material that simply needs to be dug up, moulded and baked. The cathedral's main structure is built of these bricks, and was then clad in a white Carrara marble, as well as a dark green serpentine marble that oxidises when exposed to air and looks almost black. These marvellous black and white stripes, which carry on to the interior of the church, represent the *balzano*, or the colours of Siena – and are deeply connected with the city's symbol, the she-wolf, mired in the legends surrounding the founding of the city. One tale describes the sons of Remus, Aschius and Senius, escaping Rome and the ire of their murderous uncle Romulus along the Tressa Torrent until they found three hills on which to build a new city, bringing with them a sculpture of the she-wolf to remind them of Rome. Here they founded Castelsenio (Senius's castle), which would eventually become Siena, and lit a pyre to beg the protection of the gods Diana and Apollo, from which rose plumes of white smoke sent from Diana, and black smoke from Apollo. Another version has it that, as the two brothers were very young when they fled Rome, the gods intervened and protected them from Romulus by sending down white fog to conceal them during the day, and black fog at night, until they came of age and could found the city of Siena.

Whatever the truth, images of wolves and black and white stripes are very much those that I associate with the town. Siena has always had an aptitude for colour, with the Palio flags and all the wonderful *contrada* outfits bearing testament to this historic flair for design. The red, black and white of Civetta ('The Owl'), the yellow, red and blue of Chiocciola ('The Snail'), the white and sky-blue of Onda ('The Wave'), or the yellow and blue of my parents' old *contrada*, Tartuca ('The Tortoise'), are all fabulous and have inspired many fashion designers, including Emilio Pucci, who designed gorgeous collections based on the colours of the Palio. The *contrada* designs are particularly lovely when painted onto ceramics, and my mum and I both collect 'Palio plates' – something that would be incomprehensible to a local, who would never dream of having rival colours anywhere near their house. Illustrating how, at times, personal allegiances might trump aesthetics in a town where traditions run deep.

SIENA

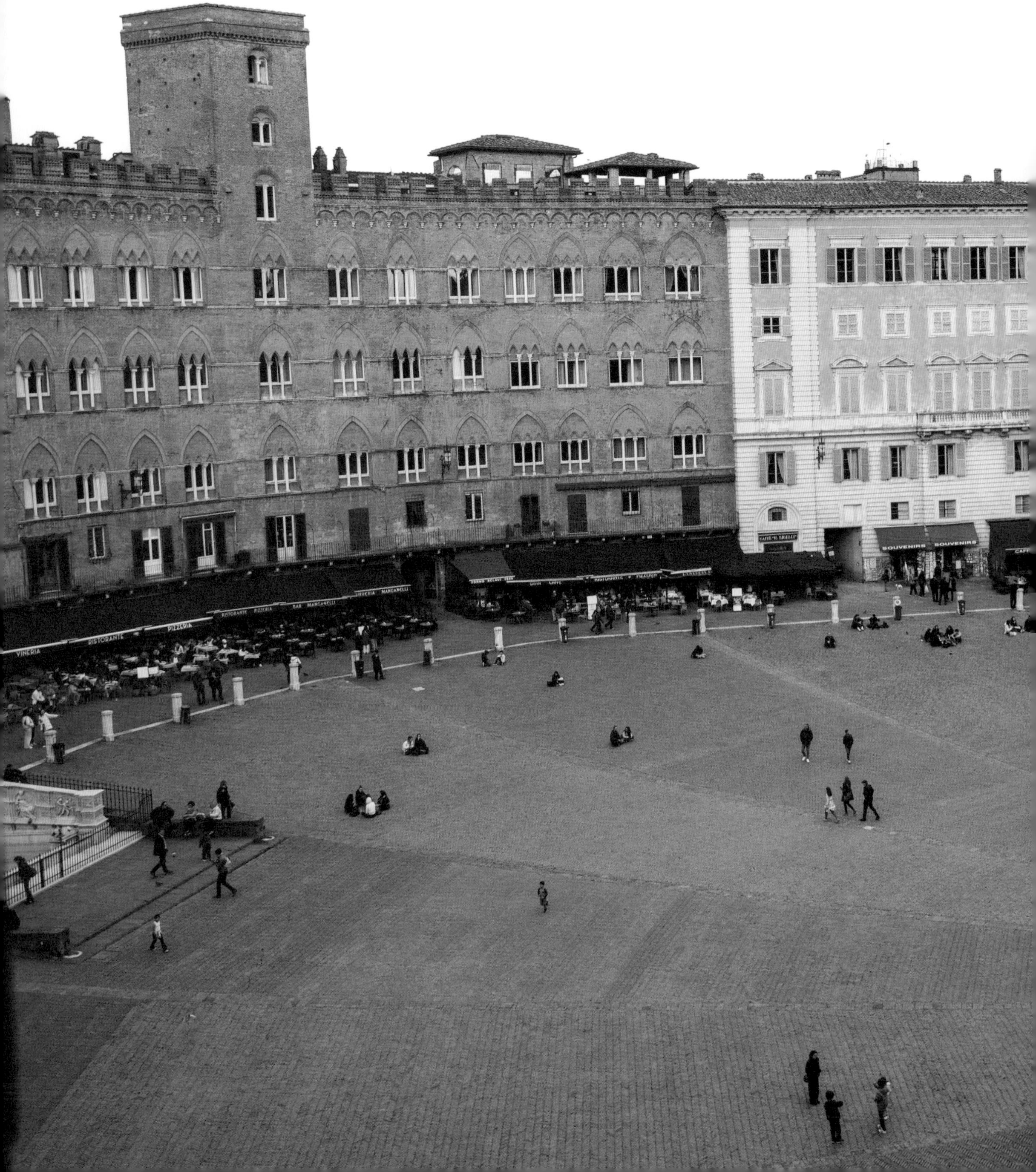
VINERIA
RISTORANTE
PIZZERIA
SOUVENIRS
SOUVENIRS

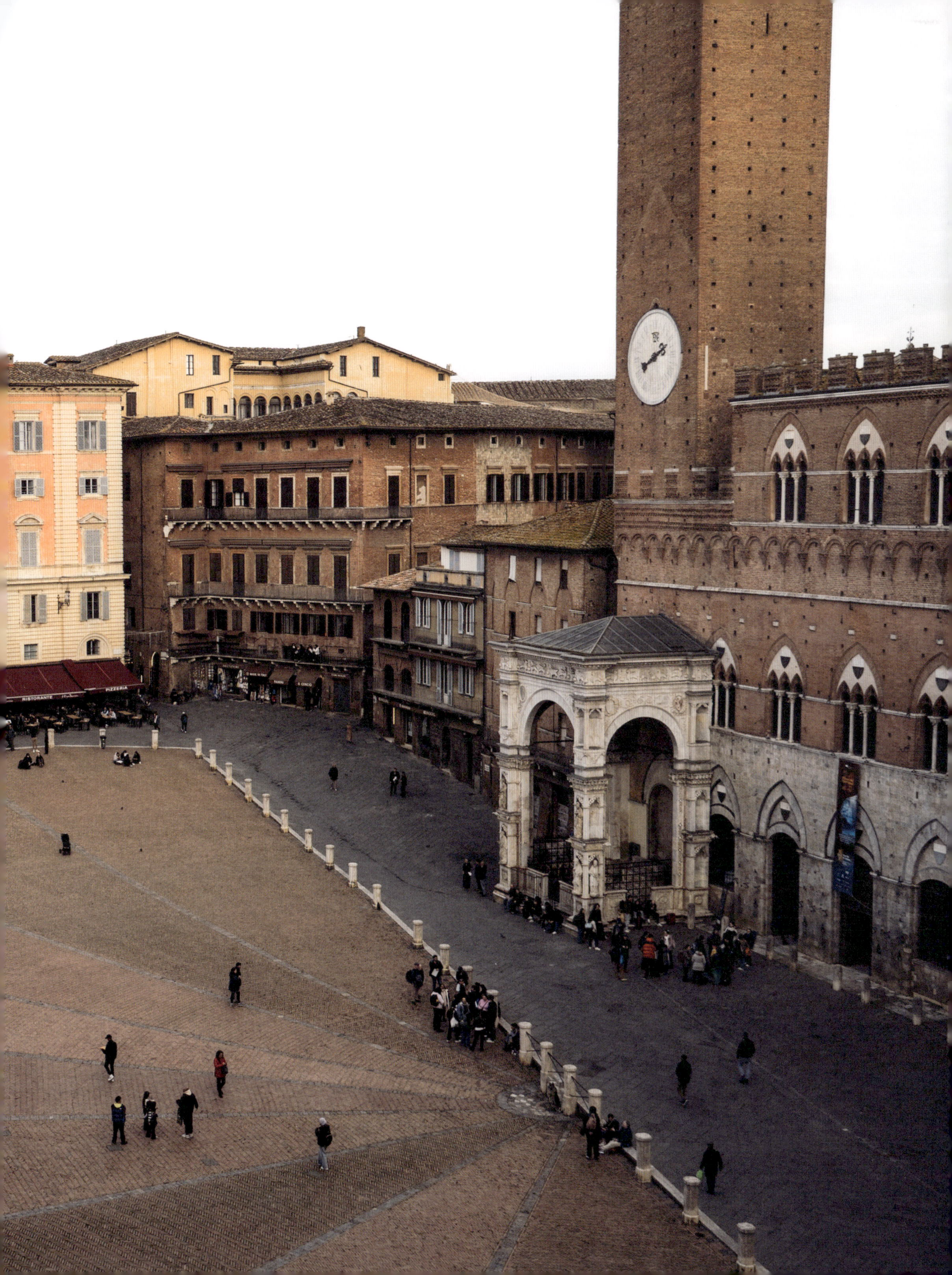
RISTORANTE
PIZZERIA

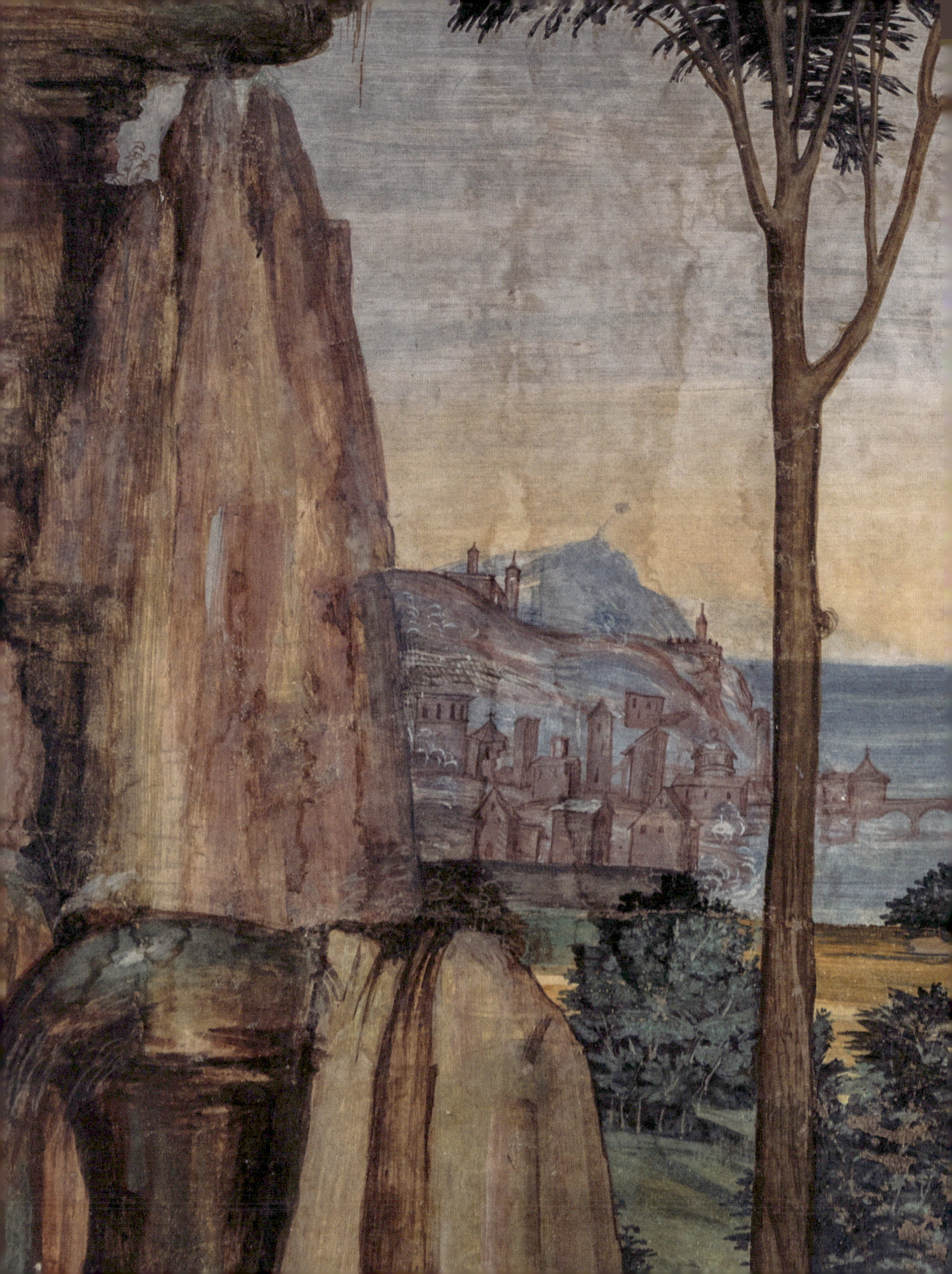

DOLCI

SWEETS

I TALIANS LOVE SWEETS, particularly at breakfast. They are more likely to have a slice of cake, a *budino di riso* (little rice pudding tart), or a brioche laden with *crema pasticcera* (custard) almost to the point of collapse, than they are to have a boiled egg. Shortcrust pastry plays a big role: tarts filled with fruit jam then baked (*crostate*) are a classic gift to bring for lunch, as is Tuscany's most traditional dessert, *torta della nonna*, a shortcrust pastry tart filled with custard topped with pastry and pine nuts – it's basically a baked hug. These are the kind of desserts that are on most restaurant menus in Tuscany, those of the rustic, homemade variety as opposed to fancier and more imaginative desserts made by a *pâtissier*. As with much Tuscan food, the desserts are notable for their simplicity and for their deep links with the past, territory and traditional local ingredients.

Pudding wine also plays its part in the form of the Tuscan speciality, vin santo (holy wine). The smallest and finest grapes are hung up to dry for months in special cellars known as *vinsantaia*, then aged for years in barrels to make the unctuous and sweet vin santo for which the region is known. Bakers turned to the vineyards for another Florentine sweet which is made in autumn when the grapes are being harvested, to make the city's famous *schiacciata all'uva* – a focaccia topped with tiny grapes and sugar and baked in the oven.

Many of the characteristic sweets on offer around us in Siena are quite spartan and dry, as they were developed hundreds of years ago before the arrival of the fridge, and when honey, nuts and spices were the prized ingredients of the day. These desserts were designed to have a relatively long shelf life, such as panforte, the Sienese cake made from almonds, candied fruit and honey, documented as far back as 1205. Cantucci, another of Siena's baked goods, also falls into this category. Made with blanched almonds, egg white, butter and honey, it is baked in a log, then cut into long strips on a diagonal. A plate of almond cantucci served with a glass of vin santo in which to dip the dry biscuit – an action known as to '*inzuppare*', to soak or flood something with liquid – is possibly the most Tuscan way to end a meal. I love this classic combination of flavours so much I've married them into a semifreddo, which you'll find on page 229.

Another reinvention of a classic is my friend Chiara's delicious *frittelle di castagne* (Chestnut flour fritters, page 245), which are a take on *castagnaccio*, another ancient dish that was originally invented from necessity and want, but has become a sought-after dessert in its own right. *Castagnaccio* was a clever way for poor communities in the Apennine Mountains and on our local mountain of Monte Amiata to enjoy a sweet treat, by baking a cheap, locally available ingredient – chestnut flour – into a dense cake enriched with raisins and pine nuts.

The following pages bring together some of my favourite traditional sweets that I like to make for family and friends. Some are classics with a twist, and others aren't traditional at all – the ones I make with what I have to hand, such as a tarte tatin with quince from the garden (page 227), and a chocolate and rosemary olive oil mousse (page 230) made with our local olive oil and rosemary sprigs I've snipped from the bush. And while I don't usually find myself eating spoonfuls of chocolate mousse with my morning coffee, on a dark winter's morning you too might find yourself nibbling at some of these cakes and biscuits for breakfast, as the Italians do.

OPPOSITE:– Having breakfast with Milo in Piazza Santo Spirito

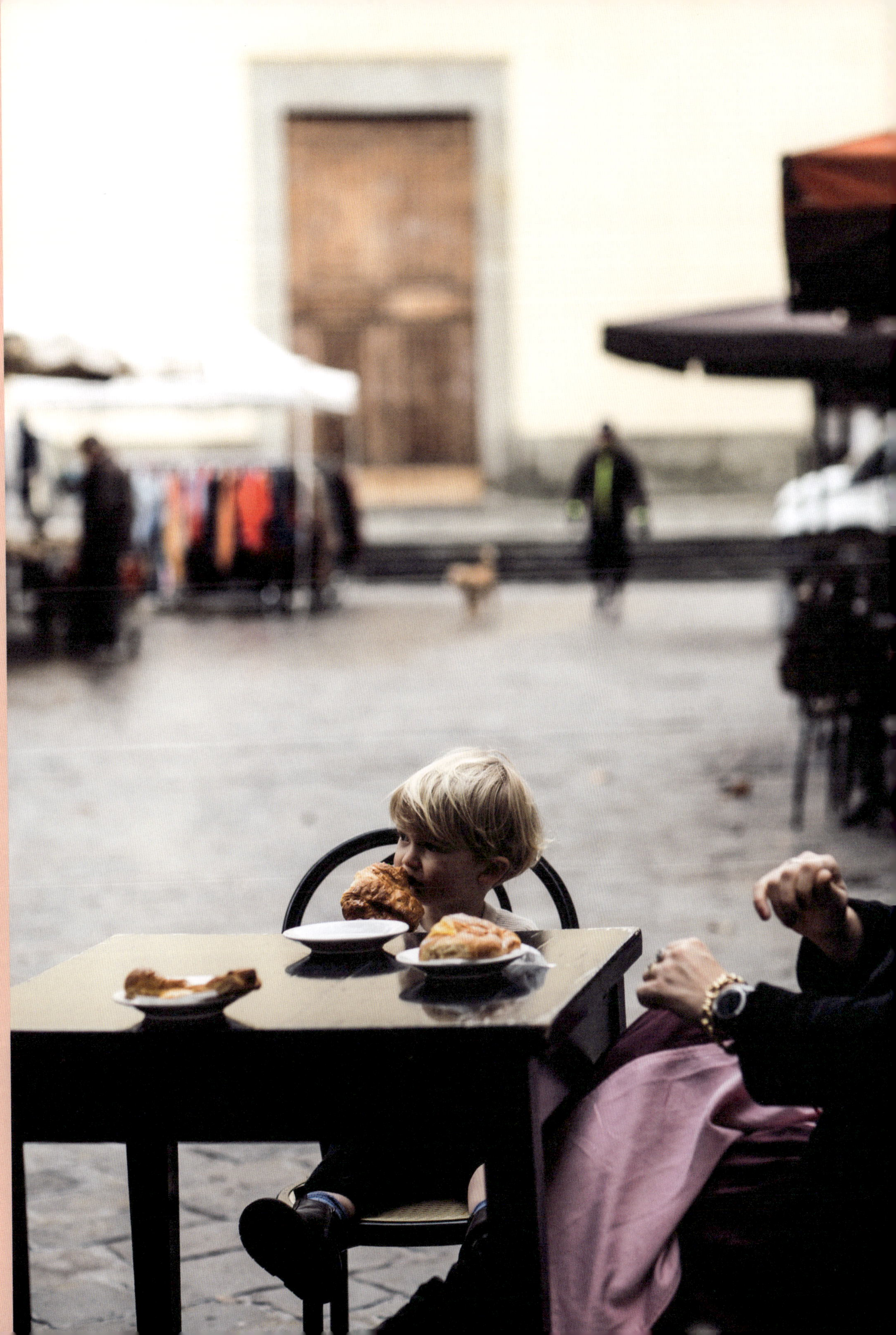

CLOCKWISE FROM TOP LEFT:—
Panforte at Nannini in Siena; Matthew at
Cantina del Brunello in Montalcino; Early
morning coffee at Rivoire in Piazza Signoria

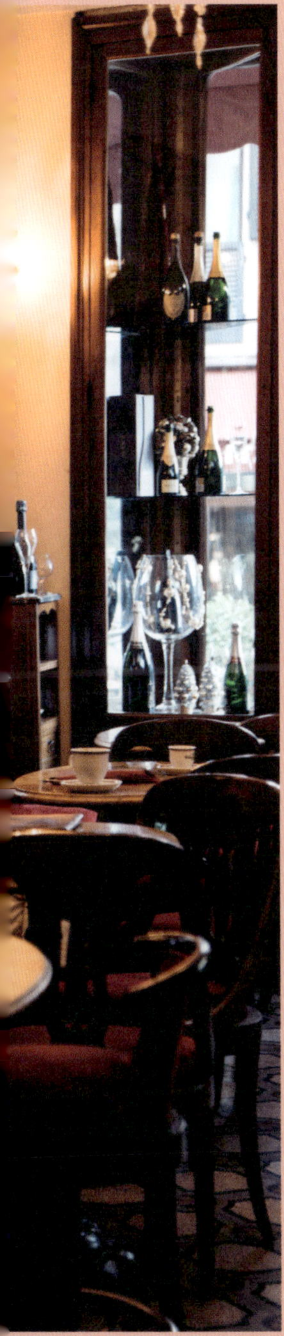

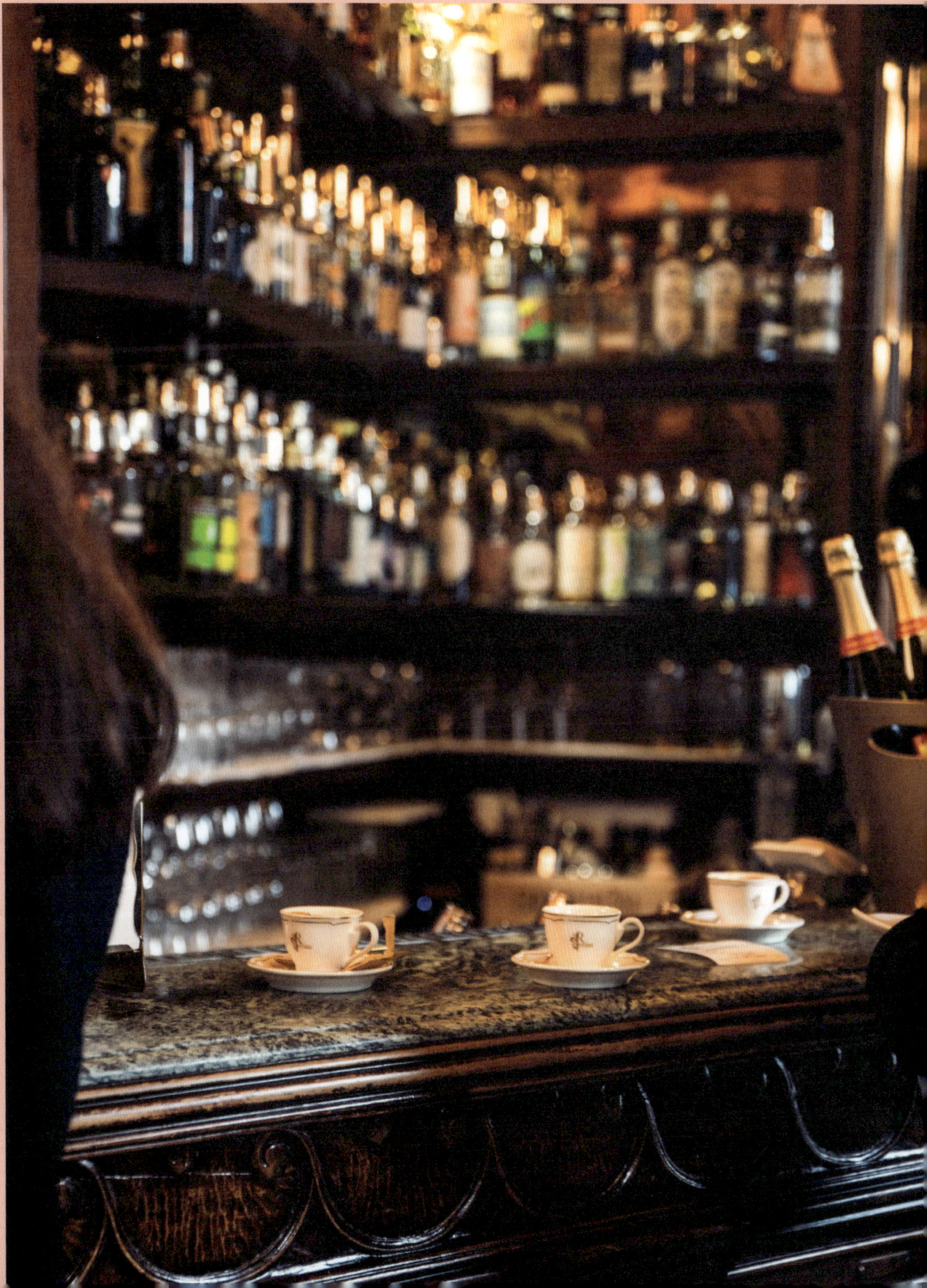

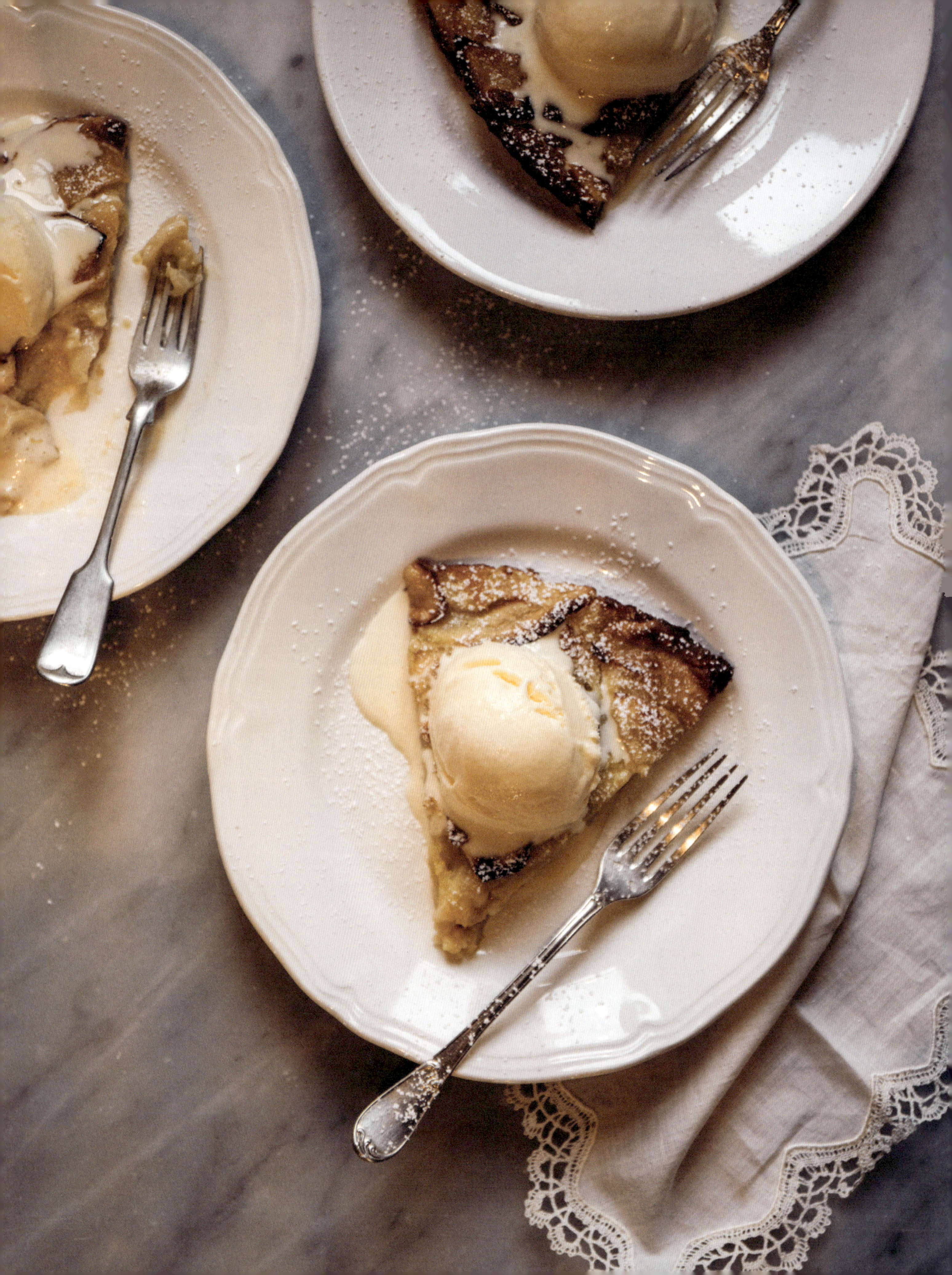

Torta di mele

Florentine apple 'pancake' cake

SERVES 4

3 large firm apples, peeled
squeeze of lemon juice
50 g (1¾ oz) caster sugar, plus extra for sprinkling
zest of ½ lemon
1 organic egg
½ teaspoon baking powder
50 g (1¾ oz) '00' flour
50 ml (1¾ fl oz) full-fat milk
50 g (1¾ oz) unsalted butter, melted

TO SERVE

2 tablespoons icing sugar
vanilla ice cream

This cake is one of the best things on the menu of Alla Vecchia Bettola, a bustling trattoria on the south side of Florence. Its peculiarity is that it isn't a risen sponge with apples in it, but the apples are the main ingredient and are just held together by the cake mix. That's why you mustn't be surprised by the proportion of apple slices to batter in the recipe. At the restaurant they make this in an enormous circular flat copper pan, but I've scaled down their original recipe to make it more manageable at home. You want the cake to be about 1 cm (½ inch) in height, so make it in a large cake tin or even a rectangular roasting tin that allows you to smooth it out to a thin cake – the shape it ends up won't affect the taste. The thinness is what results in the characteristic charred and caramelised apple pancake feel.

It's heaven on its own, or topped with vanilla ice cream.

PREPARATION:– 20 minutes
COOKING:– 50 minutes

Preheat the oven to 200°C (400°F) fan-forced. Butter a 24 cm (9 inch) tart or cake tin and line with baking parchment.

Cut the apples into quarters, remove the cores, then thinly slice. Toss in a bowl with a squeeze of lemon juice to stop them browning.

In a large bowl, using hand-held electric beaters, whisk together the sugar, lemon zest and egg for 1–2 minutes, until thick and pale.

Gently fold the baking powder and half the flour through. Once smooth and amalgamated, add the rest of the flour. Mix the milk through, followed by the melted butter.

Once you have a smooth, amalgamated cake batter, add the apple slices, mixing well to ensure each one is well coated in the batter.

Pour the mixture into the tart tin. There is very little batter, so use a spatula to scrape it all out of the bowl. Spread all the apples and batter out evenly with the spatula, pressing down to make sure the apples are well compacted – you should end up with a 1 cm (½ inch) high cake. Smooth any additional batter over the top of the apples, then sprinkle an extra tablespoon of sugar over the cake.

Bake for 40 minutes, until the corners of the cake start to darken and caramelise. If it starts going very dark on top, you can cover the cake with foil for the last 10 minutes of baking.

Remove from the oven and leave to cool in the tin for at least 10 minutes. While cooling, sieve over a light dusting of icing sugar from a height.

Transfer to a large plate or wooden board; the 'cake' will be much more like a thick pancake than a traditional sponge.

Serve warm or at room temperature in slices, topped with a scoop of vanilla ice cream. The cake will keep for up to 3 days if stored in an airtight container in the fridge.

Panna cotta al vino con miele e pere

Red wine panna cotta with Jessica's grilled pears

SERVES 4

60 g (2 oz) flaked almonds
1½ gelatine leaves (3 g or 1/10 oz)
150 ml (5 fl oz) red wine
2 tablespoons runny honey
250 ml (8½ fl oz) double cream
150 ml (5 fl oz) full-fat milk
30 g (1 oz) icing sugar
1 vanilla pod

FOR THE GRILLED PEARS

2 large pears, ripe but firm
3 tablespoons red wine
4 teaspoons caster sugar
4 teaspoons runny honey

> **VARIATIONS:—** To make a plain vanilla panna cotta with just the right amount of wobble, skip the first step of making the wine syrup. Add the honey straight into the cream and proceed as described above.
>
> Panna cotta is also delicious with poached quince (page 227).

You'll find panna cotta on most trattoria dessert menus, firstly as it's delicious and secondly because it is supremely easy to make in large batches ahead of time. It's just a matter of heating the ingredients, then chilling them in individual ramekins to be turned out as needed. I love a plain vanilla panna cotta, but infused with red wine and honey and served with pears – classic ingredients that usually accompany cheese during a Tuscan *aperitivo* – it's even better. Adding a wine syrup to the panna cotta lends a mellow wine-y note and a pretty pale violet hue. Our friend Jessica's method of grilling the pears is both beautiful and delicious with a wobbly, smooth panna cotta.

COOKING:— 30 minutes
CHILLING:— 6 hours

Preheat the oven to 180°C (350°F) fan-forced. Spread the flaked almonds on a baking tray and roast for 5 minutes. Remove from the oven and set aside to cool.

Using scissors, cut the gelatine leaves into a small bowl and cover with cold water, making sure they are fully submerged. Leave to soak for 5 minutes.

Pour the wine into a small saucepan and stir in the honey. Leave to bubble over a medium heat for about 5 minutes, so that the wine reduces by about two-thirds to a thick sauce. Pour the syrup into a small glass to cool down for 5 minutes.

In the meantime, add the cream, milk and icing sugar to the pan. Split the vanilla pod and scrape out the seeds with a knife, adding them straight into the pan with the vanilla pod. Stir together and leave over a medium heat for a minute or so. Stir in the wine syrup and leave until the mixture is just on the point of boiling – as soon as you see any bubbles, take the pan off the heat.

Remove the gelatine leaves from the water and squeeze out any excess liquid. Stir the gelatine into the hot cream mixture until completely dissolved.

Pour your panna cotta mixture into four individual ramekins, moulds or low-rimmed glasses. Leave to cool completely out of the fridge (this prevents the gelatine and cream splitting). Once cooled, leave in the fridge to set for at least 6 hours.

Meanwhile, prepare the pears. Preheat the oven grill to 200°C (400°F) fan-forced. Using a sharp knife, remove the stems from the pears, then cut the pears lengthways into five or six slices about 1–2 cm (½–¾ inch) thick. (Don't worry if they vary in size a little or end up uneven.) Find a roasting tin or two large enough to hold all the pear slices in one layer and line with baking parchment. Pour in the wine and spread the pears out in a single layer. Evenly sprinkle each pear slice with the sugar, then drizzle with the honey.

Roast on the highest shelf in the oven under the grill for 30 minutes, until the tops are browned and some of the sugar is bubbling and caramelised. Remove from the oven and set aside to cool until you're ready to serve. (To make this dessert very speedy to pull together, the pears can be roasted a day ahead.)

When ready to serve, gently run a small knife around the inside rim of the panna cotta moulds (or pierce the base if using foil ramekins). Place your serving plate securely over the panna cotta and invert. Leave for another few seconds before removing the mould, and you should be left with a perfectly wobbly panna cotta. Sprinkle with some almonds.

Arrange a few slices of grilled pear on each plate and serve immediately, with a fork and a spoon.

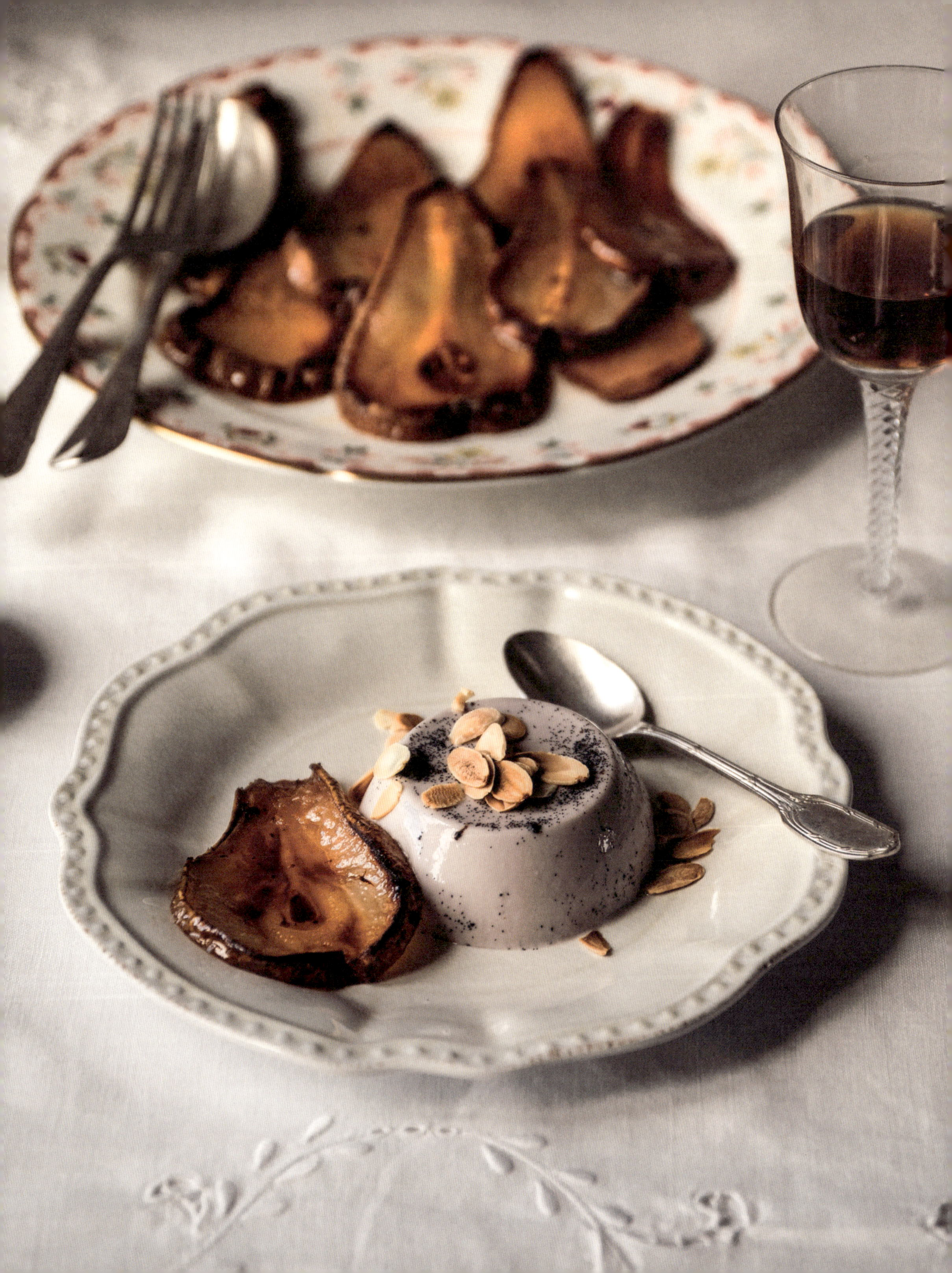

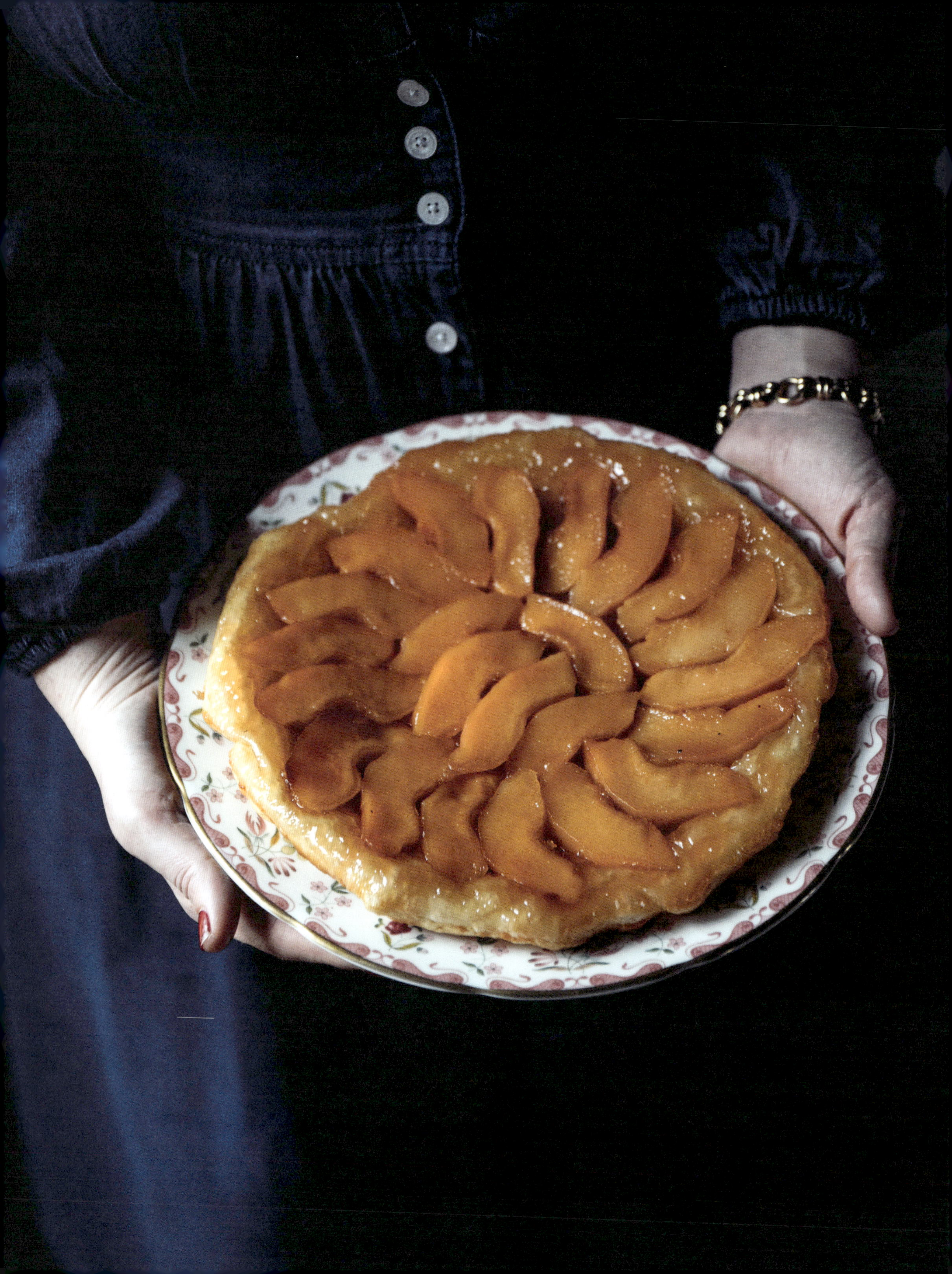

Crostata di mela cotogna

Quince tarte tatin

MAKES 6 SLICES

3 large quinces

300 g (10½ oz) caster sugar

juice of 1 lemon

40 g (1½ oz) unsalted butter

1 sheet of ready-rolled puff pastry

cream or vanilla ice cream, to serve

Mela cotogna – the cross between an apple and pear that in English we call quince – grows in abundance in southern Tuscany. We have a quince tree in our garden at Arniano, which some years is so prolific it is difficult to know what to do with the surfeit of fruit, so horrid when raw, but so very delicious when cooked. One autumn, my mum and I decided to try the very French dessert of a tarte tatin in our Tuscan kitchen. The result was fabulous and much aided visually by the rosy colour cooked quince takes on. If you don't want to bake a tart, the poached quince and its cooking liquid are delicious with panna cotta (page 224) or simply with cream. You could also cook down the poaching liquid for another 30 minutes and let it set into a delicious quince jelly (the fruit is rich in pectin so this is a fairly quick and easy process) to serve with cheese, particularly pecorino. Or, turn it into *cotognata* – little soft candies made from solidified quince jam rolled in sugar – as the monks at nearby Monte Oliveto Maggiore famously do.

PREPARATION:– 1 hour
COOKING:– 25 minutes

Peel the quinces. Using a sharp knife, and taking great care as the flesh is dense and tough, cut off the stems and cut the quinces into quarters. Cut out and discard the core and seeds.

Combine the sugar, lemon juice and 1 litre (34 fl oz) water in a saucepan and bring to a gentle simmer over a medium heat. Add the quince quarters and turn down the heat. Cut a piece of baking parchment into a circle about the same size as the pan and cut a little steam hole in the middle. Place this sheet over the quince and leave to poach for 20–25 minutes, or a little longer if they are particularly tough. Keep an eye on them: you want them to be tender and easy to pierce, but to still retain their shape rather than turn mushy. Once tender, using a slotted spoon, and leaving the liquid in the pan, transfer the quince pieces to a bowl to cool.

Bring the poaching liquid back to a gentle boil and allow to reduce for 30–40 minutes, until it has turned slightly pink and looks bubbling and sticky, but is still quite liquid. Turn off the heat. (At this point you can use the quince and poaching liquid for other desserts.)

Preheat the oven to 180°C (350°F) fan-forced. Pour the poaching liquid into an overproof frying pan or skillet. (If it has solidified into a jelly, don't worry – it will soon return to a thick sweet syrup.) Place over a medium heat and stir in the butter until well amalgamated and liquid. Turn off the heat.

Arrange the poached quince pieces in the pan in a tight formation. Cut a steam hole in the middle of your puff pastry sheet, or pierce it all over with a fork, then drape the pastry over the quince, gently pressing down and pinching or folding the edges over to enclose the quince.

Bake for about 25 minutes, until the top of the tart looks golden, and caramel is bubbling over the sides. Carefully remove from the oven and leave to cool for 5 minutes.

Turn the tart out by placing a plate securely over the top and flipping it over, being careful to avoid hot caramel splatters. Serve hot or at room temperature, with ice cream or cream.

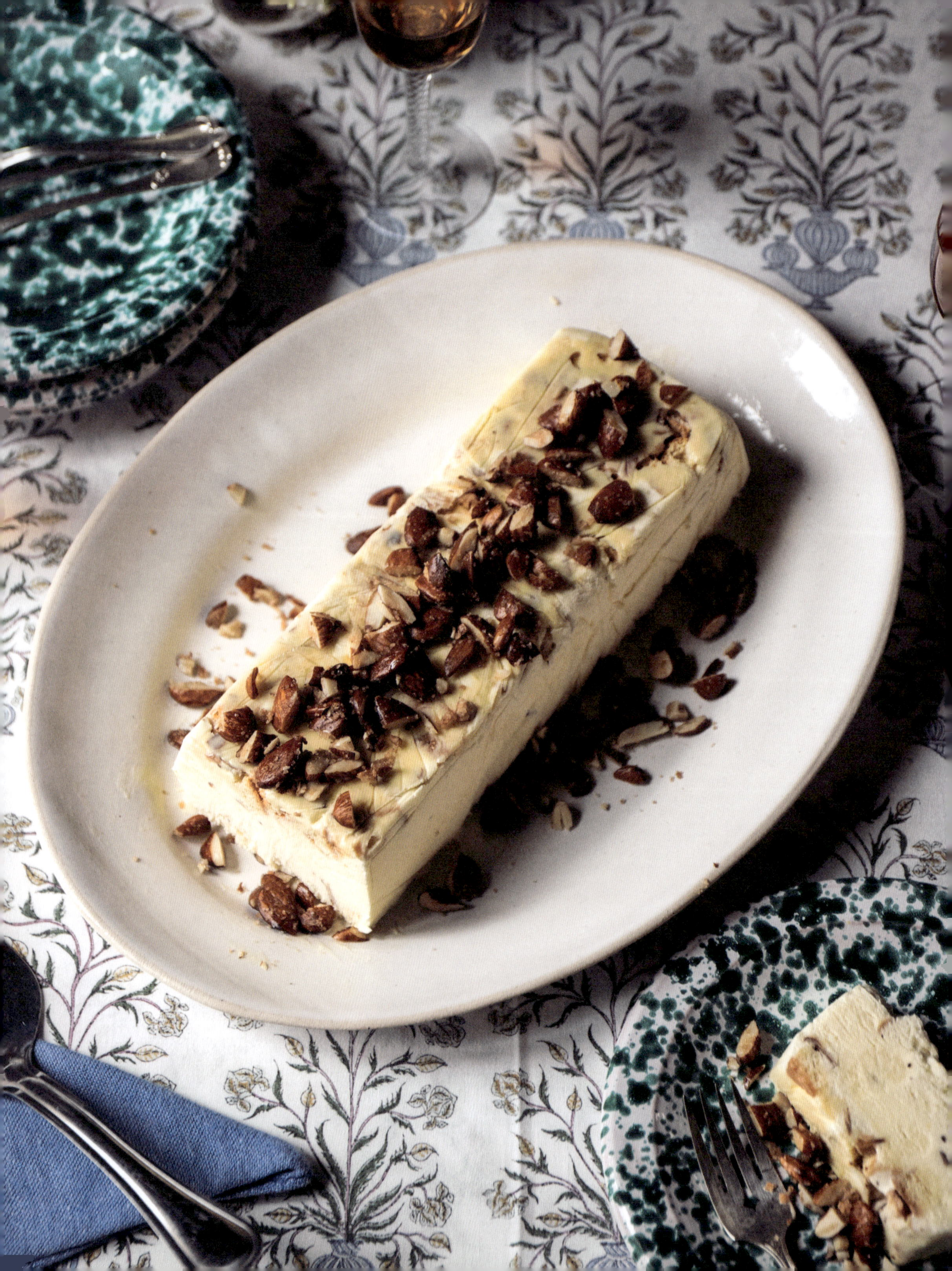

Semifreddo al vin santo e cantucci

Cantucci & vin santo semifreddo

MAKES 6–8 SLICES

4 tablespoons flaked almonds
1 teaspoon unsalted butter
8 tablespoons caster sugar
5 almond cantucci biscuits
white wine vinegar
2 organic eggs
400 ml (13½ fl oz) double cream
3 tablespoons vin santo, plus extra to serve (optional)
sea salt

There is no way to end a meal that is so representative of Tuscany as dipping cantucci (very dry almond biscuits) in vin santo (sweet pudding wine). A little glass of vin santo accompanied by several biscotti is the easiest after-dinner treat, but when I'm after something a little creamier and want to make a bit more of an effort, I bring this famous duo together in another popular local dessert: semifreddo, meaning 'semi-frozen'.

PREPARATION:– 20 minutes
CHILLING:– 3 hours

Preheat the oven to 160°C (315°F) fan-forced. Put the flaked almonds in a small roasting tin. Dot the butter over the almonds and sprinkle with 2 teaspoons of the sugar. Bake for 5–7 minutes, until the almonds are golden and smell nutty, and the butter has melted. Remove from the oven and set aside to cool.

Line a loaf tin with cling wrap so that the bottom and sides are completely covered, and some cling wrap is hanging over the sides.

By hand, roughly chop the cantucci into small pebble-like pieces. You want them to still retain some texture, rather than turning them into a dust or crumbs, as these will get soggy. Scatter the cantucci evenly over the bottom of the loaf tin, followed by half the cooled roasted flaked almonds.

Get a clean metal bowl and rub the inside with the corner of a clean tea towel dipped in white wine vinegar.

Separate the eggs, putting the egg whites in the cleaned metal bowl, and the yolks in a separate bowl. Pour the cream into a third bowl.

Add the remaining sugar to the egg yolks and, using hand-held electric beaters, beat for about 2 minutes, until thick, pale and smooth. Mix in the vin santo.

Give the beaters a rinse and dry thoroughly with a tea towel. Whisk the egg whites with a pinch of salt until stiff peaks form.

Give the beaters another rinse, then whip the cream until smooth and cloud-like.

Using a clean metal spoon, gently fold the egg whites into the cream, then fold this mixture through the beaten egg yolks with the remaining almonds.

Pour the semifreddo mixture into the loaf tin, gently smoothing out the top with the back of a spoon until evenly distributed.

Move to the freezer and make sure the tin is sitting flat. Leave to firm up for at least 3 hours, or up to 3 days.

Remove from the freezer 10 minutes before serving in slices, with another little splash of vin santo over the top if you like.

Mousse al cioccolato all'olio di oliva e rosmarino

William's chocolate & rosemary olive oil mousse

SERVES 4

4 rosemary sprigs

120 ml (4 fl oz) very good olive oil

150 g (5½ oz) very good dark chocolate

sea salt

4 organic eggs

5 tablespoons caster sugar

TO SERVE

olive oil

sea salt

This mousse is a wonderful celebration of two of the mainstays in our garden at home at Arniano, rosemary and olives. It is a particular joy to make in November using the rich and unctuous new season's olive oil. Olive oil replaces the usual cream of a traditional mousse, making it simultaneously lighter and yet richer, a happy oxymoron giving a texture like a sweet chocolatey mayonnaise. It's a combination that was first suggested to me by my dear friend and maestro on our painting courses, William Roper-Curzon. He lives in Greece, where he first tried this dessert, and we often have lively discussions as to the merits of Italian versus Greek olive oil.

Serving the mousse with a drizzle more olive oil and a sprinkling of sea salt is an inspired touch suggested by another friend, Duncan, a quintessential *buongustaio* (gourmet) who excels at making things just that little bit more delicious, and it does indeed bring this pudding to dizzying new heights.

PREPARATION:– 35 minutes
CHILLING:– 1 hour

Put the rosemary sprigs in a small saucepan and cover with the olive oil. Gently warm over a low heat for about 5 minutes, until a few little bubbles appear. You don't want the oil to boil or cook too furiously. The moment you see a bubble, immediately turn off the heat and leave the rosemary to infuse for about 20 minutes. (If you're short on time, don't worry, just continue with the recipe – your mousse will just be a little less 'rosemary-y'.)

Pour a little water into a small saucepan and bring to the boil over a high heat. Break the chocolate into pieces and place in a large heatproof bowl with a pinch of salt. Place the bowl over the saucepan, making sure the bottom of the bowl doesn't have any contact with the boiling water. Leave the chocolate to melt over the boiling water, stirring occasionally. Once almost completely melted, remove the bowl from the heat and stir the chocolate until melted and smooth. Set aside to cool a little.

Separate the eggs, putting the whites into a very clean, dry mixing bowl, and the egg yolks and 4 tablespoons of the sugar into a large serving bowl from which you can serve the mousse later.

Discard the rosemary sprigs and add the olive oil to the melted chocolate bit by bit, stirring well to make sure it's well amalgamated and smooth.

Using hand-held electric beaters, whisk the egg yolks and sugar for about 2 minutes, until thick and pale. Give the beaters a rinse and whisk the egg whites with a pinch of salt until frothy. Add the remaining tablespoon of sugar and whisk until stiff peaks form. Set aside.

While the melted chocolate mixture is warmish, rather than still very hot, gradually mix it through the beaten egg yolks using a spatula or large spoon. The mixture will be quite thick and dense. Once amalgamated, add a tablespoon of the beaten egg whites, gently folding the rest in bit by bit. I find the best way to do this is to scoop around the rim of the bowl and then cut down through the centre to fold the chocolatey mass with the whites. Repeat until all the egg white is incorporated into the chocolate.

Once amalgamated, scoop off any mousse clinging around the top of the bowl and drop it into the main batch. Give the rim a wipe with a clean tea towel.

Leave to set in the fridge for at least 1 hour, or loosely covered overnight.

Remove from the fridge 15 minutes before serving alongside some very good olive oil for drizzling and sea salt for everyone to sprinkle over their mousse.

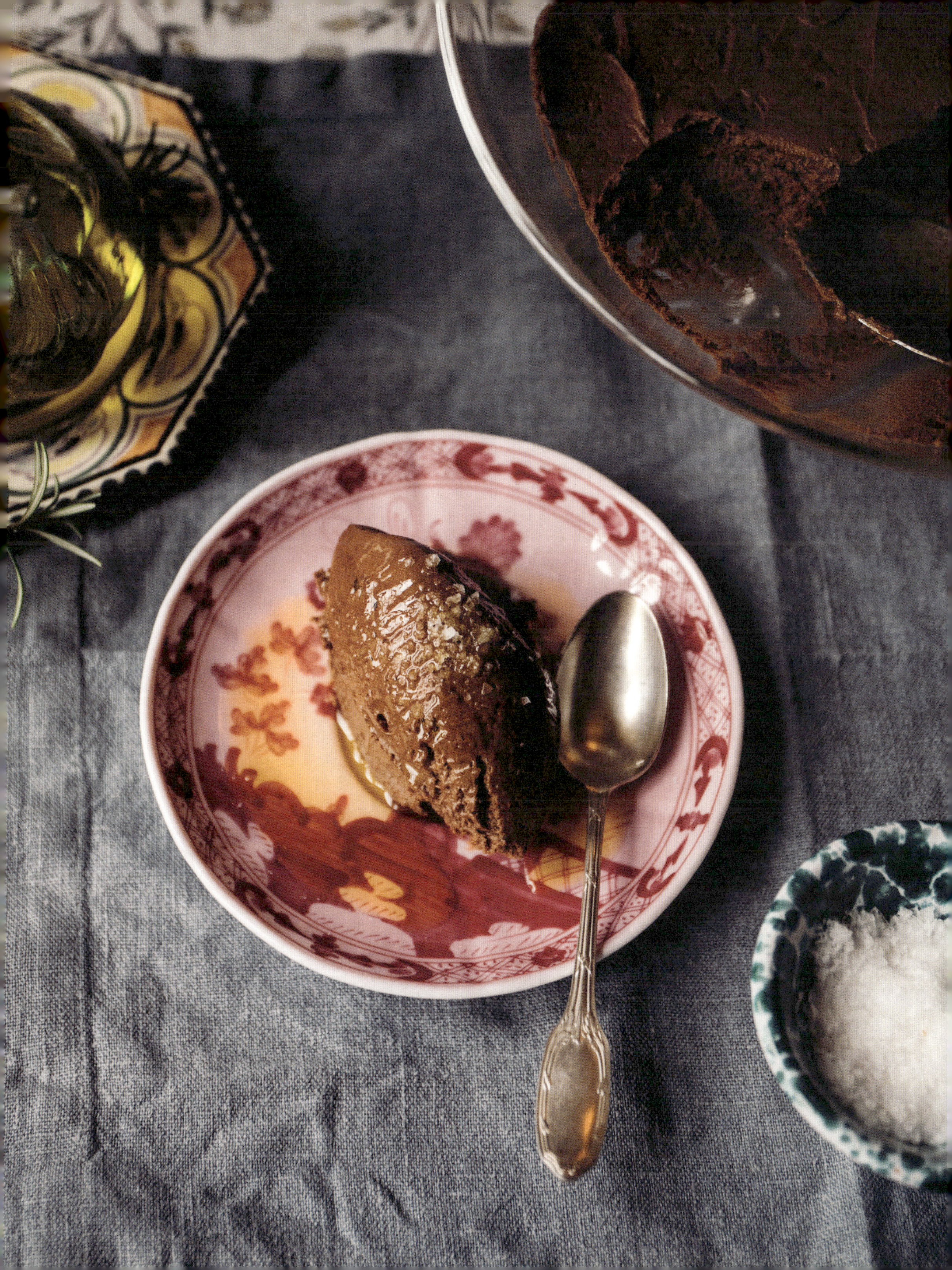

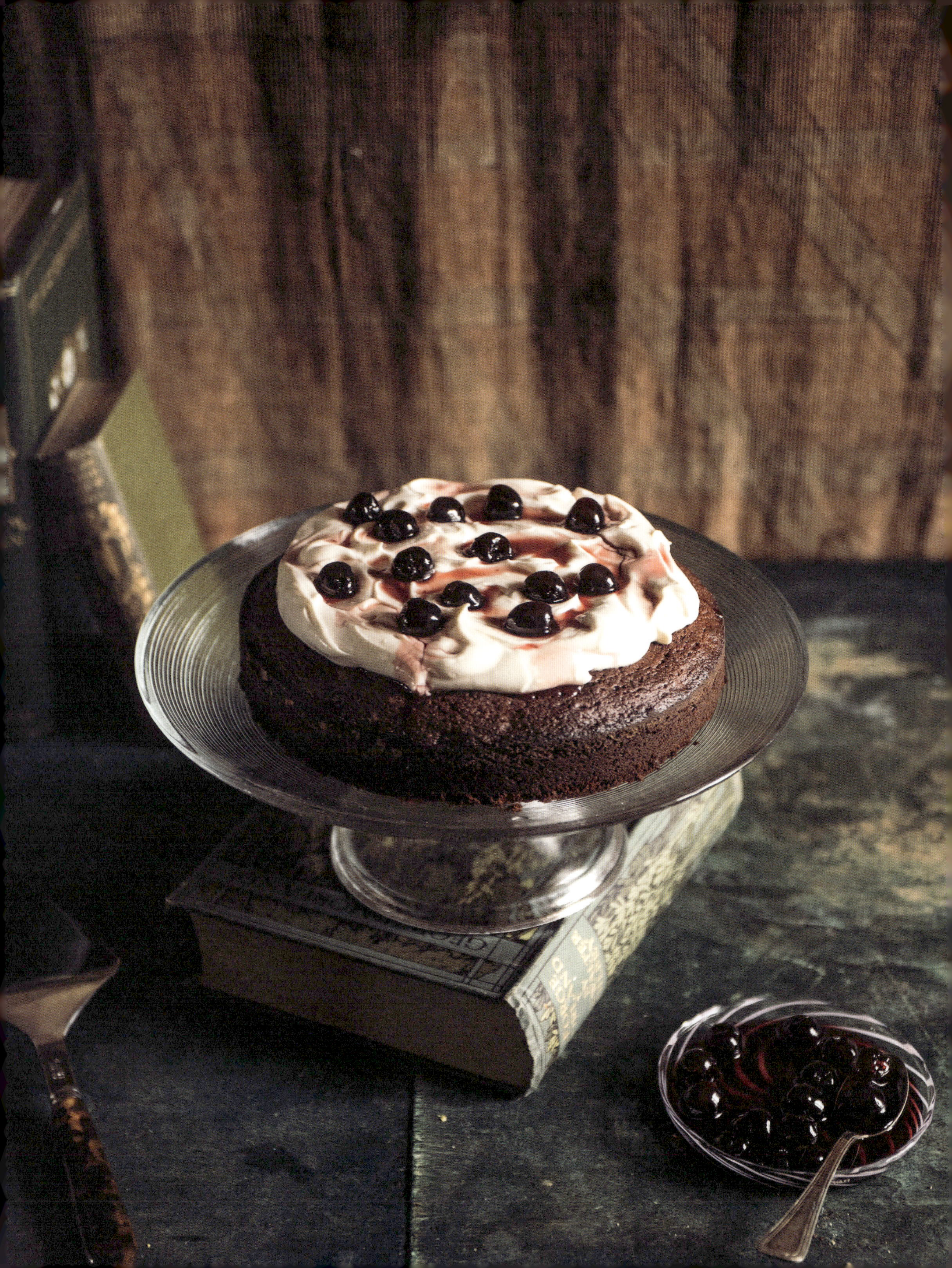

Torta al cioccolato con amarene

Chocolate & Amarena cherry cake

SERVES 4

125 g (4½ oz) unsalted butter, plus extra for greasing

125 g (4½ oz) self-raising flour

120 g (4½ oz) dark chocolate, broken into small pieces

pinch of sea salt

100 g (3½ oz) Amarena cherries, roughly chopped, plus 3 tablespoons of the cherry syrup (see note)

200 g (7 oz) cherry jam

100 g (3½ oz) caster sugar

2 large organic eggs, beaten

FOR THE TOP

250 g (9 oz) fresh ricotta, drained

1 tablespoon icing sugar

2 tablespoons Amarena cherries, plus 2 tablespoons of the cherry syrup (see note)

NOTE:– If you can't find Amarena cherries or baulk at their cost, you can leave these out of the cake batter and use 300 g (10½ oz) cherry jam instead. For the topping, gently warm about 3 tablespoons of cherry jam for a few minutes until liquid, and simply drizzle it over the ricotta from a height using a teaspoon.

This is a dense, cherry-infused chocolate cake which can be mixed in one pan. It has developed as a variation over the years from a favourite recipe in our house, queen Nigella's spectacular chocolate and marmalade sponge from her book, *How to Be a Domestic Goddess*. I love it as it's pretty failsafe, quick and the ingredients are normally in my cupboard, perfect for a winter's night when I want something indulgent but can't face braving the cold to go to the shops. Amarena cherries are black cherries from Emilia–Romagna and preserved in cherry syrup. They are very easy to find in supermarkets in Italy and are sold in pretty Art Nouveau–style jars. They are available in delis outside Italy, but are expensive; the cheapest I have found abroad are the 600 g (1 lb 5 oz) jars that can be bought online. They are a useful thing to have in the cupboard as you can throw together a last-minute dessert in seconds – if you have a tub of vanilla ice cream in the freezer, simply spoon over some of the Amarena syrup and a few black cherries.

PREPARATION:– 10 minutes
COOKING:– 50 minutes

Preheat the oven to 150°C (300°F) fan-forced. Butter a 20 cm (8 inch) cake tin or loaf tin and line with baking parchment.

Melt the butter in a saucepan, then remove from the heat. Add the chocolate and salt and stir well until completely melted. Stir in the cherries and cherry syrup, then add the sugar and mix in the eggs. Bit by bit, mix in the flour.

With the help of a spatula, pour the batter into the cake tin and bake (without opening the oven door) for 45–50 minutes, until a cake tester inserted in the centre comes out cleanish.

Remove the cake from the oven and leave in the tin to cool completely.

While the cake cools, drain the ricotta in a colander to rid it of excess moisture. Transfer to a bowl and whisk using hand-held electric beaters for about 1 minute, until velvety and smooth. Sift in the icing sugar and whisk again for about a minute, until shiny and smooth.

Once the cake has cooled, transfer it to a serving plate or cake stand, ready for topping. Spoon the ricotta on top of the cake in a heap in the middle, smoothing out the edges with the back of a spoon. Dot the cherries around the top of the cake, then drizzle the cherry syrup over from a height.

Serve in slices, at room temperature.

The cake will keep for up to 3 days in an airtight container. If keeping in the fridge, bring up to room temperature before serving.

Torta di polenta all' arancia e timo

Orange, polenta & thyme cake

MAKES 6–8 SLICES

200 g (7 oz) unsalted butter, softened, plus extra for greasing

200 g (7 oz) almond flour

150 g (5½ oz) coarse polenta

20 g (¾ oz) cornflour

1 teaspoon baking powder

handful of thyme sprigs, leaves picked

150 g (5½ oz) caster sugar

zest of 4 oranges

3 organic eggs

juice of 1 orange

SYRUP

3 tablespoons runny honey

juice of 1 orange

a few thyme sprigs, leaves picked

This is a lovely light and floral cake to enjoy at any time of the day; I'll often have it at breakfast (Italians love cake for breakfast) or with a cup of coffee in the afternoon. It's also a great dessert served alongside a dollop of crème fraîche. I use thyme sprigs from the garden in this recipe, but you can leave these out if you don't have any to hand, for a classic orange and polenta cake. The cake also happens to be gluten free, being made with almond flour and polenta (cornmeal).

PREPARATION:– 15 minutes
COOKING:– 45 minutes, plus cooling time

Preheat the oven to 160°C (315°F) fan-forced. Butter a 20 cm (8 inch) cake tin or loaf tin and line with baking parchment.

In a bowl, mix together the almond flour, polenta, cornflour and baking powder. Set aside.

Melt 1 tablespoon of the butter in a small saucepan with the thyme leaves. When sizzling, stir to help the thyme infuse. Remove from the heat once the butter is completely melted.

In a large mixing bowl, cream the remaining butter with the sugar until thick and pale, using hand-held electric beaters. Add the orange zest and melted butter (including the thyme leaves).

One by one, mix in the eggs, then stir in the orange juice. Bit by bit, stir the dry ingredients through using a spatula, until fully incorporated.

Pour the batter into the cake tin, then bake for 40–45 minutes (without opening the oven door), until the cake is golden on top and well risen. If a cake tester comes out covered in batter and the cake needs a little more time, bake for another 5 minutes and test again.

Remove the cake from the oven and leave in the tin to cool completely.

Meanwhile, make the syrup by heating the honey in a small saucepan with the orange juice and thyme leaves for about 5 minutes, until fully liquid and bubbling.

Prick the top of the cake all over with a fork, pour the syrup over and leave to soak in while the cake cools.

Once cooled, turn the cake out onto a serving plate. Serve alongside a spoonful of crème fraîche, yoghurt or whipped cream.

The cake will keep for up to 5 days in an airtight container. If keeping in the fridge, bring up to room temperature before serving.

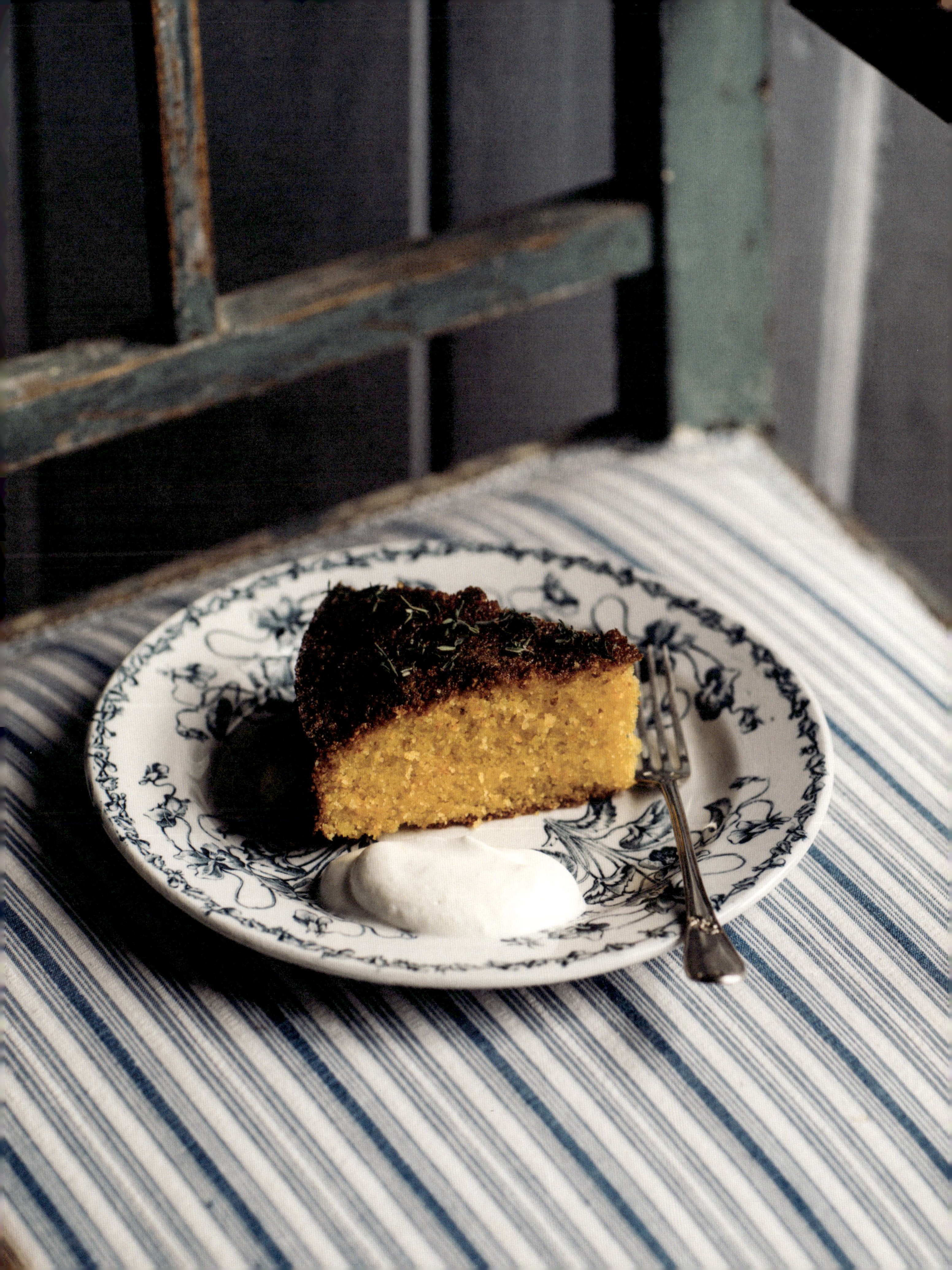

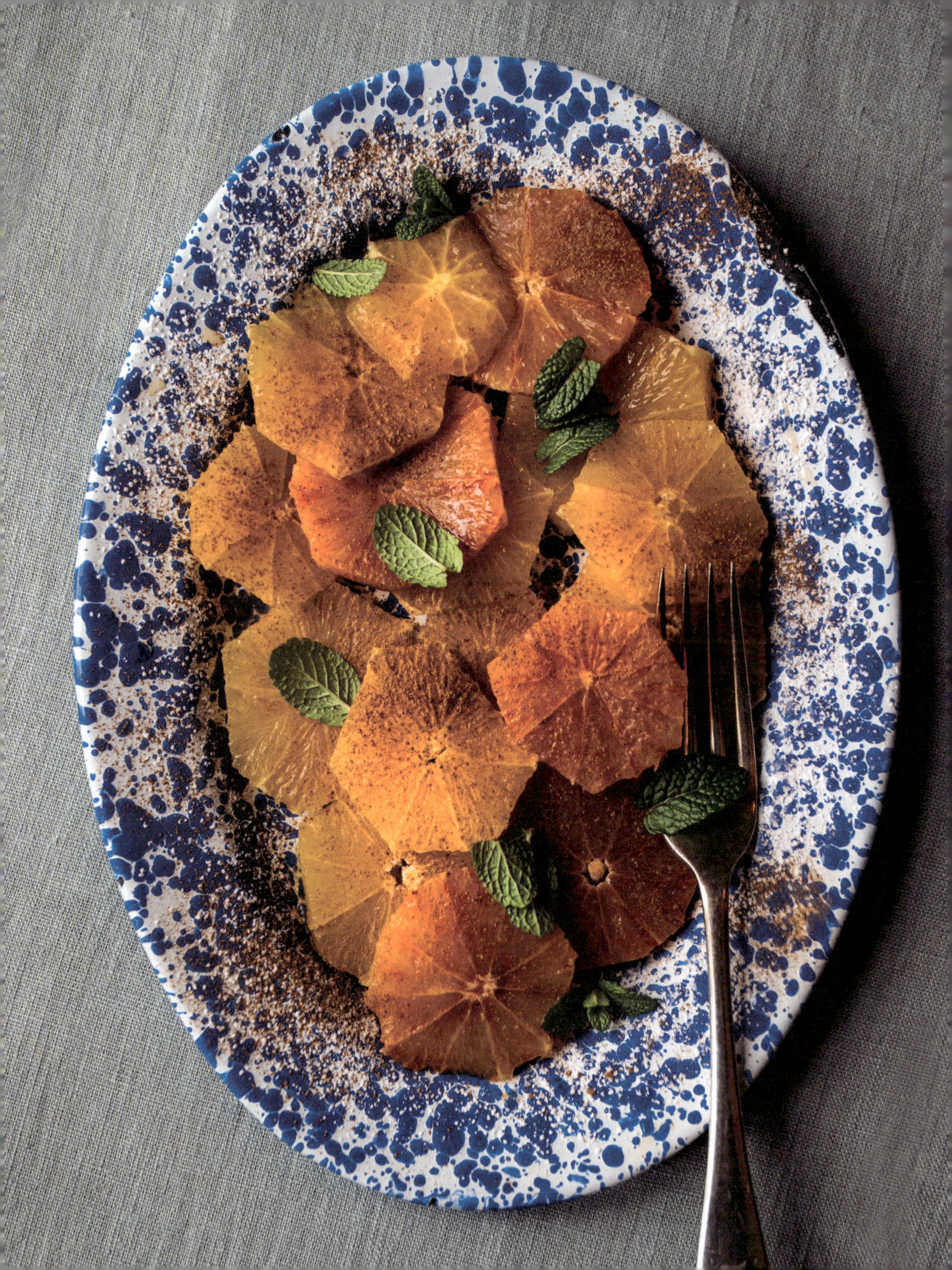

Arance con cannella

Matthew's orange & cinnamon salad

SERVES 4

1 orange per person (preferably blood orange)
1 tablespoon ground cinnamon
100 g (3½ oz) icing sugar
handful of mint leaves

Whenever I am stuck for a dessert, especially after an elaborate or rich meal, I turn to this simple but aesthetically pleasing dish devised by my husband. He maintains that one of the great luxuries in life is to have an orange peeled and sliced for one, as they are so delicious to eat but so messy to prepare. He was once served this dessert in Fez while driving through Morocco to The Gambia, where oranges grow in abundance, and says the addition of cinnamon and icing sugar elevates the simple orange to something really special. I particularly love this dessert in deepest winter, when oranges are at their best – but if for some reason your oranges are not very sweet or of good quality, the icing sugar and cinnamon will lift them to sublimely delicious heights.

Another great thing is that you can prepare this dish before dinner and let it sit until you're ready to serve it.

PREPARATION:– 5 minutes

Using a sharp knife, cut off the top and bottom of each orange so that you can stand them upright. Starting from the top, slice away the orange peel in strips, following the shape of the orange, and working all the way around.

Cut the oranges into neat and reasonably thick slices and arrange them in an attractive fashion on a large shallow platter. Liberally sprinkle the cinnamon and icing sugar over the oranges, using a sieve if you have one to hand.

Just before serving, decorate with a few mint leaves. We usually eat this dessert on its own, but it's also fabulous with a drizzle of cream or a dollop of vanilla ice cream.

Ricciarelli

Sienese Ricciarelli

MAKES 16

200 g (7 oz) almond flour
200 g (7 oz) icing sugar
2 organic egg whites
zest of 1 orange
seeds from 1 vanilla pod
squeeze of lemon juice

Ricciarelli are soft Sienese biscuits made from almond flour, egg whites and sugar. They date back to the 15th century, when sweets made of almond, such as marzipan, began to come into fashion. There are many theories as to how these pastries made their way to Siena, one being that it was due to an influx of Sicilian immigrants, another that they were brought by Arab spice traders passing through the city. Originally they were known as *marzapetti*, little marzipans, but around 1800 they developed into what we now recognise as *ricciarelli*.

They are extremely easy to make, with the added bonus of being gluten free and dairy free. Delicious with a cup of coffee after lunch, they also make a perfect house present when nicely wrapped – though they don't keep long, so try to eat them within two days. One usually does.

PREPARATION:– 2 hours
COOKING:– 15 minutes

Mix the almond flour in a bowl with 120 g (4½ oz) of the icing sugar. Reserve the remaining icing sugar for shaping the biscuits later.

Using hand-held electric beaters, whisk the egg whites in a large metal bowl for a couple of minutes, until they start frothing. Add the orange zest, vanilla and lemon juice and whisk again; it should look like a liquid froth.

Using a spoon, stir in the almond flour mixture until you have a smooth, thick mixture that resembles marzipan.

Put the dough in a sealed container, or a bowl topped with a plate, then leave to rest in the fridge for at least 2 hours.

Preheat the oven to 150°C (300°F) fan-forced. Line a large baking tray with baking parchment.

Retrieve the dough from the fridge. Now that it has cooled and rested, the dough should be denser and easier to handle. Spread the reserved icing sugar on a plate. Using a tablespoon, scoop off a walnut-sized piece of dough and roll it between your hands into a ball, then lengthen and shape it into a long diamond. Repeat with the remaining dough.

Once you've shaped all the *ricciarelli*, dust them liberally in the icing sugar so that the biscuits are completely white all over.

Place them on the baking tray, spacing them apart. Pat any leftover icing sugar over the top of each one so they are topped with a thick layer.

Bake for 5 minutes, then turn the oven up to 170°C (325°F) and bake for another 9 minutes, until cracks start forming in the icing sugar.

Remove from the oven and leave to cool completely, before storing in an airtight container. The *ricciarelli* are best enjoyed within 2 days.

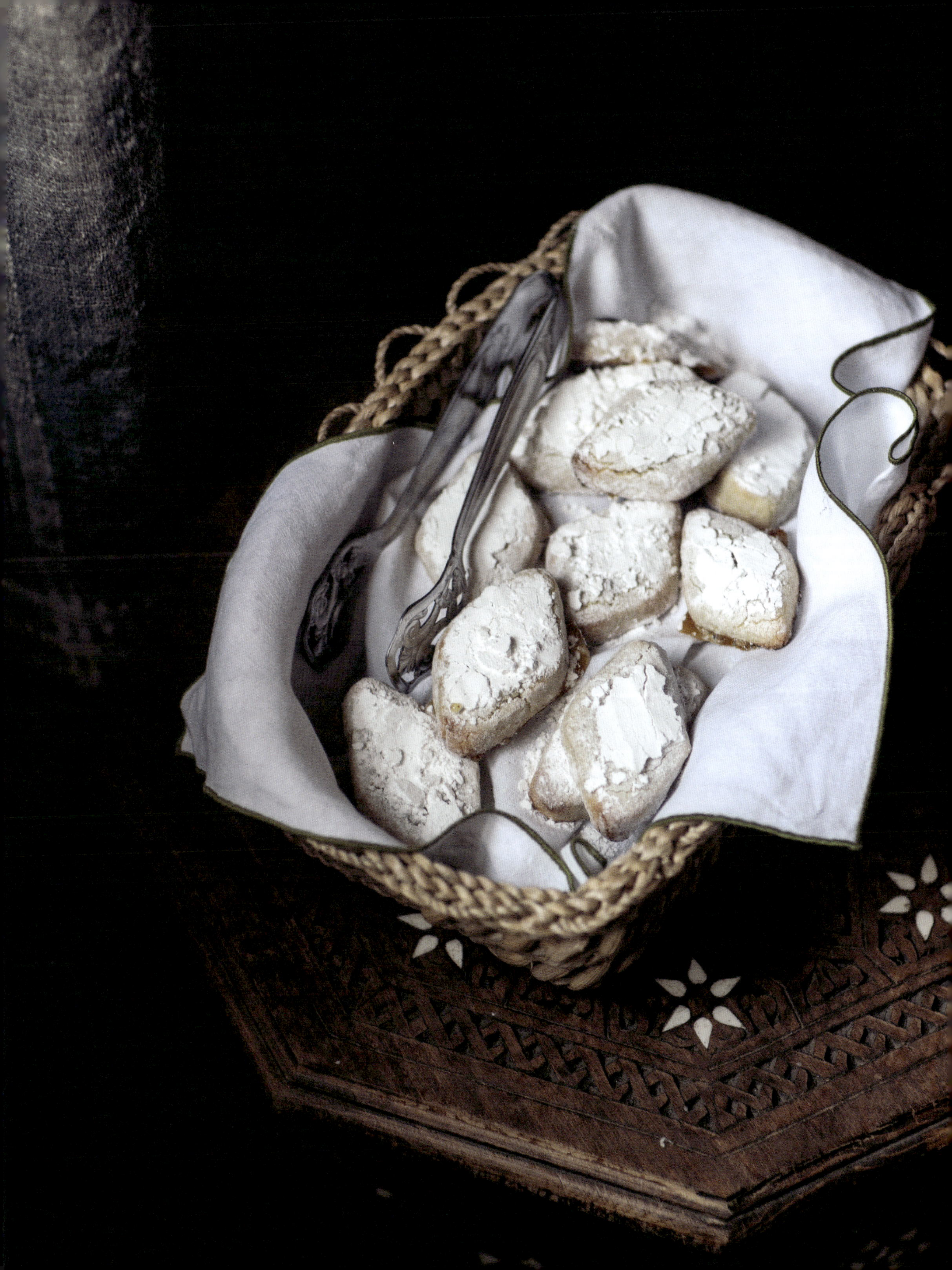

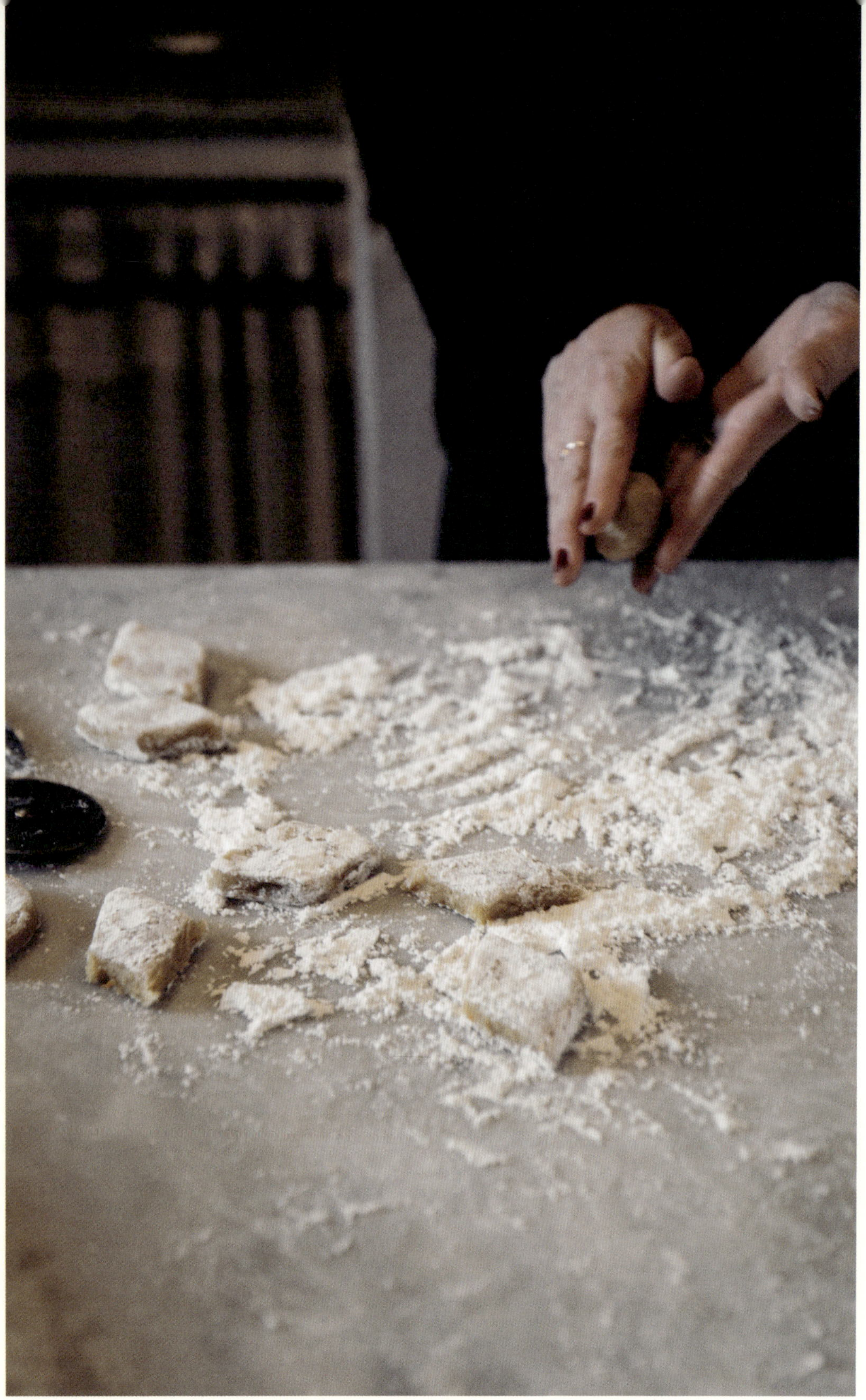

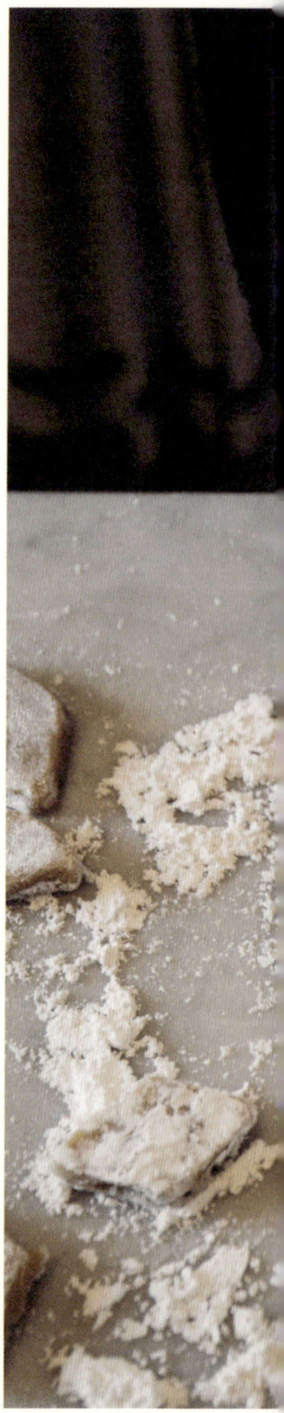

DOLCI

Panforte senese

Sienese spiced honey & nut cake

SERVES 4

300 g (10½ oz) almonds

100 g (3½ oz) hazelnuts

150 g (5½ oz) caster sugar

75 g (2¾ oz) runny honey

200 g (7 oz) mixed candied orange and lemon peel

4 whole cloves, finely crushed, or ⅓ teaspoon ground cloves

½ whole nutmeg, finely grated

½ teaspoon ground cinnamon

a few grinds of black pepper

3 tablespoons plain flour

200 g (7 oz) icing sugar

Nothing makes me think of Siena more than panforte. Literally meaning 'hard bread', panforte is an aromatic cross between a cake and candy, being made predominantly of nuts and candied fruit, held together by a honey and sugar syrup with hardly any flour. It dates back to the 11th century, when spices were king, and so is highly spiced with nutmeg, cloves, cinnamon and a little black pepper. Containing no dairy or eggs, it also had the benefit of keeping for a long time.

The beauty of panforte is that you can play around with it. Some people add a few finely chopped dried figs, or substitute the hazelnuts with walnuts. You can play around with the spices or add a tablespoon of cocoa powder to make it chocolatey. Or make it vegan friendly by using maple syrup instead of honey.

The version below is a classic Panforte Margherita, named after Queen Margherita's visit to Siena in 1879 to see the Palio horse race. It makes a wonderful Christmas gift, as it's fairly low effort, and wrapped in nice wrapping paper or presented in a pretty tin box, it keeps for months in a sealed container. I often serve it with a cup of coffee after lunch.

PREPARATION:– 15 minutes
COOKING:– 25 minutes, plus setting time

Preheat the oven to 180°C (350°F) fan-forced. Line the base and sides of a 24 cm (9 inch) loose-bottomed cake tin with baking parchment.

Spread the almonds and hazelnuts on a baking tray and roast for about 10 minutes.

Meanwhile, combine the caster sugar and honey in a small saucepan and set over a medium heat until the sugar has dissolved and the honey is totally liquid, stirring occasionally. This should take about 3 minutes. You want the sugar and honey to amalgamate into a thick syrup, not to caramelise. As soon as you see bubbles or the mixture starts boiling, remove from the heat and stir well.

Remove the nuts from the oven and turn the oven down to 160°C (315°F) fan-forced.

Toss the warm roasted nuts into a large mixing bowl. Add the candied peel, spices and flour and mix well.

Pour the honey syrup over the mixture and stir. After a minute or so – and a bit of elbow grease – the flour should look like it's disappeared and everything should come together in a lovely sticky mass. It's important that the nuts are still warm at this stage as it will help the mixture come together.

Pour or spoon the batter into the cake tin and press down using the back of a wet spoon – the liquid will prevent the mixture sticking. Once it's all in, wet your hands and use your fingers and palms to push the mixture down hard into the tin and smooth out the top, so that it's level and well compacted. Sprinkle with 2 tablespoons of the icing sugar, rubbing it into the top.

Bake for 25 minutes, until the cake smells nutty and the icing sugar has dried out.

Remove from the oven and leave in the tin to cool completely. Leave to set for a few hours or overnight in the cake tin, then drape a tea towel over the top once it has cooled completely.

Once completely cooled and set, turn the panforte out of the cake tin. Rub the top and sides with the remaining icing sugar until it's white all over.

Panforte keeps in an airtight container for up to 1 month. Cut into thin slices to serve.

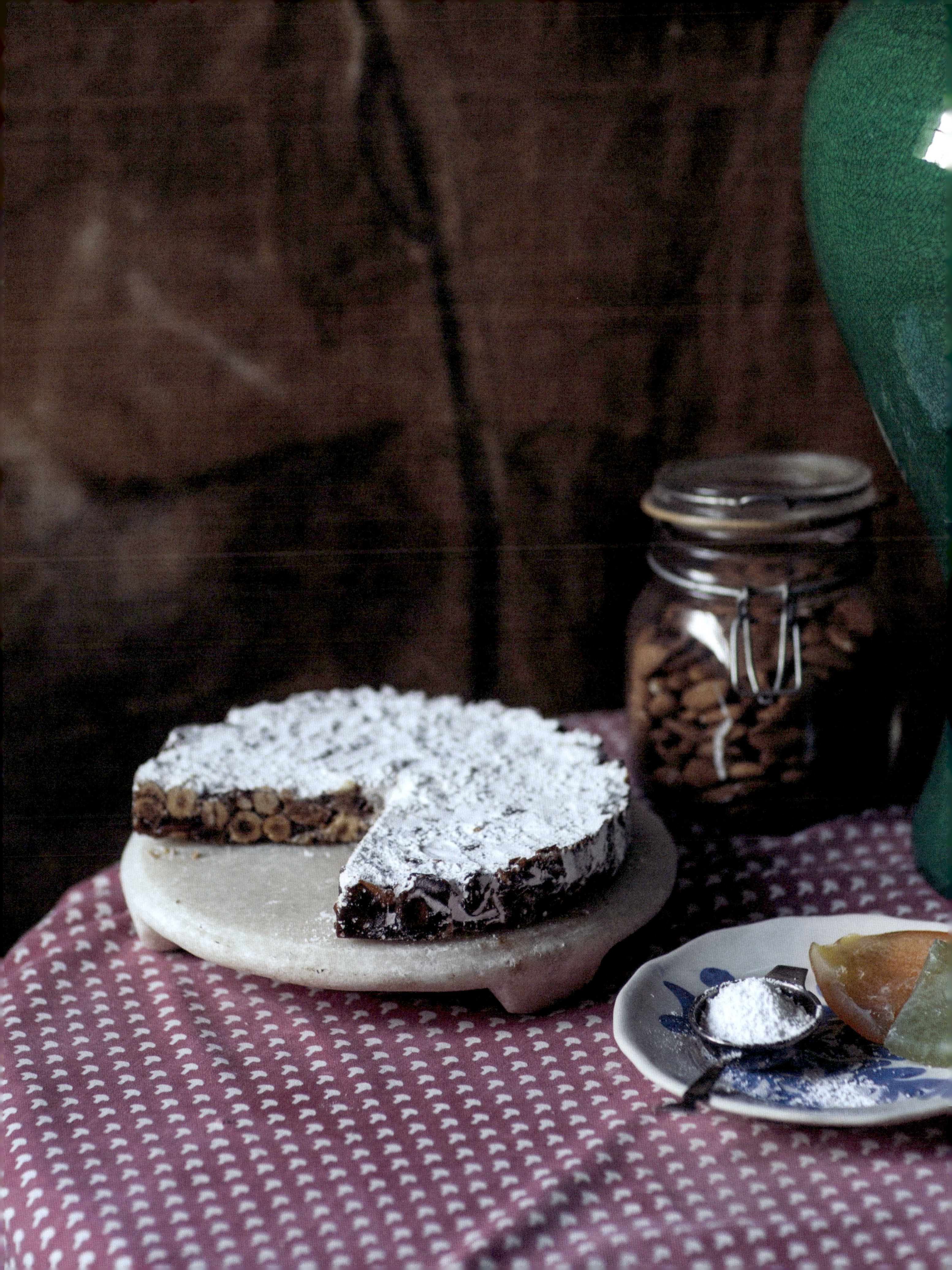

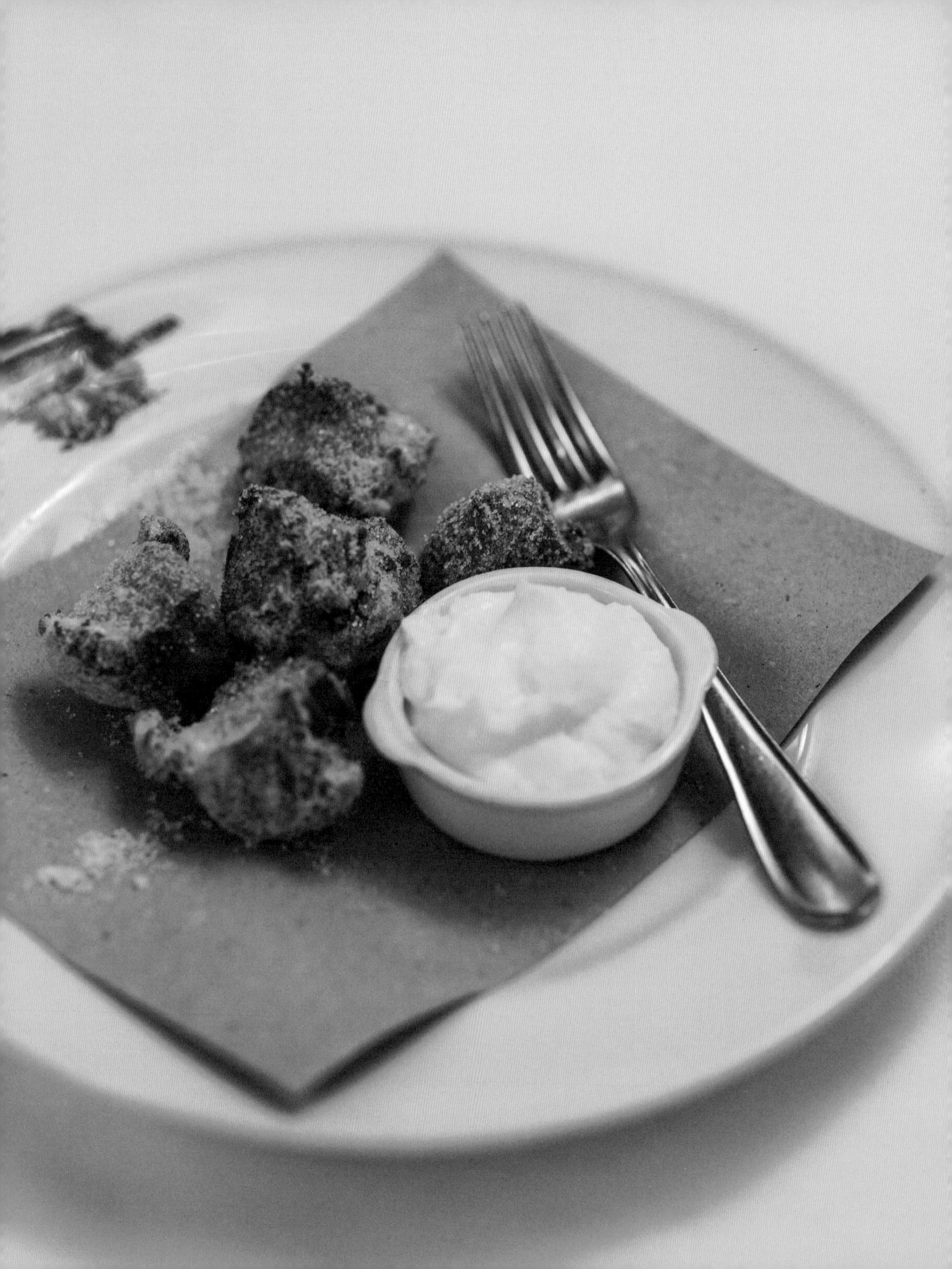

Frittelle di castagne con ricotta al rum

Chestnut flour fritters with whipped ricotta

SERVES 4

250 g (9 oz) chestnut flour

pinch of sea salt

75 g (2¾ oz) walnuts, roughly chopped

1 tablespoon raisins, roughly chopped if large

sunflower oil, for deep-frying

1 organic egg white

50 g (1¾ oz) caster sugar

FOR THE WHIPPED RICOTTA

125 g (4½ oz) fresh sheep's ricotta, drained

2 tablespoons double cream

2 tablespoons sugar

1 tablespoon sweet rum, vin santo or marsala

TO SERVE

100 g (3½ oz) sugar

These fritters are my friend Chiara's reinvention of the traditional Tuscan dessert *castagnaccio* (chestnut flour cake), which is made in most bakeries, homes and restaurants in late autumn and winter. I am not mad on *castagnaccio*, finding it a bit cloying, but Chiara's version, which turns the mixture into little deep-fried sugar-coated fritters served alongside a sweet and boozy ricotta dip, has converted me to chestnut flour desserts. She normally only makes them with a special flour made of smoked chestnuts produced by a friend of her husband, Massimo. While this eye to detail is why they run one of the best restaurants in Florence – Trattoria Cammillo – I have found that her recipe, which she has kindly shared, works beautifully with regular chestnut flour from the shops. An unintended bonus of chestnut flour is that it is naturally sweet, so there is little sugar in the mixture – and it is also gluten free, making this is a good indulgent option for those avoiding gluten.

I usually fry the *frittelle* just before sitting down for dinner, then serve them warm as dessert.

PREPARATION:– 10 minutes
COOKING:– 5–10 minutes

Start by preparing the whipped ricotta. Place the ricotta, cream and sugar in a bowl and whisk until smooth and velvety, using hand-held electric beaters. Add the rum and whisk until incorporated. Set aside in the fridge while you make the *frittelle*.

In a large bowl, mix together the chestnut flour, salt, walnuts and raisins. Slowly start adding 175 ml (6 fl oz) water and mixing it into the flour. You want all the flour to be wet, but you're after a coarse, dry-looking dough that isn't too wet. If it looks too dry, add a splash of water, bearing in mind that the egg white will add a little more moisture later.

Pour enough sunflower oil into a wide, deep heavy-based saucepan to come about two-thirds of the way up the sides. Set the heat to medium.

Meanwhile, in a clean metal bowl, whisk the egg white using hand-held electric beaters until frothy. Add a tablespoon of the sugar and keep beating, gradually adding the rest of the sugar until you have stiff peaks.

Using a clean metal spoon or spatula, gently fold the egg whites through the dough mixture, being careful not to knock the air out, until it is all incorporated.

Once the oil has heated up, drop a little piece of dough into the oil: if it sizzles and floats to the top, your oil is ready. Use 2 teaspoons to scoop up some of the dough and shape it to the size of a walnut, dropping it directly into the oil. Repeat to make more *frittelle*, being careful not to overcrowd your pan. After 30 seconds, use a slotted spoon to flip them over so they cook evenly. Cook for another 30 seconds, turning down the heat if they are looking too dark. Once uniformly golden caramel brown, transfer to a plate lined with paper towel and leave to drain while frying the next batch.

Tip the 100 g (3½ oz) sugar in a large bowl. While still hot, toss the *frittelle* in the sugar to coat.

Transfer to a serving plate and serve hot, with the whipped ricotta.

THIS SPREAD:— Being taught to make *frittelle di castagne* by Chiara

247

Cenci

Fried carnival 'rags'

SERVES 4

145 g (5 oz) '00' flour

½ teaspoon baking powder

pinch of sea salt

1 organic egg yolk

1 tablespoon caster sugar

50 ml (1¾ fl oz) vin santo (or grappa, marsala or white wine)

zest of 1 orange or lemon

15 g (½ oz) unsalted butter, melted

sunflower oil, for frying

icing sugar, to serve

Light, moreish and not overly sweet, *cenci* are made of dough that has been rolled as thinly as fine translucent poplin, sliced into long thin 'rags' and deep-fried, left to cool, then dusted liberally with icing sugar. They appear all over Italy with various names, and are only made during Carnevale – the month leading up to Lent when observers of religion tend to gorge ahead of the 40 days of deprivation that precede Easter. Our village of Buonconvento took Carnevale very seriously when I was a child. Each *quartiere* (neighbourhood) had their own themed float, which we would all ride around town on, scattering the streets with confetti, and the children would all be kitted out in costumes sewed diligently by local ladies who volunteered their time. Carnevale was the bane of my mother's life: not only did we come home with our shoes, hair and pockets full of confetti which went all over the house, but she detested the cheap nylon tackiness of it all. Looking back, the themes set by the *quartiere* for our outfits on the float were sometimes quite odd: one year we were 'mad cow disease', which meant dressing up as a hot-pink spotted cow; another year we were the 'summer of love' and dressed as pink-spangled hippies, complete with plastic spliff. I think my mother had a different vision for our bucolic Tuscan upbringing.

PREPARATION:– 45 minutes
COOKING:– 5–10 minutes

In a bowl, mix the flour with the baking powder and salt. In another large bowl, whisk the egg yolk with the sugar using a fork until amalgamated, then mix in the vin santo, orange zest and butter. Bit by bit start adding the flour, mixing together as you go.

Once you have a rough dough, tip it out onto a clean surface and knead for 5–8 minutes, until homogenous. Roll into a ball and place on a plate with an upturned bowl on top. Set aside to rest at warmish room temperature for at least 30 minutes; this is key to allowing the signature air bubbles to form during frying.

Divide the rested dough into two even pieces. Using a rolling pin and a little more flour so the dough doesn't stick, roll the dough out as thinly as you can – to a very thin, translucent pasta dough. You can also do this using a pasta machine, gradually going from the widest to the thinnest setting. (Rolling the dough very thinly is also key to getting those air bubbles during frying.)

Using a serrated rolling cutter or knife, cut the dough into rectangular pieces about 20 cm × 5 cm (8 inches × 2 inches). No need to get out the ruler here.

Pour enough sunflower oil into a wide, deep heavy-based saucepan to come about two-thirds of the way up the sides. Heat the oil to 175°C (345°F) over a medium heat. Once bubbles begin to appear, the oil is hot enough to start frying your *cenci* – a piece of dough gently dropped into the oil should sizzle.

Fry the *cenci* in batches for a few seconds on each side, until light golden and bubbly looking. They need hardly any time in the hot oil. If they go dark brown, turn down the heat and wait a moment. Transfer each batch to a plate lined with paper towel to soak up any excess oil, then transfer to a serving plate and leave to cool completely.

Once cooled and ready to serve, dust liberally with icing sugar.

The *cenci* will keep for 2 days in an airtight container. If you are taking them somewhere as a gift, don't dust them with icing sugar until the last minute.

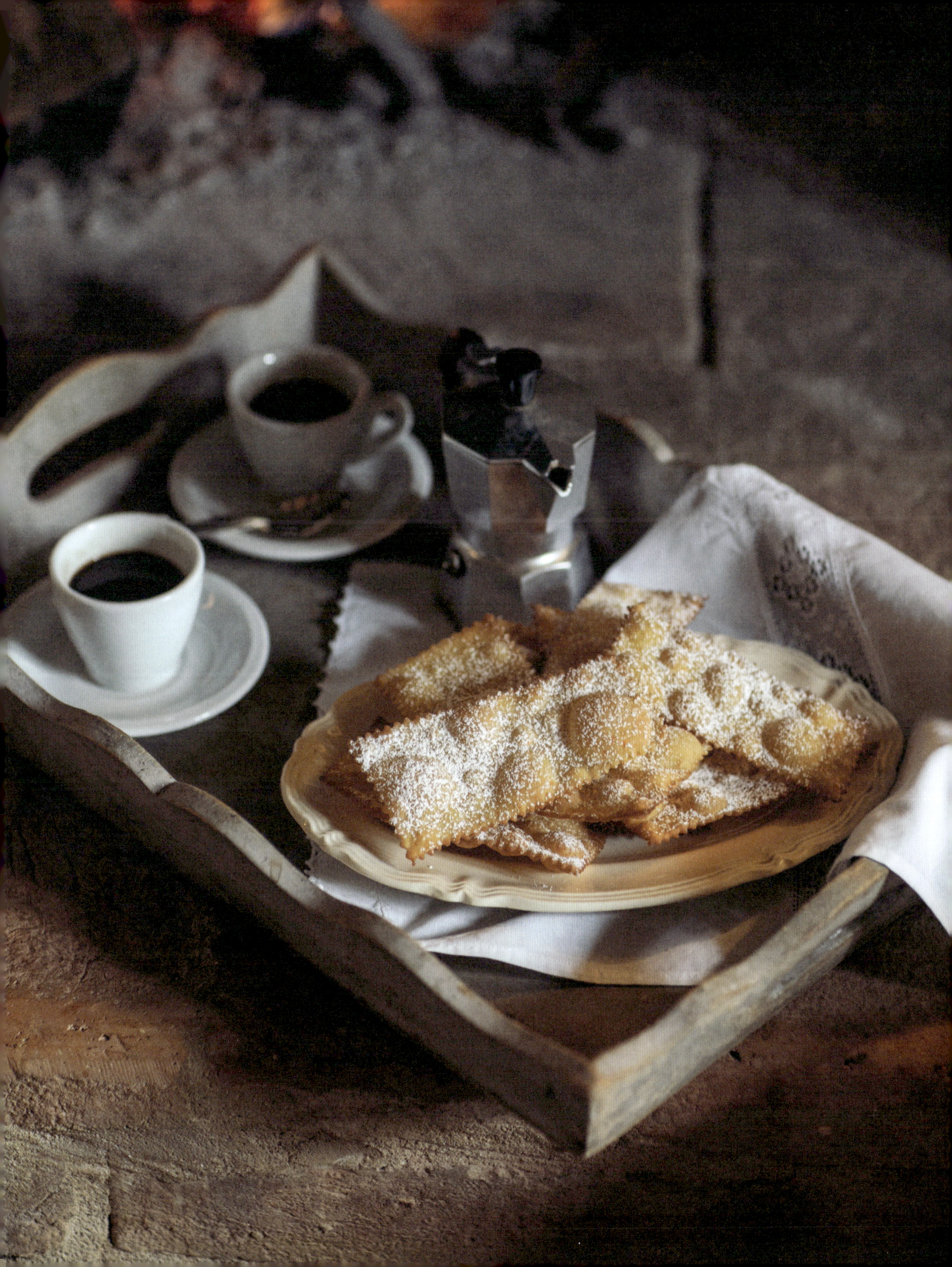

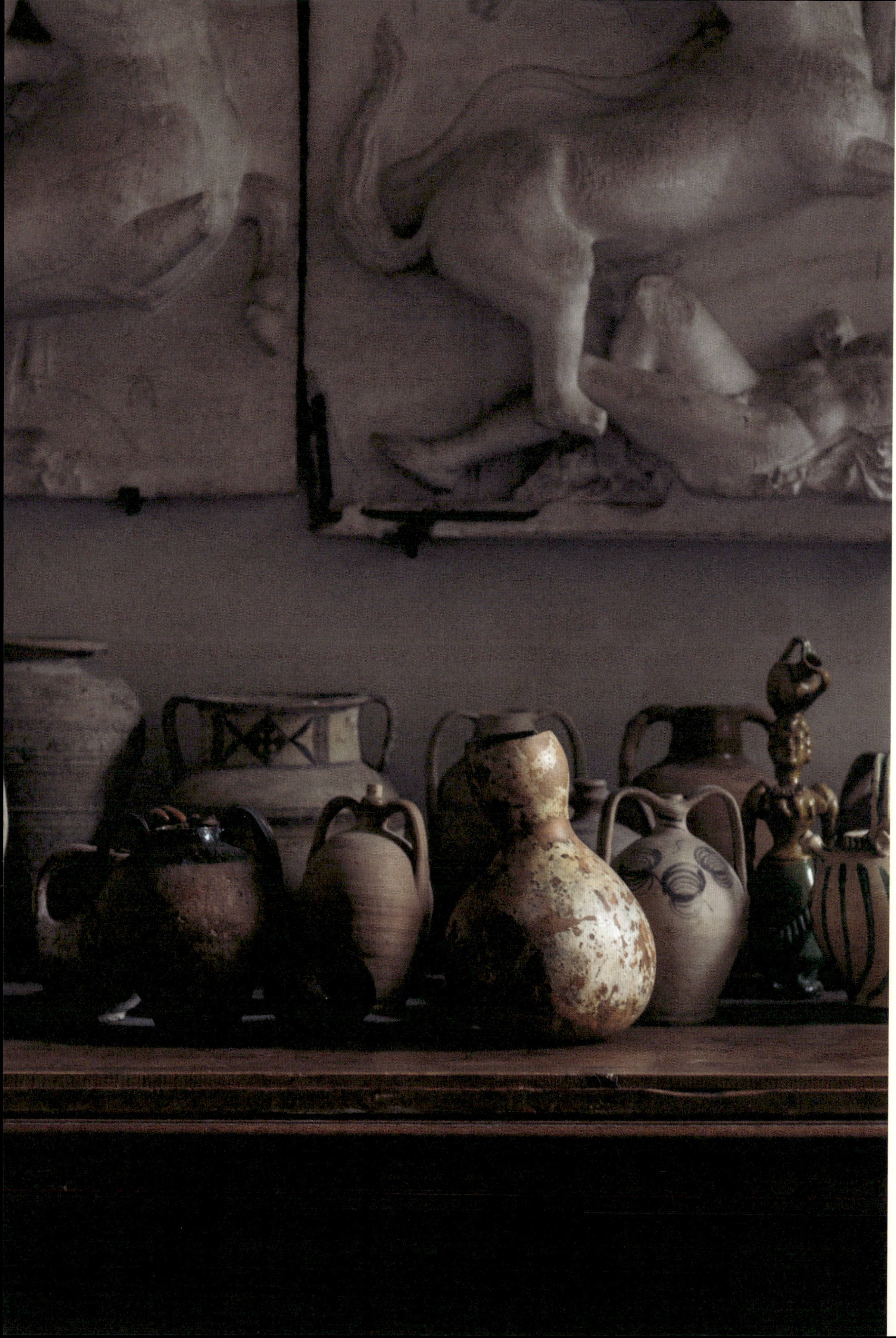

ACKNOWLEDGEMENTS

I would first like to thank my husband, Matthew, for whose seemingly endless patience and support I never stop being grateful. I am so lucky to have you cheering me on, as my in-house editor, creative partner and taste tester - your brutal honesty and constructive criticism are invaluable and keep me laughing. To my publisher, Kirsten Abbott, your sense, good taste and steady hand on the tiller elevate all things you touch. To our designer, Ashlea O'Neill, for her thoughtful, beautiful and inspired design. To Fay Helfenbaum, Shannon Grey and everyone at Thames & Hudson, thank you for keeping me and the book on track in a very tight turn around. Huge thanks also to my wonderful editor Katri Hilden. Your fine tuning of the text and marshalling of my thoughts were invaluable.

To our unstoppable photographic team, thank you for bringing my recipes and words to life and for making a very full-on, ambitious shoot so enjoyable. To Valentina Solfrini for your gorgeous photography, to Benedetta Canale and Gaia Lochetti for your organisation and flawless food styling and Alice Adams Carosi for the beautiful props. To my fabulous agent, Laurie Roberston, thank you for being my sounding board and for all your creative support, encouragement and input.

This book is a collection of cosy family recipes, not just from my family, but also from friends, old and new. I would like to thank the team at Da Mario in Buonconvento, known locally as 'Nara's' - Anna, Cristian, Fonzie, Francesco, thank you. Other local friends who helped bring this book to life are Pamela at Il Paradiso and Gianfranco and Signora Paola from Ristorante la Torre at Monte Oliveto. To my oldest friend Carolina Bracalente and her husband Nicola Voltolini, thank you for being the best greedy companions, friends and recipe tasters and to Carolina for her mum's polpettone recipe.

In Florence, I want to say a huge thank you to Chiara Masiello and Massimo Pettini of Trattoria Cammillo. Your food is always an inspiration and I am thrilled to be able to share two of your recipes in this book. Thank you to Massimo Stagi from Alla Vecchia Bettola, for finally disclosing how to get the softest, tastiest polpette possible and the secret to the Florentine apple cake.

To Andrea and everyone at Casalinga in Santo Spirito for two of the best cavolo nero recipes and thank you to the team at Trattoria del Carmine. A huge thank you also to the fabulously talented Poppy Bertram, who tested many of these recipes and to Rachael Allen of Ballymaloe for putting us in touch.

I'm thrilled and feel very lucky to have been able to use the beautiful frescoes from the Abbey of Monte Oliveto Maggiore as the chapter openers of this book, a privilege which feels all the more special as I have been visiting them all my life and for which I would like to thank the Right Reverend Abbot Dom Diego Gualtiero Rosa, Don Andrea Pintus and Dott.ssa Francesca Giannino of the Sopra Intendenza Belle Arti of Siena. Don Andrea in particular was unbelievably generous with his time and enthusiasm for the project and I am very grateful for his having shared one of the abbey's signature recipes for 'speltotto'. Thank you also to my old friends, the Peploe and Brewster families for allowing us to photograph their beautiful grounds in Florence and to Caterina de Renzis Sonnino for allowing us to photograph Castello Sonnino.

To my friends and family whose support makes everything feel possible: my sister Claudia, Savannah Alvarez, Ben and Juliette Ashworth, Nick and Olwen Bell, Vanessa Garwood, Beata Heuman & John Finlay, Duncan Campbell and Luke Edward Hall, Niccolò Calabrese de Feo and Remy Renzullo, Emily FitzRoy, Grazia Flores, Robyn Lea, Rossana Lippi, David Macmillan, Henry Machin, Liberty Nimmo, William Roper-Curzon and Panos Varoutsos, Jessica Ramirez Canal, George Smith, Grace Pilkington, Tom Richards and Tara Zivkovic, Marcella Testai and, for her endless support and wise counsel, Sue Townsend.

And finally, to my mum, Camilla, and my late dad, Jasper, for our funny upbringing on a Tuscan hilltop, for introducing me to delicious food and good company, and for teaching me to delight in the seasons.

OPPOSITE:– Hilderbrand's sculptures and Cloclo Peploe's collection of pottery in the studio at San Francesco

INDEX

A

abbeys 90, 93, 96, 114
aglione 22
al volo dishes, menu of 38
Alla Vecchia Bettola, Italy 152–153
almonds
    Ricciarelli 238
Amarena cherries
    Chocolate & Amarena cherry cake 233
anchovies
    Burro e acciughe 45
    Fennel in lemony anchovy sauce 54
antipasti 38–39, 44–45, 188
    Baked porcini 57
    Burro e acciughe 45
    Chiara's bruleed pecorino 50
    Crostini 61
    Crostini with cavolo nero & cannellini beans 65
    Crostini with chicken liver pate 62
    Fennel in lemony anchovy sauce 54
    Fettunta 45
    Fried salty 'cuddles' with prosciutto & stracchino 49
    Juliette's mustardy artichoke crostini 66
    Pecorino con pere, miele e noci 45
    Pinziminio 45
    Sausage & stracchino crostone 58
apples
    Cabbage, apple & walnut salad 202
    Florentine apple 'pancake' cake 223
Arniano, Italy 12, 87–90
Arno river, Italy 156, 158
artichokes 22
    Artichoke frittata 133
    Artichokes with parsley & garlic 192
    Chicken with artichokes 184
    Juliette's mustardy artichoke crostini 66
    Tonnarelli with artichokes & prosciutto 109
Asciano, Italy 90, 93

B

Baked fennel & pasta with bechamel 144
Baked fennel with chilli & parmesan 195
Baked porcini 57
beans 17 *see also* cannellini beans
bechamel *see* sauces, dips and dressings
beef
    Black pepper stew 176
    Carolina's meatloaf 180
    Chicken & beef bone broth 73
    Florentine steak 166–167
    Lemony escallops 183
    Lemony meatballs 179
    Penne bolognese 116

biscuits
    Cantucci & vin santo semifreddo 229
    Ricciarelli 238
black pepper
    Black pepper stew 176
    Pici with cheese & pepper sauce 127
blood orange *see* oranges
broths *see* soups, stews and broths
brussels sprouts
    Orecchiette with brussels sprouts & pancetta 110
Buonconvento, Italy 87–90
button mushrooms
    Claudia's chestnut & mushroom 'peposo' 140

C

cabbage *see also* cavolo nero
    Cabbage, apple & walnut salad 202
Caffe Melloni, Italy 152
cakes
    Chocolate & Amarena cherry cake 233
    Florentine apple 'pancake' cake 223
    Orange, polenta & thyme cake 234
    Sienese spiced honey & nut cake 242
cannellini beans 17, 22
    Crostini with cavolo nero & cannellini beans 65
    Garlicky rosemary cannellini beans 198
    Nara's spelt & cannellini bean soup 84
Cantucci & vin santo semifreddo 229
Carolina's meatloaf 180
Casalinga, Florence 153
Castiglion del Bosco, Italy 88
cavolo nero 22
    Crostini with cavolo nero & cannellini beans 65
    Fussiloni with cavolo nero, walnut & pecorino pesto 106
cheese *see also* parmesan cheese; pecorino cheese; ricotta cheese; stracchino
    'Good time' radicchio, gorgonzola & walnut lasagne 143
cherries
    Chocolate & Amarena cherry cake 233
chestnuts 22–23
    Chestnut flour fritters with whipped ricotta 245
    Chestnut gnocchi with butter & sage 120
    Claudia's chestnut & mushroom 'peposo' 140
    Etruscan chestnut & chickpea soup 83
Chianti 28
    Drunkard's spaghetti 105
Chiara's bruleed pecorino 50
chicken
    Chicken & beef bone broth 73
    Chicken with artichokes 184
    Crostini with chicken liver pate 62
chickpeas 23
    Etruscan chestnut & chickpea soup 83
    Sausage, lentil & chickpea stew 172
chilled desserts
    Cantucci & vin santo semifreddo 229
    Red wine panna cotta with Jessica's grilled pears 224

    William's chocolate & rosemary olive oil mousse 230
chocolate
    Chocolate & Amarena cherry cake 233
    William's chocolate & rosemary olive oil mousse 230
churches 149, 205 *see also* Duomo di Siena, Italy
cinnamon
    Matthew's orange & cinnamon salad 237
crostini 44
    Crostini 61
    Crostini with cavolo nero & cannellini beans 65
    Crostini with chicken liver pate 62
    Fettunta 45
    Juliette's mustardy artichoke crostini 66
    Sausage & stracchino crostone 58
cucina povera 12–13

D

Dada's baked leeks in bechamel 134
dark chocolate *see* chocolate
desserts 38–39, 218 *see also* biscuits; cakes; chilled desserts; fritters
    Matthew's orange & cinnamon salad 237
    Quince tarte tatin 227
dinner menus 36–37
Drunkard's spaghetti 105
dumplings
    Chestnut gnocchi with butter & sage 120
    Mama's malfatti in broth 76
Duomo di Siena, Italy 205, 208–209, 212–213

E

eggs 23
    Artichoke frittata 133
    Egg & parmesan 'shreds' in broth 79
    Sage, spinach & quail egg pie 137
elephant garlic 22
Emergency rosemary & garlic spaghetti 113
entrees *see* antipasti; primi
Estruscans 17
Etruscan chestnut & chickpea soup 83

F

fennel
    Baked fennel & pasta with bechamel 144
    Baked fennel with chilli & parmesan 195
    Fennel in lemony anchovy sauce 54
Fettunta 45
fish *see* anchovies
Florence, Italy 212–213
    Arno and Ponte Vecchio 149, 158–159
    churches 149, 213
    food 152–153, 158
    galleries 149
    history 158, 212–213
    inhabitants 152, 155–156, 158
    mountains 152
    rivalry with Siena 212–213
    weather 149, 152
Florentine apple 'pancake' cake 223

Florentine peas with ham **191**
Florentine steak **166–167**
flours **23** *see also* polenta
fridge staples **21–25**
Fried carnival 'rags' **248**
Fried salty 'cuddles' with prosciutto & stracchino **49**
fritters
    Chestnut flour fritters with whipped ricotta **245**
    Fried carnival 'rags' **248**
frugality **12–13, 18**
fruit *see names of fruit*
Fussiloni with cavolo nero, walnut & pecorino pesto **106**

G

garlic **22**
    Artichokes with parsley & garlic **192**
    Emergency rosemary & garlic spaghetti **113**
    Garlicky rosemary cannellini beans **198**
    Pici with garlicky tomato sauce **126**
gelatine
    Red wine panna cotta with Jessica's grilled pears **224**
gnocchi
    Chestnut gnocchi with butter & sage **120**
gnudi
    Mama's malfatti in broth **76**
'Good time' radicchio, gorgonzola & walnut lasagne **143**
gorgonzola cheese
    'Good time' radicchio, gorgonzola & walnut lasagne **143**
Grazia's radicchio, sausage & rice timballo **174**
Greens tossed 'in the pan' **197**

H

ham *see* pancetta and prosciutto
herbs *see also* rosemary; sage
    Artichokes with parsley & garlic **192**
    Herby roast pork loin with potatoes **170**
    Orange, polenta & thyme cake **234**
Hildebrand family **156**
honey
    Pecorino con pere, miele e noci **45**
    Sienese spiced honey & nut cake **242**

I

ice cream
    Cantucci & vin santo semifreddo **229**

J

Juliette's mustardy artichoke crostini **66**

K

kale *see* cavolo nero

L

larder staples **21–25**
lasagne *see* pasta
leafy greens *see also* cabbage; lettuce
    Greens tossed 'in the pan' **197**
leeks
    Dada's baked leeks in bechamel **134**
lemons
    Fennel in lemony anchovy sauce **54**
    Lemony escallops **183**
    Lemony meatballs **179**
lentils **17, 23**
    Sausage, lentil & chickpea stew **172**
lettuce
    A very good green salad **189**
    Pink radicchio & blood orange salad **201**

M

Mama's malfatti in broth **76**
Matthew's orange & cinnamon salad **237**
meat **17–18** *see also* beef; chicken; offal; pork; sausages; secondi di carne
menus **36–39**
Mille Miglia **87**
minestre *see* soups, stews and broths
monasteries **90, 93, 96, 114**
Montalcino, Italy **12, 28, 90**
Monte Oliveto Maggiore, Italy **90, 93, 96, 114**
mousse
    William's chocolate & rosemary olive oil mousse **230**
mushrooms
    Baked porcini **57**
    Claudia's chestnut & mushroom 'peposo' **140**
mustard
    Juliette's mustardy artichoke crostini **66**

N

Nara's restaurant **90**
Nara's spelt & cannellini bean soup **84**
nuts *see also* chestnuts; walnuts
    Ricciarelli **238**
    Sienese spiced honey & nut cake **242**

O

offal **18, 34, 164**
    Crostini with chicken liver pate **62**
olive oil **23–24**
    William's chocolate & rosemary olive oil mousse **230**
Oltrarno, Italy **158**
onions
    Roasted baby onion **194**
oranges
    Matthew's orange & cinnamon salad **237**
    Orange, polenta & thyme cake **234**
    Pink radicchio & blood orange salad **201**
Orecchiette with brussels sprouts & pancetta **110**
Origo, Iris **89**
Ortigia **156**
Osteria Le Logge, Siena **208**
Osteria Vini e Vecchi Sapori, Florence **153**

P

Palazzo Pubblico, Siena **205, 208**
Palio race **205, 208–209, 212–213**
pancetta and prosciutto **24**
    Florentine peas with ham **191**
    Fried salty 'cuddles' with prosciutto & stracchino **49**
    Orecchiette with brussels sprouts & pancetta **110**
    Tonnarelli with artichokes & prosciutto **109**
panna cotta
    Red wine panna cotta with Jessica's grilled pears **224**
pantry staples **21–25**
parmesan cheese **24**
    Baked fennel with chilli & parmesan **195**
    Egg & parmesan 'shreds' in broth **79**
    Grazia's radicchio, sausage & rice timballo **174**
parsley
    Artichokes with parsley & garlic **192**
passata *see* tomatoes
pasta **100–101** *see also* dumplings; pici
    Baked fennel & pasta with bechamel **144**
    Drunkard's spaghetti **105**
    Emergency rosemary & garlic spaghetti **113**
    Fussiloni with cavolo nero, walnut & pecorino pesto **106**
    'Good time' radicchio, gorgonzola & walnut lasagne **143**
    Orecchiette with brussels sprouts & pancetta **110**
    Penne bolognese **116**
    Rigatoni with 'fake' meat sauce **102**
    Tiny pasta in broth **75**
    Tonnarelli with artichokes & prosciutto **109**
pastries *see* pies and pastries
pears
    Pecorino con pere, miele e noci **45**
    Red wine panna cotta with Jessica's grilled pears **224**
peas
    Florentine peas with ham **191**
pecorino cheese **24, 96**
    Chiara's bruleed pecorino **50**
    Fussiloni with cavolo nero, walnut & pecorino pesto **106**
    Pecorino con pere, miele e noci **45**
    Pici with cheese & pepper sauce **127**
Penne bolognese **116**
Peploe family **156**
pepper *see* black pepper
pesto
    Fussiloni with cavolo nero, walnut & pecorino pesto **106**
Piazza del Campo, Siena **205, 208–209**
pici **100–101**
    Pici with cheese & pepper sauce **127**
    Pici with garlicky tomato sauce **126**
    Sienese pici **122, 124**
Pienza, Italy **96**
pies and pastries
    Quince tarte tatin **227**
    Sage, spinach & quail egg pie **137**

Pink radicchio & blood orange salad 201
Pinziminio 45
polenta 24
    Orange, polenta & thyme cake 234
    Polenta with bechamel & ragu 119
Ponte Santa Trinita, Florence 158–159
porcini mushrooms
    Baked porcini 57
pork *see also* pancetta and prosciutto
    Grazia's radicchio, sausage & rice timballo 174
    Herby roast pork loin with potatoes 170
    Penne bolognese 116
    Sausage, lentil & chickpea stew 172
potatoes
    Herby roast pork loin with potatoes 170
    Tuscan roast potatoes 199
primi 38–39, 100–101 *see also* pasta
    Saffron 'speltotto' from the monks of Monte Oliveto 114
prosciutto *see* pancetta and prosciutto

Q

quail eggs
    Sage, spinach & quail egg pie 137
'quanto basta' method 33–34
quick dishes, menu of 38
Quince tarte tatin 227

R

radicchio
    'Good time' radicchio, gorgonzola & walnut lasagne 143
    Grazia's radicchio, sausage & rice timballo 174
    Pink radicchio & blood orange salad 201
ragu *see* sauces, dips and dressings
red wine
    Drunkard's spaghetti 105
    Red wine panna cotta with Jessica's grilled pears 224
Rigatoni with 'fake' meat sauce 102
Ricciarelli 238
rice 100
    Grazia's radicchio, sausage & rice timballo 174
ricotta cheese
    Chestnut flour fritters with whipped ricotta 245
    Mama's malfatti in broth 76
Rivoire, Florence 152
Roasted baby onion 194
rosemary 24–25
    Emergency rosemary & garlic spaghetti 113
    Garlicky rosemary cannellini beans 198
    William's chocolate & rosemary olive oil mousse 230

S

Saffron 'speltotto' from the monks of Monte Oliveto 114
sage
    Chestnut gnocchi with butter & sage 120
    Sage, spinach & quail egg pie 137

salads
    Cabbage, apple & walnut salad 202
    Matthew's orange & cinnamon salad 237
    Pink radicchio & blood orange salad 201
    A very good green salad 189
Sant'Antimo, Italy 90
Santo Spirito, Florence 158
sauces 100
    Baked fennel & pasta with bechamel 144
    Carolina's meatloaf 180
    Chestnut gnocchi with butter & sage 120
    Crostini with chicken liver pate 62
    Dada's baked leeks in bechamel 134
    Fennel in lemony anchovy sauce 54
    Fussiloni with cavolo nero, walnut & pecorino pesto 106
    Grazia's radicchio, sausage & rice timballo 174
    Penne bolognese 116
    Pici with cheese & pepper sauce 127
    Pici with garlicky tomato sauce 126
    Polenta with bechamel & ragu 119
    Rigatoni with 'fake' meat sauce 102
sausages 25
    Grazia's radicchio, sausage & rice timballo 174
    Sausage, lentil & chickpea stew 172
    Sausage & stracchino crostone 58
secondi di carne 164–165
    Black pepper stew 176
    Carolina's meatloaf 180
    Chicken with artichokes 184
    Florentine steak 166–167
    Grazia's radicchio, sausage & rice timballo 174
    Herby roast pork loin with potatoes 170
    Lemony escallops 183
    Lemony meatballs 179
    Sausage, lentil & chickpea stew 172
secondi carne 38–39
semifreddo
    Cantucci & vin santo semifreddo 229
sheep's cheese *see* pecorino cheese
side dishes 188 *see also* salads
    Baked fennel with chilli & parmesan 195
    Florentine peas with ham 191
    Garlicky rosemary cannellini beans 198
    Greens tossed 'in the pan' 197
    Tuscan roast potatoes 199
Siena, Italy
    food 208, 212
    Palio race 205, 208–209, 212–213
    relationship with Montalcino 90
    rivalry with Florence 212–213
    sights 205, 208–209, 212–213
    Sienese pici 122, 124
    Sienese spiced honey & nut cake 242
soups, stews and broths 38–39, 70–71
    Black pepper stew 176
    Chicken & beef bone broth 73
    Claudia's chestnut & mushroom 'peposo' 140
    Egg & parmesan 'shreds' in broth 79
    Etruscan chestnut & chickpea soup 83
    Mama's malfatti in broth 76
    Nara's spelt & cannellini bean soup 84
    Sausage, lentil & chickpea stew 172

    Tiny pasta in broth 75
    Vegetable minestrone 80
    Vegetable stock 72
spaghetti *see* pasta
spelt 17, 23, 100
    Nara's spelt & cannellini bean soup 84
    Saffron 'speltotto' from the monks of Monte Oliveto 114
spices *see also* black pepper
    Baked fennel with chilli & parmesan 195
    Juliette's mustardy artichoke crostini 66
    Matthew's orange & cinnamon salad 237
    Saffron 'speltotto' from the monks of Monte Oliveto 114
    Sienese spiced honey & nut cake 242
spinach
    Mama's malfatti in broth 76
    Sage, spinach & quail egg pie 137
staple ingredients 21–25
starters *see* antipasti; primi
stews *see* soups, stews and broths
stracchino 25
    Fried salty 'cuddles' with prosciutto & stracchino 49
    Sausage & stracchino crostone 58
supper menus 36–37

T

tarts
    Quince tarte tatin 227
    Sage, spinach & quail egg pie 137
thyme
    Orange, polenta & thyme cake 234
tinned tomatoes *see* tomatoes
Tiny pasta in broth 75
toast *see* crostini
Tolomei, Bernardo 93
tomatoes 25
    Penne bolognese 116
    Pici with garlicky tomato sauce 126
Tonnarelli with artichokes & prosciutto 109
Torre del Mangia, Siena 205, 208–209
Trattoria Cammillo, Florence 158
Tuscan roast potatoes 199
Tuscany, Italy
    access to produce 17–18, 130
    antipasti 44
    Autumn and Winter atmosphere 11–12
    cooking principles 12–13
    fridge and pantry staples 21–25
    geography 87
    history 12–13, 17–18, 88–89, 164
    industries 87–88, 164–165
    meat 164–165
    soups 70
    wine 27–28

V

Val d'Ombrone, Italy 12
vegetables 17–18, 100 *see also* names of vegetables; salads; side dishes; vegetarian meals
vegetarian meals 38, 130
    Artichoke frittata 133
    Baked fennel & pasta with bechamel 144
    Claudia's chestnut & mushroom 'peposo' 140

Dada's baked leeks in bechamel 134
'Good time' radicchio, gorgonzola
 & walnut lasagne 143
Pinziminio 45
Rigatoni with 'fake' meat sauce 102
Sage, spinach & quail egg pie 137
Vegetable minestrone 80
Vegetable stock 72
A very good green salad 189
vin santo 218
Cantucci & vin santo semifreddo 229

W

walnuts
Cabbage, apple & walnut salad 202
Fussiloni with cavolo nero, walnut
 & pecorino pesto 106
'Good time' radicchio, gorgonzola &
 walnut lasagne 143
Pecorino con pere, miele e noci 45
War in the Val d'Orcia 89
waste and frugality 12–13, 18
white beans *see* cannellini beans
William's chocolate & rosemary olive oil
 mousse 230
wine 218 *see also* red wine
Cantucci & vin santo semifreddo 229
World War II 88–89, 158

First published in Australia in 2025
by Thames & Hudson Australia
Wurundjeri Country, 132A Gwynne Street
Cremorne, Victoria 3121

First published in the United Kingdom in 2025
By Thames & Hudson Ltd
6–24 Britannia Street
London WC1X 9JD

First published in the United States of America in 2025
By Thames & Hudson Inc.
500 Fifth Avenue
New York, New York 10110

Winter in Tuscany © Thames & Hudson Australia 2025

Text © Amber Guinness 2025
Images © Valentina Solfrini 2025
Frescoes from the Abbey of Monte Oliveto Maggiore on pp. 42–3, 68–9, 98–9, 128–9, 163–3, 186–7 reproduced with thanks to the Ministero della Cultura, Soprintendenza Archeologia, Belle Arti e Paesaggioper, le Province di Siena

28 27 26 25   5 4 3 2 1

The moral right of the author has been asserted.

All rights reserved. No part of this publication may be reproduced or transmitted in any form or by any means, electronic or mechanical, including photocopy, recording or any other information storage or retrieval system, without prior permission in writing from the publisher.

ISBN 978-1-76076-475-3
ISBN 978-1-76076-521-7 (U.S. edition)
ISBN 978-1-76076-546-0 (U.K. edition)

EU Authorized Representative: Interart S.A.R.L.
19 rue Charles Auray, 93500 Pantin, Paris, France
productsafety@thameshudson.co.uk
www.interart.fr

A catalogue record for this book is available from the National Library of Australia

A CIP catalogue record for this book is available from the British Library

Library of Congress Control Number 2024953029

Front cover: Ashlea O'Neill | Salt Camp Studio
Design: Ashlea O'Neill | Salt Camp Studio
Editing: Katri Hilden
Printed and bound in China by C&C Offset Printing Co., Ltd

Thames & Hudson Australia wishes to acknowledge that Aboriginal and Torres Strait Islander peoples are the first storytellers of this nation and the Traditional Custodians of the land on which we live and work. We acknowledge their continuing culture and pay respect to Elders past and present.

Be the first to know about our new releases, exclusive content and author events by visiting
thamesandhudson.com.au
thamesandhudson.com
thamesandhudsonusa.com

AMBER GUINNESS

AMBER GUINNESS is an English cook and food writer who lives in Florence, Italy. She was born in London but raised at Arniano, the Tuscan farmhouse her parents restored near Siena. She has a first class Masters degree in History and Italian from the University of Edinburgh, and has worked as a cook in both London and Italy. Amber's first book, *A House Party in Tuscany*, featured family recipes and stories from her internationally acclaimed residential painting school at Arniano. Her second book, *Italian Coastal*, was culinary journey across the Tyrrhenian Sea, from Tuscany to Sicily. *Winter in Tuscany* is her third book. Amber is married with a son.